The psychology of gender and sexuality

The psychology of gender and sexuality

An introduction

WENDY STAINTON ROGERS
AND
REX STAINTON ROGERS

Open University Press
Buckingham · Philadelphia

Open University Press
Celtic Court
22 Ballmoor
Buckingham
MK18 1XW

email: enquiries@openup.co.uk
world wide web: www.openup.co.uk

and
325 Chestnut Street
Philadelphia, PA 19106, USA

First Published 2001

A catalogue record of this book is available from the British Library

ISBN 0 335 20225 X (hb)   0 335 20224 1 (pb)

Library of Congress Cataloging-in-Publication Data
Stainton Rogers, Wendy.
The psychology of gender and sexuality : an introduction / Wendy Stainton Rogers and Rex Stainton Rogers.
p.   cm.
Includes bibliographical references and index.
ISBN 0-335-20225-X (hardcover) — ISBN 0-335-20224-1 (pbk.)
1. Sex (Psychology) 2. Sex. 3. Sex differences (Psychology) I. Stainton Rogers, Rex. II. Title.
BF692.S72 2000
155.3—dc21   00-035614

Typeset by Graphicraft Limited, Hong Kong
Printed in Great Britain by Biddles Limited, Guildford and King's Lynn

Contents

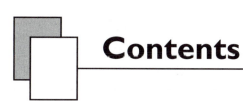

Acknowledgements

In the usual way I would like to thank Rebekah Stainton Rogers, Luke Wray and Susannah Chappell for help with the bibliography. Also the people who reviewed the original proposal, and Robin Long, Harriett Marshall and Paul Stenner who reviewed the final manuscript. Their comments and suggestions were so useful that we acted on most of them.

But I would also like to add my thanks to all those who made completing the book possible. I should mention here both the long-suffering Justin Vaughan at Open University Press, and my friends and colleagues at the Open University, especially Pam Foley, Stan Tucker and Jeremy Roche, who took on large sections of my work to give me the space and time to devote to the book.

Finally, though, I would like to thank all the many people who have supported me over the past year – my daughters Amanda, Karina and Rebekah; my sisters Sally and Pam; my wider family, my friends, my neighbours, my doctor, my chiropractor, my gardener, my heating engineer, my cleaner and my builders. I'm sorry I can't name you all, for fear of missing anybody out – you know who you are. But I could not have got through the months since Rex died without all of your love, tenderness, thoughtfulness, kindness and help. I will remain always deeply grateful.

Wendy Stainton Rogers

Preface

Rex and I worked on this book throughout most of 1998. It would be true to say that it dominated our lives that year. For most of the time Rex was on sabbatical, and he divided his time between what came to be called 'Rex's Erection' (a deck and greenhouse he built – although neither of these words conveys the reality of the amazing structure he created) and writing first drafts of many of the chapters. I put in most evenings and weekends, as well as vacation times – we worked through all three. I cannot count the hours we spent beavering away, him upstairs, me down, meeting regularly in the kitchen to confer, to plot and plan, to talk through what we would each do next, and, of course, to argue – it was out of our arguments that our best writing came.

We gave up on taking a holiday that summer. But I do remember the autumn day when we decided that the sun was shining so gloriously that we had to go out and enjoy it. We walked by Wittenham Clumps to Dorchester, saying to one another: 'Blow the book' (or words to that effect) 'there are too few days like this in life, and they should not be spent at the desk.' That day was a precious one.

It was not always easy writing as a couple. I remember wryly commenting several times to my friends that whereas most co-authors have to catch you on the phone to nag you – 'How's Chapter 3 getting on then?' – with Rex this usually happened when he dug me in the ribs in bed in the morning, just as I was waking up. My replies were far from polite, although usually after breakfast together and several cups of coffee the negotiation would be calmer and more constructive. It was hard work, but I have many happy memories of those times – writing a book with someone you love can be an incredibly rewarding experience.

The first draft of the book was completed in December 1998, and a couple of weeks into the new year Rex and I began to work on the amendments suggested by our editor at Open University Press, Justin Vaughan. But Rex was taken seriously ill in January, and, indeed, his last contributions to the manuscript were made while he was recovering in hospital. Two weeks later, on 8 February 1999, Rex died. This book will be his last published work, completing an incredibly diverse and influential publishing career.

Not surprisingly, it has been very painful for me to finish the book, and it has taken some time before I could face this task – thank you, Justin, for being so understanding. But now I have, and I hope I have not done too much violence to Rex's text in the changes and deletions I have made. I would have given anything to have had him here to argue and battle its completion. We had spent more than 26 years writing together. The battles were hard, the arguments often heated – but they were such enjoyable battles, such marvellous arguments! I will miss, dreadfully, his sheer intellectual vivacity, his inventiveness and his wicked, wicked way with words – and I am not the only person who feels like that.

Rex was often not an easy man to work with (or indeed to live with). At times he drove me crazy with frustration, and I know he was a thorn in the flesh of many others. He would never have wanted to be sanctified or put on a pedestal, and I am not going to pretend he was a saint. But he was the most amazing, incredible man – an inspirational man; a man of immense warmth, generosity, kindness and charisma. Like so many others, I miss him dreadfully. But he lives on, in the lives he influenced, in the gifts of hope and courage and inspiration he gave to so many – the students he taught, the many psychologists (and others) to whom he gave such a hard time.

Rex also lives on in Beryl Curt – that extraordinary collective author, maker of mischief, singer of songs, dreamer of dreams, dancer superb, player of games, consumer of indulgences, water-pistol aficionado, snatcher of crates of wine (some of it from Open University Press – sorry Justin). With her incredible intellectual gifts, her zest for life, with her determination to make trouble and to have such fun, such fun, doing it, how could she not? She was Rex's invention, and gave him so much happiness in the last years of his life. Being acorporeal, Beryl cannot die – and will be his most lasting legacy and tribute. Long may she prosper and continue to make trouble.

And Rex will endure in the words he wrote. The words that follow are his last. I hope that despite my fiendish editing, you can get some little measure from them of just what a remarkable man he was.

Wendy Stainton Rogers
Long Wittenham
January 2000

Introduction

In terms of psychology textbooks, 'gender' and 'sexuality' are comparatively new kinds of language. Their use in psychology today reflects recent changes in the way that psychology is taught, studied, researched and practised. These changes include a growing sensitivity to the politics of the discipline, which has been prompted by inputs from critical and feminism-informed scholars. Many mainstream psychologists are strongly resistant to the idea that psychology has any engagement with politics. Psychology is generally assumed to be a science and, as such, outside of politics. But as you will see as you progress through this book, there are a number of movements both within and outwith psychology that have challenged this claim, notably feminism, social constructionism and postmodernism. Indeed, all of these movements pose an even more extensive challenge to science itself. They argue that science is profoundly political, not in a party politics sense, but in terms of the politics of power.

This concern with the politics of power has led to a fuller awareness of the reflexive relation between language, knowledge and power. This too has been a major stimulus to the introduction of gender and sexuality into psychology's domain. Both of these are areas of human experience and action in which language, knowledge and power are played out. To give just one example, this is how one psychologist began to open up the question of how language and gender are connected:

> 'man' and 'person' have been synonymous in Western, patriarchal thought, as is evidenced by the use of the terms 'man', 'mankind', and 'he/him' as universals. As women we can strive to be 'people'

> and 'women'. Logically there is no contradiction. However, because 'person' actually consists of the attributes which are meant to be characteristic of men, there is an underlying contradiction.
>
> (Hollway 1984: 22)

If you want to get a sense of the point Hollway is making, go and look at almost any psychological text that was written in the 1970s or earlier. You will find that it almost certainly uses the term 'man' to mean 'people', and 'he' and 'him' to refer to both men and women. We were told, at the time, that this was no more than a grammatical convention. And yet, slips of the pen often showed that the convention worked in only a superficial way. Miller and Swift (1981) illustrate this with the following quotations:

> As for man, he is no different from the rest. His back aches, he ruptures easily, his women have difficulties in childbirth.
>
> [M]an can do several things which the animal cannot do. . . . Eventually, his vital interests are not only life, food, access to females, etc., but also values, symbols, institutions.
>
> (cited in Miller and Swift 1981: 12)

Hollway is suggesting that when language like this was commonplace, women were being excluded and made to feel that they did not 'belong' to the human race. Thus the very way that language is used is powerfully implicated in the way people perceive and think about men and women. And, crucially, the way people perceive and think about men and women affects how they treat men and women. This brings power into the equation, since the different treatment of men and women has considerable consequences.

In 1972 a fascinating study was published (Broverman *et al.* 1972) which explored the way mental health professionals thought about men and women. This was interesting in itself – psychologists do not usually put their own thinking under scrutiny. But the results they got were even more instructive. They asked a large number of practising mental health professionals (both men and women) to describe the qualities of:

1 the mature, healthy, socially competent *adult*
2 the mature, healthy, socially competent *man*
3 the mature, healthy, socially competent *woman.*

The descriptions of the 'mentally healthy man' and the 'mentally healthy adult' were virtually identical. Both were characterized as having strong instrumental qualities (that is, being able to do things) and some of the more desirable expressive traits (that is, about their feelings and ways of connecting with the social world). But the description of the 'mentally healthy woman' was quite different. She was characterized as more submissive, more easily influenced, as excitable in minor crises, concerned with her appearance and more likely to have her feelings hurt. She was less independent, less dominant, less aggressive, less objective and less adventurous.

These findings showed that mental health professionals equated 'men' with 'adults'. Effectively, they saw them as one and the same – to be a mentally healthy man is to be a mentally healthy adult. But this was not true of their ideas about women – to be a mentally healthy woman was *not* seen as the same as being a mentally healthy adult. Rather, for a woman to be viewed as mentally healthy, she needed to 'feminine'. If she failed to conform to accepted feminine qualities, then she could not be a mature, healthy, socially competent woman.

It was this kind of work that forced (somc) psychologists to take another look at the assumptions about the qualities of men and women – sex differences, as they were then called – that underpinned the discipline of psychology. This in turn led to the introduction of gender as a topic, and, more generally, to the consideration of the interplay of language, knowledge and power in psychology's approach to its subject matter – people. Once this happened, sexuality also came to be addressed as a topic. This was because once the whole can of worms of language, knowledge and power was opened up, then it was not just psychology's sexism that came under fire, but its homophobia too. It was at about this time (as we describe in the Introduction to Part II) that psychologists in the USA conceded that homosexuality was not a disease.

But we are getting a bit ahead of ourselves. The aim of this book is, primarily, to give you a basic introduction to the psychology of gender and sexuality as it is now pursued within what has come to be called 'critical' psychology (see, for example, Stainton Rogers *et al.* 1995; Fox and Prilleltensky 1997; Ibáñez and Íñiguez, 1997). However, to be able to make sense of what it is that psychology is critical *about*, you need to have a basic grounding in the mainstream approaches that have been taken in psychology in these fields.

We have therefore divided the book up into three parts. Part I sets out the three mainstream paradigms in which psychology has researched and theorized about gender and sexuality: biological paradigms (Chapter 1); social and cultural paradigms (Chapter 2) and interactive paradigms (Chapter 3). It needs to be said that these are still, for many psychologists (probably the majority), the ways in which they continue to be conceived. But these paradigms are under fire from critical psychologists – in which camp we would place ourselves. So, as an overtly critical text, in our book we have included in the first three chapters some critique of the mainstream approaches, and have then set out the main challenges that have been directed to them (although, you will notice, our criticality pops up from time to time even in the first three chapters).

Part II covers the three main kinds of challenge that have been directed towards this mainstream work: liberatory challenges (Chapter 4), feminist challenges (Chapter 5) and postmodern challenges (Chapter 6). These chapters each provide a detailed account of the theory-base from which their challenge is mounted, and each introduces some of the main criticisms that have been directed towards psychology's research and theorization.

Part III then takes a different tack. It contains five chapters on a range of different topics: research into sexual behaviour (Chapter 7), alien sex (Chapter 8), bodies (Chapter 9), sex crime (Chapter 10) and 'new men' and 'new women' (Chapter 11). These chapters draw on critical – mainly feminist and postmodern – theorizing, and show how they can be applied to subjects, issues and topics for which gender and sexuality are salient. Our reason for doing this has been that feminist and postmodern theorizing can often be quite inaccessible. All too often they are written in obscure language, in which it is all too easy to get lost. By concentrating on particular topics and issues, we hope we have been able to show (rather than try to explain) what they can do, and how they do it. And, to be honest, it is a more interesting way to approach this work – well, it was for us, and we hope it will be for you too.

More specifically in Part I, Chapter 1 reviews biological paradigms, and provides a fair amount of the basic, underpinning knowledge that you need to know in relation to things such as the physiology of the body and body architecture. It contains details, for example, of what can go wrong genetically in relation to 'bodily sex', and information about research into the biological basis of what goes on in the body during sexual intercourse. It also summarizes recent developments in this field, including sociobiology and evolutionary psychology. Chapter 2 reviews social and cultural paradigms – those that concentrate on social, social psychological and cultural influences on, for example, how children acquire their understanding of what it means to be a boy or a girl. It is mainly based around psychology, looking, for example, at social learning theory explanations of how boys learn to behave like boys and girls to behave like girls. But it also includes important work from anthropology and sociology. Chapter 3 examines interactive paradigms – those where psychologists have sought to understand gender and sexuality through the interplay between biology and culture. These approaches cover a lot of ground, including the work of Eysenck, Freud and Kohlberg. It looks in particular at theories of gender development, especially those that focus on moral development. This was one of the first areas to receive a critical challenge from feminists, and the chapter ends by looking at the work of Carol Gilligan, and her claim that women approach ethical issues from 'a different voice' from men.

In Part II we begin, in Chapter 4, by looking at the liberatory movement which influenced psychology in the 1960s and 1970s, especially in humanistic psychology. The chapter leads into this through the history of liberatory movements more generally, and includes an account of the influential work of Willhelm Reich. Chapter 5 sets out the basis of the feminist challenge. A fair amount of the chapter is devoted to describing where and how feminist ideas emerged, and explaining the differences between first wave and second wave feminism. The chapter also details the many different forms and approaches of feminism, including some of the conflicts between them. It then looks at three main challenges that feminism poses for psychology: to psychology's epistemology, to its modes of inquiry and to theorization. The chapter explores the first two of these in some detail. Feminist challenges to theorization are taken up in Part III.

Chapter 6 sets out the challenges presented by postmodern theorizing. Again, we have had to adopt a fairly superficial approach, both because this is a wide (and growing) theoretical field and because, quite frankly, much writing in this area is at best 'difficult' and at worst downright obscure and impenetrable. This is not just a matter of its theorists being bloody-minded and deliberately cryptic, though it has to be acknowledged that some do seem to take a kind of mischievous pleasure in being incomprehensible. Postmodernism is fundamentally concerned with language, and how language can be used to beguile us into seeing things in particular ways – sometimes it talks specifically about 'language games'. A good example is the description given at the beginning of this section of the use of 'he' and 'man' as generic – *as if* they represent both male and female. As we hope we have shown you, they are not actually experienced in that way, either by the people who say or write the terms or those who hear or read them. Language, according to postmodern theory, powerfully constructs the way people see the world, and the way they make sense of their experiences, of themselves and of others. Consequently, postmodern theorists argue, it is necessary to take enormous care in the language used to 'do' theory. It needs to be precise, and it *needs* to be difficult to understand – it *needs* to make the listener or writer think hard about what is being said, for that is the purpose of the exercise. What we have tried to do in Chapter 6, therefore, is to outline the main elements of postmodern theory, how they apply to psychology, and, specifically, the challenge they present to mainstream approaches to the psychology of gender and sexuality.

At first sight, Part III might look like a bit of a 'rag-bag'. Each chapter is on a different topic, and their approaches are different too. However, there is some purpose in all of this. We have chosen each topic because we thought it would be interesting to you. But we have also used each one to demonstrate a particular strategy that can be used to approach these kinds of topic from a 'critical' perspective. Chapter 7, 'Where's the action?', begins with mainstream research into sexual conduct – who does what, with whom and how often? It then goes back and examines what this research is doing: what are its consequences?, and what are the implications of the conventional way in which such research is usually reported? It explores the idea that science can be viewed as a 'story-telling practice', and examines why we need to be deeply suspicious, sometimes, of the stories that science tells. Chapter 8, 'Aliens and others', makes a foray into the way in which sex and gender have been construed in science fiction in the form of 'aliens' (that is, beings from other planets and dimensions). It also briefly examines how sex, sexuality and gender can, today, be manifested and manipulated in cyberspace. Chapter 9, 'Bodies', takes a brief and selective look at a topic which is of growing interest in psychology, and indeed in theory more broadly. It focuses, in particular, on the ways in which warranting is used in claim-making and argument. It looks at the way in which psychologists make use of warrants to, for example, justify their claims that people who are unhappy with their bodies – who suffer from 'syndromes' and 'conditions' (such as anorexia nervosa) – 'need' therapy. Chapter 10, 'Sex crimes', looks in particular at rape, both female and male. Here, in particular, feminist theorization is applied to the 'myths' that surround these crimes (for example, that men are driven to rape through an excess of testosterone) and is used to explore some of the dangers inherent in sociobiological theorizing. Finally, Chapter 11, 'New men, new women, new relationships?', explores how gender and sexuality are undergoing change, and the consequences for the lives, life experiences and life opportunities of today's young men and women.

Some ideas about how to approach the book

Our aim in this book has been to offer you something of a textbook, in the sense that we have tried to cover the ground that you need to know about, at a basic level, to 'get into' the psychology of gender and sexuality. We have also included some aids to understanding and using the book in your studies:

1 Suggestions for further reading (at the end of each chapter).
2 A glossary of key terms (these are marked in bold, and you will find the glossary at the end of the book).
3 Summary boxes (at the end of each section of Chapters 1–6).
4 Boxes summarizing 'implications for psychology' (at the end of Chapters 7–11).

As a textbook, the chapters follow a logical sequence. Part I builds up a case for a critical approach (as well as giving you a basic grounding in psychology's conventional approaches to what we now call gender and sexuality). Part II then sets out the three main paradigms that challenge the mainstream approach from a critical perspective. Part III then applies these approaches to a variety of topics. So, if you want a thorough grounding in this field of work, you will do best to read the chapters in Parts I and II in the sequence in which we have presented them. The chapters in Part III are independent of each other, and can be read in any order. But do remember that they take up ideas and theories that have been introduced in the first two parts. You will get much more out of them if you read them after you have worked through the beginning of the book. But, having said that, you may want to begin by 'dipping into' Part III – just to whet your appetite. At least it will give you some sense of what you are getting into.

However, you, the reader are in control now. We have done our bit. So you can read in any order you like, and as much as or as little of the book as you want. We hope you at least sometimes enjoy it, and feel when you have read it that you have learned something from it. Believe it or not, we got a lot of pleasure in writing it. Certainly we learned a lot in its writing – sometimes from quite unexpected sources. But that's another story – enjoy this one.

Part I

Mainstream psychological approaches to gender and sexuality

1 Biological paradigms

> Many studies have shown that there is a marked difference in how well men and women register and remember details, and to a man dust on a shelf or a scum ring around a bath are just that – details. Even if he does notice them, he may simply not accord them the importance a woman does. To her dirt is offensive, to him it is part of the natural world. From very early childhood males have a greater tolerance for, and even liking for dirt. What a man perceives as 'clean' a woman might find dirty, and what he finds merely 'dirty' she might find utterly disgusting. His sense of smell is different too; the stale socks and sweaty shirt don't bother him because they are among the pheromone-related smells that women are acutely aware of but men simply do not detect.
>
> (Moir and Moir 1998: 252)

Recently, biological explanations of the differences between the way men and women act and see the world have become hugely popular. They argue – often very convincingly – that the reason why men are more promiscuous than women, and why men are more aggressive and win more Nobel prizes, is that their biology is different. In this book we directly challenge such biological explanations of people's social behaviour, and ask why, just now, they have such appeal. Before we can do that, though, we need to 'begin at the beginning' by seeing what biological explanations do have to tell us about sex, sexuality and gender – in particular about some of the differences between the sexes. This is what we will be doing in this chapter.

Psychology, the bio-social science?

From its beginning, psychology has differed from the other social sciences in taking many of its ideas and theories directly from natural science, biology in particular. Indeed, psychology is sometimes described as a bio-social science or even as **biopsychology** (see Pinel 1993), with the stress very much on the 'bio'. As Burr has recently argued in relation to the nature–nurture debate:

> there is a common sense assumption (which may have no factual basis) that biological factors exert a powerful 'push' in particular directions, and that (weaker) environmental influences have a merely moderating effect. Biological influences are assumed to be deeper and stronger than societal forces, which are seen as more superficial. It is significant that the study of the biological sciences has often seemed more relevant to the education of psychologists than has sociology.
>
> (Burr 1998: 32)

Mainstream psychology has concentrated on discovering and understanding the biological processes through which humans came to acquire the qualities and capacities that make them human – the biological bases of human behaviour and experience. Four main interlocked processes have been identified as making up these biological foundations.

Box 1.1 The biological bases of human behaviour and experience

Evolution: the process through which humankind, as a species, is seen to have originated. It is this process which is seen to have constituted the basic qualities that all human beings possess.

Genetic inheritance: the process through which individuals are seen to acquire at conception, and hence be born with, particular qualities (such as their sex, pigmentation of skin, hair and eyes, susceptibility to certain diseases). These qualities, being 'wired-into-the-genes', are seen as largely enduring and unchangeable.

Physiology: the body's chemical processes, through which the genes are seen to exert their influence on human behaviour. Of particular importance in relation to sex are the operations of hormones, which differ (albeit in highly complex ways) between males and females.

Morphology: the processes through which body form is seen to develop as a result of physiological influence. In terms of sex, two aspects are particularly important. The first has to do with visible bodily differences (including the development of genitals, breasts, differences in height and overall body shape and size) between men and women. The second has to do with the 'architecture' of the brain, which affects cognitive performance.

This chapter looks at each of these. We begin by explaining the processes involved, and then we set out the biologically grounded theorization that has been developed to explain the differences between the sexes. Given that some of you may not have studied biology in any depth before, we have included some basic information. If you are already familiar with this material, you may find you can skip over these sections quite rapidly.

The theory of evolution

It was Darwin's great achievement to put the ideas of evolution – ideas that had been around for some time – on to a scientific basis. This he achieved through his observations of the natural variety of living species. His evolutionary theory proposes that change among living things happens through the combination of the natural occurrence of 'sports' – offspring which are different from their parents – and their subsequent struggle for survival. Those individuals which are well adapted to their environment tend to survive and reproduce. Those which are not tend to die before they can reproduce, and hence their 'blood-line' dies out. In this way living things adapt to their environment, generation by generation. Darwin called this '**natural selection**', the process by which nature selects the 'fittest' to survive.

The theory of genetic inheritance

However, for all the power of Darwin's theory of evolution, it remained incomplete until there was a theory about how the mechanism of biological inheritance worked. The foundational work was conducted in parallel with Darwin's work (but in obscurity) by Gregor Mendel, a Polish monk working in Brno, now in the Czech Republic. In the monastery garden, between 1855 and 1868, Mendel bred different varieties of garden pea and meticulously documented how different characteristics were passed on from one generation to the next. When this work was rediscovered by three independent investigators in 1900 it led directly to the science of genetics as we know it today.

Mendel had shown that the key to inheritance lay in *pairs* of factors that exist in each organism, which divide before fertilization and recombine during fertilization. He found that these pairs of factors produce, on large-scale samples, a mathematically precise ratio of different physical outcomes at maturity. For example, he looked at peas that differ in their colour (they can be green or yellow) and in their shape (they can be round or wrinkled). Mendel bred together yellow and green, round and wrinkled peas, and demonstrated that under carefully controlled conditions he could predict precisely how many round-yellow, wrinkled-yellow, round-green and wrinkled-green plants would be produced in the next generation.

Genetic inheritance

This information about inherited characteristics, when rediscovered in 1900, fitted extremely neatly into the then-current state of cytology (the study of animal and plant cells). Cytologists had recently found out that the nucleus of living cells contained threads of material which were intimately involved in cell division: these were named **chromosomes**.

Using microscopes, cytologists found that they could, with some organisms (such as fruit flies), see each chromosome, and that they could be sorted into pairs. Moreover, they observed that whereas in ordinary cell division (called **mitosis**) each pair is simply reproduced, in the cell division in which sperm and ova are produced (called **meiosis**), only one of each pair is generated and only, therefore, a half set of chromosomes. These sets then combine, when sperm and ovum meet at fertilization, to produce a full set of paired chromosomes, one of each pair coming from the sperm and one from the ovum.

Mendel's 'pairs of factors' could now be identified with chromosomes. These factors were called **genes**, although it was not until later that the mechanisms by which genes work was discovered. In 1944 Avery, MacLeod and McCarty identified the active agent as a nucleic acid, but it took until 1953 for the full picture to emerge through the research of Watson and Crick. They identified the molecular architecture of how genes function. They were able to show that genetic material (called **DNA**, short for deoxyribonucleic acid) consists of a spiral structure (usually called a 'double helix') rather like a ladder that has been twisted. The 'sides' of the ladder are made of long molecules of sugars and phosphates, and the 'rungs' are made up of pairs of interlocking nitrogenous bases: adenine, cytosine, thiamine and guanine.

Since only adenine will fit with thiamine (and vice versa), and only cytosine will fit with guanine (and vice versa), when the 'ladder' is split (as happens when cells divide), each side can act as a template for the exact production of the other side. In this way, through the sequence-patterns of the bases along the sugar-phosphate strands of the DNA, information is stored in chemical form (in a manner that is similar to the way computers store information electronically). This information is like a series of computer programs, which enable and regulate the processes by which living organisms develop and operate. In simple terms, they work chemically. They provide blueprints for, say, constructing the precise form of various body organs – the colour of your eyes, your skin colour, whether your hair is naturally curly or straight, your height and whether or not your ears stick out or your nose turns up. Equally, they provide the operating codes for digesting food, eliminating waste, breathing and so on.

The process of producing females and males

Humans generally have 46 chromosomes. Forty-four of these can be organized into 22 homologous pairs (look-alike couplets) of chromosomes. However, the other two come in two distinctive configurations: either an XX set or an XY set (this nomenclature reflects their alternative shapes, like an X and like a Y). In most instances, people possessing an XX pair are female; people possessing an XY pair are male.

This genetic distinction now allows an alternative definition of sex to the traditional obvious observational means (boys are born with a penis, girls with a vagina) and is called **chromosomal sex**. It is on this basis, for example, that 'sex testing' is carried out when there is a dispute about an athlete's sex. The configurations arise through the half-set of chromosomes from each parent. Females produce only X chromosomes in their ova; males produce about half X-carrying and half Y-carrying sperm. Where an X chromosome from the male meets the X chromosome from the female, the resulting **foetus** is female. Where a Y chromosome is in the sperm that fertilizes the egg, the result is a male foetus.

Once an egg is fertilized it begins to divide to produce more cells. First a hollow ball of cells develops, and soon this begins to fold and differentiate to construct an embryo. For the first six weeks or so of development, male and female embryos are the same – except at the genetic level. At this point both have the capacity to develop into either a boy-form or a girl-form, since both build up two structures: one with the capacity to generate a male reproductive system (called the **Wolffian system**); one with the capacity to generate a female reproductive system (called the **Müllerian system**). But at around the third month, things begin to change.

Where the embryo has an XY (male) pairing of sex chromosomes, two kinds of hormones (see below) are produced. One stimulates the Wolffian male-reproductive-system-to-be, to make it begin to grow, and, at the same time, the other inhibits the Müllerian female-reproductive-system-to-be, to make it degenerate. Where the embryo has an XX (female) pairing of sex chromosomes, there is hardly any secretion of hormones to control the production of the girl's reproductive system, and it is the Müllerian female-reproductive-system-to-be which develops. Biologically speaking, femaleness is the default state – an embryo develops a female reproductive system unless it is masculinized by hormonal action.

Sex differences and physiology

The genetic differences between men and women are made manifest by the action of hormones, which result in differences in physiology. We will look at hormones first, and then examine other physiological sex differences.

Box 1.2 Hormones

Hormones are sometimes called 'chemical messengers' – this gives a good clue as to what they are and what they do: they are chemicals which are produced by endocrine glands (*endocrine glands* secrete into the body, as opposed to exocrine glands that secrete out) and travel around the body in the bloodstream. Particular organs in the body are receptive to particular hormones – they possess a biochemical receptor site which, when activated by a hormone, 'turns on' or 'turns off' a particular process. You have just met an example of a hormone working in this way, where hormonal action causes the male reproductive system to develop.

The hormonal system is controlled largely by a gland in the brain, the **pituitary gland**. This gland produces a number of hormones, which, in turn, stimulate the release of other hormones. For example, the action of the pituitary stimulates the sex organs (called **gonads** – the **testes** and the **ovaries**) to secrete gonadal hormones. The action of the pituitary is affected by a nearby brain structure – the **hypothalamus** – which produces hormones that trigger the pituitary into action. Hormones control a large number of body processes. One that you may know already is adrenaline, which is produced in response to arousal (for example, being frightened or excited). The impact of adrenaline is to 'prime' the body to take action (to fight, or to run away, say, from danger) by making the heart beat faster and moving the blood supply to where it is needed to take swift action. But here we are interested in **sex hormones** (sometimes called gonadal hormones).

Sex hormones

Sex hormones can be divided into two main classes: **androgens** and **oestrogens**. It is often assumed that androgens are 'male hormones' and oestrogens are 'female hormones', as if only men have androgens and only women have oestrogens. But this is not so – *both* sexes produce *both* types. What is true is that, in general, men have more androgens and fewer oestrogens operating in their bodies; and women have more oestrogens and fewer androgens. The most common of the androgens is **testosterone**, and the most common oestrogen is **oestradiol**. The gonads also secrete a third type of hormone, the **progestins**, the most common of which is **progesterone**. Progesterone's main function is to prepare a woman's body for pregnancy following fertilization, although men also secrete it in small quantities (its function for them is, as yet, uncertain).

Hormones and puberty

During infancy and childhood, the level of sex hormones circulating in the body is low. But at puberty a number of hormones come into play. The pituitary releases growth hormones, which results in the **adolescent growth spurt**, when bones (especially the long bones in legs and arms) and muscles fairly suddenly begin to grow faster, so that the child relatively rapidly gains adult size and proportions. The pituitary also releases two other hormones: **follicle-stimulating hormone** (FSH) and **luteinizing hormone** (LH). These stimulate the gonads to increase the production of oestrogens and androgens, which results in the maturation of the gonads and the development of secondary sexual characteristics – body hair in both sexes, and the distinctive body shapes of adult females and males.

In adolescent boys and in men the production of androgens is proportionately higher than their production of oestrogens; in adolescent girls and women the situation is reversed, with relatively more oestrogens and fewer androgens being produced. Again, it is important not to assume that androgens are simply 'male hormones' and oestrogens 'female hormones', since one of the androgens, for example, is responsible for the growth of pubic and underarm hair in both boys and girls. Equally, FSH and LH are involved in both the development of eggs (ova) in women and the production of sperm in men, and LH contributes to the maturation of the egg in women and the maturation of sperm and the production of testosterone in men. From puberty onwards, throughout their fertile years, women's hormones operate cyclically – they have a cycle of fertility, which passes through a sequence of stages controlled by hormones (this is described in more detail later). In boys the production of hormones is not cyclical, but neither is it entirely steady.

Hormones and sexual activity

In animals, sex hormones are often clearly linked to sexual activity. In many mammalian species females are sexually receptive only at certain

> **Box 1.3 Biology is not destiny**
>
> This certainly seems true in relation to decline in hormone levels. For example, many women experience an *increase* in sexual interest after the menopause, even though their oestrogen levels will be much lower. This is assumed to be much more to do with no longer having to worry about pregnancy or contraception than having anything to do with hormone levels. And it is worth noting that it is a lot easier to have an active sex life in an 'empty nest' than one full of teenage children.

points in their cycle of fertility – they are sexually receptive only when 'primed' by their homones. But in humans the relationship is much more complex. It seems that puberty is an important trigger for developing an appetite for sex; individuals who do not undergo the hormonal changes that result in puberty generally fail to engage in sexual relationships (Meyer-Bahlburg 1980). But this is not sufficient in itself, and hormones are certainly not the only factor (nor even, probably, the most important factor) in determining whether an individual human becomes interested in sex or is sexually active.

Problems with sexual differentiation

The way in which sex unfolds in the embryo is a complex process. The description provided earlier simplifies it a lot. Researchers have gained some understanding of how it works by looking at what happens when there are problems with the process. The reproduction of chromosomes does not always work perfectly, and the consequence may be that there are, in effect, 'bugs' in the 'program' encoded in the DNA. These originally arise spontaneously, although some get reproduced and passed on (leading to certain inherited dysfunctions, such as haemophilia). Many such spontaneous errors are so harmful that the foetus dies (or may never develop beyond a few cells) and is either reabsorbed or is miscarried (the technical term is a spontaneous abortion). Other errors may be so trivial as to be unnoticed. In the middle range lie a number of conditions, some of which have an effect on the new individual's sex-linked architecture. When the chromosomes differ from the norm, this leads to dysfunctions in the usual hormonal system, which can lead to problems in sexual differentiation. So too can hormonal factors alone. Some of the main syndromes associated with these are set out in Box 1.4.

Box 1.4 Genetic and hormonal syndromes which affect sexual architecture

Klinefelter's syndrome is the most common sex chromosome misconfiguration, occurring in about 2 per 1000 male births. It results from having one or more extra chromosomes – 47 or more instead of the usual 46. An extra X chromosome, making an XXY configuration, disturbs male physiology. Although individuals with this syndrome have male internal and external genitalia, their testes are small and cannot produce sperm, so they are infertile and have a lowered libido. Boys may also develop a more female body shape at puberty. Like other people with extra chromosomal material, males with this syndrome are more likely to have a learning disability.

Occasionally there are even more extra chromosomes – XXXY and XXXXY configurations have been found. Such individuals often have more severe problems with their reproductive and skeletal systems, and a higher probability of severe learning disability.

'Super Males' is where an XYY pattern is found, which usually leads to the male being taller and also raises the possibility of learning disability. This pattern has been subject to a great deal of publicity, with claims being made that such people are 'super-males' with strong aggressive tendencies, based on the finding that such men are relatively more likely to end up in prison. However, Witkin *et al.* (1976) have refuted this claim, showing that prison inmates with an XYY pattern were no more violent than other inmates. They suggested that the effect is a result of the men's learning disability and great height (which, in making them distinctive, means that they are more likely to be caught committing crimes).

Turner's syndrome is rarer, found in about 1 in 10,000 female births. Here an X sex chromosome is missing from its couplet and this is usually denoted as XO (O = absence). Many embryos with this configuration are spontaneously aborted (Mittwoch 1973) but some are not. Typically, the external genitalia are female in form but internally the ovaries fail to form. Hence, ovulation is absent and there are no ovarian hormones to trigger puberty – although this can be treated with hormone supplements. Without ovaries women with this syndrome are infertile.

'Super Females'. Occasionally females are born with one or more extra X chromosomes. They are more likely to have a learning disability and some have menstrual irregularities and are sterile. But there have been cases of women with an XXX configuration having children (Mittwoch 1973). Again, there are a few rare cases of women having XXXX and even XXXXX patterns, and these are usually associated with severe developmental problems and serious learning disability.

Intersexuality (sometimes called hermaphroditism) is where a person is born with characteristics of both sexes. It is extremely rare, with no more than 60 cases being identified in Europe and North America in the past 100 years (Money 1986). It occurs when an individual has, say, an ovary on one side of the body and a testicle on the other, or where both tissues combine together to produce a structure called an oveotestis.

Pseudohermaphroditism occurs much more frequently. It can arise from a variety of genetic 'bugs', the most common being androgen insensitivity syndrome, androgenital syndrome and kwolu-aatmwol.

Androgen insensitivity syndrome. Here the chromosomal structure shows the usual 46-chromosome, XY male pattern. However, the androgen receptors in the body do not recognize the circulating androgens: they are there, but, as far as the body is concerned, when the foetus is in the uterus, they are not – so the foetus develops, by default, as a female. The outcome is a baby with an XY (i.e. male) chromosome pattern, but without the corresponding male genitalia. The baby *looks* female and is identified as a girl at birth. The Müllerian system does not develop. Interestingly, their (internal) testes produce enough oestrogen to stimulate breast development at puberty, but insensitivity to the androgen that mediates underarm and pubic hair in both sexes means that this hair does not grow. Individuals with this syndrome are infertile and do not menstruate.

Adrenogenital syndrome can affect both XX and XY foetuses. It results from a reduction in adrenal cortisol (hydrocortisone), which in turn leads to an increase in adrenal androgens (male hormones). For boys the main impact is an accelerated onset of puberty, but, other than this, males with this condition experience few problems. In females, however, the excess of androgens leads to a masculinization of the body – an enlarged clitoris at birth (which may look like a penis) and the development of a sac resembling a scrotum. Confusions as to the sex of an infant have occurred, but these days early surgical 'correction' is used and with oral cortisol given in childhood typical adolescent development follows. The internal sex organs are usually unaffected.

Kwolu-aatmwol is the New Guinea name given to a form of pseudohermaphroditism which is found there and in the Dominican Republic. It means 'female thing-transforming-into-male thing' and arises through a genetic disorder arising from a deficiency in the enzyme 5-alpha ructase, which prevents testosterone from producing the usual male genitalia at the foetal stage of development. Individuals born with this condition have genitals that are ambiguous – their penis looks more like a clitoris and their scrotum is unfused and looks like **labia** (Herdt 1990). Often such individuals are raised as girls, although they are genetically XY. At puberty they produce testosterone and become masculinized. Their penis grows, their testes descend, they grow facial hair and their musculature takes on a male shape. Such individuals seem to transform from girl children into men as they become adult.

These and other conditions are sometimes regarded as 'natural experiments'. They have been studied by psychologists to explore issues about the development of gender identity, sexual orientation and 'normal' sexual development.

Hormones and menstruation

One of the most important functions of hormones in adult women, once they begin to ovulate and until the **menopause**, is the control of their cycle of fertility: the (about) monthly production of an ovum and the preparation of the uterus for pregnancy if that ovum is fertilized.

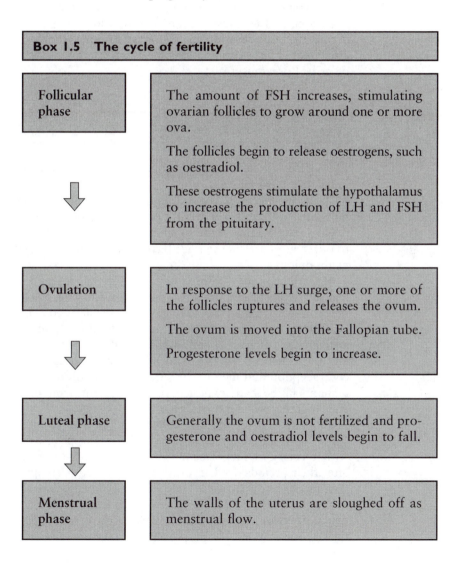

Box 1.5 The cycle of fertility

Follicular phase	The amount of FSH increases, stimulating ovarian follicles to grow around one or more ova. The follicles begin to release oestrogens, such as oestradiol. These oestrogens stimulate the hypothalamus to increase the production of LH and FSH from the pituitary.
⇩	
Ovulation	In response to the LH surge, one or more of the follicles ruptures and releases the ovum. The ovum is moved into the Fallopian tube. Progesterone levels begin to increase.
⇩	
Luteal phase	Generally the ovum is not fertilized and progesterone and oestradiol levels begin to fall.
⇩	
Menstrual phase	The walls of the uterus are sloughed off as menstrual flow.

Premenstrual syndrome

In the 1960s Dalton (see Parlee 1973 for a review) first suggested that women experience a variety of negative emotional, cognitive and physical effects as a result of the hormonal changes that precede menstruation – what became known as the **premenstrual syndrome** (PMS). The list of symptoms associated with this syndrome extends to more than 150, including headache, backache, abdominal bloating, irritability, depression and tension. Blechman *et al.* (1988) reviewed the various symptoms and concluded that they are far too diverse to constitute a 'syndrome'. None the less, throughout the 1960s and 1970s many studies were reported which claimed to find evidence for 'moodiness' associated with the menstrual cycle: women typically showing heightened feelings of wellbeing around ovulation, and feelings of depression, tension and irritability during the period just before and during menstruation. These effects have been attributed to the hormonal changes associated with the cycle of fertility described previously.

Research evidence Biology is not destiny

Although excess oestrogen, falling progesterone and oestrogen/progesterone imbalance have all been proposed as possible causes of negative mood, no clear evidence has been found for any link between any of these hormone levels and reports of mood effects (see Rubin *et al.* 1981, for a review). Studies that claim to show systematic mood changes in relation to different phases in the cycle have been heavily criticized for their poor methodology.

McFarlane *et al.* (1988) conducted a detailed, lengthy and methodologically sophisticated study to try to address these problems. For example, they told participants that they were looking at 'mood changes over time' rather than that it was a study of 'premenstrual syndrome effects'; they used instruments to measure mood which did not prime negative responses; and they included women who had normal cycles, women taking oral contraception and men in the study. Their main result was that all participants in the study experienced mood swings from one day to another and, indeed, over a day.

But there were no systematic effects on mood as reported in a daily diary which were different for the three groups, except just one – the women with normal cycles reported more pleasant moods during and immediately after their periods. McFarlane *et al.* also asked participants to report on their moods retrospectively. They filled in a questionnaire about their moods at the end of the 70 days over which the study took place. Interestingly, their responses here did show a PMS effect in women's recollections of their moods. Women reported in this questionnaire that they had had

PMS-linked 'moodiness', even though this was inconsistent with the diary entries they had made at the time. The most significant mood effect found in the whole study was to do with a weekly cycle – generally all groups reported more negative moods on Mondays and more positive moods on Fridays (perhaps this should be called the TGIF syndrome).

Slade (1984) also found no associations between mood and cycle of fertility, although she did find that pain and fluid retention were more common in the premenstrual and menstrual phases. Blechman *et al.* (1988) suggest that these physical symptoms, together with apprehension about them, may well be the basis for women seeing themselves as 'feeling premenstrual', rather than any hormonal effect.

Testosterone and aggression

In many animal species testosterone has been shown to play an active role in aggressive behaviour (Kalat 1992). Its effects in humans, however, are less clear. Although press reports of studies conducted on the possible link have generally made unequivocal claims – Goleman, writing in the *New York Times*, for example, entitled his piece 'Aggression in men: hormone levels are the key' (Goleman 1990) – academic commentators are usually much more circumspect. Brannon (1996), for instance, summarizes the situation thus:

> researchers have used different approaches to investigate the actions of testosterone on various behaviours and the reaction of testosterone to various experiences. All of the studies found some relationship between testosterone and behaviour, but the relationships were very complex. Research on human subjects does not confirm a clear cause-and-effect relationship between hormone levels and aggressive behaviours.
>
> (Brannon 1996: 63)

This complexity is evident, for example, in a number of studies carried out by Dabbs and his colleagues. One study produced what seem at first sight to be fairly clear-cut results. It examined testosterone levels in military veterans (Dabbs and Morris 1990). The men whose testosterone levels were in the top 10 per cent of the 4462 tested were found, compared with the rest of the sample, to more often report:

> having trouble with parents, teachers and classmates; being assaultive towards other adults; going AWOL in the military; and using hard drugs, marijuana and alcohol. They also reported having more sexual partners. The overall picture is one of delinquency, substance abuse, and a general tendency towards excessive behaviour.
>
> (Dabbs and Morris 1990: 209)

But these results were not as clear-cut as this assertion implies. The data obtained showed an interaction with socio-economic status. Men with higher income and more education were, on average, significantly less likely to have high levels of circulating testosterone than men with low income and less education. Only in those men with lower socio-economic status was there a tendency for high levels of testosterone to be linked to antisocial behaviour. These data can be interpreted in many different ways. Dabbs and Morris concluded that high-status men learn to cope with their antisocial behaviours in a way that low-status men do not. But Brannon (1996) points out that high-status men could, just as easily, simply be in a position not to get into trouble. As soon as an attempt is made to tease out cause-and-effect, interpretation gets very difficult.

Dabbs and his colleagues (Dabbs *et al.* 1988) have also studied testosterone in women, looking at samples of prison inmates and college students. They found that among the prison sample, women with the highest levels of testosterone were more likely to have records of unprovoked violence, whereas those who were serving sentences for defensive violence (such as murdering an abusive partner or spouse) had the lowest levels of testosterone. But the average levels of testosterone were the same for the prison and student samples. Again, these data can be interpreted in a number of different ways, requiring consideration of social and cultural factors as mediators of biology.

Possibly the data from Dabbs and his colleagues that are the most difficult to interpret (Dabbs *et al.* 1990) are from a study looking at male testosterone levels in relation to different professions. They found that the highest average levels of testosterone were found in football players and actors, and the lowest in church ministers. Salesmen and firefighters, who they assumed would have high testosterone levels, did not have high levels. The researchers' attempts to account for the patterns they found begin to look more and more confused: 'ministers tend to be self-effacing and actors self-aggrandising. Ministers praise the glory of God, whereas actors keep the glory to themselves' (Dabbs *et al.* 1990: 1264).

Other sex differences in physiology

The hormonal differences between males and females lead to different development at puberty. Boys' bodies develop more muscle and less fat than girls' bodies. The average male body has 15 per cent fat, whereas the average female body has 27 per cent fat. In men about 40 per cent of body weight consists of muscle; in women it is 23 per cent. Men also tend to have a higher metabolic rate – they 'burn' more calories whether they are just resting or taking exercise. One consequence is that men usually find it easier than women to lose weight. For men, exercise alone can result in weight loss, whereas women usually need to reduce their food intake as well (Meijer *et al.* 1991; Gleim 1993). The higher level of androgens circulating in the male body also leads to differences in metabolism. For example, men have higher levels of protein synthesis, and hence need more protein in their diet (Phillips *et al.* 1993).

This difference in physiology may contribute to men's greater susceptibility to a number of diseases, including, for example, cardio-vascular disease (CVD) and cancer. Men have higher mortality than females across the lifespan (Strickland 1988). This has been true for at least the past century, and the pattern is found worldwide. However, once more, it is difficult to tease out what may be biological from other influences. For example, stress is a risk factor for cardio-vascular disease (CVD), and men are much more likely to die from this cause than women, especially between the ages of 35 to 75. But how far is this a matter of straight physiology (when subjected to stress, males tend to release more adrenaline than females, and adrenaline raises blood pressure and heart rate)? And how much is it to do with lifestyle and gender roles? Helgeson (1990) found that men were more likely than women to respond to stress in ways that are dysfunctional (that is, are risk factors for CVD).

Summary box Do hormones affect human behaviour?

Although there is a body of research evidence to show that hormones have a direct and significant impact on the behaviour of lower (that is, lower in an evolutionary sense) animals, the evidence for their influence on human behaviour is much less clear.

- There is good research evidence that a lack of sex hormones at puberty interferes with the acquisition of a desire for sex. It seems that hormones are required to trigger human sexuality, in the sense of making people want to have sex.
- Sex hormones also clearly have a direct influence on physiology, and, through this, on morphology too. This means that male and female bodies are differently shaped (although there is an enormous range in both male and female body forms) and work somewhat differently at a biological level. These physiological and morphological differences can have an impact on behaviour. For example, they may lead to men and women using different strategies for losing weight.
- More subtle aspects of human sexuality seem to be mediated more by social and cultural influences than by hormones. Research evidence indicates that all sorts of factors come into play, including expectations (for instance, in relation to premenstrual syndrome), worries (such as concern about becoming pregnant), opportunities (such as when it is possible to have spontaneous sex) and social class (which affects, for example, the likelihood of getting into trouble for misbehaviour).

Sex differences in brain architecture

As we saw earlier, men's and women's bodies typically possess distinguishing characteristics (you probably don't need us to tell you that!). Men tend to be taller and heavier, although there is considerable diversity. Other obvious morphological divergencies are the distinctive genitals of each sex, and the different patterns of breast development, body-hair and hair-loss.

What are less obvious are differences in the architecture of the brain. From the subject's beginning, psychologists have claimed that there are differences between men's and women's brains. At first their claims simply mirrored popular 'wisdom' of the time – women were seen as intellectually inferior to men and as having brains unsuited to scholarship (although such claims did not go unchallenged at the time; see Shields 1975, and Lewin 1984b for reviews). At first the arguments for difference were based on the observation that women's brains tend to be smaller than men's. It took until the late 1960s before researchers began to examine the possibility that the brains of men and women might be organized differently, with the first support provided by a study conducted on rats by Raisman and Field (1971).

Much of the work in respect to human brains has concentrated on differences in **lateralization**. The **cerebral cortex** of the brain is divided into two halves – two hemispheres – joined by a large bundle of nerves, the **corpus callosum**. In adult humans each hemisphere has developed a specialist function. Typically (the pattern is somewhat different for left-handers) the left hemisphere specializes in language skills, and the right hemisphere specializes in spatial skills. This was first discovered by examining the effects of strokes (a stroke to the left hemisphere tends to interfere with language, whereas one to the right hemisphere tends to interfere with skills involving spatial relationships).

Research data point to the possibility that men are more lateralized than women: the specialization of each hemisphere is more complete. For example, Shaywitz *et al.* (1995) used magnetic resonance imaging (MRI) to map neurological activity in the brain while men and women were solving verbal problems. In all of the men in the study, only the left hemisphere was seen to be active when working on these problems. The women, however, seemed to be using both hemispheres. They concluded that: 'Our data provide clear evidence for a sex difference in the functional organization of the brain for language. . . . We have demonstrated remarkable differences . . . between normal males and females' (Shaywitz *et al.* 1995: x).

This difference is consistent with the observation that women are much less likely than men to experience speech deficits following a left hemisphere stroke (see Springer and Deutsch 1989). Brannon (1996), however, points out that the magnitude of the difference is limited, and many studies have failed to find it. It would seem, she suggests, that the differences in lateralization are small but real. Different theories have been proposed to explain how the difference comes about. Waber (1976) suggests that it arises because girls tend to mature faster than boys. Geschwind and Galaburda (1987) propose that it is produced by the extra testosterone circulating in the male foetus before birth, which slows down the growth of the left hemisphere, allowing the right hemisphere to develop faster. Kimura (1992) has questioned whether women are less lateralized, and suggested, instead, that the difference has more to do with the organization of the language centres in the front and back of the cerebral cortex.

Other work has explored the possibilities of sex differences in other parts of the brain, including the **hypothalamus**, the **thalamus** and the corpus callosum. Again, studies on rats led the way, with the discovery in the 1970s that a small area of the hypothalamus, called the **sexually dimorphic nucleus**, is much larger in males than in females (see Gorski 1987 for a review of these studies). Evidence for a similar difference in humans has been claimed by Swaab and Fliers (1985). This area is very sensitive to testosterone and oestrogens, and in rats it is associated with sexual response and mating behaviour. Swaab (quoted in Gibbons 1991) has suggested that the operation of this structure might be involved in the development of male identity. However this claim is controversial. Brannon (1996), for example, points out that 'gender identity is a complex concept relating to feelings . . . that are not limited to or congruent with sexual behaviour' (1996: 81) and concludes that we simply do not know what this structure does or how it works in humans.

Even more controversial is a claim by LeVay (1991) that there are structural differences between the brains of male homosexuals and heterosexuals; that, in effect, homosexuality is a genetic predisposition – or, as popularly expressed, that there is a **'gay gene'**. Comparing autopsies on brains of heterosexual men, homosexual men and women, he found that another area of the brain (the interstitial nuclei of the hypothalamus) was twice as large in the heterosexual men compared with both the homosexual men and the women. But there may be other explanations for the difference. All of the homosexual men that LeVay studied died of AIDS-related illnesses, whereas less than half of the heterosexual men had died of AIDS, and only one of the women. So the difference may reflect, in part at least, differential damage related to AIDS. A number of other differences have been claimed, but evidence for them is generally fairly weak, often taken from quite small samples (see Brannon 1996 for a fuller review of these data).

Differences in mental capacities

As mentioned at the beginning of this section, historically, psychology started from the preconception that men are more intelligent than women. Yet one of the earliest intelligence tests devised by psychologists had to be 'modified' to make sure that men scored, on average, the same as women. Otherwise, the average scores for women proved higher than the average scores for men. This 'adjustment' was still going on in the 1950s and 1960s in the UK, to make sure that as many boys as girls 'passed' the 11+ test (the test used to select pupils for grammar schools).

What gradually became apparent, as tests were made more sophisticated, was that women and girls consistently scored higher, on average, on tests of verbal intelligence, and men and boys scored higher on tests of mathematical and spatial ability (see Maccoby and Jacklin 1974 for a review). More recent work suggests, however, that the difference in verbal skills is more complex than was first thought, and the differences seem to be lessening over time. Brannon (1996) suggests that the difference is small, and shows up only in some verbal abilities (such as spelling) and not in others (such as verbal reasoning). Equally, recent work on mathematical ability indicates a much more complicated picture than was originally apparent. Boys' and men's advantage is concentrated in mathematical skills that involve spatial reasoning. On spatial tasks, men and boys seem to have a consistent, but small, advantage over women and girls in just some skills (Kimura 1992).

Overall, Hyde (1981), using a more sophisticated form of statistical analysis than used in other studies, suggests that only about 1 per cent of variability in performance on aptitude tests can be attributed to sex, with 99 per cent a result of a complex mix of other factors. However, she points out, it is impossible to tease out what may be the contribution of biology (that is, arising from differences in brain architecture and physiology) and what may be due to a host of other influences – such as different expectations, experiences and interests – all of which are socially and culturally mediated. We will come back to this issue in Chapter 2.

Summary box Do men and women have different brains?

- The research evidence suggests that there are some small differences in the way men's and women's brains are organized, leading to small average differences in their mental function. At least some of this may well be a result of biological differences, particularly as they affect the development of the brain in infancy and early childhood. The process of lateralization seems to progress slightly differently in men and women.
- As a consequence, women tend, on average, to show a small superiority in language skills, and men in spatial skills.
- However, these differences are small. They cannot be used to account for much greater differences in men's and woman's performance – for example, that there are many more male than female mathematical 'geniuses'. Social and cultural factors play a significant part. As social attitudes and expectations change, and as girls gain greater opportunities to engage in 'male' subjects (such as mathematics and engineering) during their education, these performative differences seem to be getting less and less.

The sexual response

In 1966 Masters and Johnson published *Human Sexual Response*. This work addressed the physiological features of sexual arousal and sexual activity. The people who took part in the studies (382 women and 312 men) were volunteers and mostly married couples. More than 10,000 sexual responses were examined, including sexual intercourse, masturbation and 'artificial coition' (self-stimulation using instruments that allowed direct viewing and film recording). From this work Masters and Johnson went on to develop a model of sexual response divided into four phases: the excitement phase, the plateau phase, orgasm, and the resolution phase.

It is usually accepted that these different components of the sexual response are biologically pre-programmed – they do not need to be learned and happen automatically given the right stimulation. It is not

Box 1.6 Masters and Johnson's four stages of sexual response

Excitement. The first biological indicator of sexual excitement in women is vaginal lubrication, which typically appears within 30 seconds of stimulation. This, Masters and Johnson discovered, is exuded from the semi-permeable vaginal walls in response to an increase in blood supply. In men, erection can be even faster – but also much slower. Erection also results (mechanically speaking) from an increase in blood supply. Both sexes show genital engorgement and both also experience patterns of muscle contraction. Women also show erectile responses both in the clitoris and of the nipples. Changes also occur in the two sets of genital lips (the major and minor labia) yielding a blooming effect, and the vaginal barrel begins to oscillate with distensions exceeding constrictions: its inner two-thirds can increase in diameter by 300 per cent. In men the scrotum is raised and the spermatic cords shorten. Both sexes (women much more often than men) can show a 'sex flush' or rash (which, unlike blushing, begins on the abdomen).

The plateau phase covers some further changes that follow excitement (for example, raised pulse rate) which can be regarded as precursors to any subsequent orgasm. This phase is more marked in women than in men. The most remarkable is the 'orgasmic platform' – the swelling of the lower vagina, reducing its diameter and increasing its penile 'grip'. In parallel the clitoris retracts and is lifted away from the vaginal entrance. In men the testes enlarge and are pulled further into the scrotum. When they are fully elevated the man is on the verge of orgasm.

The orgasm. If they climax, women experience marked, fast, rhythmic contractions of the lower vagina, gradually reducing in intensity and increasing in interval. The uterus and sometimes the anal sphincter also join in these contractions. In men, the sperm which have moved into the seminal vesicles and ampullae are expelled by contractions into the urethra. Simultaneously, the prostate gland spasms, releasing prostatic fluid. This mixture is held in the urethral bulb. Ejaculation results from contractions of the penis and urethral bulb. Pulse rate and blood pressure peak during orgasm and breathing becomes panting. Some quite extreme muscle spasms and facial grimacing are commonplace. Subjectively, sensations of orgasm tend to slightly precede contractions in women and ejaculation in men.

The resolution phase. Within a few seconds of the end of orgasm, the body begins to return to 'normal', although some signs (for example, partial penile erection) take longer to subside. Men show a 'refractory period' of between a few minutes and hours before re-arousal is possible. Many women do not have a 'refractory period' and can re-orgasm rapidly. Some may manage quite a number, the 'multi-orgasmic response'.

surprising that, at a physiological level, sexual response should tap into pre-programmed patterns, given how crucial it is to evolutionary survival. However, as the recent massive sales of the erection-inducing drug Viagra have shown, even here instinct is by no means the whole story. The enormous interest in the drug shows that many men feel that they have problems in getting a satisfactory erection. Although this can be a consequence of medical disorders and the side-effects of some forms of medical treatment, erection is notoriously sensitive to social and situational factors. Some men, for example, cannot be aroused except in particular ways – for example, by viewing certain erotic stimuli, such as bondage.

Equally, for women, although the machinery for sexual response may be in working order, biologically speaking, being turned on (and hence able to respond) has much more to do with non-biological factors. And although it is often assumed that women's arousal is much more dependent on emotional stimuli than it is for men, the evidence for this is largely anecdotal. Certainly, women as well as men can become fixated (that is, dependent for sexual arousal) on particular stimuli – as evidenced by the material available on the internet. One website, for example, is devoted to a woman who gains sexual satisfaction from having fish hooks inserted into her breasts.

Summary box Biology and sexual arousal

As with other aspects of human sexuality, people's sexual response seems to have a clear biological foundation. It appears to be a biological mechanism which, once triggered, goes through a sequence of genetically programmed stages of response. However, given the human qualities that people possess, this mechanism does not operate in any simple way. It is highly mediated by expectations and experience. A good example is 'performance anxiety' in men. Men who have had sexual encounters in the past where they have failed to achieve an erection or have lost it during sex often can become anxious during sex, and this anxiety affects their ability to achieve or maintain erection. This can become problematic, since the more it happens, the likelier it is to go on happening. The good news is, however, that the cycle can be broken, either through formal therapy or by simply finding a sympathetic partner who is able to help them overcome the anxiety. Equally women can develop aversion to sex following bad experiences, which can stop them becoming sexually aroused and hence prevent them from being able to engage in and enjoy sex. At its most extreme this can lead to **vaginismus** – a conditioned response (see Chapter 3) in which the vagina clenches up when any attempt is tried to make her sexually aroused. This makes penetration impossible. Again the good news is that this response is reversible, once more either through therapy or finding a sympathetic and caring partner to help her overcome her anxiety.

Sociobiology and evolutionary psychology

In this section we will look briefly at more recent theorization which has expanded the kinds of behaviours considered to be biologically driven: sociobiology and evolutionary psychology.

Sociobiology

Sexual reproduction itself is a key driver of evolution. As Gribbin and Gribbin neatly state, '[i]n everyday language, sex speeds up evolution' (1998: 250). It is sexual reproduction that creates the genetic variability that enables change. The crucial implication of this for psychology has been that evolution has come to be seen as encompassing wider aspects of sexual behaviour. Darwin himself made this connection:

> Sexual Selection . . . depends, not on a struggle for existence in relation to other organic beings or to external conditions, but on a struggle between the individuals of one sex, *generally the males*, for the possession of the other sex.
>
> (Darwin 1859: 65; emphasis, added)

The rationale for suggesting that sexual behaviour is a feature of evolution is that it is reproduction that is what really matters for evolutionary survival – it is the *only* way for an inherited characteristic to be passed from one generation to the next. Thus evolution favours those organisms that get to reproduce, and whose offspring themselves get to reproduce. In other words, having sex which results in the birth of offspring is the sole way of achieving evolutionary 'success'. Living things have evolved a wide range of different instinctual behaviours to optimize reproduction. In this sense, sex really is about 'the birds and the bees' – think, for example, of the 'courtship display' of the male peacock. It is not surprising, then, that a number of theories have been developed about the ways in which human instinct may be involved. These theories propose that there are 'natural' differences in the behaviour of men and women that are related to giving each sex a potential evolutionary advantage over others of the same sex.

This idea has been neatly encapsulated in the term 'selfish genes' (Dawkins 1976), within a development of evolutionary theory called sociobiology. Its theorization proposes that organisms are predisposed, because of the force of evolution, to behave in ways that increase the probability of producing offspring, and to maximize the number of offspring produced. Sociobiologists (such as Dawkins 1976, 1982, 1988; and Wilson 1980) have argued that this leads to rather different forms of social behaviour in men and women.

Men, according to this argument, are pre-programmed for promiscuity: men's selfish genes will maximize their (that is, their genes') chances of surviving by the man having sex at every opportunity and with as many women as possible. Women, on the other hand, are, according to this theory, pre-programmed for selectivity and settling down. Women's selfish genes will maximize their (that is, their genes') chances of surviving by the woman carefully selecting a mate who will produce the strongest, most-able-to-survive children, and who will stay around to protect and feed her and the children until they reach sexual maturity. The difference, it is proposed, comes about because, relatively speaking, women can produce only a limited number of children in their child-bearing years, whereas men can inseminate large numbers of women and hence have many children.

In sociobiology, direct links are often drawn between evolutionary adaptive strategies and highly enculturated social behaviour. As we saw at the beginning of the chapter, this includes housework. Gribbin and Gribbin provide another typical example:

> In terms of evolutionary success, the prime requirements that a man should seek in a marriage partner are youth and health. . . . A woman, on the other hand, requires rather different attributes in a partner. . . . She needed a male that had proved himself fit . . . And a man proves himself fit firstly by surviving to a reasonable age, and secondly by achieving wealth or status within society. A woman who mated with a successful older man was likely to leave more descendants, in the long run, than a woman who chose a young, unproven male as her partner.
>
> (Gribbin and Gribbin 1998: 269–70)

Baker (1996), in his book *Sperm Wars*, has taken this idea of genes directly and profoundly affecting behaviour even further. In it he claims that there is an evolutionary advantage to infidelity. He argues that a woman's body, unconsciously primed by instinctive evolutionary forces, leads her into situations where she has sex with two men at the time when she is most fertile. Baker accords the body's instinct an amazing level of insight and cunning. Having described a situation where a woman has a one-night stand with an ex-boyfriend, he suggests the following:

> The underlying strategy her body was pursuing was that, no matter who fathered the child, the man best suited to help her raise the child is her partner. It was vital to this strategy, therefore, that any infidelity should not be discovered. . . . When she gets home, she works very hard to have sex with her partner. Consciously, she will have seen this as helping to avoid detection. If she can get her partner to inseminate her, any tell-tale damp patch on the sheets or any smell of semen will not arouse his suspicions. What her conscious mind will not realise, though, is that having collected sperm from her ex-boyfriend, her body is now very keen to collect sperm from her partner. Her body has already decided that, on balance, her ex-boyfriend would make a better genetic father than her partner. The one thing it does not know is how the ejaculates compare. She wants to have her egg fertilized by her ex-boyfriend only if his ejaculate is also the more fertile and competitive. The way for her to discover this is to pit one ejaculate against the other. In other words, her body wants to promote *sperm warfare* between the two men.
>
> (Baker 1996: 43–4; emphasis in the original)

Early sociobiological theorization (see, for example, Alexander 1974) speculated that the drives towards particular behaviours were directly encoded in the genes. A rather more subtle kind of theorization has now been developed as evolutionary psychology (see, for example, Buss 1990, 1996; Gribbin and Gribbin 1998; Wright 1996).

Evolutionary psychology

The key element to evolutionary psychology is the idea that natural selection operates on expressed behaviours. In this way it can impact on underlying psychological mechanisms, favouring those that promote successful reproduction and militating against those associated with non-reproduction. Of course, because we cannot inherit acquired characteristics, any such process must have a grounding at a genetic level. The psychological mechanisms and their expression (for example, altruism) need to have a level of predisposition in the genes.

Proponents of evolutionary psychology argue that their theory helps to make sense of empirical findings from experimental social psychology. For example, some research suggests that people are more likely to help (be altruistic towards) strangers who look, act and think like themselves. Such strangers, they claim, are more likely to have a genetic resemblance. In other words, propinquitous altruism indirectly favours the genetic profile of the helper through supporting the person helped (Rushton 1989).

Men across a range of cultures have been shown to favour youthful-looking women (Cunningham 1986; Buss 1989). They also find women more attractive if their waists are about a third narrower than their hips (Singh 1993). If such preferences are the result of a partially inherited mechanism, as evolutionary psychologists would suggest, then men would seem to be 'wired up' to choose reproductive partners whose youthful fertility offers the best chance of genetic profiles being reproduced.

It is worth noting that a problem with this kind of theorization is that a plausible story can be told to explain almost any 'facts'. Were the result otherwise – for example, if men showed a preference for rather more mature women who have already given birth – it could be argued that their choices were for experienced, 'better' mothers. The theory, moreover, is completely untestable.

Similar problems apply to research into women's notions of male attractiveness. Buss (1994) has argued from an evolutionary psychology perspective that this is mediated by selection for protection and support (that is, men who seem mature and dominant). However, more recent research (Perrett 1998) using image 'morphing' suggests that women prefer men's faces that are *not* over-masculine (in the sense of strong jaws and heavy brows). However, he did also confirm a male preference for more 'feminine' women's faces. Again, Perrett's finding about men's faces can be explained in evolutionary psychology language. 'High testosterone' faces just might signal violent, unstable partners, and to avoid them might bring a man with better parenting potential. However, the evidence for such a link is far from clear, and the ability of evolutionary psychology to assimilate contradictory contentions (for example, between Buss and Perrett) is not encouraging.

Summary box Sociobiology and evolutionary psychology

It is worth reiterating that sociobiology and evolutionary psychology fall at the first post when it comes to scientific method. Both are inherently untestable. Their claims cannot be subjected to empirical test, and, crucially, cannot be falsified. They operate only at the level of speculation.

Moreover, both sociobiology and evolutionary psychology are highly selective in the range of human behaviour on which they base their speculations. They focus on the most banal of 'normal' sexual behaviour, mainly that of the stereotypical heterosexual couple engaging in penetrative sex, albeit taking infidelity into their remit. The sheer diversity and range of people's sexual interests, behaviours and turn-ons raises serious doubts about the ability of thee theories to explain human sexuality. It is, for example, hard to see how **sadomasochism** can have any possible evolutionary advantage. And yet this practice is much more common than most people realize. Sadomasochism is less about pain than it is about playing around with power, dominance and submission – the sexual pleasure to be gained by acting in either (or, at different times, both) submissive or dominant roles. As such it highlights the subtle qualities of insight, desire and knowledge that make us human, and separate us from lower animals. While both humans and animals can be sexual, only humans can be erotic. Indeed, the very word 'erotic' conveys what is most human about human sexuality, stressing the cultural features of human desire. Whether we are talking about sexy underwear, leather gear or red roses, it is hard to see how these can have anything other than symbolic meanings. Certainly their ability to seduce and arouse cannot, surely, be programmed into the genes?

What is at stake, here, however, is not just a matter of poor science and limited theorization. As was mentioned at the beginning of this chapter, biological explanations of human sexuality and gender are currently becoming popular, and are actively favoured by the media. It is interesting to speculate why. One reason is that they are highly plausible and offer neat and simple explanations. Another, more worrying, is that they feed into the anxieties and preoccupations of those with the power to determine what is written and broadcast (and, indeed, researched). Generally these are middle-aged and older men who have a stake in promoting the idea that it is 'natural' for men to be sexually predatory, especially on younger women. Equally, such men have a stake in fostering the perception that women are nagging harpies who constantly complain about men's untidiness and disinterest in housework.

In other words, we should not just look at theories in terms of their scholarly adequacy. We need also to consider their impact upon how people live their lives. Sociobiological and evolutionary psychology theories have largely been formulated in highly misogynist terms, in that they serve male interests and prejudices. Accepted uncritically they encourage us to view certain aspects of human sexual behaviour as 'natural' and thus, by implication, as irresistible. They draw attention away from the ethics of how people *should* behave. As you will see in Chapter 10, this is now happening in relation to rape, with claims being made that it is a product of evolutionary force. We would argue that such a claim insults men as much as it can contribute to creating conditions that, at the least, devalue women and, at the worst, may increase their vulnerability to sexual assault.

Significant differences

Adopting a biopsychological approach need not, and should not, be taken as saying the same thing as 'biology is destiny'. Indeed, neo-Darwinian evolutionary theory *requires* an environment through which change is mediated and genetic potential is manifested. Increasingly, that environment is human-made rather than 'natural'. Only over quite long periods of time do such changes (sometimes) become a permanent feature of the species, as was the case for the variations Darwin noted on the different Galapagos Islands. Human evolution, in the sense of stable, non-reversible developments, takes place over long time-scales. The population of present-day Rome is not more evolved in any significant biological sense than the population who lived in the city in the days of the Roman Empire – any differences are the result of cultural change. However, it is equally true that biological differences (for instance, whether a particular inhabitant of Rome is female or male) led to major differences in life possibilities 2000 years ago, and that remains the case (if not so dramatically) today.

From the beginnings of modernism, both human biology and the human environment were seen as sites of intervention whereby the human condition could be improved, and this dual focus still operates today. However, it easily slips into a tension or an ideological choice, with the disfavoured site being reduced to a trivial or subsidiary possibility – conservatives favouring biology as the site of action, progressives favouring the environment. Both possibilities can marshal research evidence and common sense into a compelling, and singularizing, story. The case for environmental centrality follows in the next chapter.

Further reading

Burr, V. (1998) *Gender and Social Psychology*. London: Routledge.
Trew, K. and Kremer, J. (1998) *Gender and Psychology*. London: Arnold.

2 Social and cultural paradigms

[T]he first and most momentous step of primitive men [*sic*] towards civilization must have been the evolution of rigid customs, the enforced observance of which disciplined men [*sic*] to the control of the immediate impulses.

(McDougall 1942: 244)

In this chapter we examine ways in which gender and sexuality are constituted through social and cultural influences. We will look at how our experiences of being male or female, gay or straight, sexually active or celibate are mediated by the society and cultures in which we live. We will explore how they open and close various possibilities for what we can be and do, and for how we think and feel about ourselves and others. We will look in particular at psychological theory and research which informs our understanding of the social and cultural forces at play in gender and sexuality, but will also consider what anthropology and sociology can offer.

Internalizing the external

When psychology was first emerging as a discipline, people were preoccupied with the conflict between nature – 'sharp in tooth and claw' – and civilization. This was the time when the British had established an empire, in the belief that they were 'civilizing' the 'savages' of other nations. The self-help books of the time were full of advice to people about how to control their 'brute animality' and 'baser instincts' in order to achieve the rational, spiritual and educated qualities of an authentic human being. More generally, early twentieth-century human science was preoccupied with the desirability of progress, both of individuals – to become better people – and of societies – to become more civilized. It was believed that progress depended on the external becoming internal – the civilizing customs of society being incorporated into individual minds and into shared beliefs and ideologies, allowing people to control their innate impulses. In other words, there was a deep interest in the mechanisms of control (and hence progress) by **internalization** of progressive human values (cf. Ross 1991).

Box 2.1 Internalizing the external

The social science disciplines are all concerned with how the external – culture, society and their rules and mores – becomes internalized into people's thinking and hence influences how they act and feel and how they experience the world around them. But they tend to concentrate on different aspects of this:

Anthropologists tend to attend to the role that culture plays in internalization. Examples are the rites of passage through which male and female adult identities are conferred, and the way in which, in many cultures, different genders live segregated lives, with a clear demarcation of tasks, roles and responsibilities.

Sociologists tend to focus on internalization as the product of broader social processes, such as the way that socio-economic forces shape the roles of men and women. Marxist theorization, for instance, argues that capitalism requires a plentiful supply of compliant male workers, enabled to devote a majority of their time to their work by the efforts of their wives taking care of domestic life, including child-rearing. Thus the system is seen to rely on boys aspiring to becoming 'the breadwinner' and girls to becoming 'a good wife and mother'. It is seen to work because boys and girls internalize different gender identities.

Psychologists tend to concentrate on internalization as a process of socialization. This is the process whereby children gain from their family (often called the agent of primary socialization) and, somewhat later, other social institutions such as schools (thus called agents of secondary socialization) a knowledge and understanding of the social rules governing their behaviour and determining their role, position and identity. Gender role theory, for example, is concerned with the way that children learn how to behave appropriately in respect to their gender – as boys and girls, men and women.

In this chapter we will look at the contributions of all three of these disciplines to our understanding of the role played by social and cultural influences on gender. We begin by illustrating the approaches of anthropology and sociology, and then move on to examining psychological approaches in more detail.

The contribution of anthropology: the role of culture

It was in anthropology, in the 1920s and 1930s, that one of the first challenges was made to the assumption that gender differences are a product of biology. At that time in the United States anthropology had taken a turn which distinguished it from British social anthropology – namely, a concern with individuals and their **enculturation** (that is, the way in which socialization is culturally mediated) rather than an emphasis on society and culture *per se*. Two leading lights in this US tradition were Ruth Benedict and Margaret Mead. The fact that they were women was important, because, unlike male anthropologists, they talked to women as women and about women's lives and experience.

The work of Margaret Mead

This was very clear in Mead's two famous books *Coming of Age in Samoa* (1928) and *Growing Up in New Guinea* (1930). In both books young women's culturally specific experience got a clear voice, and Mead was able to show that there was considerable diversity in the way that gender operates in these cultures – and large differences from mainstream US culture. Equally, Benedict reported on cultures where, for instance, the 'double standard' over marital fidelity did not operate and, in one case (the Zuñi), where it was the wife and mistress who exchanged blows rather than the husband and his wife's lover (Benedict 1935: 77). However, it was Mead who really put the cat among the pigeons with her classic *Sex and Temperament in Three Primitive Societies* (Mead 1935) which described three New Guinea tribes: the Arapesh, the Mundugumor and the Tchambuli.

Box 2.2 Different gender roles in different cultures

Mead reported that in *Arapesh* society both men and women behaved in what western culture would see as a decidedly 'feminine' manner. The opposite held for the *Mundugumor*, where both men and women demonstrated what western culture would see as a decidedly 'macho' way of behaving. This was not to say that men and women were the same. They could, and did, have gender-specific roles and statuses. Rather, the social behaviour of men and women in these cultures was, she claimed, evidence that temperament was the result of cultural conditioning and was not innate. But most salient to Mead's theorizing were the lake-dwelling *Tchambuli*:

> The Tchambuli have . . . used the obvious fact of sex as an organizing point for the information of social personality, even though they seem to us to have reversed the normal picture. While there is reason to believe that not every Tchambuli woman is born with a dominating, organizing, administrative temperament, actively sexed and willing to initiate sex-relations, possessive, definite, robust, practical and impersonal in outlook, still most Tchambuli girls grow up to display these traits. And while there is definitive evidence to show that all Tchambuli men are not, by native endowment, the delicate responsive actors of a play staged for the women's benefit, still most Tchambuli boys manifest this coquettish play-acting personality most of the time. Because the Tchambuli formulation of sex-attitudes contradicts our usual premises, we can see clearly that Tchambuli culture has arbitrarily permitted certain human traits to women, and allotted others, equally arbitrarily, to men.
>
> (Mead 1935: 211–12)

Mead was to go on to become something of cultural guru in the USA, having considerable impact on popular culture, most notably through her book *Male and Female* (1949). But it was the thesis concerning the relativity of our notions of femininity and masculinity that truly stirred and provoked academic thought. If what it means to be a woman or a man can differ so markedly from one culture to another, then surely this must mean that masculinity and femininity are the products of culture and not of biology?

Culture can be defined as the network of customs, rituals and rules that provide social coherence in a group – to 'belong' to the group requires following the group's rules and engaging in its rituals and customs. It can be applied as much to groups in industrialized societies as to 'exotic' groups like the tribes studied by Mead. Indeed, cultural theorists often talk of 'subcultures' in this context. Examples include groups such as 'crusties' and 'bikers'. Other examples are groups defined by a common religious faith (such as Roman Catholics or Muslims). Within the rules, rituals and customs of these kinds of cultures and subcultures are particular expectations and requirements about how men and women should behave, and what it means to be 'male' and 'female', and so on. These differ from one culture or subculture to another.

We come back to look at cultural influences several times later in the book. For example, in Chapter 9, 'Bodies', we explore circumcision, male and female; and in Chapter 10, 'Sex crimes', we look at the subcultures within which gang rape occurs.

Summary box The role of culture

- Margaret Mead's work demonstrated that culture has a significant influence on what constitutes gender for a particular group. Groups vary considerably in their expectations about and understandings of appropriate behaviour in terms of gender.
- Culture does not influence gender only in 'exotic' tribes like those studied by Mead. It operates within cultures and subcultures in all societies.
- Although culture is not the only determining factor – individuals in a culture vary enormously in how they behave – it does provide a powerful pressure to conform. Behaviour that does not conform is often subject to sanctions.

The contribution of sociology: the role of social forces

Sociologists are particularly interested in **gender roles**, usually defined as that which is indicated by performative differences in the way men and women act (see Williams and Best 1990). Robert Brannon (1976) has argued that its origins come from the terminology of the theatre, where it is accepted that performing a role does not mean that the 'part' a person plays is them-as-a-person. Rather, all that an actor needs is sufficient cultural understanding of the character they are playing to pass as that person in a convincing manner. From this perspective male and female roles are akin to 'scripts' that people learn and follow. Brannon therefore defined the social science usage of 'role' in terms of the socially encouraged patterns of behaviour that people are expected to perform in specific situations. Gender roles are about the ways that men pass as men, and women pass as women, in a convincing manner. An acute example is the test that is sometimes given to people who want to change their gender. Many doctors require **transsexuals** to spend a period passing as the gender that they want to be – dressing, talking, moving, sitting and interacting appropriately – before they will change their genitals surgically (Raymond 1980).

The work of Talcott Parsons

Role is one of several concepts in social psychology that reflect their dual origin in sociology and in psychology. The key figure in the development of **sex role theory** in sociology (as gender role was then called) was Talcott Parsons. In his earliest writings he framed socialization mainly in the context of the family, although he did acknowledge that, at the time, female roles were opening up and diversifying. Somewhat later he extended his theorization, bringing together a structural account of kinship, a somewhat watered-down psychoanalytic account of personality formation, an analysis of interaction patterns of the household, and the gender-based division of labour (Parsons and Bales 1953).

Parson rejected the possibility that gender differences can be explained in terms of biology. Rather, he saw gender differentiation as a product of **structural functionalism** (the theory for which he is best known). This is a process by which social organization seems to come about through a form of social evolution, in which particular social practices and customs evolve because they benefit the cohesion and smooth working of social groups and communities. Parsons drew on psychoanalytic theory to explain how role acquisition occurs through a process of internalization. According to this theory, each gender gains a **gendered identity** – both competence in and commitment to the role appropriate to their gender:

> relative to the total culture as a whole, the masculine personality tends more to the predominance of instrumental interests, needs and functions, presumably in whatever social system both sexes are involved, while the feminine personality tends more to the primacy of expressive interests, needs and functions. We would expect, by and large, that other things being equal, men would assume more technical, executive and 'judicial' roles, women more supportive, integrative and 'tension managing' roles.
>
> (Parsons and Bales 1953: 101)

Structural functionalism assumes that these different gender roles of men and women perform different but complementary functions, operating together to make society 'work' effectively. By dividing up expressive and instrumental functions, each gender makes its contribution to the smooth running of social organization. Structural functionalism takes a **consensus view of gender** – that these differences are manifestations of humankind's capacity to co-operate for the common good. By contrast, other sociological theories take a **conflict view of gender** – that the different roles and positions of men and women arise out of a conflict of interests. Marxism is a theory concerned with the way that power is wielded by capitalism to the detriment of workers. Most important in the context of gender is feminism, a theory fundamentally concerned with the way in which male patriarchal power is wielded to the detriment of women. Feminist theory will be looked at in more detail in Chapter 5.

Summary box Sociological explanations of gender roles

Sociology seeks to understand the way that gender is influenced by broad social forces.

- Consensus theories like structural functionalism view gender roles as functional – they help society to 'work' effectively. In such theories the different roles played by men and women are mutually beneficial.
- Conflict theories such as Marxism and feminism view gender roles as arising out of conflicts of interests: between different social positions in the case of Marxism; between the patriarchal power of men and the interests of women in the case of feminism.

The contribution of psychology: the role of socialization

Two main kinds of psychological theory have been applied to the question of how children acquire their understanding of gender and learn to behave in gender-appropriate ways: social learning theory and gender schema theory (a development of cognitive developmental theory, which we will examine in the next chapter). In this section we will look at both of these.

Social learning theory

Social learning theory was developed from the general orientation of **behaviourism**. By claiming that human behaviour is learned, behaviourism offered the main challenge to theorization that prioritized the role of 'nature'. It is relatively easy to see how learning could influence the development of gendered behaviour. For example, if when a 2-year-old girl plays with dolls she gets a lot of attention, smiles and approval from those around her, behaviourism argues that she is likely to play with dolls more and more. If she gets ignored or even teased whenever she plays with 'boyish' toys she is likely to gradually lose interest in them. In this way 'feminine' behaviour will be reinforced, and 'unfeminine' behaviour will be, if not always punished, certainly undermined.

Drawing on several simple elements of Hull's learning theory (cue, drive, reinforcement and response), Miller and Dollard (1941) set out to produce an empirical, hypothetico-deductive account of the ideas Freud had formulated, including the mediation of imitation. They called their text *Social Learning and Imitation*. The fundamental axiom underpinning more recent social learning theory (and one that is clearly central to ideas of gender and sexuality, although this was not its main initial concern) is that individual differences in behaviour are the result of social variations in the conditions of learning. This differs from the original theorization of behaviourism by emphasizing the importance of human meaning-making – the way in which the meaning and significance of an event or an experience may make it reinforcing or punishing.

Observational learning and modelling

The first specifically *social* learning theory was produced by Bandura (for example, Bandura and Walters 1963). His starting point was the conviction that human qualities such as gender are primarily the product of socialization rather than biology: 'Although biological characteristics form a basis for gender differentiation, many of the social roles that get tied to gender are not ordained by biological differences. . . . Gender-role development is, therefore, largely a psychosocial phenomenon' (Bandura 1986: 2).

Crucially, he asserted that human learning is much more complicated than the kinds of formulation envisaged by early behaviourists such as Hull, stressing the importance of cognitive and symbolic features of human learning. Probably his most enduring contribution was the idea of **observational learning** – that much human learning consists of first watching and then imitating the behaviour of another. Bandura's is thus an internalizing model of learning, involving the encoding of experience. Another way of approaching this is to locate Bandura as part of the '**cognitive revolution**' that was eventually to overthrow behaviourism as the dominant paradigm in psychology.

Bandura and Walters looked at how children in various cultures develop gender roles. In traditional cultures with highly demarcated gender division of labour they observed that girls tended to stay with their mothers, watching and imitating their domestic activities. The boys accompanied their fathers, and were often given child-size tools so that they could copy their fathers' work activities. Hence Bandura and Walters rejected the idea that all that was going on was learning in the strict behaviourist sense. Rather, they argued, learning is a profoundly *social* experience, involving complex internalization processes:

> While playing with toys that stimulate imitation of adults, children frequently reproduce not only the appropriate adult-role behaviour patterns but also characteristic or idiosyncratic parental patterns of response, including attitudes, mannerisms, gestures, and even voice inflections. . . . Children frequently acquire, in the course of imaginative role-playing, numerous classes of inter-related responses *in toto*, apparently without proceeding through a gradual and laborious process of response differentiation and extinction or requiring a lengthy period of discrimination training.
>
> (Bandura and Walters 1963: 48)

They gave the term **modelling** to this process where children imitate the behaviour of the people around them.

The acquisition of gender roles

Maccoby and Jacklin (1974) have suggested that there are four major themes running through the arguments presented for this kind of learning in relation to the acquisition of gender roles.

1 *Differential reinforcement, on its own, cannot account for the speed and comprehensiveness of the acquisition of gender roles, and so imitation must be involved.*

Sears *et al.* (1965) express this well:

> Gender roles are very broad and very subtle. It would be difficult to imagine that any kind of direct tuition could provide the learning of such elaborate behavioural, attitudinal and manneristic patterns as are subsumed under the rubrics of masculinity and femininity. Furthermore, these qualities are absorbed quite early and are highly resistant to modification.
>
> (Sears *et al.* 1965: 171)

2 *Because parents are easily available, nurturant and powerful, they are the people most likely to be modelled by children in their acquisition of gender roles, particularly in a child's early years.*

This is a fairly commonsense idea, and it may well be less true today than when it was formulated, given the greater access children now have to alternative **role models** through media such as television.

3 *Children are more frequently exposed to models of their own gender than of the other gender.*

Even 30 years ago Maccoby and Jacklin pointed out that this differs between cultures, referring to the way that some cultures practise strict gender segregation and hence increase the degree to which this is the case. But the opposite is also true. For example, for complex sociopolitical and historical reasons, black women of African Caribbean origin in the UK and African origin in the USA are more likely than the average not to live with their children's fathers (see Bryan *et al.* 1985 for a discussion of the British situation, and Marable 1983; hooks 1984 for the USA). Thus their children will have rather different experiences in relation to male and female role models, compared with other groups. Equally, Cheater (1969) describes how many cultures that were once gender segregated are undergoing rapid change, with a consequent impact on children's early experiences. When fathers leave their families to work away from home (a common experience in many poor countries) this, overall, reduces the amount of contact that children have with men. This formulation is thus highly context, culture and subculture specific.

4 *Children tend to imitate role models they see as similar to themselves, and so same-gender models are more imitated than opposite-gender ones.*

This assertion brings the idea of **identification** centrally into the process. Modelling is not just about copying, but also involves higher cognitive processes by which children are selective about the models that they imitate. This formulation argues that gender is an important, even decisive, factor determining a child's role models. A large number of studies have provided empirical evidence to support the contention that children tend to model themselves on a person who is the same gender as themselves. For instance, studies by Raskin and Israel (1981) showed this happening in relation to the people with whom children interacted; Ashton (1983) demonstrated it in relation to characters portrayed in books; and McGhee and Frueh (1980) showed it in relation to television portrayals.

In the 1960s there was a great deal of fine-grained research examining in more detail the characteristics of a person that may influence whether they are the targets for children's modelling. These studies tended to show that children imitate the more dominant, powerful person when more than one person is available (Busey and Bandura 1984); and that the amount of nurturance offered is also a factor (Bandura and Huston 1961; Hetherington 1965; Hetherington and Frankie 1967).

Shifts in identification for boys

The situation is complicated because even in societies that are less gender segregated, young children tend to spend much more time with women than with men. Not only are they more likely to be cared for by their mothers, but nannies, childminders, nursery staff and primary school teachers are almost always women. Thus for both boys and girls, their first primary model is likely to be their mother. For the formulations above to work, at some stage boys must shift their identification to their father and/or other males, to acquire competence at performing a male gender role. The question then arises – how, and for what reasons, does this shift come about? It typically happens well before boys enter into a world in which men are their most usual carers and companions, so it cannot simply be a matter of role-model availability. Two other main explanations are possible:

- at about the age of 3 or 4 years, boys reach a 'wired-in' developmental stage (rather as a tadpole is pre-programmed, genetically, to develop into a frog) which predisposes them to shift their identification; or
- other social influences come into play, which steer boys towards a shift in their identification.

The first of these is a biosocial explanation. A good example of this type of theorization is Kohlberg's work on gender role, in which he argues that age-related shifts cannot be explained simply by changes in power or nurturance: 'The power theories of identification cannot account for

. . . age shifts in terms of family structure variables as such, because the family's power structure does not change regularly according to the age of the child' (Kohlberg, 1966). We will come on to look at this developmental theorizing in the next chapter.

The second explanation focuses on the influence of social learning. Although social learning theory stresses that, for people, learning amounts to much more than simple **conditioning**, it none the less acknowledges that the processes of modelling and identification are influenced and augmented by operant learning. Proponents of social learning theory point out that, as described above, parents and other carers, and indeed other children, generally do praise and reward children for behaving 'appropriately'. A girl who cries when she is hurt is likely to get a cuddle and comfort, but even quite small boys can be ticked off for crying, and told to 'stop behaving like a baby' (indeed, a boy's playmates may tease him for 'crying like a girl'). In a now-classic set of studies, Archer and Lloyd (1982) showed that children as young as 3 years old criticize and are less willing to play with children who take part in activities associated with the other gender. However, social learning theorists believe that reinforcement and punishment may seldom act directly, more often acting vicariously. When children observe a behaviour being rewarded, they are more likely to imitate it than if they see the same behaviour being ignored or punished (Brannon 1996).

This may help to account for the shift that boys make in identification. Studies by Bussey and Bandura (1984) and Nicholas and McGinley (1986) both provided evidence that boys between the ages of about 3 and 5 years tend more than girls to imitate the more powerful of two potential role models. Men tend to be more often rewarded than women for acting 'powerfully'; women tend to be more often rewarded than men for acting 'nurturantly'.

Bandura argued that as children observe many models, they notice the consistencies among some models. Children thus learn to connect certain kinds of behaviour with one or other gender – they learn that 'this is how men and boys behave' and 'this is how women and girls behave'. 'Young children thus learn to use gender as an important characteristic for classifying persons and activities and to use gender features as a guide for selective modelling' (Bandura 1986: 96).

The way that parents and other carers behave is thus clearly important. Fagot *et al.* (1992) conducted a study that showed that 2- and 3-year-old children whose mothers were more endorsing of gender-segregated roles and gender-typed play were more able to use and understand the labels 'boy' and 'girl'. When children start to get together with other children, as we have seen, their own behaviour also starts to exert an influence. Well before they start school, children tend to segregate themselves by gender.

They also begin to behave differently. For instance, Jacklin and Maccoby (1978), in a study of the behaviour between same- and mixed-gender pairs of 33-month-old children found that the same-gender pairs interacted more with one another than the mixed-gender pairs. Girls placed with boys tended to watch the boys play, or withdraw and seek their mothers, while the boys tended to ignore them. Jacklin and Maccoby speculated that even at this young age, the children had come to understand and act out gender differences when faced with another child of the other gender.

Summary box Social learning theory's explanations of the acquisition of gender roles

- The processes through which children acquire gender roles are more complex than simple learning (for example, operant conditioning). They involve higher-order cognitive processes including imitation and modelling.
- Parents act as particularly powerful role models.
- In general children tend to be more exposed to same-gender role models. They are also more likely to model themselves on them.
- Crucial to this is the process of identification – children tend to imitate role models they see as similar to themselves.
- Boys between the ages of 3 and 5 years tend to imitate the role models they see as the most powerful. This is given as an explanation of why boys come to identify with male role models.
- As they get older, children gain an understanding of gender as a concept and learn to classify the behaviour of others (including their role models) in gendered terms. This developing conceptual understanding comes into play in the way they select role models.
- Children do not just directly imitate the behaviour of role models. They also observe whether the behaviour of others is rewarded, punished or ignored. They tend to imitate behaviour that is rewarded.

Gender schema theory

A number of psychologists have been highly critical of social learning theory's conceptualization of the acquisition of gender roles. Bem (1985), for example, has argued that it casts children as far too passive. She pointed out that their behaviour shows evidence of developing complex, schematic cognitive categories for gender, which form a framework for gaining their gender-related knowledge. This kind of theorization, which places a stronger emphasis on cognitive organization, results in cognitive-developmental theories. Since these are interactive, they will be addressed in the next chapter. We will look at **gender schema theory** here, however, since its emphasis is very much on social and cultural influences:

> Gender schema theory proposes that sex typing derives in large measure from gender-schematic processing, from a generalized readiness on the part of the child to encode and organize information – including information about the self – according to the culture's definitions of maleness and femaleness. Like cognitive-developmental theory, then, gender schema theory proposes that sex typing is mediated by the child's own cognitive processing. However, gender schema theory further proposes that gender-schematic processing is itself derived from the sex-differentiated practices of the social community.
>
> (Bem 1985: 186)

The term **schema** was first developed by Bartlett (1932) to describe the conceptual frameworks through which people perceive and make sense of the world around them. Bartlett was particularly interested in memory and conducted a number of studies on how people remember stories they are told. He found that when asked to recount a story they had heard some time ago (anything from a day or so to years ago), people tended to tell a distorted version. The story was not only shorter (a lot of detail was omitted) but, in particular, aspects of the original story that were at all strange or unfamiliar were 'ironed out' – made more plausible according to the individual's own world view and experience. Bartlett saw this as providing evidence that when people take in information they interpret it through their existing knowledge, and store this *interpreted* version in their memory. He proposed that the way in which this is done is that remembered knowledge is organized into schemata (strictly, *schema* is the singular form and *schemata* the plural; in practice, schema and schemas are widely used). It is these schemata, he argued, that enable us to make sense of what happens around us and to us.

Schemata are thus seen to 'guide information processing by structuring experiences, regulating behaviour, and providing bases for making inferences and interpretations' (Martin and Halverson 1981: 1120), and are therefore central to the way in which people make sense of gender, including their own. A number of studies have shown support for this contention. Stangor and Ruble (1987) have provided a review, concluding, for example, that children whose gender schemata are well developed tend to remember pictures of men and women acting in traditional, gender-stereotyped ways much better than they remember pictures that are counter-stereotypical. Moreover, their recall tends to be distorted. Their descriptions from memory of the counter-stereotypical pictures were often altered from what they had seen to make them more consistent with their gender schemata. For example, they reported that the picture they had seen was of a woman who was ironing, when, in fact, the picture was of a man. Janoff-Bulman and Frieze have argued that gender schemata are crucial to people's identity construction: 'our gender schemas represent deeply embedded assumptions that we hold about maleness and femaleness in our society, and that we use to evaluate ourselves as well as others' (Janoff-Bulman and Frieze 1987: 169).

Indeed, a number of theorists have claimed that gender schemata have influence well beyond simple, day-to-day cognition, extending into a person's whole world-view and life choices. Frable (1989) examined the possible connections between gender schemata and what she called 'gender ideology'. In a study using college students, she found that those who adopted strongly gendered self-schemata (that is, women who saw themselves as strongly feminine and men who saw themselves as strongly masculine) were more likely to endorse gender rules about behaviour, and to discriminate against women when asked to evaluate applications for jobs and college places. Lavallee and Pelletier (1992) looked at the gender schemata of women in gender-traditional and gender-unconventional jobs, and found that those women who were employed in gender-unconventional jobs were more likely to express non-traditional gender schemata. Finally, Martin and Halverson (1981) have made the obvious point that the development of strong gender schemata, with the accompanying tendency to see the world and interpret the actions of others through 'gendered lenses', can lead to gender stereotyping.

Summary box Gender schema theory's explanations of the acquisition of gender roles

- Children's acquisition of gender roles involves complex cognitive processing. They develop schemata – conceptual blueprints – of femininity and masculinity, through which they perceive their own and others' character and behaviour.
- These schemata profoundly affect the way that children process information. They structure children's experiences, act as a basis for making inferences and interpretations, and thereby affect the way that children not only see the world and make sense of it, but also how they act within it.
- Gender schemata persist into adult life, and continue to influence the way men and women think, feel and act throughout their lives.
- Gender schemata can lead to gender stereotyping.

Gender stereotyping

Parsons' writing is an example of **gender stereotyping**. A gender stereotype is a schematized set of beliefs about the psychological traits and characteristics and the behaviours expected of (and seen as appropriate for) men and women. Linda Brannon makes the point that:

> [g]ender roles are defined by behaviours . . . gender stereotypes are beliefs and attitudes about masculinity and femininity . . . but they tend to be related. When people associate a pattern of behaviour with either women or men, they may overlook the individual variations and exceptions and come to believe that the behaviour is inevitably associated with one, and not the other gender. Therefore gender roles can become gender stereotypes.
>
> (Brannon 1996: 168)

As we have seen in the previous section, according to social learning theory, gender stereotypes can have a profound influence on children, since they establish social categories for gender. And, Brannon argues, they do not only have an effect on children, but pervade social categorization throughout the life-span.

A number of commentators have argued that the dominant perceptions of what constitutes 'true womanhood' and 'true manhood' (in the Western, industrialized world at least) are historical legacies. Pleck (1984) has explored the historical origins of 'true manhood'. He has argued that one of its central themes is the prohibition against being a 'sissy'. Robert Brannon (1976) has taken this argument further, suggesting that the contemporary persona of a 'real man' is woven around four main themes (we have changed Brannon's wording somewhat to suit contemporary UK audiences):

*How to be a **real** man*

No girlie stuff!	All feminine qualities are to be avoided.
Be a winner	Gain status, success and respect.
Be a tough guy	Be self-reliant, strong and confident.
Give 'em hell!	Never let anybody get the better of you, and use aggression or even violence if you need to.

Welter (1978) has drawn connections between contemporary idealization of femininity with what she calls 'the cult of true womanhood' established in the nineteenth century. Drawing on religious texts and magazines of that time, she suggested that the concept comprised four cardinal virtues: piety, purity, submissiveness and domesticity. Although things have changed, we can see resonances in today's traditional stereotype of femininity. If we draw up a list similar to that for 'real men', then:

Today's 'real woman'	*Historical image*
Is warm and caring	Piety, in the sense of being religious, no longer holds as a dominant cultural value, but the belief in women's moral superiority still applies, translated into care for others, especially those who are weak and vulnerable.

Today's 'real woman'	*Historical image*
Does not sleep around indiscriminately	Purity, in the sexual sense, still has some grip – the 'double standard' that makes a promiscuous woman a 'slag'.
Treats her body 'as a temple'	But purity in the sense of being clean and wholesome (no unwanted body odours or body hair), and determined to discipline the body by diet and exercise, continues to be salient (look at women's magazines such as *Red*, *She*, *Cosmopolitan* or *Elle*, if you are not convinced).
Gets her way by coy 'feminine wiles' rather than blunt aggressiveness	Overt submissiveness to the point of servility is no longer valued, although women are still expected to put the needs and feelings of others before their own, and to get what they want through gentle persuasion and 'fluttering their eyelashes'.
Loves children and is a good home-maker	Domestic responsibilities are still seen as primarily women's work, and there is still much more censure for a mother who leaves her children than a man who does so.

This traditional stereotype has recently come under direct attack, especially in the popular media – ladettes, girl power and gutsy women are offered as alternatives. But it can be argued that such images gain their potency only through contrast. The archetypal feminine icon of our age, Princess Diana – as icon at least – fitted the blueprint, albeit not quite perfectly.

Men are from Mars, women are from Venus?

Gender stereotypes are pervasive. If you need evidence of this, then it is amply provided by the phenomenal sales of John Gray's book *Men are from Mars, Women are from Venus* (Gray 1993). Six million copies of this book were sold between 1992 and 1997. It has been translated into 38 languages, and four million copies of the sequels – *Mars and Venus in the Bedroom*, *Mars and Venus in Love*, *Mars and Venus on a Date* and *Mars and Venus Together for Ever* – have been sold. The original book has sparked a whole industry of workshops, board games, audio- and video-tapes, greetings cards and calendars. Gray has appeared on numerous television programmes in the USA, including a series of slots on prime-time news programmes, and has presented his work in a one-man Broadway show (see Crawford 1998, for more details). Gray introduces his book thus:

> *Men are from Mars, Women are from Venus* is a manual for loving relationships in the 1990s. It reveals how men and women differ in all areas of their lives. Not only do men and women communicate differently but they think, feel, perceive, react, respond, love, need, and appreciate differently. They almost seem to be from different planets, speaking different languages and needing different nourishment.
>
> (Gray 1993: 5)

He then goes on to describe men as 'Martians' and women as 'Venusians', elaborating their different characters in great detail.

> Martians value power, competency, efficiency, and achievement. They are always doing things to prove themselves and develop their power and skills. Their sense of self is defined through their ability to achieve results. They experience fulfillment primarily through success and accomplishment. . . . They are more concerned with outdoor activities, like hunting fishing, and racing cars. They are interested in the news, weather, and sports and couldn't care less about romance novels and self-help groups.
>
> (Gray 1993: 16)

> Venusians have different values. They value love, communication, beauty, and relationships. They spend a lot of time supporting, helping, and nurturing one another. Their sense of self is defined through their feelings and the quality of their relationships. They experience fulfillment through sharing and relating. . . . Rather than building highways and tall buildings, the Venusians are more concerned with living together in harmony, community, and loving cooperation. Relationships are more important than work and technology. . . . They do not wear uniforms like the Martians (to reveal their competence). On the contrary, they enjoy wearing a different outfit every day, according to how they are feeling. Personal expression, especially of their feelings, is very important. They may even change outfits several times a day if their mood changes.
>
> (Gray 1993: 18)

We rest our case.

The development of gender stereotypes

In a review of studies examining the influences on children's development of gender stereotypes, Linda Brannon (1996) summarizes the main factors thus:

Influence	*Study*	*Children who tend to express strongly gender-stereotypical attitudes and beliefs*	*Children who tend to express more flexible beliefs and attitudes about gender*
Parental attitudes	Weisner and Wilson-Mitchell 1990	have parents who hold traditional, gender-stereotypical attitudes and beliefs	have parents who challenge gender stereotypes and have less traditional attitudes
Parents' beliefs about gender	Bem 1989	have parents who see gender mainly in terms of how people behave	have parents who accept that there are biological sex differences, but do not assume that there are gender-related differences in behaviour
Interaction with parents	Levy 1989	interact more with parents	interact less with parents
Family size	Levy 1989	tend to have more siblings	tend to have fewer siblings
Mother's role	Levy 1989	tend to have mothers who stay at home	tend to have mothers who work outside the home

Overall, these results are what you would expect. Children seem more likely to develop gender-stereotypical perceptions of men and women if they grow up in families in which the roles of breadwinner and home-maker are divided along traditional lines, where such stereotypical attitudes are held by parents and where the parents' influence is marked. But Sandra Bem's work has a more interesting aspect. It was conducted with an explicit agenda – how to raise gender-aschematic children in a gender-schematic world (Bem 1985). She concluded that to do this, as well as exposing children to role models that challenge gender stereotypes, parents should actively teach children about sexual anatomy. She argues: 'In the American context, children do not typically learn to define sex in terms of anatomy and reproduction until quite late, and as a result they . . . mistakenly treat many of the cultural correlates of sex as definitional' (Bem 1985: 10). We will be looking at this work further in Chapters 4 and 5.

Gender stereotyping in psychological studies of femininity and masculinity

In Chapter 5 we will be looking in detail at the feminist challenges that have been mounted against traditional theorizing in this field. A mark of their success is that it is impossible here to consider the traditional work carried out by psychologists to examine such 'sex differences' (as gender differences were originally conceived) without being aware that it has been shot through with gender stereotyping from its very beginnings. This has been particularly the case in areas usually included in personality and social psychology.

One of the most important early **psychometricians** was Lewis Terman. It was Terman who transformed Binet's pragmatic device for detecting scholastic learning difficulties (the older term educational subnormality is probably clearer here) into a test of intelligence (the Stanford-Binet Test). Later in his career, Terman turned his attention to examining individual differences in terms of masculinity and femininity (the non-alphabetic ordering was his) and set the tone for work to come (Lewin 1984a). In 1936, with Catherine Cox Miles, he produced the Attitude Interest Analysis Survey. It consisted of 456 items, most of which had been shown to be answered, on average, differently by men and by women. Terman and Miles called those items which were more endorsed by men M items. Those which were more endorsed by women they called F items. Their implicit assumptions are evident even in the way they expressed masculinity/femininity: a final score was derived by subtracting the F scores from the M scores, with a positive result showing masculinity and a negative result showing femininity.

The history of the widely used Mf (again, the designers' implicit assumptions show up in the way they express this) subscale of the Minnesota Multiphasic Personality Inventory (MMPI) is even more weird. The MMPI has become one of the most ubiquitous personality scales – frequently used (and still in use) for selecting people for jobs and college entry and in applied research. The Mf subscale was even included in a personality test constructed to measure psychological disorders (Lewin 1984b). Yet only men were used to 'validate' the Mf subscale. Heterosexual soldiers (or, at least, soldiers who had not come out as gay) were used to provide the masculine response criterion, and only 13 homosexuals' responses were used to supply the feminine criterion! Gough's California Personality Inventory also confused gender and sexuality in seeking to construct a single dimension of femininity which could both distinguish between more and less feminine women and, at the same time, identify homosexual men.

The problem with these attempts to measure femininity/masculinity was not just one of appallingly bad methodology, but was conceptual as well. First, all such scales are inherently tautological – masculinity is defined by the statements that men commonly endorse, and measured by the extent to which men agree with them more than women do. Femininity is defined by the statements that women commonly endorse, and measured by the extent to which women agree with them more than men. They work, of course, and have an apparent face validity. But scales like this are not measuring anything other than responses that conform to stereotypes. The whole body of psychometric work on sex differences which used such scales lacked any conceptual (as opposed to purely operational) definition of masculinity or femininity (see Constantinople 1973 for a more detailed critique). Looking back at this work, still popular in the 1970s, it comes across as a bad joke. Lips and Colwill sum it up neatly:

> [O]n one recently developed test (Sechrest and Fay 1973), one of the items that discriminates between men and women is: 'I tend to become irritated when I see someone spit on the sidewalk' (men tended not to). This is hardly the stuff of which distinctions between darkness and light, or intuition and logic are made.
>
> (Lips and Colwill 1973: 130)

This is compounded by the way that in early theorization gender roles were seen as manifestations of sexuality (as described above, that homosexuality was a matter of being effeminate). Colley (1959) sought to operationalize this concept by dividing gender roles into three factors: **biomode**, **sociomode** and **psychomode**. This kind of framework enabled large amounts of research information (and common sense) to be integrated into digestible chunks.

Biomode	This refers to the degree of match between gender and physique – for example, the way in which a powerful, muscular body typifies masculinity.
Sociomode	This refers to the extent to which people behave in gender-appropriate ways – for example, the way in which being 'warm and caring' typifies femininity.
Psychomode	This refers to the extent to which attitudes are gender appropriate – for example, the way that not liking people spitting typifies femininity.

This division may seem common sense, but it is as shot through with preconceptions as previous formulations. This is evident, for example, in the picture McCandless paints of what this means for men: 'The appropriate, conflict-free psychology of maleness includes: easy, unselfconscious masculinity, heterosexual preference and practice, and pride in one's sex and sexuality' (McCandless 1970: 160).

In this formulation it was widely assumed that it was more of a challenge for a woman to have 'pride in one's sex and sexuality' and that women experienced more role conflict and role incompatibility. A pioneering study by Komarovsky (1982) into female US college students seemed to back this up. Her research revealed considerable tensions between the role of professional-woman-in-the-making and intellectual, and that of marriage-seeker and the 'social graces'. Some 40 per cent of her interviewees reported that they 'dumbed down' as a route to resolving role conflict. A final criticism of the social psychological research into gender differences, then, has to be to ask just how far the demand characteristics of the studies led people to respond 'normatively'.

Masculinity and femininity – one or more dimensions?

An extended and painstaking – and highly critical – review by Constantinople (1973) put the final nail in the coffin for this work. Constantinople challenged, in particular, two of its main assumptions: unidimensionality and bipolarity. Unidimensionality is the assumption that masculinity/femininity is a single, one-dimensional trait. Bipolarity is the assumption that masculinity and femininity are opposite ends of this scale. This assumption can be schematized like this:

Femininity ———————————— Masculinity

Instruments such as the Mf scale view gender as a continuum, with extreme femininity at one pole and extreme masculinity at the other. Constantinople argued that implicit within this formulation were the following assumptions:

(a) any score that deviates from the 'appropriate' pole is undesirable;
(b) masculinity and femininity are logical reversals of each other: having a high degree of masculinity means having a low degree of femininity, and vice versa;
(c) biological sex is the criterion which should be used for item selection and the development of measures (that is, the scale was deemed successful if it clustered men's and women's responses at the two poles).

Constantinople argued that these measures, and their implicit assumptions, were highly problematic – basically, they do not do what they are supposed to do and they do not support the assumptions on which they are based. She referred to factor-analytic studies (Engel 1966; Lunneborg 1972) which tended to produce a number of factors, indicating that what was being tapped was not a single trait but a number of independent, separate clusters of beliefs and attitudes. Although Constantinople acknowledged that bipolarity was more difficult to assess, given that it was built into the design of the scales, she argued that if gender differences are multidimensional, then gender differences cannot, logically, be bipolar in any simple sense. The problematic question of just what the gender-differentiating items might signify has also been raised by Pleck (1975).

He argued that the items which do discriminate may be of only vicarious importance to gender itself. One response to these conceptual problems was the development of multidimensional scales, most notably scales that included the concept of androgyny. We will look at these in Chapter 4, since this move was part of the liberatory challenge.

Summary box Gender stereotyping

- A gender stereotype is a rigid set of beliefs about what men and women are like – it defines what it means to be a 'real man' and a 'real woman', and views those who deviate from these expectations as odd or unnatural.
- Children are more likely to develop gender stereotypes if their father fulfils the traditional role of breadwinner and their mother that of the housewife, where their parents themselves have gender-stereotypical attitudes and where their parents have a strong influence on them.
- Strong gender stereotypes also seem to be associated with an upbringing which stresses the behavioural rather than the biological differences between the genders.
- Early psychological research into masculinity and femininity was shot through with gender stereotyping.
- Gender stereotypes are alive and kicking in many popular psychology texts today.

Chapter review

In this chapter we have examined some of the ways in which social and cultural influences contribute to the construction of gender, and reviewed traditional theories that were developed to account for their influence. We have also explored the ways in which assumptions about gender can lead to gender stereotyping, and how this, in turn, has influenced theory and research. You will have detected that we take a rather jaundiced view of this early work, and that we are concerned by the continued influence of stereotypical thinking, especially on 'pop' psychology, epitomized by John Gray's *Men are from Mars, Women are from Venus*. Crawford (1998) argues – and we agree – that psychology needs to take more notice of the 'self-help bandwagon' which is filling the psychology shelves of bookshops in the USA (and the UK) and the 'gender-differences-are-natural-so-stop-fighting-them' world-view which seems to be becoming dominant in popular discourse. It is for this reason that we have designed this book around the *challenges* to this kind of thinking. We will move on to this in the next section, but before we do we have one further paradigm – the interactionist paradigm – to examine.

Further reading

Brannon, L. (1996) *Gender: Psychological Perspectives*. Boston, MA: Allyn and Bacon.

3 Interactive paradigms

[T]hroughout development there is an essential tension between the biological and the social. The infant and his [*sic*] social world are in constant interaction; just as the biological infant structures and modifies his social environment, so he is socially structured by it and his biology is modified.

(Richards 1974: 1)

In this chapter we will look at theorization about gender and sexuality based around the interplay between 'nature' (that is, biological bases of behaviour) and 'nurture' (that is, the influences of the social and cultural environment). This move towards a focus on interaction reflected the ***Zeitgeist*** of the late 1960s and the early 1970s, interweaving two sets of ideas that became popular at that time. The first arose out of a more general interest with systems theory, which was fashionable in what was coming to be called cognitive psychology (see, for example, Neisser 1966). The second was the 'make love not war' ideology of the 1960s (which we will look at in more detail in the next chapter), a liberal humanism which sought to get away from antagonistic ways of thinking and move towards theories and models which integrate and offer 'the best of both worlds'. Together these encouraged psychologists to explore the possibilities of explaining human behaviour and experience in terms of the products of interaction between different influences. The dominant idea was that 'the whole may be more than the sum of its parts'; that with something as complex as human behaviour and experience, the causative influences are likely to be multifactorial, co-actional and complex.

We will be looking at four quite different interactive models of gender and sexuality: Eysenck's extraversion/introversion theory; Freud's psychoanalytic theory of personality and of psychosexual development; cognitive developmental theories; and theories of moral development. Each offers an illustration of a much more extensive body of theory in each of these different paradigms. The chapter also compares three theories of gender development: two of which you met in Chapter 2 (social learning and gender schema theories) and one that you meet here (cognitive developmental theory). Including a section on moral development may seem to be a somewhat strange thing to do. We have included this aspect of development because the field is a contentious one in relation to gender, since the best-known theories (Freud's and Kohlberg's) claim that women, on average, are unable to achieve the same degree of maturity as men.

Eysenck's theories of gender and sexuality

Hans Eysenck is perhaps the UK's most internationally famous psychologist. In the period immediately following the Second World War, eugenic and behavioural genetic modelling was, understandably, out of fashion. Eysenck was in a good position to help in its rehabilitation, however, as he was a Berliner whose family had left Germany shortly after Hitler's rise to power. He achieved this rehabilitation through a theory based on the co-action between physiology (and ultimately genetics) and environment (including the social environment). It is clear from Eysenck's own writings that his goal was to redress what he saw as a drift towards theories that emphasize social and cultural effects, and to draw nature back into the frame:

> Difficult as it may seem to deny the importance and relevance of hormonal and general physiological differences between the sexes, many modern writers seem to stress overwhelmingly the importance of 'sex roles' and their determination by society – without asking themselves whether perhaps society imposes these roles because nature has so ordained.
>
> (Eysenck 1978: 240)

Extraversion–introversion/stability–emotionality

In the simplest version of Eysenck's model, individuals are seen to have genetically 'wired in' physiological differences in both their need for stimulation and in their emotional stability or instability (Eysenck 1967). These differences, Eysenckians argue, result in personality differences along two dimensions: introversion–extraversion and emotionality–stability.

The explanation for these personality differences is that **extraverts** are physiologically 'dampened'. They are much less sensitive to external stimulation than introverts, whereas **introverts** are highly sensitive to external stimulation: 'The extravert consequently requires greater external stimulation in order to arrive at an optimal level of arousal than the normal (ambivert) person, while the introvert requires less external stimulation than the normal (ambivert) person' (Eysenck 1978: 17).

	Extraverts tend to be	*Introverts tend to be*
If they are stable	sociable, outgoing, gregarious, talkative, responsive, easy-going, lively and carefree.	careful, thoughtful, peaceful, self-controlled, reliable, even-tempered and calm.
If they are emotional	touchy, restless, aggressive, excitable, changeable and impulsive.	moody, anxious, rigid, reserved and unsociable.

One result of this, according to Eysenck, is that introverts are more susceptible to conditioning (described in Chapter 2) and may also be more sensitive to punishment. So, for example, introverts are more likely to be law-abiding and to follow conventional rules of behaviour; extraverts are more likely to take risks and seek excitement. The emotionality–stability dimension is held to relate to individuals' physiological responses to emotional stimuli, and the efficiency of their physiology in maintaining equilibrium. Individuals high in emotionality are more likely to show 'emotional lability and overreactivity' and will tend to be 'emotionally overresponsive and to have difficulties returning to a normal state after emotional experiences' (Eysenck and Eysenck 1964: 6). Individuals high in stability, by contrast, have well-tuned emotional responsiveness. They react to emotional stimuli in a measured way, and their biofeedback mechanisms return them rapidly to a stable state.

The co-actional basis of the model takes off from here, with extraverts and introverts physiologically primed to respond differently to the social environment. Extraverts, for instance, require a much firmer socialization regime to internalize their culture's social standards than do introverts. Stable individuals, because they cope better than emotional individuals with feelings of anger or depression, are more likely to get on well with others and to be liked.

Eysenck's theory applied to sexual behaviour

Eysenck (1978) specifically applied his theory to sexual behaviour, and made three main predictions in relation to extraversion/introversion:

- introverts, because they seek less stimulation than extraverts, are likely to approach sex in a circumspect manner, and to shy away from the more stimulating forms of sexual behaviour. Conversely, extraverts are likely to approach these stimulating forms of sexual behaviour eagerly and passionately;
- extraverts, because they form conditioned responses more slowly and less effectively than introverts, are likely to be less well socialized than

introverts and are more likely to indulge in sexual behaviour that is considered to be antisocial (Eysenck mentions perversions, and pre-marital and extra-marital intercourse);
- extraverts, because they habituate faster than introverts – they soon get used to stimulation and respond less and less – are more likely than introverts to seek out novelty in their sexual behaviour (that is, new and different ways of having sex) and in their relationships (having new and different partners).

Eysenck reported evidence to support all three contentions. He cited, in particular, a study by Giese and Schmidt (1968) which surveyed 6000 German students, asking them to report on their sexual experience and behaviour, and also testing them for extraversion/introversion. Among the data they obtained were the following:

Reported behaviour (%)	*Males*		*Females*	
	Extraverts	*Introverts*	*Extraverts*	*Introverts*
Sometimes masturbate	72	86	39	47
Sometimes 'pet' to climax with a partner	78	57	76	62
Have sexual intercourse sometimes	77	47	71	42
Average number of times per month that they have sexual intercourse	5.5	3.0	7.5	3.1
Have had sex with more than four partners in the past 12 months	25	7	17	4
When having sex, engage in long periods of foreplay	28	21	18	21
Sometimes engage in cunnilingus	64	52	69	58
Sometimes engage in fellatio	69	53	61	53
Have had sex in more than three positions	26	10	13	12

Eysenck concluded from these data that extraverts masturbate less, pet to orgasm more, have sex more frequently, have sex in more different positions, engage in foreplay for longer and practise **fellatio** and **cunnilingus** more frequently. Looking at the data, he seems to have good evidence for this conclusion. But it is important to recognize where these data come from. They look impressive and strongly support the idea that introverts and extraverts behave differently in terms of their sexuality. But remember that no physiological testing was carried out. Extraverts and introverts were identified by simply asking people to complete scales which asked them, for example, whether or not they were sociable and enjoyed taking risks. Those who ticked response boxes saying they were and did were categorized as extraverts; those who said they were not and did not were categorized as introverts. Then respondents filled in similar boxes to report on their sexual behaviour. So all that these data show is that people are consistent in the responses they give in questionnaires. People who say that they are sociable and enjoy taking risks report having more sexual partners than people who say they are not sociable and don't enjoy taking risks. These more private and risk-avoiding individuals tend to masturbate more.

However, Eysenck also offered evidence from an unpublished study in which 40 men were fitted with a penile **plesthysmograph** (a device for measuring erections). These men were shown short sex films edited from what Eysenck calls 'commercial material', each film concentrating on one kind of sexual activity (for example, cunnilingus, ***soixante-neuf***, what Eysenck refers to as 'orgies'). The films were shown over a period of several days, each man watching nine films in blocks of three on three different occasions. The data obtained, according to Eysenck, 'showed that Extraverts showed significantly more **habituation** [i.e. a reduction in their penile erection] during the showing of each film, from film to film, and from occasion to occasion' (Eysenck 1978: 20; emphasis added).

Eysenck also commented on links to emotionality, which he describes as 'strong, labile emotionality, predisposing a person to develop neurotic symptoms' if subjected to excessive stress. He predicted that emotionally labile individuals would be 'less likely to indulge in sexual contacts, to worry more about sex and to have fewer contacts with sexual partners', and so 'sexual relations, to the neurotic, should present a conflict-laden area' (Eysenck 1978: 20).

Eysenckian theory thus offers a plausible, face-valid explanation for differences in people's sexual behaviour. It is not difficult to see why his model is so compelling – the personality types are instantly recognizable and the links to sexual behaviour and 'sex crimes' come across as highly credible. His theory has, however, been widely criticized. His own preoccupations and prejudices are clear in the way that he expressed himself.

Eysenck's position on women

Eysenck's writing was extremely sexist in its assumptions. He described the stable extravert as 'a happy philanderer' who has 'considerable social facility with the opposite sex, likes and enjoys his sexual activity, is contented with it and has no worries or anxieties regarding it' (Eysenck 1978: 236). At the time he was writing (recall the Richards quote at the beginning of the chapter) the term 'he' was used generically to mean both men and women. Yet, as Miller and Swift have pointed out, writers who use terms such as 'he' and 'man' generically 'often slip unconsciously from the general meaning to the limited one' (Miller and Swift 1981: 11). This description of Eysenck's is obviously about a man, although, in principle, he is supposed to be writing about both male and female extraverts. It gets worse. Eysenck also commented that 'we found that females had done [sexual] things they disliked almost four times as frequently as males' (Eysenck 1978: 238). He reported that women were more 'sexually prudish' than men, and that the more sexually shy and prudish they were, the more likely they would be to report having done sexual things that they did not like. So, he implied, that was the explanation – women who didn't like the sexual things they did, didn't like them because of their prudery and shyness.

Although he admitted that this link needed further study, it seems not to have occurred to him that women may not have liked the sexual things they had done because, for example, they had been coerced or persuaded into them by men. Or that they were more worried about the risks (in those days the fear was of pregnancy rather than disease). Or that some sexual practices (such as **bondage**) tend to position women as the objects of male action – they are more usually done *to* women rather than *by* them. Or that other practices (such as oral sex and masturbating a partner) were (at that time, certainly) viewed as skills that women were expected to develop in ways in which men were not. Comfort's (1972) *The Joy of Sex*, for example, devotes two and a half pages to instructing women on how to give '**slow masturbation**' to a man, and just half a page to advising men on how to do this to women.

Eysenck seems oblivious to the sexual 'double standard' that was highly prevalent at the time, and to the power imbalance between men and women (again more prevalent then than now). His writing is a prime example of the **androcentrism** (male-centredness) of psychology, which we will come on to discuss in more detail in Chapter 6. Today, Eysenck's theory is generally seen as over-simplified and naive, very much a mirror of its (more misogynist but also more liberally naive) time, when psychologists could do experiments involving showing pornographic films, in the disingenuous belief that all that was at stake was the measurement of male sexual arousal.

Summary box Eysenck's theories of gender and sexuality

Differences in people's 'wired in' physiology affect how much stimulation they want and how emotionally stable they are. Both affect their sexual predilections and behaviour.

- Extraverts crave more stimulation than introverts, and are less susceptible to conditioning. So they are more likely to take risks, seek excitement and new experiences, and engage in sex that is viewed as 'deviant' or 'kinky'. Overall, extroverts tend to have more varied sex than introverts.

- Emotionally stable people tend to enjoy sex more and approach it in a guilt-free manner compared with emotionally labile people – who worry about sex more and have more sexual 'hang-ups'.
- Although at first sight the data Eysenck uses to support these contentions are impressive, they are mostly based on correspondence between questionnaire responses. People who claim to take risks, to seek adventure and to crave stimulation *in general* (extraverts) also claim to enjoy taking risks and seeking variety and stimulation in their sex lives. This consistency is not really very surprising, and shows no more than that people see themselves as behaving consistently. It does not 'prove' that physiological differences underpin differences in sexual behaviour.
- Eysenck was a man of his time. Like the work reviewed in the last chapter, his theories incorporate gender stereotyping. Women's greater sexual 'prudishness', for example, he attributed to a personality difference between men and women, with no apparent awareness of the issues of the power differentials between men and women and the way this may influence sexual preferences and behaviour.

Freud's psychoanalytic theories of personality and psychosexual development

Eysenck's theory was a good place to start this chapter, since it is formulated clearly enough to make the idea of co-action relatively easy to grasp. However, it is neither the first nor the most influential co-actional model – either in general or as specifically applied to human sexuality. That place belongs to Freud's psychodynamic theory of half a century earlier. This may help to contextualize why Eysenck (for example, Eysenck and Wilson 1974) devoted considerable energy into seeking to demolish and replace Freudian theory.

Freud's theory of personality development and function

Freud's work was very much grounded on the assumption that human behaviour is fundamentally 'wired in' in some way (although, of course, he would not have used that analogy); that the things people do are, at root, instinctive and driven, rather than being learned or otherwise acquired from culture. The biological basis of Freud's theory is consistent with his training and early biography. He had worked as a neurologist, a physiologist and a pharmacologist and, for example, conducted research into stains that would show up eels' gonads under the microscope. So it is hardly surprising that the theories of human development that he produced drew considerably on biological ideas.

We have, elsewhere (Stainton Rogers and Stainton Rogers 1992), suggested that it is instructive to recast theories as particular kinds of stories, to get a general sense of their focus and what is being claimed. Indeed, Haraway has argued specifically that this is, indeed, what theories are: '[L]ife and social sciences in general . . . are story-laden; these sciences are composed through complex, historically specific storytelling practices. Facts are theory-laden; theories are value-laden; values are story-laden. Therefore facts are meaningful within stories' (Haraway 1984: 79).

If you apply this to Freud's theory of development it can be read as 'The Tale of Jack the Dragon-Slayer'. In this tale the child, from birth, is faced with a sequence of hazards to be overcome – psychic 'dragons' that have to be slain – to attain the prize of fully functioning, healthy adulthood. Embedded in this story is the *leitmotif* of the warrior who gains his (and here it is *his*) strength through being tested. Facing his fear and finding the courage to slay the dragon against the odds is a necessary transformative experience, the only way in which the hero can achieve his destiny. In Freud's theory these hazards are fixed by biology. The sequence of tasks, what has to be achieved for each one and how each has to be accomplished are all seen as predetermined. But what makes this a co-actional model is that the outcome for each individual depends on whether and how each dragon is slain. If the individual fails at any point, he or she will remain entrapped, unable to fully progress further. Freud's theory thus views development as a biologically grounded process that is modified by experience and socialization, working through a series of predetermined stages as an individual matures from infancy to adulthood.

As such it has a lot in common with other developmental theories, such as that of Piaget, which we will come on to later in the chapter. Freud's psychodynamic theory was, however, much more concerned than Piaget's with the development of gender and sexuality. Freud's general theory is sufficiently well documented elsewhere that we need not set it out in detail here. Instead we will concentrate on what Freud had to offer in the spheres of gender and sexuality.

The development of Freud's theory

Freud's patients were mostly female: girls and women who were experiencing **somatizations** (bodily manifestations of psychic distress) such as hysteria (it is worth noting that the term 'hysteria' translates as 'womb sickness', which gives a clue its origins). Freud began his clinical work by adopting the standard modernist equation:

Diagnosis of Problem + Intervention = Solution (or at least amelioration)

This paradigm had proved fairly successful throughout the nineteenth century, as medicine grew into a more scientific discipline and technology provided more effective interventions. However, then, as now, less tractable conditions attracted some fairly dubious treatments, and Freud was no exception – he tried cocaine as a **psychotropic drug, hydrotherapy** and even **electrotherapy**. Gradually, though, he shifted to more psychological forms of intervention, first hypnosis (at which he proved largely useless) and then **free association** – which became one of the building-blocks of what he came to call psycho-analysis.

Freud described the basic energy for personality development and functioning with a word that in German is usually translated as 'instinct', but is also sometimes translated as 'drive' or 'impulse' (Feist 1994). Freud argued that a number of **instincts** – such as instincts for life and for death and sexual and aggressive instincts – provide psychic 'energy' (hence the term 'psychodynamics'). It is this energy that drives the development of personality, and that regulates how personality functions. Freud believed that most of the work that this energy does happens at an unconscious level. People are not aware of it, and it is possible to know what is happening only through observing its manifestations in a person's character, experiences (such as dreams) and behaviour. Freud did not 'invent' the unconscious (see Ellenberger 1970) but he was responsible for the idea that the unconscious is a dynamic entity, and that conscious psychic events are determined by unconscious processes.

He found the 'royal road' (as he called it) to the unconscious in dream symbols and their interpretation. Freud developed his system by listening to what his patients told him, both in direct terms about events in their lives, and indirectly through the dreams they recollected and their free associations. Gradually Freud developed his theory that the psychological problems that people experience in adulthood are caused by traumatic events in their childhood. This idea has so permeated our understanding of the world, it has become so taken for granted, that it is now difficult to recognize just how innovative it was in Freud's time – but it was. In terms of our analogy, Freud saw these problems as the consequences of psychic 'dragons' that had not been properly slain, and so they continued to lurk around in the unconscious, causing all manner of trouble.

Freud's theory of psychosexual development

Freud claimed that the sexual instinct acts as a 'driver' throughout life, starting in infancy. It is important to recognize that by 'sexual' he meant a much wider definition than we would give it today, as he saw it as something more like sensual pleasure. He hypothesized that the site of this sensual pleasure shifts sequentially as the child develops, moving the child through a series of psychosexual stages.

The oral stage

This is the first stage the infant experiences. The mouth is the site of sensuous pleasure, which infants gain through sucking and chewing.

The anal stage

By the time children are about 1 year old, the anus becomes the site of their sensuous pleasure, which they gain through the physical sensations of excretion. The 'dragon' to be fought here is toilet training and, if not accomplished properly, an 'anal personality' can develop – an obsession with neatness, stubbornness and holding on to possessions.

The phallic stage

By about 3 to 4 years old, the child's genitals become the site of sensuous pleasure – which is achieved through masturbation. This, according to psychodynamic theory, is a very active phase, and differs for boys and girls. Two main things happen, according to Freud:

- Boys notice that they have a penis and girls do not; girls notice that boys have a penis and they do not.
- The focus on genital pleasure stimulates sexual attraction to the parent of the opposite sex: boys became attracted to their mothers and girls to their fathers.

These experiences have a different significance for boys and girls; their impact is different, and they resolve them in different ways.

The phallic stage for boys

When boys realize that they have a penis and girls do not, they become fearful and suffer castration anxiety. This realization is shocking, disturbing and threatening. Some may even fear that their fathers will cut off their penis as a punishment, a fear that can be exacerbated by parental disapproval of their masturbation. At the same time the boy begins to feel sexual attraction towards his mother, and this too releases powerful emotions, here towards his father – jealousy, hatred and aggression – because he sees his father as a rival. This potent mixture of emotions faces the boy with perhaps the most terrifying 'dragon' he will ever have to confront. The boy experiences intense trauma because he is overwhelmed by his feelings, and he has to do something to resolve them.

Freud gave the name **Oedipus complex** to this confrontation, after the Greek myth in which Oedipus ends up marrying his mother and killing his father. The boy resolves it by creating a powerful identification with his father. This reduces his castration anxiety, because he gives up the sexual competition for his mother. At the same time his identification with his father allows him to gain a degree of vicarious sexual satisfaction. And it removes his feelings of hostility and replaces them with admiration. There are other benefits too, according to Freud. Identification with the father enables boys to develop a strong superego, and hence a strong sense of morality. More generally, identification with their father, together with their continued feelings of superiority because they have a penis, allow boys to develop a strong masculine identity in which they feel competent, assertive and powerful.

The phallic stage for girls

When they realize that boys have a penis and they do not, girls experience **penis envy**. They think of their vagina as the wound arising from the removal of their penis (Freud 1925/89). According to Freud, this sense of 'having something missing' makes girls feel inferior. Girls blame their mother for their lack of a penis and feel hostility towards her. Freud used the term **Electra complex** for this experience. However, for a girl the transferral of her affections to her father is much easier than it is for a boy; so too is her subsequent surrender of her sexual desire for him and her identification with her mother. So although girls do face difficult emotions and frustrations during the genital phase, these are not as intense as those that boys experience. Consequently, Freud argued, their identification with their mother is weaker. Girls therefore develop a weaker superego, and hence a weaker sense of morality. Moreover, the feelings of inferiority linked to lacking a penis remain, and girls develop a feminine identity which is more passive and acquiescent and less powerful than the masculine identity.

The latency stage

After the resolution of the Electra/Oedipus complex, children move into a period of latency, during which sensual pleasure assumes much less importance.

The genital stage

At puberty, physiological changes lead to a reawakening of sexual desire. Initially this is **homoerotic**, but through more 'dragon-slaying' it is soon 'normalized' into heteroeroticism. Once again, Freud theorizes different processes for males and females. Young men find this transition easier, since, as at the phallic stage, their attention is focused on the penis. Young women, however, have a much more difficult time, as they must make the transition from gaining sensual pleasure from the **clitoris** (in masturbation) to achieving it through the vagina (in sexual intercourse). Freud thought that a girl has little awareness of her vagina until puberty, and that the redirection of her sexual energy to the vagina is therefore a difficult hurdle for her. If she cannot overcome it, and remains fixated on clitoral orgasm (from childhood masturbation), Freud believed that a woman remains immature.

Freud and the position of women

Freud was born in 1856 in Moravia (then part of the Austro-Hungarian Empire, now part of the Czech Republic) into a Jewish middle-class family. His identity as Jewish is significant, because in Moravia at that time there was widespread and deep-seated anti-Semitism. So Freud enjoyed male, middle-class advantages and yet also suffered considerable prejudice and **social exclusion**. His move into private medical practice was both financially driven (he wanted to marry – an expensive business at that time for those in his position) and a response to institutional practices that effectively blocked professional advance for Jews within the mainstream.

This does not seem to have made Freud any more sensitive to the position of women at the time. He largely took for granted the gendered structure and division of labour in Victorian families, and reproduced them in his own marriage. More significantly, given his importance in the history of twentieth-century thought, his theories have been widely charged with treating women as psychodynamically inferior. Women are inferior in Freudian theory because:

- women's development is seen as grounded on discovering that they lack a penis (and hence on penis envy), leading to feelings of inferiority;
- to reach sexual maturity women are seen as having to move from siting sexual pleasure on the clitoris to experiencing it through the vagina, once they have matured sufficiently to be ready for heterosexual relationships with men;
- their weaker identification with their mother, and the fact that this identification is with a weaker role model, limits women's capacity to develop a strong superego, which thus renders women morally inferior to men.

It is this last point, perhaps, which is the most shocking to contemporary sensibilities. It is quite clear that Freud *did* see women as incapable of fully mature development:

> The fact that women must be regarded as having little sense of justice is no doubt related to the predominance of envy in their mental life; for the demand for justice is a modification of envy and lays down the condition subject to which one can put envy aside . . . There are no paths open to further development; it is as though the whole process had already run its course and remains thenceforward insusceptible to influence – as though, indeed, the difficult development of femininity had exhausted the possibilities of the person concerned.
>
> (Freud 1933/64: 134–5)

Freud's theory is haunted by the leitmotif of the brave knight who can 'gain his spurs' only by being severely tested and then triumphing over the most terrifying of dragons. It casts women in the role of frail maidens who can only wait to be saved, who have 'no paths open to further development'. Yet, as Feist (1994) has pointed out, Freud's attitudes to women were inconsistent. Although domestically and in his writings he was **misogynist**, at a time when women had few opportunities to enter professional life he admitted them to psychoanalytic training (Tavris and Wade 1984). This included his daughter Anna Freud, who carried on his work after his death.

Freud's denial of sexual abuse

But Freud is also seen as guilty of a further betrayal of women in denying the possibility that the childhood traumas that some of his patients told him about were what we would now call 'child sexual abuse'. In the process of listening to his patients talk about their childhood experiences, several of them told him about incidents in which they were 'seduced' by their fathers or other close relatives or members of the household. At first Freud took these accounts at face value, and viewed them as having somehow disrupted the patients' normal development. However, his reports of these incidents scandalized Viennese society, especially his medical colleagues, who protested that Freud's patients could not possibly be telling the truth. Under this pressure Freud recanted, and instead suggested that what he was hearing from his patients were fantasies reflecting the vivid sexual subjectivity of children. Not surprisingly, this sequence of events has led in our own times to the charge that Freud thereby 'silenced' information that pointed to the widespread sexual abuse of girls. We will examine in more detail this aspect of Freud's work in Chapter 10. We will also return to Freud in Chapter 6, since, not surprisingly, his work (and particularly his portrayal of women as inferior) has been strongly challenged by feminists. We will, however, take up one aspect of his work here a little later in this chapter – his claims about differences in moral development.

Summary box Freud's theories about gender and sexuality

- Freud's theory of personality development can be viewed as a 'Jack the Dragon-Slayer' parable, in which healthy development is achieved through successfully overcoming a sequence of obstacles – 'slaying dragons'. Biology sets the obstacles, but the outcome is determined by how well they are surmounted.
- In Freudian theory much of the activity involved in development is seen to operate at an unconscious level.
- The sexual instinct is seen as a driver throughout an individual's life, although its focus changes developmentally from the mouth, to the anus, to the phallus (or its lack); then, after a stage of latency, it shifts in adulthood to the genitals.

- Because of their lack of a phallus, because the dragons they have to slay are less powerful, and because the shift from a focus on the clitoris to a focus on the vagina is more difficult to achieve, girls are seen as having inferior development compared with boys. Freud therefore saw women as inherently incapable of achieving the full adult maturity of men.
- Freud's theory has been particularly criticized today because he changed his position over what we now term child sexual abuse. In his early work he attributed certain psychic disturbances (such as hysteria) to the trauma caused by sexual 'seduction' in childhood. But under pressure from his peers he recanted, changing his theory to one in which children (mainly girls) were seen to have fantasized about being seduced.

Cognitive development

The best-known theorist of cognitive development is undoubtedly Piaget, and the narrative analogy we have applied to Freud can also be applied to Piaget's work. Piaget's cognitive developmental theory can be read as 'The Entomologist's Tale'. It treats intellectual development as akin to the sequence of distinct body forms found in animals such as frogs and butterflies which undergo metamorphoses – changes in form – as they progress though their life cycle. A butterfly starts life as an egg. It next becomes a caterpillar and then turns into a chrysalis before the mature adult form (the imago) emerges. The analogy is that Piaget's theory sees development of the intellect as a similar kind of sequence of transformations between different ways-of-knowing-in-the-world. Again, Piaget's theory is sufficiently well known from general psychology for us not to need to spell it out here. For our purpose, the most important feature of the theory to grasp is that Piaget saw children as '**cognitive aliens**' – as understanding the world, and the people in it, in a fundamentally different way from adults. This conception of the child runs through all theories of cognitive development.

In fact it was Kohlberg rather than Piaget who most explicitly applied cognitive developmental theorizing to children's acquisition of cognitive competencies in relation to gender. He suggested that this has three main aspects:

- **gender labelling** – being able to accurately attribute terms such as 'boy' and 'girl';
- **gender knowledge** – knowledge about the characteristics of female and male gender;
- **gender constancy** – recognizing that gender is unchanging.

Kohlberg regarded babies and toddlers as having so limited a sense of self that they cannot consistently apply the labels 'boy' and 'girl' to themselves or to others. To Kohlberg the small child fails at gender labelling. This they begin to reach at around 3 years of age. This, he argued, does not signal the development of gender identity, as mistakes are often made. He observed that some children at this stage, for example, label all the people they like as one gender, and all those they do not like as another gender. Only somewhere between the ages of 4 and 9 (but usually around 5 or 6) did hc think that gender constancy is achieved.

According to Kohlberg's theory, from this point on, cognition becomes more and more sophisticated. But unlike social learning theory (which views this as an ongoing process), cognitive developmental theories such as Kohlberg's see children as passing through a series of cognitive metamorphoses, shifting from one kind of cognition to another. Cognitive developmental theory thus regards the acquisition of gender-related behaviours as resulting from the development of gender identity: children begin to behave in gender-appropriate ways *because* they adopt a gender identity. (This contrasts with social learning theory, which sees gender identity as coming from acting in gender-appropriate ways.)

One important corollary of this is that because cognitive developmental theory argues that younger children are less competent at categorization than older children, younger children will adopt highly stereotypical conceptions of gender. There is evidence to support this contention. Kuhn and colleagues (1978), for example, were able to show that children as young as 2 years old evinced gender stereotypical knowledge, and the more such knowledge they showed, the more likely they were to have begun to develop gender constancy and gender identity.

As cognitive developmental theory is a stage theory, heavy emphasis is placed on foundational achievements. For Kohlberg, gender identity was largely built up from gender constancy. This contention has, however, been challenged by Martin and Little (1990), who have offered a somewhat different interpretation of the development of cognition around gender. Testing children aged 3 to 5 years old, they came up with the following sequence of children gaining cognitive competencies:

	Gender labelling	*Gender knowledge*	*Gender constancy*
Stage 1	Not acquired	Not acquired	Not acquired
Stage 2	**Acquired**	Not acquired	Not acquired
Stage 3	**Acquired**	**Acquired**	**Possibly acquired**
Stage 4	**Acquired**	**Acquired**	**Acquired**

Martin and Little have argued that gender constancy may not be an all-or-nothing acquisition. They separated out gender stability (the understanding that gender is a stable personal characteristic) from gender consistency (the understanding that people retain their gender, even when they behave in a way that is, or have superficial characteristics which are, gender incongruent) and suggested that they are acquired separately.

Some research in this field has been used to contend that gender development may differ for boys and girls. Kuhn *et al.* (1978) found that the girls in their study tended to attribute more positive characteristics to girls than to boys, whereas boys showed the reverse effect. Martin *et al.* (1990) found that children tend to learn about the attributes of their own gender first, and only later learn about those of the other gender. In a study by Levy and Fivush (1993) data were obtained that suggested that the knowledge that young children have about gender tends to be much better organized and understood when it relates to events and behaviours stereotypically associated with their own gender.

There has been much less research into gender development in adolescence, even though general cognitive developmental models span into this age group. This is mainly because it is usually assumed that cognitive competence in regard to gender is complete by the end of childhood. There have been, however, a few exceptions to this generalization. Urberg (1979), for example, has shown that in the early teenage years there is typically a fair degree of gender stereotyping which is more extreme than in younger children (that is, before gender knowledge is fully acquired). Only once the late teens are reached, she claims, do young people gain sufficient flexibility in abstract thinking to move beyond these stereotypes and gain insight into the issues raised. However, she found that this flexibility is more marked in relation to one's own gender, with a fair amount of stereotyping still applied to the other gender.

This finding was partially supported by a study by Katz and Ksansnak (1994) of US secondary school students. There were some differences, but the age groups studied were not the same and the time lag between the two studies was 15 years, which alone may account for the differences. Katz and Ksansnak's study found a complex pattern of gender-role flexibility, and examined what might be affecting this. They concluded that the most important influences came from the peer group and from siblings, especially same-sex siblings.

It is often concluded that cognitive developmental theory diminishes in utility with the age of the individuals to which it is applied (see, for example, Archer and Lloyd 1982). Once children gain certain cognitive capabilities, it would seem that social and cultural influences rapidly overshadow any stage development of new cognitive capacities. In other words, theories that emphasize the impact of social factors (which we examined in the last chapter) gain in explanatory utility.

Criticisms of cognitive developmental theory

But there are other problems with cognitive developmental theorization. Probably its most vocal critic, Sandra Bem, challenges its very basis, particularly its naive assumption that sex is just another category: '[t]he theory fails to explicate why sex has primacy over other potential categories of the self, such as race, religion and eye colour' (Bem 1985: 184). Linda Brannon expands on this: '[t]his theory fails to explain why children chose gender as a primary domain around which to organize information' (Brannon 1996: 150), suggesting that it is this problem which led to the development of gender schema theory (which we looked at in the last chapter). This is the key question. Many recent theorists argue that it can only be the socially constructed meaning of gender which makes it so central and important to the way that children come to make sense of the world. This idea will be taken up in Chapter 6.

Summary box Theories of cognitive development

- Piaget's theory of cognitive development can be viewed as an 'Entomologist's Tale', in which a child is seen to mature through a series of distinct transformations in their thinking.
- In regard to the development of gender and sexuality, a crucial concept is that of the child as 'cognitive alien' – that is, of thinking in a very different way from adults.
- Kohlberg specifically applied cognitive developmental theorizing to children's acquisition of cognitive competencies in relation to gender. These competencies include gender labelling, gender knowledge and gender constancy. These abilities, according to Kohlberg, undergo a series of distinct shifts as children develop.
- Cognitive developmental theory is most useful when applied to younger children. Once competencies have been acquired, social and cultural influences seem to become much more important.
- More recently, theorists such as Bem have challenged the basis of cognitive developmental theory applied to gender, arguing that it fails to address the question of why gender is so salient for categorization.

Comparing theories of gender development

Before we move on to the final section of this chapter, it may be helpful to briefly review and summarize the three main theories of gender development that you have met so far: social learning theory and gender schema theory (in Chapter 2) and cognitive developmental theory here. This is set out in the table, which we have modified from Brannon (1996). Her book covers all three in much more detail than we have been able to do here, and is an excellent source of additional information.

Social and coactive theories of gender development

	Social learning theory	*Gender schema theory*	*Cognitive developmental theory*
Site of influence:	emphasizes social influences	emphasizes social influences	stresses co-action of biological basis of development and social influences
Gender differences develop through:	observation and modelling, with some influence of reinforcement	development of gender-specific schemata	stages of cognitive development, especially gender constancy
Children's perception determines:	which models are imitated	the schemata which are specific to gender	how information is organized
Gender development begins:	as soon as agents of socialization have an impact	once the cognitive capacity is there	once the child is capable of developing schemata
Gender development:	is a gradual, ongoing process	proceeds through the development of schemata	proceeds through a series of discrete stages
Gender development is complete:	in adulthood, although always subject to change	mainly in late childhood, but may continue into adulthood	usually during late childhood
Girls and boys:	will often develop quite different gender knowledge and gender-related behaviours	may develop different schemata, especially where there are strong influences from family and peer group	will tend to develop similar cognitive understandings of gender

Moral development

In developmental psychology, few fields of study have raised hackles more than that of moral development. As you have seen, Freud's work set this off, with his contention that women lack the capacity to attain the highest levels of moral thinking. This was, if not excusable, at least understandable at a time when this was a commonly held viewpoint, even among women. What is less understandable (or excusable) is that this prejudice persisted into the 1970s in the work of Kohlberg.

The work for which Kohlberg is best known is his extension of Piaget's theory of moral development. Kohlberg used stories – moral dilemmas – to assess children's moral reasoning. On the basis of answers given to the moral dilemmas, Kohlberg developed a stage theory of moral development (Kohlberg 1958). His scheme has three levels, each of which has two stages:

Levels and stages	*Orientation of moral reasoning*	
Preconventional level		
Stage 1	Punishment and obedience	Wrong things are those that are punished, and you obey rules to avoid punishment.
Stage 2	Hedonism	Good and bad are to do with satisfying your own needs. You do what is best for you.
Conventional level		
Stage 3	Interpersonal concordance	Being good is about being loyal and looking after the interests of those you care about, who show empathy and affection towards you.
Stage 4	Law and order	Being good is about obeying the law and following the rules, which may be statutory or religious.
Principled level		
Stage 5	Social contract	Being good is about fostering the welfare and well-being of others.
Stage 6	Universal ethical principles	Being good is defined by your own conscience, in accordance with self-determined ethical principles.

Kohlberg proposed that, like other forms of cognitive development, moral development progresses through each of these stages sequentially. To reach stage 6 (which Kohlberg clearly saw as superior) an individual must move through stages 1–5. Kohlberg's formulation is quite clearly arguing for a particular set of values, and claiming certain values to be superior. He has, not surprisingly, been criticized for this.

Much of Kohlberg's theory was derived from a longitudinal study in which he repeatedly tested a group of *boys*, from their early years in school into adulthood. Moreover, all of the characters in the moral dilemmas are men. So it is not surprising that when young women are tested, they perform, on average, less well than young men. For instance, Haan *et al.* (1968) found that whereas 28 per cent of the young men in their study performed at stages 5 and 6, only 18 per cent of young women were assessed as having done so. The modal stage for young women was stage 3, whereas it was stage 4 for young men. Kohlberg explained this discrepancy as arising from women's greater allegiance to children, and to the stronger socialization pressures on them.

Gilligan's theory of 'a different voice'

The main criticism of Kohlberg's work has come from feminists, most notably Carol Gilligan (1982). Gilligan argued that as well as having methodological flaws, Kohlberg's theory is conceptually biased against the type of moral reasoning that girls and women tend to use. In particular, she pointed out that in downgrading moral reasoning which emphasizes human relationships to an earlier and lower stage (stage 3), women are portrayed as inferior. Gilligan argued that this reasoning is not worse, but is simply different. Women are perfectly capable, she contended, of applying the kinds of abstract principles that Kohlberg valued so much. They simply do not see them as so important, in many situations, as values of loyalty, concern and care. Indeed, other feminists (for example, Johmann 1985) have argued that it is this system which is superior, especially in jobs and in roles where caring for people is important.

Originally, Gilligan proposed that women differ from men in the basis of their moral judgements – men being more concerned with 'justice' and women with 'care'. More recently, she has shifted to argue that these two are alternative perspectives, adopted by both men and women in different contexts. Although women are more likely to adopt the care perspective, this is by no means always the case, and, at least in part, reflects the different life worlds of women and men:

> Our analysis of care and justice as distinct moral orientations that address different moral concerns leads us to consider both perspectives as constitutive of mature moral thinking. The tension between these perspectives is suggested by the fact that detachment, which is the mark of moral judgement in the justice perspective, becomes the moral problem in the care perspective – the failure to attend to need. Conversely, attention to the particular needs and circumstances of individuals, the mark of mature moral judgement in the care perspective, becomes the moral problem in the justice perspective – failure to treat others fairly, as equals.
>
> (Gilligan and Attanucci 1988: 82)

Summary box Theories of moral development

- As we have seen earlier, Freud made the claim that women are unable to achieve the same level of maturity as men in relation to making moral judgements. Kohlberg, the best-known theorist of moral development, made much the same claim.
- Critics have pointed out that Kohlberg's work was methodologically flawed – for example, he used male characters in the moral dilemmas for testing his theoretical formulations.
- Gilligan, however, has gone further. She has suggested that there are two quite different approaches that can be taken to making moral judgements – one based on the notion of justice and the other on that of care. Kohlberg's results, she argued, arise because men tend to prioritize justice and women to prioritize care. More recently, she has argued that the main difference may have less to do with gender *per se* than with the situations in which moral judgements are made, with women being more likely to operate in settings where care is more relevant.

Chapter review

Co-actional models of gender development and sexual behaviour have, as we have noted already, a great deal of plausibility. Also, in seeking to address the complexity of human action and experience, they at least caution us to resist the allure of the simplistic explanations we met in Chapter 1, which explicitly and emphatically continue to attribute the differences between men and women almost entirely to biology. Equally, they draw 'nature' back into the frame compared with the theories described in Chapter 2, which do not so much dismiss biology as ignore it.

Yet, as we have argued elsewhere (Stainton Rogers and Stainton Rogers 1992), co-actional models in developmental psychology are based on an alembic myth, a myth which suggests that psychologists know how nature and nurture can be compounded together, just as chemists know how the elements sodium and chlorine can react together to form a compound – sodium chloride, commonly called salt. Whereas chemistry has a theory of electron rings to explain how the chemical reaction between sodium and chlorine makes salt, psychology has no such theory about how nature and nurture interact, and it still does not have one as we write today. Nor is one in prospect. Unlike chemical reactions (such as forming sodium chloride) that are often once-and-for-all events, any interplay between individuals and their environment is a complex, ongoing process, involving a large number of inputs. To give just one example, acting in a caring manner has a meaning and significance that differs markedly from one context to another. What may be appropriate behaviour in the setting of caring for a sick child would be quite inappropriate in the cut-throat world of share dealing. What would be seen as a man acting powerfully might well be perceived in a woman as 'bossy' behaviour. Both are profoundly influenced by expectations, assumptions and meanings.

Nevertheless, we would stand by the claim that psychology has proceeded *as though* there were a clear theory of interplay between environment and heredity. We (among many others) would argue that the problem lies in even seeking to come up with a co-actional model. This endeavour is central to the modernist approach that continues to dominate psychology today. We regard it as a wild goose chase, seeking for something that can never be found.

Further reading

Brannon, L. (1996) *Gender: Psychological Perspectives*. Boston, MA: Allyn and Bacon.

Part II

The challenges to mainstream approaches

Introduction to Part II: Challenges

In this section of the book we move on from the traditional paradigms that have been adopted in mainstream psychology to study gender and sexuality, to look at more recent work which challenges them. We have divided these into three challenges, and devote a chapter to each one:

- liberatory challenges
- feminist challenges
- postmodern challenges.

Before we can examine these in detail, we need to set the scene by looking at the underpinning philosophy within which psychology (as one of the social sciences) came into being, which is usually referred to as modernity. The bio-social sciences are both very much the products *of* modernity and crucial contributors *to* it.

Our Modern world is thoroughly permeated with ideas constructed through social science: ideas about individuals in society, interpersonal relationships, 'selves' and social forces. In particular we live in a psychologized world, where ideas such as sex differences, sociobiology, unconscious desires and extraversion/introversion have been made so meaningful to us, so much a part of common sense, that they have become things we see as really-real. Indeed, more than that, they have become the crucial building blocks for constructing our understanding of the world. It would be, quite simply, impossible to function effectively as a person in our time and culture without a familiarity and fluency with psychological concepts. In order to understand how and why psychology created itself around ideas like this, and hence to make sense of its more recent challenges to them, we therefore need to examine Modernism itself.

Modernism

What we mean by **Modernism** in this context (it has a different meaning in the arts) is the set of values and practices which emerged out of the historical period of the eighteenth-century Enlightenment. Modernity is sometimes called the post-Enlightenment project, since it was (and is) motivated by the conviction that humankind can – and, crucially, *should* – create a better world through its *own* efforts (rather than, say, relying on the benevolence of God). It sought to replace irrationality and disorder with reason and rationality; to move on from ways of knowing based on superstitious beliefs (whether informed by religion, magic or the arcane) to knowledge gained by rational means, primarily through scientific methods of empirical inquiry. Central to the emergence of Modernism, then, was the desire to improve the human condition.

The central tenets of Modernism

Modernism is based on the beliefs that:

- people have certain fundamental entitlements as human beings;
- institutions (such as governments) should serve human interests and respect human rights;
- action needs to be based on rational knowledge;
- scientific methods and the practice of science hold the key to gaining such knowledge.

Those of us who live in 'the West' (a term generally taken to mean Europe, North America and Australasia) very much live in a Modern world – although, with global communication systems reaching all over the world, today there are few people on earth untouched by Modernism. At the same time, its influence is by no means absolute. You have only to think of the popularity of television programmes such as *The X Files* or of horoscopes to recognize that many people continue to be superstitious. Religion still has a significant influence, generally stressing the duty and obedience owed to God. And governments do not always respect human rights. None the less, the liberal humanism that Modernism promotes has become the dominant ideology of our times. It is epitomized, for example, in the United Nations Convention on the Rights of the Child. And its prioritization of science has come to dominate what is generally taken as scholarship, not only in explicitly scientific fields (such as biology and physics) but also in areas like medicine, engineering and disciplines which study the social world.

So pervasive is the Modern world-view that it is almost impossible to conceive of what life must have been like before its ideas and practices came to be taken for granted. But looking back at history can help. To give just one example, before the Enlightenment people almost universally believed that disease was a punishment from God, the result of magic or arose as a consequence of plotting by some marginalized group (such as the Jews). For instance, in 1665 Daniel Defoe wrote about the enormous number of amulets and talismans that were being used by the people of London to ward off the plague. He also described in detail the dreams and portents that were seen to have predicted its coming, especially the appearance of a comet (see Herzlich and Pierret 1984/87: 13). Yet, as Herzlich and Pierret have pointed out, today 'in our society the discourse of medicine about illness is so loud it tends to drown out all the others' (Herzlich and Pierret 1984/87: xi). Although some superstition still surrounds our ideas about the causes of disease, it is difficult to conceive of how the inhabitants of London in the seventeenth-century must have thought about the plague at a time when scientific medicine, as we know it, did not exist.

All men are created equal? Modernity and its discontents

The desire to promote human happiness and well-being is, of course, much older than Modernism; it can, for instance, be traced back to Plato's *Republic*. What makes modernity different is that it became what, in German, is called a *Zeitgeist* (the dominant world-view of a particular time and place). It arose from a number of historical events, of which one of the most important was the Second Continental Congress in the British American Colonies, which, on 4 July 1776, approved the Declaration of Independence. However, its call for emancipation was highly partial, as one US text entitled *The American Achievement* describes: 'It is . . . certain that a greater proportion of the American population was eligible to vote than was true in any other country at that time. Of course, no state seriously considered allowing women or Negroes to vote or hold office' (Brown *et al.* 1966: 86).

To cut a long story short, the rhetoric of Modernism, for all its new language of human rights, co-existed with a much older tradition of male power and racism. The declaration that 'all men are created equal' was specifically intended to challenge aristocratic governance – the system within which some men were seen as born to wield power and authority, whereas others were seen as born to serve and obey. The new form of governance introduced by Modernism, not only in the American colonies but also in revolutionary France, restricted its emancipation to a selected portion of the population that specifically excluded women. However, its **misogyny** did not go unchallenged, as this nineteenth-century declaration shows:

> We hold these truths to be self-evident: that all men and all women are created equal . . . when ever any form of government becomes destructive of those ends, it is the right of those that suffer from it to refuse allegiance to it . . . such has been the patient sufferance of the women under this government, and such is now the necessity which constrains them to demand the equal station to which they are entitled.
>
> (The Seneca Falls Convention 1848)

It has taken a long time for Modernism to lead to even notional universal suffrage, and its heralding of equality is still far from complete. In the UK it has taken about 200 years to achieve the most basic level of legal protection against sexual and racial prejudice and discrimination, and there is still a long way to go. Thus, although Modernism *seems* to offer the promise of universal good for all humankind, in terms of actual, on the ground, practice there is still a considerable gap to be bridged between the Utopian rhetoric and the lived experience of people's lives.

Frustration with this gap has led to a number of reformist and revolutionary movements, agendas and speculations. Some have not worked out too well (notably Marxism as it was translated into the Marxism-Leninism of the Soviet Empire). Others (for instance, the women's suffrage movement) have, within the democracies, largely achieved equality at the ballot. But they have not been as successful in opening up opportunities in the workplace and other institutions of power. Our concern here is with the particular history of gender and sexuality, and the question is – has Modernism actually fostered 'liberty and the pursuit of happiness'? And, if it has, for whom?

Modernism as a progressive project

A central claim of Modernism is that it has brought about progress. It is often told as an 'up the mountain story' (Rorty 1980) in which primitive belief in magic was superseded by religious belief, which was then superseded by the rational knowledge of science (see, for example, Douglas 1965 for a more detailed account of this historical progression; see also Chapter 6). This story reflects a kind of intellectual Darwinism – an epistemological survival of the fittest – where, over time, weak and dysfunctional ways of knowing have given way to one that is strong and functional.

We can think of this progress as having two main elements. First, there is the progress made possible by the practical and epistemological achievements of **techno-science** (that is, science and the technology it made possible). Second, there is the progressive ideology of liberal humanism, which emancipated groups of people who had previously been oppressed and excluded, and changed social institutions to make them serve human interests better. Let us look briefly at how each of these has affected gender relations and human sexuality.

The progress enabled by techno-science

New technologies have profoundly affected both gender relations and human sexuality. An illustration is provided by developments in rubber technology starting in the nineteenth-century, which generated:

- A quantum leap in the availability and reliability of contraception, through improved quality of condoms (pigs' small intestines were the previous raw material) and the production of the 'Dutch cap'. This, in enabling women to exert control over their fertility, was a major factor in their emancipation.
- The inflatable tyres for bicycles, which both opened up women's mobility and also influenced women's clothing towards less restrictive styles. Together these allowed women to gain greater freedom of movement, and greater participation in activities (such as sport) from which they had been excluded.
- Trivial though it may sound, the invention of elastic also opened up a range of possibilities in underwear and corsetry, which also increased women's freedom of movement and ability to participate.
- Rubber tyres and hosing were also crucial for the development of motor vehicles, which made possible the introduction of efficient public transport. This played an important role in enabling urban women to increase their employment opportunities and social mobility. More recently, greater access for young people to the back seats of cars (particularly in the USA) is widely credited with their growing sexual experience over the twentieth century.

There have also been, of course, downsides to technological progress. For instance, the technology which made possible fast and accessible global travel for large numbers of people has also contributed to the spread of the HIV virus, with its devastating impact on sexuality, especially among the gay community in the West.

The progress enabled by liberal humanism

Progressive ideas have contributed to emancipation in a number of ways. For example, throughout the Western world in the late twentieth century there was a liberalization of views towards homosexuality. From about the 1950s laws that criminalized homosexual acts have gradually been repealed (although they still remain in places such as the Cayman Islands and Singapore). In parallel, public opinion has also gradually changed. What occurred in psychology is indicative of this trend.

Historically, homosexual acts, particularly anal intercourse (called buggery in the UK and sodomy in the USA), were regarded as sinful. Once cast within the medicalizing gaze of psychology, they were at first seen not so much as sinful as 'sick' – as manifestations of a psychological disorder. And then in 1973, the American Psychiatric Association, following a series of disruptions of its earlier meetings by gay activists, collectively conceded that homosexuality was not a disease, and voted to remove it from its *Diagnostic and Statistical Manual of Mental Disorders* (DSM-III). What happened next is perhaps even more instructive. Within a few years it was **homophobia** – the 'irrational, persistent fear or dread of homosexuals' (Macdonald 1976) – which had become the sickness. Kitzinger (1987) comments that this reversal – from classifying homosexuals as sick to classifying homophobes as sick – is just one of several such about-turns in the history of psychological theorization about sexuality. It is, however, one of the most dramatic and well documented. Morin (1977) has estimated that about 70 per cent of pre-1974 psychological research on homosexuality was sited within discourses of deviance and dysfunction, devoted to three questions: 'Are homosexuals sick?', 'How can homosexuality be diagnosed?' and 'What causes it?' The early 1970s then saw a proliferation of studies on homophobia (see Kitzinger 1987 for a detailed account) and a flurry of scales designed to measure it, yielding clear 'evidence' that it is linked to a host of other forms of personality defect (such as authoritarianism). As we write, work is burgeoning under the headings of 'Lesbian and Gay Studies' and 'Queer Theory' (see, for example, Medhurst and Hunt 1997; Nardi and Schneider 1998) and, stemming from this, there is a move to theorize heterosexuality (see, for example, Wilkinson and Kitzinger 1993; Richardson 1996).

Homophobia has not, however, been magically eradicated simply because psychologists have come to regard it as a disorder. Sigelman *et al.* (1991), in a survey of the attitudes of heterosexual men, reported that 47 per cent evinced a purely negative reaction to gay men, with comments such as: 'I don't like them', 'I want nothing to do with them' and 'I hope AIDS wipes them out', with a further 45 per cent expressing mildly anti-gay attitudes, such as '[gays] generally don't bother me so long as they don't try and press their beliefs on me'.

Humaneering

We can observe, then, that social sciences such as psychology tend to be more imbued with liberal humanism than is popular opinion. Indeed, this has been explicit for some time, as evidenced by this early 'mission statement':

> The value of learning more about ourselves and human nature is obvious. Our social, political and economic theories rest ultimately upon our understanding of human nature. Upon sound knowledge of human nature depends the possibility of directing social changes, so as to make social institutions and practices better suited to human needs. As citizens, then, we need to make our beliefs about human

> nature as sound and rational as possible. The nineteenth century was marked by great achievements in engineering. Advances in psychology, sociology, and physiology should lead to as striking advances in 'humaneering' during the twentieth century.
>
> (Tiffin *et al.* 1940: 23–4)

The **humaneering mission** pervades psychology (see Stainton Rogers *et al.* 1995 for a more detailed examination), which has adopted a commitment to using its knowledge 'to make social institutions and practices better suited to human needs'. But just as it has come to be recognized that techno-science's engineering has not brought unalloyed benefits to humankind, some psychologists have begun, since about the 1970s, to argue that humaneering has its downside too.

Challenges to Modernism: the climate of perturbation

In other books to which we have contributed (Curt 1994; Stainton Rogers *et al.* 1995) we have argued that in about the 1970s the social sciences began to experience what we have called a **climate of perturbation**. In psychology this stirred up rebellion, dissent, trouble and doubt about both its praxes and its epistemological, methodological and philosophical foundations. This began to happen against a backcloth of more general questioning and challenge directed towards 'the Establishment' that had begun in the 1960s. On both the streets in Europe (most explosively in Paris and Prague, but also in London) and US campuses (at Kent State, three students were shot dead by state troopers), university students and some of their more radical teachers either led or joined political protest movements – in the USA most notably against the Vietnam war, in Europe in a broader rebellion against various forms of state power.

This atmosphere of rebellion was reflected in an upsurge of intellectually radical thought – indeed, a number of academics (including social theorists such as Noam Chomsky, Michel Foucault and Tomas Ibañez) were active on the streets and at the barricades. Central to this movement was a growing disenchantment with the 'system'. Established wisdom was subjected to critique and challenge throughout the social sciences and across the arts and humanities.

However, even in their beginnings, these critical voices had little in common beyond discontent. And as the Western world began to swing from 'you have never had it so good' economic boom to times of 'bust', as unemployment rose, as traditional powers reasserted themselves, and as the dreams of revolution faded, the intellectual landscape of disillusionment shifted and mutated further, splintering into a panoply of dissenting voices. In terms of the labels we use today, these include second-wave feminism, critical theory, queer theory, postmodernism, poststructuralism and social constructionism.

The term 'disillusion' is an expressive one, for it encompasses two common themes: disquiet and cynicism towards the dominant order; and a desire to escape from cosy 'illusions' – the illusion that there are any simple solutions to problems, that there is any kind of hot-line to the truth, that there are any simple certainties which can be trusted. Beyond that there is considerable variation. If we focus on those disillusions which relate most to issues of gender and sexuality, we can, however, make some broad categorizations, in terms of what is viewed as the dominant order that needs to be challenged, and the aims to be achieved:

	See the dominant order that needs to be challenged as:	*Aim to:*
Liberatory challenges	repressive institutions, including religion and the state.	set people free, enable them to discover themselves and to achieve their full potential.
Feminist challenges	social institutions which oppress, exclude and devalue women.	emancipate women and offer alternative world-views that are not based on male power.
Postmodern challenges	the dense network of power which permeates the whole of human society.	disenchant – to reveal the 'enchantments' that beguile us into seeing the world in a particular way, and to expose the ways in which power is operated and can be resisted.

The three chapters in this section each examine one of these.

4 Liberatory challenges

Perversion
In books prior to the seventies, this meant, quite simply, any sexual behaviour which the writer himself [*sic*] did not enjoy. . . . The commonest perversions in our culture are getting hold of some power and using it to kick other people around, money-hunting as a status activity, treating other people, sexually or otherwise, as things to manipulate, and interfering with other people's sex lives to ensure that they are as rigid and as anxious as the interferer.

(Comfort 1972: 209)

Over its history, psychology's varied theoretical, empirical and ideological involvement in issues of gender and sexuality has not only been a matter of changes in the discipline itself. It has also reflected disputes over and shifts in broader cultural values in relation to sex and sexuality. In political terms these can be mapped on to a tension that began in the late eighteenth century as a divide between conservatives (who grounded themselves in the 'natural' power of elites) and liberals (who saw political power going to the most politically able). Nineteenth-century socialism added a third element to the politics of Modernism.

Liberalism

The form of democratic government that is now becoming the global model (in theory if not always practice) is generally called liberal democracy because it assumes that people of divergent self-interests share a bedrock of common interests. It is now conventional to regard (party) politics in the liberal democracies as a continuum from 'Left' through a 'Liberal Centre' to 'Right' (Lipset 1963). At various points psychologists have suggested that at least one additional dimension is also operating, variously termed: 'hard'/'soft' mindedness (Eysenck 1954); open-mindedness/closed-mindedness (Rokeach 1960); 'life-loving'/'anti-life' (Maccoby 1968). Over time, an issue (say, women's right to vote) can move across the spectrum and even drop off the end into consensus. Maccoby's work (drawn from Fromm) is very helpful in understanding a tension in Modernism from its foundation that became highlighted in society and in psychology in about 1960. On the one hand, Modernism centres on values such as freedom and equality; on the other hand, it seeks to better the human condition through what Tiffin *et al.* (1940) termed humaneering. This was exactly the polarity that Maccoby (1968: 2) worked on:

> A person with intense love of life is attracted to that which is alive, which grows, which is free and unpredictable . . . he [*sic*] dislikes sterile and rigid order. He rejects being mechanized, becoming a lifeless part of machine-like organizations. . . . At the other pole, there are individuals attracted to that which is rigid, ordered, mechanical and unalive. These people do not like anything free and uncontrolled.
>
> (Maccoby 1968: 2)

The first of these poles is obviously humanistic – in the same sense that humanism is used in humanistic psychology. But it also had another interesting characteristic, namely that it cut across traditional markers that tend to link to voting behaviour (such as social class). This forum, favouring (at that time) such things as ending the Vietnam war, ending poverty and aiding underdeveloped countries could be called 'liberal': in the sense that the *Guardian* is a 'liberal' newspaper. (In the present-day USA, by contrast, the term 'liberal' carries pejorative overtones implying thinly disguised 'socialist' sympathies!) Maccoby, in other words, has tapped into an ideology that attracts the label: liberal humanism. Liberal humanism is the modal ideology that is institutionalized into disciplines and practices such as psychology; so much so, indeed, that it has a taken-for-granted quality. However, it is not without its critics, including psychologists working in the area of gender and sexuality (for example, Kitzinger 1987).

In the context of this book (and this chapter in particular) political liberalism and liberal-humanistic ideology are not distinguished only from one another, but also from radical politics which valorize freedom. 'Free love' and 'sexual liberation' are slogans of liberatory sexual politics that, traditionally, seek deregulation of aspects of gender and sexuality. However, as we shall see in the next chapter, the received view of liberatory sexual politics is not the only view of liberation around.

To return to this chapter, however, here we will explore the challenge presented to mainstream psychology's treatment of gender and sexuality by liberal humanism. To do this we will begin with a more general examination of the sexual liberation attributed to the 1960s and 1970s, before moving on to a more specific review of psychology's response to this movement. We will focus on three main elements: humanistic psychology, work on the concept of androgyny and research on the effects of erotica and pornography.

Regulation and liberation

As we have argued elsewhere (Stainton Rogers *et al.* 1995), social psychology as we know it today has its foundation in the liberal democratic values of individual autonomy and citizenship rights. But liberal democracy also draws from Modernism a commitment to social progress – the humaneering mission of human betterment (Tiffin *et al.* 1940) which you met in the introduction to this section. This places Modernism under tension – a tension between its powerful commitment to individual freedom and its equally strong commitment to making the world a better place. This tension is manifested in two opposing social pressures: regulation and liberation, which operate at both a social and a personal level.

At a social level, regulation is seen to be required in order to ensure a well-ordered society – to prevent crime and disorder, to protect the weak against the strong, to ensure the smooth and efficient running of social institutions. At a personal level, regulation is seen to be necessary to hold in check the uncontrolled forces of our base instincts; technologies of self-control are seen as the key to being a civilized and rational human being – if you remember, this notion was introduced in Chapter 2. Liberation, on the other hand, is also viewed as essential to human progress – necessary to free humankind from the prejudices and bigotry of pre-modern ideologies. It also operates at a social and personal level. At a social level, liberation is about opening up opportunities to groups that had been denied them – the women's liberation movement is a good example. It is also about creating social changes that remove oppression and counter social exclusion – such as challenging racism. At a personal level, liberation is seen to free the individual from their neuroses and complexes, enabling them to 'discover themselves' and reach their full potential.

In the ***realpolitik*** of government, liberalism has often taken precedence over democracy with the result that liberation has taken the back seat to control. However, Crawford (1984), a sociologist, has suggested that capitalism – another element of Modernism – needs two tensional social metaphors to function effectively. He calls these 'control' and 'release'. The notion of control, he says, is essential for motivating people to work hard and act responsibly. Capitalism, he argues, needs people to sign up to what has otherwise been called 'the Protestant work ethic' in order to produce goods and services. By contrast, the notion of release is about feeling that we deserve to indulge ourselves and seek pleasure. Capitalism, Crawford claims, also needs people to seek gratification in order to be consumers of goods and services. 'Control' and 'release', according to Crawford, are what oil the wheels of the reciprocal cycle of production and consumption on which capitalism is based. From this, we can deduce that gender and sexuality too come under the mandates of control and release. Gender and sexuality are both *controlled* to produce a work force (see also Marxist and socialist feminism in Chapter 5) and *released* as commodities to be consumed.

Bowdler and Grundy

A good example of the interplay of control and release, regulation and liberation, is their manifestation in respect to censorship. The emerging modern democracies of the nineteenth century (particularly Great Britain and the USA) showed a marked 'Victorian' attitude towards sexuality in the arts and in popular entertainment. The term **bowdlerize** (to censor) has its origins in the name of the editor Thomas Bowdler (1754–1825) who produced an expurgated edition of Shakespeare, in which all the 'rude bits' were discreetly removed to protect the sensibilities of, particularly, women and children. He is often partnered in discourse by Mrs Grundy (hence **Grundyism**: narrow-minded, busybody concern with the sexual morals of others). She derives from the play *Speed the Plough* by T. Morton written in 1798. Together, bowdlerizing and Grundyism are used to characterize much that marked the Victorian perspective on sexuality, and which continued well into the twentieth century.

They are still with us in the form of film censorship and certification, in television 'watersheds' that lay down when, say, the word 'fuck' can be heard, and in the 'Mull of Kintyre' criterion, determining at what angle an erect penis becomes an unacceptable image in a film or video. According to Dewe Mathews (1998) there have, to date, been only two exceptions to this, the best known of which is in Derek Jarman's *Sebastiane* (apparently, Jarman himself was unaware that in one scene a Roman centurion was shown with a clearly erect penis, as it had not been evident in the original 16 mm version of the film).

The legal tradition in most English-speaking countries regarded certain language and images as having the capacity to 'deprave and corrupt'. It was then left to the courts to find such a charge either proved or not proved. You might think that this was an evidential question – just the sort of assertion that research could support or reject. But in the heyday of sexual censorship, cases were decided largely on the rhetorical powers of lawyers and at the whim of judges. There were also a number of controls that were not mediated by the courts. Until quite recently in the UK, theatre performances were censored by the Lord Chancellor and local events were under the remit of Watch Committees. Today still the importation of pornography remains the province of Customs and Excise.

The economic consequences of bans and prosecutions also ensured a fair level of self-censorship. Finally, some acts (such as public nudity) became specific offences (English-speaking countries, in particular, have tended to police their beaches) and other acts (for example, kissing in public) may be an offence if the actors are of the same sex. At the same time such attempts to censor are now becoming increasingly undermined by the free availability of material on the internet, which is impossible, in practice, to control.

What is often most telling about censorship is what constitutes the disputed territory between what 'passes' and what 'fails'. When we were children, the only photographs of breasts we saw were restricted to the 'exotic' (as in, 'chocolate coloured beauties' – seriously, this terminology was used). Naturist magazines could be published, but could only show nudity that had been air-brushed to obscure pubic hair. The sexological works of Van de Velde were allowed to be published in the 1920s by printing on the dust cover that sales were restricted to 'the medical profession' or 'the medical and legal profession'. Forel's work *The Sexual Question* (1906) was open to a slightly wider audience: 'Members of the Medical, Legal, Clerical [that is, priests and ministers] and Teaching Professions, and to such responsible adult persons who have a genuine interest in Social Science, Eugenics and Education' (it is nice to know you would have qualified, isn't it?). Lesbianism was another 'no go' area, and the publication of Radclyffe Hall's *The Well of Loneliness* led to a successful prosecution in Britain in 1928 even though there are no descriptions of sex in the book. Levels of 'tasteful' explicit heterosexuality gradually crept into mainstream writing, but anything beyond that (such as D.H. Lawrence's *Lady Chatterley's Lover*) were only published abroad.

The 'Trial of Lady Chatterley' in 1960 – in which Penguin Books successfully defended its paperback publication – marked a broader watershed. Richard Neville's *Play Power* (1970) is another example of this liberalization, although Neville (and colleagues) did a spell in jail for the 'obscenity' of one edition of the magazine *Oz* (which was, interestingly, in terms of recent developments, the 'schoolkids' issue' which featured a highly phallic *Rupert the Bear*). Nevertheless, the broader die was cast. By the late 1960s, in the UK public entertainment could, within limits, offer 'soft erotica'.

Or, if you prefer it, 'soft' pornography. Over the past three to four decades, the nature of liberal-democratic censorship, we would argue, has been renegotiated rather than shifted fundamentally. Perhaps most noticeably, the category of 'soft erotica' has been somewhat opened to adult homoerotic material (mostly, but not exclusively male) in line with changing public and legal sensibilities (and the power of the 'pink pound') while the law has been strengthened towards greater control over material that involves children. Production and publication of such material is now a criminal offence.

Psychology's 'progressive' credentials

These shifts over censorship (among other things) have led some people to argue that contemporary society is much more liberated than it was in the past; that there has been a historical progression from regulation to liberation, from control to release. This, we think, is an over-simplification. So too is the idea that there is some kind of historical pendulum that swings between the two. Rather, we would suggest that they are both always present, although manifested in different ways and in relation to different aspects of life at different times and in different cultural and subcultural locations. Even so, the notions of regulation/liberation and control/release are important themes which help us to make sense of the debates in psychology about gender and sexuality and how psychologists have tried to understand them, and you will find these tensions appearing regularly throughout this chapter.

In the remainder of this chapter we shall examine the impact of 'progressive' values on psychology's understandings of and approaches to gender and sexuality, especially as they have been used to challenge the gender stereotypes built into early work on sex differences. We will also look at how contemporary interpretations of progressive values led to the sexual liberation of the 1960s, and its impact on psychology. To do this we need to cover some more history, albeit briefly.

Public and private

The separation between public and private is another central theme in liberal democracy – it is one of the ways in which the tension between regulation and liberation is managed. In a liberal democracy the state is seen to have a legitimate interest in and the right to intervene in and regulate people's public lives. But it is seen as having only extremely limited authority to intervene in or to seek to regulate the private and personal aspects of people's lives (see Weeks 1986; Kitzinger 1987; and Martin 1989 for more detailed treatments of this aspect of liberal democracy). However, this separation is much more problematic than it might seem, especially concerning issues of gender and sexuality.

In Europe and its colonies (including what is now the USA), before Modernism sexual conduct and gender relations were seen largely as moral issues to be regulated by the (Christian) church. Modernism's progressive project introduced state regulation of those aspects of sexual conduct which were seen as threatening to social order and public health. In England this included bringing in laws against obscenity in 1857, against prostitution and homosexuality in 1885 and 1898, and against indecent advertising in 1889. Interestingly, it took until 1908 before there were secular laws against incest. Up until that point, cases of incest were prosecuted in ecclesiastical courts, since, according to a commentator at the time, the law had not dared, previously, to 'invade the sacred precinct' of the home.

Given this pressure to regulate the essentially private concerns of gender relations and sexual behaviour, liberalism's public/private distinction is somewhat paradoxical in relation to sexuality:

> Sexuality is constantly spotlighted for a public gaze, yet it is considered to be the most personal and intimate of experiences. Even where the act of 'having scx' appcars to be part of the public domain – in pornographic films and magazines, live sex shows, cottaging – a sense of the private persists, either in viewing these acts as exceptional or in the idea that the irreducibly personal and undisclosed elements are present, like individual responses and fantasies.
>
> (Harding 1998: 23)

Martin has argued that the distinction emerged during industrialization, when 'productive activity moved from the household to the factories' (Martin 1989: 16) and reached its high point in the Victorian era. Regulation was particularly applied to women but, interestingly, it was much more marked for women from the middle class. If you recall from Chapter 2, in the nineteenth century there emerged a 'cult of true womanhood' made up of four cardinal virtues: piety, purity, submissiveness and domesticity – these were the qualities expected of the Victorian 'woman of good character' who remained safely in the private domain of the home. By contrast, women who occupied the public sphere risked their reputations. Weeks describes the 'two worlds' like this:

> Victorian morality was premised on a series of ideological separations: between family and society; between the restraint of the domestic circle and the temptation of promiscuity; between the privacy, leisure and comforts of the home and the tensions and competitiveness of work. And these divisions of social organisation and ideology were reflected in sexual attitudes. The decency and morality of the home confronted the danger and pollution of the public sphere; the joys and the 'naturalness' of the home countered the 'corruption', the artificiality of the streets, badly lit, unhygienic, dangerous and immoral. This was the basis of the dichotomy of 'the private' and 'the public' upon which sexual regulation rested. . . . The private was the nest of domestic virtues; the public was the arena of prostitution, of vice on the streets. . . . The division between the private and the public sphere, which was located both in economic development (the separation of work and home) and in social ideology, was by the end of the nineteenth century at the heart of moral discourse.
>
> (Weeks 1986: 81)

The regulation of women's sexuality

What we can see going on in Victorian times was an interplay between concerns about sexuality and understandings of and assumptions about gender. Among Victorian opinion leaders (whose views informed popular wisdom among the 'chattering class' of the time) women were seen as being 'closer to nature' than men, and of therefore having a potentially dangerous and disruptive sexuality – which thus needed to be regulated and controlled (you will recognize resonances here with the kinds of ideas that informed Freud). This was accomplished by keeping women safely occupied with domesticity in the security of the home, and expecting them to be asexual. Even those who asserted a specific female sexuality articulated their arguments in biological terms. For instance, although Elizabeth Blackwell, a pioneering woman doctor, described female sexuality as an 'immense spiritual force of attraction', she mediated this claim by writing: 'The impulse towards maternity, is an inexorable but beneficent law of woman's nature, and is a law of sex' (Blackwell 1885: 87).

The bodily manifestations of women's biological nature were required to be kept private – for example, 'public conveniences' were not provided for women (even in the big department stores). This severely limited women's ability to be away from home for any length of time. Menstruation was seen as highly debilitating, so that women were expected to withdraw from public life when they had their periods. Marshall, for example, writing in a medical textbook on reproduction, described menstruation as 'belonging to the borderline of pathology' (Marshall 1910).

Thus, as we will examine in more detail in the next chapter, the Victorian era adopted an ambivalent position with regard to women. Broadly, in the public sphere it began to emancipate women. For example, up until the 1882 Married Women's Property Act, on the day a woman married all her money and belongings became the property of her husband. The 1882 Act allowed her to keep her property and money, and to own money and property she acquired after marriage. But in the sphere of sexuality the Victorian era was far from emancipatory – it regulated middle-class women by treating them as asexual and restricting their access to public life; and it regulated working-class women by, for example, stigmatizing illegitimacy and introducing Draconian legislation against prostitutes (rather than their clients). Early sexological work operated from within this orthodoxy, stressing the need for regulation. This is evident in the work of Freud. Neither in his private life nor in his theory was Freud any kind of sexual libertine. In terms of theory, he took the view that instinctual sexual energy (libido) needed regulation, and that the price of civilization was a certain level of the neuroses thereby generated.

Summary box Liberalism

- Liberalism is becoming the dominant ideology, in theory if not always in practice, across the world, manifested in the expansion of liberal democracy.
- Liberalism contains two opposing philosophies – liberation and regulation. Liberation stresses individual freedom, the right of individual citizens to live their lives as they choose. Regulation stresses the need to 'make the world a better place' by way of personal and social control, in order to protect the weak and foster social harmony. Another way of expressing this is to argue that under liberal democracy people are subject to both control and release – to discipline themselves and to be disciplined to behave in civilized ways, but also to seek pleasure and satisfaction.
- Forms of social control (such as censorship) tend to move between liberation and regulation, control and release. Although liberal democracy has often been associated with a gradual liberalization (that is, a move towards the liberation/release pole) we would argue that this is an oversimplification. For example, whereas some aspects of sexuality have become liberalized (such as the decriminalization of homosexuality), others have been subjected to greater regulation and control (such as any kind of sex which involves children).
- Psychology is very much a 'creature of its time and place' in that it has always been based on values of liberal humanism. However, we can trace shifts in the precise manifestations of its liberalism which parallel broader shifts in dominant values over time.
- Another central theme in liberal humanism is that of separating the public from the private. Generally, liberal humanism seeks to foster human betterment by regulating the public sphere, but promotes individual freedom by not interfering in people's private lives.
- However, this separation tends to break down in relation to issues of gender and sexuality. This was true in Victorian times especially in relation to women.

The liberalization of sexuality

Towards the end of the nineteenth century there were dissenting voices arguing for liberation (an informative account is provided by Elaine Showalter 1992). In many respects, the 'naughty nineties' (the 1890s, that is) were part of a broader Continental ***fin de siècle***, marked by publications such as the *Vie Nouvelle* (Sheridan 1898). In the UK in 1897 the Legitimation

League was formed to campaign for liberalizing the law over illegitimacy, marriage and divorce. It established a journal – *The Adult* – for 'The Advancement of Freedom in Sexual Relationships'. Its liberatory agenda was obvious in its first editorial:

> We recognise the paramount right of the individual to self-realisation in all non invasive directions. *The Adult* advocates the absolute freedom of two individuals of full age, to enter into and conclude at will, any mutual relationships whatever, where no third person's interests are concerned.
>
> (cited in Weeks 1981: 180)

The organization did not have a happy history. There were major disputes about the desirability of 'free love', and in 1898 its secretary, George Bedborough, was arrested and brought to trial for publishing Havelock Ellis' book, *Sexual Inversion*. Under intense pressure from the police he pleaded guilty and was bound over, and the league was effectively crushed.

It was not until 1914 that another systematic attempt was made to open up the liberalizing agenda, by the establishment of the British Society for the Study of Sex Psychology (BSSSP). Its aim was 'to organise understanding in the lay mind on a larger scale, to make people more receptive to scientific proof'. It arranged regular public talks, many of which were published as pamphlets: on sexual difficulties; sexual variety and variability among women; the erotic rights of women; the impact of hormones and the sexual life of the child. Many of the key members of the society were homosexual at a time when this was illegal and could result in a lengthy prison sentence. One of the society's objectives was to lobby for the rights of homosexuals. It was felt that the time was not yet right for changes in the law, but it did argue for greater tolerance and a more informed view. In the Introduction to Hirschfeld's English translation of a paper on 'The Social Problem of Sexual Inversion', published by the BSSSP in 1915, he wrote: 'That any courage should be needed in a demand for facts to be recognised and scientifically investigated, is in itself a condemnation of the obscurantist attitude which prevails so largely in relation to this question' (Hirschfeld 1915: 3).

By the 1920s there were about 250 members, including many of the more famous liberal intellectuals of the day – George Bernard Shaw, Radclyffe Hall and Bertrand and Dora Russell. At this time the society changed its name to the British Sexological Society. At much the same time in Germany, 1919, Hirschfeld opened the Institute for Sexual Science to carry out research in and distribute 'scientific knowledge' about sex. The institute sponsored sex education and provided sexual counselling for couples and for 'sex variants'. In 1921 it ran the first of a series of World Congresses on Sex Reform, which led, in 1927, to the formal setting up of a World League for Sexual Reform. Its aim was to make law and social policy more in line with what it saw as 'the laws of nature'. These included:

- fostering the political, sexual and economic equality of women and men;
- reforming laws on marriage and divorce to make them more humane;
- providing sex education;
- providing accessible and effective contraception;
- making abortion more easily available to those who want it;
- taking measures against prostitution;
- preventing and treating sexually transmitted diseases;
- providing support and protection for lone parents and their children; and
- developing more rational attitudes towards those whose sexuality is 'deviant' and decriminalizing those sexual acts which do not infringe the sexual rights of others.

Wilhelm Reich

Probably the best-known 'sexual radical' of those times was Wilhelm Reich (1897–1957). Reich was a psychoanalyst who challenged Freud's endorsement of the need to regulate sexuality. Reich positively celebrated the orgasm because he believed that experiencing it is not only pleasurable but positively healthy and essential to well-being. Reich saw young people as entitled to and benefiting from sexual experience (or more specifically – marking the boundaries of his radicalism – heterosexual experience). In a paper originally published in 1932 under the title 'The Sexual Struggle of Youth' and revised in 1983 as 'The Sexual Rights of Youth', Reich argued for a clear manifesto of sexual liberation for young people. He saw them as entitled to autonomy: '[t]he decision about the sexual rights of young people must be taken by the young people concerned' (Reich 1983: 164), and championed their right to engage in sex: 'As soon as masturbation no longer fulfils its function of providing gratification, as soon as it starts to be associated with disgust, guilt feelings, and unpleasure, the young person should not be afraid of moving onto sexual intercourse' (Reich 1983: 171).

Reich's deregulatory values are evident in his advice to young people concerning how they should go about having sex: '[b]efore the [sex] act is commenced [there should be] mutual caresses, kisses, touching, stroking, and other love play for which no moral rules can be set' (Reich 1983: 175). Throughout his writings he was at pains to stress that 'nothing is immoral as long as it causes no harm and helps one's partner to experience greater pleasure' (Reich 1983: 176), and that '[o]ften a boy or a girl has to look around for some time before finding a suitable partner, sleeping with this and that person and then looking some more. There is no reason to condemn this' (Reich 1983: 184). To Reich, sexual fulfilment is a major means of civilizing human conduct: '[t]he easier and more possible it is for people to lead satisfactory and well-ordered love lives, the more such factors as sexual lust and brutality will disappear' (Reich 1983: 208). Reich condemned what he saw as the misuse of sex.

For example, he criticized young people who treat sex like a competition, simply a matter of 'having' as many sexual conquests as possible: 'Such an attitude is not only damaging to the person concerned but also to all other people involved. . . . Love is replaced by the desire to dominate' (Reich 1983: 185). His values are particularly evident in his views about the way in which women have been more sexually oppressed than men:

> We are convinced that woman is not by nature inferior to man but that over the millennia suppression in the sexual and economic sphere has actually reduced women to an inferior state. We want not only to eliminate the social and sexual enslavement of women but also to establish the complete emotional friendship of the sexes.
>
> (Reich 1983: 206)

Summary box The liberalization of sexuality

- At the end of the nineteenth century there were a number of movements in Europe that pressed for sexual liberation. In the UK these included the Liberation League and The British Society for the Study of Sex.
- They campaigned across a broad front – for liberalizing the law over illegitimacy, marriage and divorce; for 'free love' (that is, sex outside marriage) and for more acceptance of homosexuality.
- In Germany the World League of Sexual Reform was set up in 1927, which campaigned to foster legal equality between men and women; for greater access to sex education, contraception and abortion; for measures to prevent and treat sexually transmitted diseases and to control prostitution; for better provision for single parents and their children; and for greater acceptance of sexual 'deviance' including homosexuality.
- A key figure in this early press for sexual liberation was Wilhelm Reich. He believed that sexual orgasm is essential to well-being and argued for the sexual rights of women and young people.

Humanistic psychology

Apart from the work of a few radicals such as Reich, up until the 1950s mainstream psychology was dominated by a regulatory view of gender and sexuality. This was challenged by people like Carl Rogers and Abraham Maslow, who were responsible for setting up what became known as **humanistic psychology**. Their aim was to bring to psychology a 'Third Force', as they were disillusioned with the psychology of the day, which was dominated by behaviourism and psychoanalysis. Maslow, for example, said that the subject matter taught in his introductory psychology course at Cornell was 'awful and bloodless and had nothing to do with people, so I shuddered and turned away from it' (Hoffman 1988: 26). The humanistic psychology they developed was strongly individualistic. They were much more interested in finding ways of exploring each individual's uniqueness than in trying to formulate universal laws of human behaviour. They stressed the rights of individuals to make their own choices about the direction their lives will take. They were, for their time and place, fairly revolutionary, viewing society as a stultifying, normalizing force that imposes petty rules and stifles personal growth. Humanistic psychology presented two main challenges to the mainstream psychology of the 1950s. First, it accused it of being too limited in its scope and of concentrating on the most negative aspects of human conduct and experience. Allport expressed this disillusionment well:

> Our methods . . . and the interpretations arising from the exclusive use of those methods are stultifying. Some theories . . . are based on the behaviour of sick and anxious people or upon the antics of captive and desperate rats. Fewer theories have derived from the study of healthy beings, those who strive not so much to preserve life as to make it worth living. Thus we find today many studies of criminals, few of law-abiders; many of fear, few of courage; more on hostility than affiliation; much on the blindness of man [*sic*], little on his vision; much on his past, little on his outreaching into the future.
>
> (Allport 1955: 18)

Second, humanistic psychologists criticized the mainstream's obsession with treating psychology as just another form of natural science and its assumption that the same methods that work in physics and chemistry can simply be transposed to the study of human experience. Humanistic psychologists argued that this profoundly misses the point – the very qualities that mark humans out *as* human (as opposed to rats or robots) are precisely those which are not amenable to natural science's methods of study. How, they argued, could you 'objectively define' or measure human experiences such as joy, wonder or love? How can you study human insight and creativity in the laboratory?

Abraham Maslow

Abraham Maslow, best known for his theories about the hierarchy of human needs, **self-actualization** and **peak experiences**, also had little to say specifically about gender and sexuality. He saw sex as one of the most basic, physiological human needs which had to be satisfied before a person could begin seeking out satisfaction for higher-order needs such as belongingness and love. But even love he divided up between what he called **D-love** (deficiency-love) – a basic, selfish need to be loved – and **B-love** (being-love) which includes the capacity to truly love and care for others.

One aspect of his work, however, was related to issues of gender and has aroused some controversy. Maslow was particularly interested in self-actualization. This, he believed, is about satisfying one's innate curiosity about oneself and reaching one's unique potential. But he pointed out that it is not always possible for people to move to this highest plane, because they fear the consequences of such self-knowledge. He called this fear the **Jonah complex** and suggested that women are particularly prone to it – they do not pursue their intellectual potential because achievement is considered unfeminine and they fear social rejection (Maslow 1962). This notion was taken up by Horner (1969) who used it to explain why women show less achievement motivation than men do. This theorization and the empirical work carried out to support it have, not surprisingly, been the subject of criticism (see Piedmont 1988 and Crawford and Maracek 1989 for reviews).

This aspect of Maslow's work illustrates how, despite its liberatory claims, humanistic psychology retained the sexism of the mainstream and was highly insensitive to issues of power, prejudice and oppression. All of the notable 'movers and shakers' of the humanistic movement were male and white – as were the vast majority of academic psychologists of that time. They saw the world from a male perspective. Maslow, for example, saw nothing at all notable in his list of self-actualizers – Abraham Lincoln, Thomas Jefferson, Albert Einstein, Eleanor Roosevelt, Jane Addams, William James, Albert Schweitzer, Aldous Huxley and Baruch Spinoza. It seems not to have occurred to him that all were white and most were male, nor did it seem to bother him that by popularizing this list he might be helping to maintain the illusion that white males are somehow, by nature, superior. But such sexism did not go unnoticed at the time. Laura Singer, former president of the American Association of Marriage Family Counselors, was cited in the *New York Times Magazine* as wryly commenting: 'I wouldn't say that marriage and self-actualization are necessarily mutually exclusive, but they are difficult to reconcile' (Lear 1972).

Carl Rogers

Carl Rogers is best known as the 'founding father' of counselling. He saw all people as having the potential for self-actualizing: 'it may become deeply buried under layer after layer of encrusted psychological defences . . . but it is my belief that it exists in every individual, and awaits only the proper conditions to be released and expressed' (Rogers 1961: 35). These conditions, he suggested, included the **unconditional positive regard** of others – being loved, valued and respected for and in themselves. Much of his working life was devoted to exploring how troubled and psychologically damaged people could, through therapy, become fully functioning people and go on to live rich and contented lives. Among humanistic psychologists, Rogers' work offers perhaps the best illustration of a particular set of liberal-humanistic values on which this movement was based. For example, in his book *Carl Rogers on Personal Power* (Rogers 1977) he set out what amounted to a manifesto for the types of qualities to which he thought people should aspire. He wrote glowingly of corporate executives who decide to give up the 'rat race', members of **communes** and countercultures and people from oppressed minorities who have learned how to become more assertive. He described them as having the following characteristics:

- being open and honest;
- being more interested in quality of life than material possessions;
- being caring, with a deep desire to help others and contribute to society;
- having a respect for the environment and an antagonism to the misuse of science;
- trusting their own experience and distrusting authority; and
- being willing and open to change.

He was equally willing to define what he saw were the desired qualities of a harmonious and healthy marriage:

- the couple are willing to face up to and explore the differences between them;
- there is good communication and each is willing to listen to the other;
- women's growing independence is recognized as valuable in the relationship;
- each of them can transcend traditional gender role expectations and choose their own way of behaving; and
- both recognize the value of separateness, including an acknowledgement that one or both may form **satellite relationships**.

It is this last element that marks Rogers' ideas out as liberatory – by satellite relationships he specifically meant extra-marital relationships which could include sex, and argued that people who had become fully functioning would have sufficient self-worth not to be troubled by jealousy (Rogers 1972). Rogers' work both reflected and contributed to a major shift in attitudes, where an **open marriage** (Williams 1974) of the form he proposed (although not necessarily including the acceptance of satellite relationships) was increasingly advocated over traditional marriage. Other theorists went further – it was during the 1960s and early 1970s that (especially in places like California) people experimented with **multilateral relationships** (DeLora and DeLora 1972 and Smith and Smith 1974 provide readable accounts) and **communes** (see Veysey 1974). However, many alternative lifestyles of the time seem to have retained many of the gender divisions of more traditional arrangements – one account of a New Mexico commune described the members as 'young bloods and kitchen-weary girls' (Hedgepeth 1972: 321). Humanistic psychology, then, was part of a more general liberatory movement, but one in which some got more liberated than others. We will come back to look at this aspect of 1960s 'alternative' culture again in Chapter 5, as it provided a major stimulus for 'second-wave' feminism.

Erich Fromm

One of the most influential liberatory theorists outside of humanistic psychology was Erich Fromm. Born in Frankfurt in 1900, he had a deeply religious Jewish upbringing, although after studying the Talmud for 14 years he graduated in sociology and then became interested in psychoanalysis. His thinking was informed by the Marxism and **existentialism** that he met at Heidelberg University. All of these influences fed into his theorization, which he developed mainly in the USA. He emigrated there in 1934, fleeing from the Nazis. Fromm, in two of his best-known books *Escape from Freedom* (1941) and *The Sane Society* (1955), set out a powerful critique of then-contemporary Western society, which he saw as profoundly sick. People, he said, had become alienated from themselves and others because of their exploitation by big business and big government. They had, he thought, been made into faceless, unthinking automata, managed and manipulated by bureaucrats, and, as a result, had become apathetic and destructive. For Fromm, a solution needed to be found in what he called 'humanistic, communitarian socialism', a social, legal, economic and political system that would enable people to become active and responsible participants in civil life. For this to be achieved, Fromm argued for a humanization of technology and government.

Fromm's theories were less to do with sexuality and gender *per se* than they were about human relations. He proposed that the most powerful motivating forces in human behaviour are the quest to make life meaningful and a powerful need for relatedness. He saw mature love as the ultimate life goal – 'union under the condition of preserving one's integrity, one's individuality' (Fromm 1956: 17) based on 'care, responsibility, respect and knowledge' (Fromm 1956: 22). This he distinguished from romantic love, which he saw as **pseudo-love**, short-lived and based only on physical attraction.

Summary box Humanistic psychology

- Humanistic psychology is based on a broad philosophy of human liberation – liberation from the stultifying constraints of a society that stifles personal growth and limits people's freedom to achieve their full potential.
- In this context, and very much within the more general liberalizing *Zeitgeist* of the 1960s, it argued for sexual liberation, although this tended to be limited to the liberation of male, heterosexual sexuality.
- Maslow is best known for his creation of the concept of *self-actualization*. Contentiously he argued that some people suffer from a *Jonah complex* – they fear self-knowledge and achievement, and that

women are more prone to this than men. So women are less able to achieve the highest plane of self-actualization.

- Rogers is famous for being the 'founding father' of counselling. He applied his ideas to marriage and argued that good marriages are ones in which a couple communicate well, acknowledge and accommodate their differences, avoid traditional gender roles and foster the woman's independence, and recognize the value of having separate identities and life goals, including the possibility of having extra-marital relationships.
- Fromm regarded romantic love as pseudo-love – short-lived and based only on physical attraction – and as much less desirable than mature love. This he defined as a relationship based on respect for each person's individuality, care, responsibility, and knowing each other well.

Liberalism as a 'best-of-all-possible-worlds' philosophy

Weeks has written of the late 1960s and early 1970s (the time at which humanistic psychology emerged) as the 'permissive moment' – a time of not just sexual, but other forms of permissiveness. Weeks specifically links this to economic events: '[t]here is no doubt that the prolonged [economic] boom depended in part on a switch in moral attitudes away from traditional bourgeois virtues of self-denial and saving ("prudence") towards a compulsion to spend' (Weeks 1981: 250). By this analysis, it was a period during which economic forces pushed for control to give way to release. Technological change was also influential, encompassing both the profound impact of the oral contraceptive and, especially for the young, increasing mobility, economic buoyancy and cultural independence (Stainton Rogers 1997). These changes were accompanied by shifting values, which were evident in both legislative changes (such as the decriminalization of homosexuality and abortion) and the move in much of the Christian Church away from absolutist positions.

At the time the shift to permissiveness was very much seen by its proponents as liberatory – freeing people from the narrow constraints imposed by regulatory laws and conventions and giving them permission to enjoy themselves and seek pleasure and fulfilment. With hindsight, however, it is clear that such freedom was made available only to some – mainly those who were affluent and who had status – and excluded many. It was also couched within a liberalism that, as we noted at the beginning of the chapter, had become so dominant an ideology that it had gained a taken-for-grantedness that effectively denied any other ideology. Minogue expresses this well: 'Many liberal opinions seem so obvious as to be unquestionable . . . its ideological roots are buried very deep, in an understanding of the world of whose bias we are hardly aware' (Minogue 1963: 7), and describes it as 'an intellectual compromise so extensive that it includes most of the guiding beliefs of modern western opinion' (Minogue 1963: vii).

Riffraff theorizing

And there, for critical theorists, lies the rub. As Celia Kitzinger (1987) has noted, liberalism promotes the seeking of compromise, the avoidance of extremes, and middle-of-the-road theories and policies which try to integrate diverse positions and opinions into a coherent whole by combining the best of them. Mainstream psychology texts and journal articles on gender and sexuality are replete with compromise positioning. Even Linda Brannon's textbook, which is in many ways more informed than most, none the less slips into compromise at times. In the summary to her chapter on gender development, for example, she concludes with the statement: 'Evaluating the social theories of gender development leads to the conclusion that each has supporting research, yet research fails to support any theory to the exclusion of the others' (Brannon 1996: 164). This sounds like the essence of liberal humanism applied to theory. We emerge with a 'feel-good' sense that the fanaticism of ideology can be avoided by acknowledging diversity but at the same time smoothing out any conflict between opposing positions:

> Liberalism is generally regarded by its defenders as an anti-ideological, and anti-metaphysical approach, which, unlike its doctrinal rivals, eschews a comprehensive world-view in favour of the principle of attempting always to see and grasp facts as they are, free from the distortions imposed on them by mediating ideologies.'
>
> (Arblaster 1972: 89)

Nevertheless, mainstream psychology, steeped in and warranted by liberalism, has not been averse to using its power to rubbish those who challenge liberalism by pathologizing them as fanatics. This started early with Kretschmer (quoted in Rudin 1969), who argued that 'fanatics bear even in their bodily structure the characteristics of the schizothymic-schizoid syndrome'. It runs through the research on the Authoritarian Personality (Adorno *et al.* 1950) and the research carried out into closed-mindedness by Rokeach (1960). A classic example is research by Eaves and Eysenck (1974) that diagnosed a personality syndrome which 'makes some people emphatic, dogmatic, authoritarian and Machiavellian, thus predisposing them to extremist positions' (Eaves and Eysenck 1974). Caplan (1970) has termed this **riffraff theorizing** – the discounting of opponents as riffraff in order to discount their challenges. Celia Kitzinger makes the point that '[t]hrough imputing pathology to adherents of ideologies other than liberalism, the riffraff theory avoids open acknowledgement and discussion of political differences' (Kitzinger 1987: 127).

This is evident, for example, in the way that the psychology establishment (in the form, for example, of the American Psychological Association in the USA and the British Psychological Society in the UK) has resisted attempts by 'radical' groups to challenge its liberal humanism. Such radicals are still very much treated as 'on the fringe', at best humoured or ignored and not allowed any power; at worst rubbished as fanatical, on the argument that psychology is not and should not be 'political'. We will look at this in more detail in Chapter 5.

Summary box Liberalism: the 'best of all possible worlds'?

- The 1960s and 1970s saw an increasing liberalization of both public life (evident, for example, in the liberalization of the law on divorce, homosexuality and abortion) and private life (manifested, for example, in more people living together before or instead of marrying, and increasing acceptance of sex outside marriage more generally).
- However, although liberalism is often presented as 'the best of all possible worlds', it is not as accepting of difference as it is purported to be. It tends to rubbish dissenting voices as fanatics, especially those that argue that liberalism is insensitive to issues of power. This is evident in the way that the psychological establishment has resisted, for example, attempts to accommodate 'radical' movements such as Marxism, feminism and separatist lesbianism.

Androgyny

Possibly the most emblematic example of liberal-humanistic theorizing on gender in psychology was the development of the concept of androgyny. You can get a good flavour of this from the following description:

> The idea of the androgynous man and woman does not mean that men and women should be expected to behave in exactly the same way, nor that the differences between men and women, of which there are many, should be altogether minimised or ignored. Similarly it does not imply that the use of gender schemas necessarily leads to sexism. What the concept does suggest is that rather than acting in ways that society deems appropriate for men and women, *people should behave in a human way, based on freely made choices.*
>
> (Feldman 1998: 110; our emphasis)

Piel Cook defines **androgyny** as 'the balanced blending of both masculine and feminine characteristics in a given person' (Piel Cook 1985: vii). She describes how it was developed as a theoretical construct by psychologists in response to growing dissatisfaction with prior theories that treated femininity and masculinity as exclusively separate and inherently different categories. This was viewed as obscuring the extent to which men and women are alike. Moreover, as Kaplan (1979) argued cogently, the consequence of treating 'similarities as inconsequential findings or, at best, unexplainable results' was a 'female-male dichotomy that failed to represent the diversity of personal qualities and the complexity of the culture'. In other words, traditional sex differences research and theorization were seen to have produced cardboard-character images of femininity and masculinity – Stepford Wives and Rambos – which bore little relationship to what men and women are like in real life. The concept of androgyny was presented as the solution:

> A more sophisticated model of sex roles was needed, one which could conceptualize similarities *between* the sexes and differences *within* each sex as well as the reverse. Such a model was available – one which posited masculinity and femininity as positive traits existing in everyone regardless of sex and which had favourable implications for all. The coexistence of positive masculine and feminine dimensions is androgyny.
>
> (Piel Cook 1985: 17; original emphasis)

It is easy to spot the liberal credentials here – androgyny is about 'positive traits', has 'favourable implications for all' and combines the best of masculinity and femininity. Piel Cook goes on to praise the way it 'filled a troublesome void in sex-theory research' and to note with approval that '[w]ith the naming of androgyny, new options for the sexes' self-descriptions and behaviours could suddenly be universally discussed'.

There was actually nothing all that new about the concept – it goes back at least as far as Greek mythology (Heilbrun 1978) and, indeed, is an idea found in a number of ancient mythical systems. It was also an important theme in the work of Jung. What was new was its adoption into mainstream psychology in the 1970s, most notably through the writing of Sandra Bem (1974). Bem specifically argued that androgyny is a psychologically healthier and more human way of being than conforming to traditional gender roles. Bem described androgynous people as independent and affectionate, assertive and understanding. Her 'warm and cuddly' intentions are highly evident in her stated hope that 'perhaps the androgynous person will come to define a more human standard of psychological health' (Bem 1974: 162). Some feminist psychologists have been less than impressed. Hollway (1989: 99) has this to say:

> While Bem's work does not any longer represent feminist psychology – indeed it has been roundly criticized – it none the less demonstrates the serious limitations in borrowing the basic methods and concepts

> of the knowledge that needs to be overturned. Her presumably feminist intentions were subverted by the methods and assumptions she reproduced uncritically as a result of her training as a social psychologist (and the lay assumptions that it uncritically reproduces). She failed to raise theoretical questions about gender at all, but followed in the atheoretical, empiricist tradition of Anglo-American psychology. Meanwhile, the idea of androgyny was taken up with enthusiasm by an oncoming generation of progressive and often feminist American social psychologists. It fitted their training and their idealistic assumptions about gender (as well probably as their sense of their own identities). If social psychology had ever evolved any historical self-consciousness, the androgyny enthusiasts would have been able to recognize that the dominant student American position concerning gender was a historically specific phenomenon and that the concept of androgyny in social psychology was a product of similar conditions.
>
> (Hollway 1989: 99)

Although androgyny is often seen as synonymous with Sandra Bem's work (as in the quote above), there have been a variety of alternative conceptualizations developed by psychologists. These illustrate effectively just what the machine of social psychology can build from humble enough conceptualization, and are summarized in Table 4.1. This psychological theorization around the concept of androgyny, albeit in different forms, presented a challenge to the assumption that people who are not appropriately sex-typed are, at best, less than healthy and adjusted and, at worst, pathological. As Burr (1998) has noted, by arguing that 'unmasculine' men and, in particular, 'unfeminine' women are actually *more* healthy and well adjusted, this work made an important contribution to challenging stereotypical thinking about women's capacities at a time when women were fighting for better opportunities in education and the workplace. None the less, since its heyday in the 1970s and early 1980s, the construct of androgyny has come under increasing fire.

Hollway (1989), for example, has criticized Bem for implying that sexism can be countered simply by individual men and women changing the way they see the world, without the need for structural changes in the organization of society. Eisenstein has criticized Bem for her unquestioning acceptance of traditional male qualities: 'the androgynous concept embodied an uncritical vision of maleness and masculinity; the qualities of aggression, competitiveness, leadership, and so on were taken to be good in themselves and therefore important for people to acquire' (Eisenstein 1984: 63). But more generally Eisenstein was most critical of the way the concept (and the scale Bem developed to measure it) allowed psychologists to ignore the power relationship between the sexes. This is a fundamental issue in feminist approaches to the psychology of gender and sexuality, and we will take it up again in the next chapter.

Table 4.1

	Main proponents	*Key features*
Conjoint models		These models focus on the interplay between feminine and masculine qualities.
Androgyny as modulation or balance	Bem 1974	Femininity and masculinity are seen as extreme tendencies, but where they are manifested together each tends to moderate the other, producing a more rounded and well-balanced person.
Androgyny as additive	Spence *et al.* (1975)	This is a 'more is better' formulation, which sees androgyny as the possession of both feminine and masculine qualities and sees having lots of qualities and capacities as more desirable than having a few.
Androgyny as multiplicative or interactive	Spence 1983; Harrington and Anderson 1981	A 'the-whole-is-more-than-the-sum-of-the-parts' model, in which the interplay of feminine and masculine qualities is seen to make androgynous people quite different from those who are either strongly feminine or strongly masculine.
Developmental models		These models view androgyny as a developmental stage, where individuals transcend the limitations of conventional sex roles.
Androgyny as the acquisition of hybrid qualities	Kaplan 1979	Here androgyny may be seen as producing desirable hybrid qualities such as assertive-dependency, or compassionate-ambition.
Androgyny as sex-role transcendence	Heffner *et al.* 1975; Olds 1981	Androgyny is portrayed as a final stage in development. Olds, for example, saw androgyny as progress beyond the duality of femininity and masculinity and the achievement of a fluid, integrated wholeness.
Cognitive schema theory	Bem 1981	Bem's later formulations viewed androgyny as a particular way of thinking, where an individual comes to categorize the world without reference to gender stereotypes.
Personality trait model	Spence and Helmreich 1979	In their later formulation, Spence and Helmreich viewed femininity and masculinity as personality traits, operating in an additive manner.
Behavioural models		Sees androgyny as what people *do*.
Androgyny as the diversifying of social skills	Kelly and Worell 1977; Yager and Baker 1979	Here androgyny is a matter of developing high levels of competence across a wide range of social skills, both those usually attributed to women and those more generally seen in men.
Androgyny as lifestyle	Orlofsky 1977	Here androgyny becomes a way of life, spanning recreational choices, vocational preferences and behaviour in relationships.

Summary box Androgyny

- One of the best examples of liberal-humanistic theorizing is the development of the concept of androgyny – the idea that the 'best way for a person to be' is neither stereotypically male nor female, but having the best qualities of both genders.
- Although Sandra Bem's work – a development of gender schema theory – on androgyny is the best known, there have been a number of other approaches to this concept: developmental, personality trait and behavioural models.
- Some feminists have criticized the 'warm and cuddly' credentials of the concept – its liberal humanism. They argue that it fails to address the power imbalances between men and women, and that it offers 'cop-out' from the need to act to counter the structural and material disadvantages that women suffer. It tends to imply that all that needs to happen is that individual men and women have to change the way they think, see the world and see themselves, and the problems of gender inequality will magically go away.

Research into the effects of pornography and erotica

As well as having a direct impact on theorization, for psychology (and, to some extent, sociology and psychiatry) the 'permissive turn' of the 1960s led to a considerable body of research about the effects of erotica and pornography. In 1970 *The Report of the Commission on Obscenity and Pornography* was published in the USA. This report had its origins under President Johnson in 1967 but was published during Nixon's first presidency. Some 85 empirical studies were commissioned by the organization at a cost of about a million dollars. The major conclusions drawn from the research were that:

In terms of people's views:

- People generally saw **erotica** and **pornography** as having only negative effects (such as predisposing someone to rape) on others. They denied that they, themselves, would be affected in this way.
- Most academics and practitioners working in the psy disciplines (for example, sociologists, psychologists and social workers, see Chapter 6) believed that erotica and pornography had no negative effects. Police chiefs, however, tended to endorse the idea that 'obscene' books had a significant role in juvenile crime.

In empirical studies of the impact of exposure to erotic stimuli:

- These produce sexual arousal in most men and women. Young people and the better educated are more likely to be aroused than older or less well educated people.
- For ordinary people, depictions of conventional sexual behaviour (rather than anything that would have been seen at that time as 'kinky') were most arousing.
- It is possible to become satiated by over-exposure.
- Exposure to explicit sexual material can enhance short-term eroticism (for example, in dreams), but established patterns of sexual behaviour are stable.
- Erotic stimuli have little or no effect on established sexual attitudes.
- Those not familiar with erotic materials can experience strong and conflicting emotions in response to explicit material (that is, feeling both disgusted *and* aroused).

Overall,

> [e]mpirical research . . . found no evidence to date that exposure to explicit sexual materials plays a significant role in the causation of delinquency or criminal behavior among youth or adults. The Commission cannot conclude that exposure to erotic materials is a factor in the causation of sex crime or sex delinquency.
>
> (Commission on Obscenity and Pornography 1970: 32)

These findings were pleasing neither to the right (including Nixon and his then vice-president Spiro Agnew) nor to many feminists. Two 'moral majority' members of the commission, in one of several minority dissensions, dubbed the report 'a Magna Carta for the pornographer' (Commission on Obscenity and Pornography 1970: ix).

It is now nearly 30 years on from this research, and some clarification of complexity of the issue is becoming evident. The view is generally taken that there is a need to distinguish between 'erotica' (sexually focused material) and 'violent pornography' (in which, largely, women are shown as willing victims and are subjected to various degrees of violence, up to and including murder – one of the most notorious depictions has a woman being fed into a food-mincer. Erotica is held to be 'more apt to *reduce* rather than to increase men's aggression against either men or women' (Lord 1997: 529, original emphasis). Violent pornography is generally seen to increase male aggression against women, particularly where it fosters the **rape myth** (that women enjoy being raped). However, this needs qualifying as 'experiments on violent pornography end with very careful debriefings that expose the fallacies of the rape myth, men who participate in such experiments are less, not more, likely to accept violence against women' (Lord 1997: 529).

This kind of research produces results that are highly local and contingent. In the USA and the UK, ethics committees (and the fear of being sued) require all such studies to include procedures such as debriefing to protect subjects from harm. This in turn produces results that are both necessary (that is, researchers need to be able to show that they made sure that the debriefing worked) and artefactual (in that they result from the debriefing). This raises the question of how, today, research on violent pornography could be done without engendering debriefing artefacts. In medical research the answer is often to export the research to poorer countries with less legal protection for their citizens. If you don't like that answer (and we don't) then the alternative may need to be a more up-front acceptance of the limits to 'experimental research' as a guide to social policy.

Summary box The effects of pornography

- Research tends to show that viewing sexually explicit erotic material has little or no impact on behaviour – it can have a short-term effect on erotic behaviour, but established patterns of sexual behaviour seem to be uninfluenced. It does not encourage rape or sexual assaults. However, material depicting women as willing victims of sexual violence – especially depictions of rape – may encourage sexual assault.
- Early research suggested that most people are more 'turned on' by explicit depictions of 'ordinary sex' than by more unusual practices (such as bondage, for example). However, given the popularity of pornography (including vast amounts of pornography showing a wide range of 'specialist' forms of sexual activity) on the internet, this conclusion may be open to doubt.
- However, it is virtually impossible to conduct empirical research in this field, because of ethical considerations about the potential impact of the research itself.

Chapter review

As we shall see in Chapter 6, there is a widely (but by no means universally) held argument that Modernism has run its course. Even if that were so, it does not mean that every issue raised under Modernism is somehow 'merely history'. Nor should we be beguiled into imagining that time is some simple, single force running through social change, such as an inexorable move away from regulation to liberation of sexuality. We in the UK have, for instance, become less censorious of homosexuality – even the *Sun* (sometimes) and certainly now most of the British population believe that there is no reason why being 'gay' should debar a person from a career in politics. Women's sexuality (albeit usually young heterosexual sexuality) is acknowledged and even celebrated for a female audience, as any cover of *Cosmopolitan* or *Just 17* makes clear. And yet we have also become much more sensitized to the issues of the sexual abuse and exploitation of children, and much more wary of presenting children and the childish (such as *Oz's* notoriously rampant Edward Bear) as in any way sexual. Even portraying children as 'cute' has become distinctly discomforting. The reasons have been neatly summarized by Gerrard, writing about the images used in the 'Miss Pears' competition:

> None of the Miss Pears from 1958 onwards has ever been sexy: their images guard the sanctity and chastity of youth. Like the golden boy in the Millais 'Bubbles' painting, they are lispy, thumb-sucking, winsome, adorable, nostalgic and wholesome images of a picture-book childhood. A far cry from Freud, you might think. And yet, of course, we are all post-Freudians now. The children are innocent, but we are not. We know all about John Berger's ways of seeing – we have an ambiguous and corrupted gaze. We know too much about child abuse, paedophiles, prurience and perverted adult desire to be entirely comfortable with the cute Miss Pears.
>
> (Gerrard 1997: 5)

In other words, in the 30 plus years since the sexual liberation of the 1960s, a new consciousness has emerged, mainly through public acknowledgement of child sexual abuse. Feminist theorists, in particular, have drawn attention to the way that 'lispy, thumb-sucking, winsome' images of adolescents (in, for example, advertisements for designer jeans) can, by their juxtaposition of childhood innocence with adult knowingness, powerfully convey an image of the 'naughty but nice', the 'look but don't touch'. Such portrayals, many feminist theorists have claimed, increase the vulnerability of children and young women to sexual abuse.

Hence it is not possible to say, in any simple way, that we are more or that we are less sexually liberated than were earlier generations. All we can say with any conviction is that the debates over sexuality have changed. Psychology has been both instrumental in these debates and affected by them. We will be looking at this interplay in more detail in Part III. In Chapter 7 we will explore psychological research evidencing shifts in people's sexual behaviour. Another new theoretical movement has grown up around the notion of 'embodiment', and we will be exploring its impact on psychology in Chapter 9. In Chapter 10 we will examine 'sex crimes', focussing specifically on rape. And in our final chapter, Chapter 11, we will consider how the constitution of gender has changed to bring us 'new men' and 'new women', and the 'new relationships' that they have together.

But before we move on to these, a bit more theory is needed. Both feminism and postmodernism have had a major impact on our understanding of gender and sexuality, and of psychology's treatment of these topics. We take up these themes in the next two chapters.

Further reading

Gilligan, C. (1982) *In a Different Voice: Psychological Theory and Women's Development*. Cambridge, MA: Harvard University Press.

Hollway, W. (1989) *Subjectivity and Method in Psychology: Gender, Meaning and Science*. London: Sage.

Piel Cook, E. (1985) *Psychological Androgyny*. New York: Pergamon.

Weeks, J. (1981) *Sex, Politics and Society: The Regulation of Sexuality Since 1800*. London: Longman.

5 Feminist challenges

If disagreement about the meaning of a word becomes fundamental and widespread it is doubtful whether it is any longer a useful term. Sadly, I suspect this fate has overtaken the word 'feminist'. What can we use instead?

(Letter to the *Guardian* 14 November 1998)

We're all postfeminists now – aren't we?

This chapter is about feminist challenges to traditional psychological theorization about gender and sexuality. But writing it in the late 1990s is not easy, as the letter above shows. In part this is because feminism has become so diversified that it is no longer possible to talk about a 'feminist analysis' of many issues (such as date rape or pornography) since these are hotly disputed between feminists adopting different theoretical positions. But it is also hard because feminism has 'got a bad press' – in three rather contradictory ways.

First, it is often presented as a worn-out cause, no longer necessary now that women have been liberated. Faludi's analysis of the backlash against feminism encapsulates this well:

> The barricades have fallen, politicians assure us. Women have 'made it', the style-pages cheer. Women's fight for equality has 'largely been won', *Time* magazine announces. Enrol at any university, join any law firm, apply for credit at any bank. Women have so many opportunities now, corporate leaders say, that we don't really need equal opportunities policies. Women are so equal now, lawmakers say, that we no longer need equal rights legislation.
>
> (Faludi 1992: 1)

There is some truth in all this. Some of us are old enough to remember when most Oxbridge colleges excluded women students, when the rare sight of a bewigged woman lawyer appearing in court brought titters of disbelief, and when married women had to have their husband's signature if they wanted to take out a loan. In the 1970s women graduates were told at job interviews that only men were recruited to management training schemes, and it was perfectly legal to pay women less than men for doing exactly the same job. Things have moved on since then, and today when we are bombarded with 'girl power' and portrayals of feisty women 'doing it for themselves', it is easy to be lulled into a sense that the future belongs to women and that it is men (especially young men) who are the no-hopers of tomorrow.

The second problem is the way in which feminism gets rubbished, mainly in newspapers but also with considerable vitriol in some 'academic' texts. Davies' diatribe on what he terms 'women's lib' is, although rather dated, a splendid example. In the book *Permissive Britain* published in the 1970s he argued that the movement was led by a 'minority of twisted females' and explained their oddities in three ways. First, he claimed that many were infertile and, unable to fulfil 'the most important of their female roles', were therefore frustrated. Second, he said that they were 'exceedingly aggressive' and again were frustrated because society would not allow them to express their aggressive tendencies. But he saved his most caustic explanation until last:

> Thirdly, many of the aggressive leaders of women's lib seem to be married to men who, far from being the passive complementary consort one might expect, are even more pathologically aggressive than their wives. They are often of lower social status than their wives, have held jobs of a distinctly tough and masculine kind, such as coal-mining, and even have criminal records involving violent offences. It is as if in a last desperate attempt to play a submissive female role the aggressive women's 'libber' deliberately marries a thug.
>
> (Davies 1975: 88)

Basically, the argument here was that, in such a marriage, the woman cannot understand that most marriages, although they may not be egalitarian, are not authoritarian. 'For her, total dominance of one partner by another is the only realizable possibility. This explains her exaggerated longing for an egalitarian world' (Davies 1975: 88).

Finally, the message being given out is that liberation and emancipation may have been won – but, according to the media, at a dreadful price. 'You may be free and equal now, it says to women, but you have never been more miserable' (Faludi 1992: 1). We are presented with the glossily packaged image of *Ally McBeal* who, for all her designer clothes and high-powered job, is frantic because her 'biological clock' is ticking (or dancing) away and she can't find a husband. Is she happy? Is she hell!

The cost of freedom is claimed to include 'burn-out' and a whole host of health problems, infertility, anomie and loneliness.

With these messages and images – of a women's movement led by sadly misguided harridans and harpies; of liberated women who are desperate, stressed and lonely; of not having to worry any more anyway, since 1990s women have 'made it' – it is hardly surprising that many women these days are not at all keen on seeing themselves as 'feminists'. You may be asking yourself, then, whether this chapter has anything to offer other than history. Have all the feminists packed up and gone home? No, they haven't. Open a women's magazine and they are still there. In the January 1999 issue of *She*, for example, Calista Flockhart, who plays the *Ally McBeal* character, is featured in an article. Billed as 'Ally McBeal answers back', she states:

> To say our generation has no feminists, that all we have is Ally McBeal, is just crap. I know in my circle of friends, we're all feminists. It's more subtle. We're not out there burning our bras, and we take going to college for granted, but I battle sexism and all that.

A large number of feminists are teaching and researching in psychology. Certainly, there needs to be some history, if only to make sense of why there has been such a strong and sustained feminist challenge to mainstream psychology; why, say, the British Psychological Society (BPS) now has a women's section; and why *Feminism & Psychology* has become one of the most successful new journals in psychology. (Although it should be noted that the women's section of the BPS was a compromise, the BPS being unwilling to allow a lesbian and gay section to be set up – at least, it had not at the time of writing.) But there is also a positive agenda, since work informed by feminism has been highly influential on recent theorizing about the psychology of gender and sexuality. It also has considerable impact on and within the growing critical movement in social psychology, which we will take up in the next chapter.

Summary box Current challenges to feminism

As we enter the twenty-first century, feminism is often seen as having run out of steam – as no longer relevant to women's lives, or as misguided. There are three main facets to this argument:

- Feminism is seen to have achieved its goals of emancipating women, and is therefore seen as no longer necessary.
- There is strong antagonism to feminism from some quarters – not just certain sections of the media, but also from some academics. Feminists are portrayed as man-hating harpies, who are simply acting out their frustration at not being able to get a man. Feminism is regarded as a paranoid viewpoint, which sees oppression where it does not exist.

- Far from having liberated women and made their lives happier and more fulfilling, feminism is presented as having actually made women's lives worse.

Despite these challenges, we would argue that feminism continues to be useful, both in its practice and its theory. Its influence on psychology has been considerable, exposing its sexism and, more generally, offering a challenge that has strongly contributed to the development of critical social psychology.

A short(ish) history of feminism

Any history of feminism depends on what you take feminism to be. It also depends on where you look. Tchambuli women (as described by Mead, and whom we met in Chapter 2) are unlikely to have arrived at their dominant position over men by some fluke of good luck. Arapesh women are unlikely to have become subservient without argument. It is hard to believe that women throughout history and across the world have simply accepted their lot with no attempts to challenge or subvert it until Western feminism came along to lead the way to liberation. The point is, we have no way of knowing. Our understanding of history relies on being able to look at records of what people said and did (and having the skills to read them). Only some societies have made such records, and few academics read beyond their own language, and, even then, women's concerns and actions have seldom been accorded the importance of men's concerns and actions. So any history of feminism is bound to be partial.

Writing a history of feminism is not helped by the common convention of talking about first-wave and second-wave feminism. **First-wave feminism** is often assumed to begin in the twentieth century, and to finish in the 1940s and 1950s (Humm 1992 locates its end with Simone de Beauvoir's 1949 book *The Second Sex*) with the emergence of **second-wave feminism**. But it is a lot more complicated than that. For a start, this ignores important events around the time of the American and French revolutions that strongly influenced what followed. Moreover, first-wave feminism did not cease once second-wave feminism gained prominence. In many ways it is better to think about first-wave and second-wave not as a historical progression, but as different *sorts* of feminism, both of which are active today. And finally, there are other ways of seeing the history. And, as you will see in Chapter 11, there are now suggestions that we are entering a third wave of feminism.

The origins of Western feminism

The letters of Abigail Adams are often quoted as the first stirrings of women's protest in what is now the USA. The correspondence between Abigail and her husband John (who was at the time involved in the establishment of American independence from Britain) give a fascinating insight into the debates going on at the time. Probably her most famous letter was written in 1776 (at a time before spelling and punctuation had been standardized):

> I desire you would Remember the Ladies, and be more generous and favourable to them than your ancestors. Do not put too much unlimited power in the hands of Husbands. Remember all Men would be tyrants if they could. If perticular care and attention is not paid to the Ladies we are determined to forment a Revolution, and will not hold ourselves bound by any Laws in which we have no voice, or Representation.
>
> (Abigail Adams 1776, quoted in Rossi 1988: 10)

John was having none of this. He replied that 'we know better than to repeal our Masculine systems' which, he said, 'would completely subject Us to the Despotism of the Petticoat'. Abigail was not amused, and wrote to a woman friend, Mercy Otis Warren: 'He is very sausy to me in return for a List of Female Greivances'. To John she replied:

> I can not say that I think you are generous to the Ladies, for whilst you are proclaiming peace and good will to Men, Emancipating all Nations, you insist on retaining an absolute power over Wives. But you must remember that Arbitary power is like most other things that are very hard, very liable to be broken – and notwithstanding all your wise Laws and Maxims we have it in our power not only to free ourselves but to subdue our Masters.
>
> (Abigail Adams 1776, quoted in Rossi 1988: 13)

The somewhat later writing of Mary Wollstonecraft is generally seen as heralding the beginnings of British feminism. Mary was a friend of Tom Paine, who wrote *The Rights of Man* (1791–2). In 1792 she wrote her book *A Vindication of the Rights of Women*. Her main preoccupation was the limitation imposed on women through their lack of education and their treatment by men:

> women, in particular, are rendered wretched . . . for, like the flowers that are planted in too rich a soil, strength and usefulness are sacrificed to beauty. . . . One cause of this barren blooming I attribute to a false system of education, gathered from books written on the subject by men who, considering females as women rather than human creatures, have been more anxious to make them alluring mistresses than affectionate wives and rational mothers.
>
> (Wollstonecraft 1792, quoted in Rossi 1988: 40)

In France this was a time of turmoil, the French Revolution beginning in 1789 with the storming of the Bastille. Women played a central role in the revolution itself and in the early days of the new republic. A number of women's political groups were set up, including the Citoyennes Républicaines Révolutionnaires (Revolutionary Republican Women Citizens) who were allied to the radical Jacobins. They organized a march of 6000 women on the Town Hall of Paris to demonstrate about the price of bread, carried arms and participated in many of the populist actions against the aristocracy, and set up political clubs for women all over France.

In the former British American colonies (that is, what is now the USA) the struggle for the rights of women was organized less around the revolution, and more around the struggle against slavery. One of its best-known pioneers was Sojourner Truth. She was born Isabella, a black slave, in 1797 and changed her name as an act of protest. At the age of 30 she ran away from her owner and got work as a maid in New York, where she became a member of the African Zion Church. Once her children had grown she 'set out walking, singing and preaching, sleeping where I could'. When she got to Massachusetts she made contact with the Abolitionists who were lobbying against slavery and, through them, she became involved in the women's rights movement. Her most famous speech was in response to the suggestion that women should not take part in politics, as they were 'too frail for public life':

> That man over there say woman need to be helped into carriages and lifted over ditches – *and ain't I a woman*? I could work as much as a man and bear the lash as well – *and ain't I a woman*? I have borne five children and seen them almost all off into slavery and when I cried out with a woman's grief, none but Jesus hear – *and ain't I a woman*?
>
> (Sojourner Truth, cited in Watkins *et al.* 1992: 18)

This speech is notable, since it makes a point which is still an important issue for feminism today – that the 'domestic tyranny' against which middle-class women have fought, which restricts them to the home and treats them as weak and vulnerable, only ever applied to a minority of women. Poor women (including women positioned in poverty through racism and other forms of prejudice) are not and have never been accorded the 'luxury' of being 'the weaker sex'. They were and are expected to undertake hard work and endure hardship. They live and work in conditions that expose them to the seedier and nastier aspects of life from which society sought to protect women 'of good character'. This aspect of women's struggle – that for slaves and other poor women exploitation and oppression were often at the hands of other women – led to an interesting alliance at the start of feminism in the eighteenth- and early nineteenth-century USA. An alliance was formed between black women (usually runaway slaves) and Quaker women who were active in the anti-slavery movement. It was mainly Quaker women who set up the first women's rights convention in 1848 at Seneca Falls in the USA, for which they drew up the 'declaration of sentiments' which you read in the Introduction to Part II.

With the (at least theoretical) enfranchisement of black Americans but not women, the alliance between the women's rights and anti-slavery movements broke up. There followed the founding of the National Women's Suffrage Association, which organized a 6000-signature petition to the New York legislature. This suffrage movement inspired other organizations, including the National Council of Women which was founded in Washington in 1888. These organizations merged in 1890 to form the National American Women's Suffrage Association (NAWS) which engaged in sustained petitioning until women in the USA gained the vote in 1920.

In Britain political activity continued after 1792, but in a muted form until the 1850s, when a number of women activists began to challenge the law's unequal treatment of women. For example, there was a campaign in 1856 for a Married Women's Property Act to allow married women to own their own property – up until then, when a woman married all she owned became the absolute property of her husband to do with as he wished. And in 1865 a national group of women, organized through the Langham Place Ladies' Institute, petitioned parliament for votes for women. John Stuart Mill presented the bill to parliament (and in 1869 he published with his wife, Harriet Taylor, *The Subjection of Women*).

These events led to the formation of a number of organizations to fight for women's suffrage – according women full citizenship rights, including the right to vote in elections. However, it was the founding by Emmeline Pankhurst and her daughters of the Women's Social and Political Union (WSPU) in 1903 which is usually seen as the beginnings of first-wave feminism.

As well as the suffrage campaign, women also began to enter into sexual politics, particularly concerning the treatment of prostitutes. Josephine Butler, for example, challenged the Contagious Diseases Act of 1864, which allowed any 'lower class' woman in the area of a barracks or naval port to be accused of being a prostitute and examined for a sexually transmitted disease. Butler's campaign was focused less on emancipation than a concern with 'social purity', which identified alcohol, domestic violence and sexual excess as masculine evils which threatened women inside the family. In the USA proponents of social purity feminism were allied with the Temperance movement. Its leaders helped them in their suffrage campaign, because they believed that women voters would be decisive in bringing in Prohibition (the outlawing of the sale of alcohol, which lasted in the USA from 1919 to 1934). However, other feminists disagreed with their stand. Elizabeth Cady Stanton, for example, argued that 'a healthy woman has as much passion as a man' and believed that women should not be liberated from men's sexuality, but allowed their own.

Summary box The origins of Western feminism

- Western feminism arose around the time of the French and American revolutions, as men were campaigning for citizenship rights against systems of elite power. Mary Wollstonecraft's *A Vindication of the Rights of Women* is generally held to mark the beginnings of feminism in the UK.
- Women were seeking to claim the same citizenship rights for which men were fighting. In particular they challenged male authority over them.
- At the end of the eighteenth century in the USA the fight against slavery was bound up with women's fight for emancipation. Once slavery had been abolished, this alliance broke up.
- At the end of the nineteenth century suffrage organizations were set up in both the USA and the UK to fight for women's civil and legal rights.

The history of first-wave feminism

The forming of the WSPU marked the widespread popularization of feminism in the UK. In 1907 the WSPU set up 3000 branches across the country. In 1908 it held a meeting in Hyde Park, and somewhere between a quarter and half a million people, mainly women, attended. The union's newspaper *Votes for Women* sold 40,000 copies a week. By 1911 it looked as though the campaign was winning. The prime minister, Asquith, agreed that he would bring in a bill giving women property-owners the vote. But he reneged on his promise. Angered by his behaviour, the campaign became vociferous and, at times, violent. Windows were smashed and women were arrested and went on hunger strike. At first they were force-fed, and when there was public outcry against the brutality of this, the government introduced what was colloquially called the 'cat and mouse' act, by which women were released once they became weak, and rearrested when they had recovered. The fight was adjourned during the First World War, but in 1918 women over the age of 30 were given the right to vote.

At this time women were mobilizing all over the world. The first International Feminist Congress was held in Argentina in 1910. In 1911 Tan Junying set up the Chinese Suffrage Society. The first women's suffrage campaign was set up in Japan in 1917. In India in 1918 women's rights campaigners got the support of the Indian National Congress. White Australian women gained the vote in 1909 (although aboriginal women remained disenfranchised until 1967).

Looked at today, it is perhaps surprising that the place which pioneered women's political emancipation was the Union of Soviet Socialist Republics (USSR). In the Bolshevik Revolution of 1917 Alexandra Kollantai became the commissar for social welfare in Lenin's government. She set up the Zhenodtel (Women's Bureau) and it was through this power base that Kollantai (who became its head in 1920) worked with other Bolshevik women such as Inessa Armand, Ludmilla Stael and Zinadia Lilina to institute radical reforms, which included:

- female suffrage and legal equality for women;
- the abolition of the old religious marriage and its replacement by an egalitarian civil union, and laws against domestic violence;
- the introduction of what was virtually 'divorce on demand', with equal grounds for either partner;
- free maternal health care in clinics and hospitals, paid maternity leave and legal abortion;
- an equal 'right' (that is, obligation) of both women and men to work, backed up by workplace and community-based childcare;
- education and propaganda campaigns against the veiling and seclusion of women in Muslim communities.

Given the highly reactionary character of pre-revolutionary Russia and the economic, internal and international fragility of the new Soviet state (and indeed its largely male leadership), these were major achievements. But this state of affairs did not last. By 1922 Kollantai had been stripped of her powers, Lenin denounced sexual freedom as 'bourgeois' and after Stalin's rise to power in 1927 the backlash introduced a return to 'family values'. Laws against abortion, divorce and homosexuality were introduced in 1936.

The aims of first-wave feminism

First-wave feminism was (and is) primarily concerned with the material conditions of women's lives. It was (and is) a *civil political* crusade to gain equal treatment for women in terms of the law, in citizenship and welfare rights and in the workplace. Humm (1992) notes that:

> First wave feminism created a new political identity of women and won for women legal advances and public emancipation. The struggle for the vote, and the later battles for family allowances, contraception, abortion and welfare rights, twists around several axes: women's domestic labour, the endowment of motherhood, protective legislation, and woman's legal status.
>
> (Humm 1992: 14)

Summary box First-wave feminism

- Although first-wave feminism preceded second-wave feminism, it is better to think of it as a different kind of feminism – since it is still active today. First-wave feminism can best be thought of as concerned mainly with improving the material conditions of women's lives. It concentrates on fostering women's civil, economic, legal and political rights.
- In the UK its origins are mainly identified with the suffrage movement. Its primary goal was gaining 'universal suffrage' – that is, votes for women on the same basis as men.
- First-wave feminism was, and is, a global movement, with women campaigning for their civil and legal rights across the world.

The history of second-wave feminism

The shift to second-wave feminism was a political realignment, away from a concern with civil politics (to do with law, rights and citizenship) to **interpersonal politics**, encapsulated in the phrase 'the personal is political'. In the USA it gained its impetus from women's experiences in the Civil Rights movement, in which the rhetoric was about equal rights, but the 'chicks' were still expected by its exclusively male leadership to make the coffee, type the leaflets and provide the sex. Feminist resolutions were repeatedly bounced off the agenda because, the men said, there were 'more important things to discuss'. At one meeting in 1967, when Shulamith Firestone challenged this dismissiveness, the chairman told her to 'Cool down, little girl'. Chapman and Rutherford (1988) comment on similar reactions in Britain among left-wing men.

It became obvious that women needed not only to challenge their traditional opponents, but also those they had assumed were their allies. Brownmiller (1975) expresses this well: 'when the women's liberation movement was birthed by the radical left the first serious struggle we faced was to free ourselves from the structures, thought processes and priorities of what we came to call the male left'. Women in the USA therefore decided to establish a civil rights organization of their own – the National Organisation of Women (NOW), which, together with other women's liberation groups, soon got into direct action. In 1968, for example, they staged a protest at the 'Miss America' beauty contest, crowning a sheep as 'Miss America' and dumping symbols of women's oppression (false eyelashes, dishcloths, corsets and bras) into a 'Freedom Trash Can' (despite the media hype, no bras actually got burnt).

In Britain women's activism arose through a strike of women workers at the Ford Motor Factory in 1968. The women were machinists, making car seats – a highly skilled job. Yet they were paid much less than the male motor mechanics. Again the fight pitched women against men – the male workers were very disgruntled when the strike led to their being laid off and they refused to accept that the women had a case. The activism in the USA also had an influence, leading to the first UK Women's Liberation Conference in Oxford in 1970. On the agenda were demands for equal pay, 24-hour childcare, free contraception and abortion on demand. There was also growing activism against domestic violence, with the first women's refuge set up in Chiswick, west London, in 1972 and the establishment of rape crisis lines.

The aims of second-wave feminism

Second-wave feminism thus took as its starting point the politics of reproduction, and extended this into the broad sphere of personal relationships and personal identity. It was concerned with issues around:

- *reproduction* – the issue of a woman's rights over her own body in terms of access to contraception and abortion, and the limitations imposed on women by their reproductive role;
- *sexuality*, including a woman's right to enjoy her own sexuality rather than simply servicing men's sexual demands; and debates about whether heterosexuality is made compulsory by social expectations;
- *sexual and domestic violence*, sexual abuse and other forms of exploitation and oppression that go on within the private sphere of the family as well as the public domain;
- the effects of *sexual and gender stereotyping*, and how these position women and constrain their activities and life opportunities;
- the *objectification of women's bodies* – treating their bodies as objects to be used; for example, in the way that advertising and art turn women's bodies into objects of desire, and pornography turns women's bodies into objects of hatred and humiliation.

In this context of the politics of the personal, second-wave feminism draws on three main analytics: an analytic of power, an analytic of difference and a new version of psychoanalytic theory.

The analytic of power

In this context the analytic of power is specifically directed to the personal. Kate Millett asked the question: 'Can the relationship between the sexes be viewed in a political light?' She said it could, if we redefine politics 'not . . . as that relatively narrow and exclusive world of meetings, chairmen and parties' but as the 'power-structured relationships, arrangements whereby one group of persons is controlled by another'. This, by her definition, is **patriarchy**, a system in which 'sex is a status category with political implications'. She then went on to define how she saw patriarchy as operating and what it constitutes:

> the military, industry, technology, universities, science, political office and finance – in short, every avenue of power within society, including the coercive force of the police, is entirely within male hands. . . . If one takes patriarchal government to be the institution whereby half the populace which is female is controlled by that half which is male, the principles of patriarchy appear to be twofold: male shall dominate female, elder male shall dominate younger.
>
> (Millett 1977: 117)

This is a specifically feminist reading of what Michel Foucault calls the **micro-politics of power**. This vision as politics operating in the private sphere, in the actions between people in their everyday lives, represented a significant theoretical shift that took place in the 1970s, not just within feminism but much more broadly – usually referred to as postmodernism. We will come on to discuss postmodernism in the next chapter. Feminists explored the micro-politics of patriarchal power in relation to a number of aspects of women's lives and experience.

Shulamith Firestone, in her 1979 book *The Dialectic of Sex*, drew attention to how *reproduction* is the pivot around which the patriarchal social system is able to exert its power. She pointed out that, historically, this worked through the limitations imposed on women by the demands of pregnancy and caring for children. But, she said, it was continuing to operate even in the 1970s, when contraception and abortion were becoming more freely available, since it was almost exclusively men (that is, the male-dominated medical profession) who controlled women's access to contraception and abortion. She argued that women's liberation from their 'biological destiny' therefore needed action to regain control over the technology of reproduction. (As we come on to discuss in Chapter 9, today this power has been extended to encompass other aspects of women's bodies, including their reactions to the pressure to be 'attractive'.)

As a result of this kind of analysis, women began to challenge the male dominance of medicine. In the UK in the 1970s, there were very few women doctors. Medical schools recruited through an 'Old Boys' network and imposed quotas on women entrants – perfectly legally, since there was no equal employment law. And the pill was not available on the National Health Service (NHS) and was prescribed only to married women (although we subverted this by passing around 'Woolworth's wedding rings' for wearing to the **family planning clinic**). That it is now (relatively) easier for women to insist on seeing a woman doctor, to get contraception and to have access to abortion is a direct consequence of the actions women took in the 1970s to gain these rights.

Another axis of patriarchal power taken on by second-wave feminism was that of sexual violence, specifically rape and its threat. The key text here was Susan Brownmiller's (1975) *Against Our Will: Men, Women and Rape*. This argument is taken up in more detail in Chapter 10. She and other feminist writers such as Susan Griffin (1981) and Andrea Dworkin (1981) drew pornography into the frame, arguing that by objectifying and degrading women it encouraged male sexual violence. Pornography, Dworkin asserted, is about male power:

> The major theme of pornography as a genre is male power, its nature, its magnitude, its use, its meaning. Male power, as expressed in and through pornography, is discernible in discrete but interwoven, reinforcing strains: the power of self, physical power over and against others, the power of terror, the power of naming, the power of owning, the power of money, and the power of sex.
>
> (Dworkin 1981: 272)

Both Brownmiller and Griffin specifically pointed out that this argument challenges liberal values. Griffin made the point that liberal ideas have been mainly formulated by men, and are insensitive to issues of power operating in the domain of the personal. Both of them challenged the kinds of liberal and liberatory arguments described in Chapter 4. One person's liberty, they argued, is often gained at the price of another person's subjugation. Second-wave feminists applied this argument specifically to the sexual liberation of the 1960s and 1970s. The availability of the pill was portrayed as a means to sexual freedom for all, they said. But often what this meant, in practice, was increased freedom for men to sexually exploit women. Before the pill women could use their fear of pregnancy as a reason to refuse sex. Once effective contraception became (relatively) easy for a woman to obtain, women who refused to have sex were accused of being 'frigid' or 'prudish'.

The argument here is that at a *material* level women were liberated from the reproductive imperative (they could avoid pregnancy). But within a liberal climate in which 'cool chicks' were 'hot for sex' with any man who asked them, at a *psychological* level they were, if anything, made even more vulnerable to exploitation. At this time one of the worst taunts that could be thrown at a woman was that she was a 'prick-tease' – she turned a man on and then refused to 'go all the way'. Brownmiller (1975: 121) described this as 'the huge grey area of sexual exploitation, of women who are psychologically coerced into acts of intercourse they do not desire because they do not have the wherewithal to physically, or even psychologically, resist'. She argued that there is not that much difference between 'a case of rape and a case of unpleasant but not quite criminal sexual extortion in which a passive, egoless woman succumbs because it never occurred to her that she might, with effort, repel the advance' (p. 121). This, she suggested, arises out of 'a female paralysis of will, the result of a deliberate, powerful and destructive "feminine" conditioning' (p. 120). These arguments are taken up in Chapter 10, when we come on to look specifically at sex crimes.

The analytic of difference

Humm (1992: 199) suggests that the movement from first-wave to second-wave feminism is a shift from emphasizing the similarity of women and men to a focus on the difference between them: 'In the first moment women are objects, sometime victims of mistaken social knowledge. In the second moment women are challenging that "knowledge" from the strength of their own experience.' Gross (1992: 379) talks of it as a shift 'from a politics of equality to a politics of autonomy' – a shift from women striving to be seen as just as competent, just as entitled as men, to women 'doing it for themselves'. Vickers describes it as a personal journey:

> [A]s we try to understand more deeply women's experience under patriarchy, it becomes apparent that our venture is more profoundly radical than most of us had imagined (or even secretly wished). Eventually it becomes clear that the venture is more than filling in the blanks with missing nuggets of information about women. No longer can we be satisfied just with critiques of the biases and blindness of our disciplinary theories, our religions and our ideologies. Finally, the frightening and exhilarating fact can no longer be denied – we are together embarked on a journey which has as its goal the complete reconstruction of human knowledge and human experience.
>
> (Vickers 1982: 28)

Second-wave feminism was thus concerned with establishing a different kind of knowledge – women's knowledge, gained through women's understanding and experience. According to this argument, masculine knowledge of the world had come to be almost universally accepted as the only form of knowledge around. This masculine knowledge was presented and generally accepted (by both men and women) as 'the truth about the world and how it works': as objective, value-free and reflecting the world as it is. But, the second-wave feminist argument went, this is not so – masculine knowledge (indeed all knowledge) is subjective and value-laden, reflecting not the world as it is, but the world as constructed from a particular standpoint. In this case the standpoint is one arising through a male gaze and is constructed in relation to men's concerns, priorities and interests. There are other knowledges, and these knowledges are no less valid. Gross (1992) has explained the impetus for this shift thus:

> It became increasingly clear that it was not possible simply to include women in those theories where they had previously been excluded, for this exclusion forms a fundamental structuring principle and key presumption of patriarchal discourses. Many patriarchal discourses were incapable of being broadened or extended to include women without major upheavals and transformations. There was no space within the confines of these discourses to accommodate women's inclusion and equal participation.
>
> (Gross 1992: 356)

Possibly one of the most influential concepts in the analytic of difference has been that of **otherness**. Black feminist bell hooks claimed it to be 'the central ideological component of all systems of domination in Western society' (hooks 1984: 29). Haste (1993) traces it to the dualistic mode which runs through Western thinking, in which things are defined in contrast to what they are not – black is not-white, female is not-male and so on. This analysis has resonances with the idea of ***différance***, invented by the French philosopher Derrida, who himself cautions against trying to define what the term means. He argues instead that it must be 'worked at' through reading his texts (is this a clever marketing ploy, we ask ourselves?). The text you need to consult is *'Speech and Phenomena' and Other Essays on Husserl's Theory of Signs* (but it is hard work – you have been warned!) (Derrida 1967).

The issue of women's otherness was first extensively addressed by de Beauvoir. Haste describes it as the way that women are conceived within male-stream knowledge as that-by-which-men-define-themselves-as-not-being. She then goes on to argue that otherness sustains gender roles and ideas of sex differences, especially for men: 'For males, the definition of self depends upon there being an Other who differs and, by differing, asserts the integrity and definition of the Self' (Haste 1993: 85). But otherness is a matter not just of difference, but of opposition:

> In either/or dichotomous thinking, difference is defined in oppositional terms. One part is not simply different from its counterpart; it is inherently opposed to its 'other'. Whites and Blacks, males and females, thought and feeling are not complementary counterparts – they are fundamentally different entities related only through their definition as opposites.
>
> (Collins 1990: 69)

The concept of 'the other' is particularly important in black feminist theory. It has been used extensively to explore the origins and operations of racism: 'Black scholars contend that defining people of colour as less human, animalistic, or more "natural" denies African and Asian people's subjectivity and supports a political economy of domination' (Collins 1990: 69). Not surprisingly, the concept of otherness has been used specifically to challenge feminism's ethnocentricity – particularly its domination by white, middle-class women who have assumed that *their* concerns are the concerns of all women and who have therefore been highly selective in the battles they fight. We will come back to this later in the chapter.

New versions of psychoanalytic theory

A major consequence of the shift to second-wave feminism was that new conceptual frameworks were drawn into feminist theorizing, including social constructionism and postmodernism. These we will look at in the next chapter. But perhaps the most influential theoretical input came from new versions of psychoanalytic theory that were beginning to emerge from France in the 1960s and 1970s, particularly that developed by Lacan. This was then taken up and further refined by feminist theorists such as Julia Kristeva, Hélène Cixous and Luce Irigaray.

Lacan's work is notoriously difficult, and we will be able to outline it only briefly here. If you want to know more, Bristow's (1997) chapter on psychoanalytic drives offers a relatively readable account of Lacan's development of Freud's original theorization, and the subsequent development of Lacan's work by feminist theorists. One of the central ideas developed by Lacan (1966) was a reconceptualization of psychodynamic forces. Rather than viewing them – as Freud did – as biologically grounded and mediated, Lacan argued that they are grounded in and mediated by culture. Lacan drew on the work of the linguist Saussure (1916), particularly Saussure's ideas about the symbolic nature of language. He theorized that instead of human behaviour and experience being driven by the biologically based forces of the id, ego and superego, they are constituted out of three 'orders' of meaning: the symbolic order, the imaginary order and the real order. Lacan formulated his theories around how these different orders influence two aspects of people's experience: how individuals construct, experience and act out their identity; and how they construct, experience and act out their sexuality.

To Lacan the unconscious emerges from 'oneiric discourse' (the discourse of dreaming) and is structured like a language. It has its own syntactical and semantic operations, and pieces together bits of meaning into something which 'makes sense' (even if this is often a rather strange and illogical kind of sense). This is the **imaginary order** of unconscious desires, motivations and significances. By interacting with the **symbolic order** – the language-based social and intersubjective world of meaning we acquire through socialization – our subjectivity is produced (see Bowie 1991 for a more detailed description). The **real order** falls outside the domain of signification – where the psychic is felt rather than understood, for example as a result of trauma. Like Freud's id, it is threatening and frightening. And also as with Freudian psychodynamic theory, Lacan viewed his three systems as in constant antagonistic flux, the real order imposing pressure on both the imaginary order and the symbolic order, which compete with one another for meaning.

For Lacan the most important signifier is the phallus, which he defined as 'the privileged signifier of that mark in which the role of logos is joined with the advent of desire' (Lacan 1977: 287 – you can see what we mean about Lacan being obscure). He saw the phallus as having immense and wide-ranging symbolic meaning, encompassing the authority of the Father and God's own word (the logos). And, like Freud, in his early work Lacan described women's experience through their 'lack'. He argued that in order to make sense of herself a woman has to reject an essential part of herself: 'It is for that which she is *not* that she wishes to be desired as well as loved' (Lacan 1977: 290; our emphasis). Later he argued, broadly, that women's experience transcends the phallic order, although his argument is a lot more complicated than that.

Feminist theorists have taken up some aspects of Lacan's thinking, especially his view that the imaginary and symbolic orders are culturally mediated. This offered them a language and a theory base for exploring how patriarchy may operate at the subjective and intersubjective levels of 'inner' personal life and relationships. But they rejected his claims for the power of the phallus, and his grounding of sexuality in early childhood experiences. Kristeva (1984) proposed a somewhat different set of three orders from Lacan – the **semiotic order**, the **thetic order** and the **symbolic order** – which, she proposed, children move through in their early development:

The semiotic order	Derived from the Greek word for 'a mark or a sign', this refers to the pre-linguistic life stage when the child is trying to make sense of the inputs coming from the family and social structure.
The thetic order	This refers to when the child starts to make sense of the world through meanings and when subjectivity and self-awareness begin to emerge.
The symbolic order	This refers to the point at which the child severs dependence on the mother, becomes aware of 'the other' and begins to construct his or her identity in relation to others. It is at this stage that the phallus becomes the dominant signifier.

This is both a developmental theory and a theory about the psychic world. Kristeva suggested, for example, that we can see in certain works of art (such as James Joyce's *Ulysses*) that the semiotic order continues to influence the way people see and make sense of the world. Irigaray, however, challenged the dominance of the phallus, and offered an alternative model that saw female sexuality as quite different from male sexuality. She asserted that because 'her genitals are formed by two lips in continuous contact . . . she is already two – but not divisible into one(s) – that caress each other' (Irigaray 1985: 24). Thus Irigaray views woman's sexuality as both multiple and inseparable, plural and autonomous. Women do not, she asserts, define themselves by their lack of a phallus, but by their possession of the two caressing lips.

Cixous too drew attention to the difference between the phallocentrism of patriarchal discourse and the ***jouissance*** of feminine consciousness (jouissance is a difficult word to translate, but contains elements of joyfulness and sensuous pleasure going beyond the purely erotic). Her writing is highly poetic, describing women's sexuality in terms of caresses, kisses and sensuality; as expressions of love rather than the domination expressed by the phallocentric imperative to penetrate. Cixous stressed the need for women to develop their own forms of knowledge: 'woman must write about herself; must write about women and being women in writing. . . . Woman must put herself into the text – as into the world and into history – by her own movement' (Cixous 1983). Irigaray also argued that women need to speak for and about themselves in order to break the bounds imposed on them by men's 'way of knowing'. She argued that

> [i]f we continue to speak this sameness, if we speak to each other as men have spoken for centuries, as they have taught us to speak, we will fail each other . . . words will pass through our bodies, above our heads, disappear, make us disappear.
>
> (Irigaray 1980: 69)

To begin with, psychoanalytic theory was most influential in areas such as media studies. For example, Laura Mulvey (1975) argued that since films are almost always made by and for men, they assume a male gaze. The view of the world that they show is through the eyes of a man. In consequence, men in films are usually portrayed as active – they do the 'doing' and the 'being'. Women are portrayed as passive – they are the objects of men's 'doing' or the adjuncts to men's 'being'. There have been a few films (*Annie Get Your Gun* is often cited as an example) which portray women as active, and more recently we have had films such as *Thelma and Louise* and *Fried Green Tomatoes*, which portray 'spunky' female leads. But even now (if not quite as much as then), Hollywood films, at least, still tend to have male leads who are 'strong, clever, merciless, lonely, successful [and] self-contained, [and who] have a conquering disposition' (Hadas 1997: 178).

A central idea here is **scopophilia**. Freud saw it as one of the instincts of sexuality – an innate pleasure in looking, in which an individual gains gratification from secretly watching the private and forbidden. Film theorists such as Mulvey have appropriated this concept and applied it to the pleasure that people gain from cinema. She writes about the way that films 'portray a hermetically sealed world which unwinds magically, indifferent to the presence of the audience, producing for them a sense of separation and playing on their voyeuristic phantasy' (Mulvey 1992: 25). She comments on how 'the brilliance of the shifting patterns of light and shade on the screen helps to promote the illusion of voyeuristic separation' and how the 'conditions of screening and narrative conventions give the spectator an illusion of looking in on a private world' (p. 25). Mulvey claims that 'sexual instincts and identification processes have a meaning within the symbolic order which articulates desire' (p. 25). In Western culture, she suggests, the symbolic order is permeated by sexual difference, where 'women are simultaneously looked at and displayed, with their appearance being coded for strong visual and erotic impact' (p. 25).

Many of the ideas stemming from psychoanalytic theory have been taken up by feminist psychologists. Ussher (1997), for instance, draws heavily on film theory to explore the 'scripts' and 'stories' through which the symbolic order constructs femininity:

> Representations of 'woman' are of central importance in the construction of female subjectivity. We learn how to *do* 'woman' through negotiating the warring images and stories about what 'woman' is (or what she should be), among the most influential being those scripts of femininity that pervade the mass media.
>
> (Ussher 1997: 13; original emphasis)

Haste (1993) writes specifically about the role that metaphors play in how people gain understanding of their world. She stresses that metaphors are not just convenient ways of portraying what people are like, but also carry 'explanatory baggage' – they say why people are as they are. Much more down to earth than the French theorists, she discusses the way that the penis/phallus acts as a metaphor for masculinity in cartoons such as *Man's Best Friend* (Joliffe and Mayle 1985) where it is portrayed as an entity with a will of his own – Wicked Willie. Haste also draws our attention to the way that in certain settings male language is permeated by sexual metaphors. She cites Carol Cohn's (1987) observations of conversations between men working at the American Center for Defense Technology. These men described weaponry in highly heterosexist language: 'vertical erector launchers, thrust-to-weight ratios, soft lay-downs, deep penetration, . . . the comparative advantages of protracted versus spasm attacks, . . . releasing 70 to 80 percent of our megatonnage in one orgasmic whump' (Cohn 1987: 693).

Summary box Second-wave feminism

- Second-wave feminism is primarily concerned with *interpersonal* politics – as epitomized by the slogan 'the personal is political'. It sees women as being disadvantaged not only in the public sphere, but also in the private worlds of families, relationships and in the social world of what goes on between individuals in interaction and in groups of people.
- It is interested in opening up issues around reproduction, sexuality, pornography and violence; and challenging sexual and gender stereotyping and the objectification of women's bodies.
- There are three main analytics used in second-wave feminism – analytics of power, of difference and of new forms of psychoanalytic theory.
- The *analytic of power* is used to explore the reasons for women's relative lower status and lack of influence in professional, social and

personal interactions and relationships. It identified patriarchy – male dominance of power – as a potent force that oppresses women, and sought to discover how it operates and how it can be resisted.

- The *analytic of difference* shifts from the focus of first-wave feminism (which emphasizes the similarity of men and women) to one that stresses the differences between men and women. Thus, instead of campaigning for equal rights, it seeks to value and celebrate the particular qualities and capabilities that women possess. It has been particularly directed towards women's knowledge.
- *New versions of psychoanalytic theory* have been developed from the work of Lacan. He challenged Freud's assumption that the unconscious is biologically driven – by innate forces of the id, ego and superego. He argued instead that behaviour is mediated through three orders: the imaginary order of unconscious desires and motivations, the symbolic order of language and meaning, and the real order of feelings. Feminists have developed these ideas, especially around the imaginary and symbolic orders, highlighting the extent to which these are culturally mediated.

Dialects of feminism

Earlier in the chapter we stressed that first-wave and second-wave feminism are not simply two stages in the development of feminist thought, but two rather different kinds of analysis. We also said that the situation is complicated. Reviewing the situation today, there are a number of different dialects of feminism which vary in their origins, concerns and priorities, and the theories which inform them. You may find it helpful at this point to consult Table 5.1, which provides a summary.

Liberal feminism

Liberal feminism originated from the liberal and liberation movements we examined in Chapter 4. It is very much a first-wave dialect, its main concern being emancipation – changing the way that society is organized, to promote the rights and opportunities of women. Liberal feminists see two main routes to emancipation: through the ballot box – and thus altering education, law and social policy to remove discrimination and foster equality; and through socialization – thus changing the social attitudes, understandings and expectations which have, in the past, forced men as well as women to live stereotypically gendered lives.

Bem's (for example, 1985) work is a good example of a liberal feminist approach in psychology, in that she was explicitly seeking ways to change

Table 5.1 Dialects of feminism

Perspective	*Informed by*	*Sees as the main site of the problem*	*Says that what needs to be done is*
Liberal feminism	Traditional liberal-humanistic theorizing	A society which is organized in ways that do not accord women their full legal rights as citizens, that exclude women from public life and that limit their economic participation in the workforce.	Political action to emancipate women and enable them to participate fully in all aspects of public life and the economy.
Marxist feminism	Marxist theory	Capitalism, which requires women to maintain the male workforce by servicing men, and to renew the workforce by producing children and rearing them.	The overthrow of capitalism, or at least subjecting it to radical change to hand back power to those whose labour is the means of production.
Radical feminism	Radical here means 'going back to basics'. Its theory is based on the assertion that 'the personal is the political'	A patriarchal system which gives men power over women in all spheres of life. It is male power (rather than the actions of individual men *per se*) which is seen as the problem.	Resistance to male power, leading to the overthrow of patriarchy. This will require a radically different organization of social relations between men and women, in which power is shared and systems are put in place to prevent the misuse of power by men.
Socialist feminism	Both Marxist and radical theorization	The way that the economic system and the system of gender relations conspire together to oppress women.	Change needs to happen in both the public and private spheres – in relation to social institutions, work, the family and relationships.
Separatist feminism/ political lesbianism	Its theory–base is the idea of compulsory heterosexuality or what Butler (1990) calls the 'heterosexual matrix'	Patriarchal social conventions and organization which create conditions in which women assume that heterosexuality is both normal and desirable – the compulsory heterosexuality acts to maintain male power over women.	Women must separate themselves from men, especially in their relationships, and make their relationships with women central to their lives – become political lesbians. This is sometimes summarized as 'ceasing sleeping with the enemy', although the lesbianism advocated does not imply (necessarily) having sexual relationships with women.
Black feminism	Theorization around the notion of 'otherness' and the way this exacerbates the oppression of women who are subjected to racism	Contemporary Western society is designed to meet the needs and promote the interests of the white majority, and treats those who do not 'fit' as 'other' – who are thereby discriminated against, marginalized and subject to social exclusion. These forms of oppression may be more discriminatory than patriarchy, and involve the oppression of black women by white women.	A reconstruction of the symbolic order which constructs certain classes of women as 'other', in order to counter their oppression (for example, racism). Such a society would be inclusive – it would respect and value diversity and would be organized in ways that would enable all women to participate fully and reach their full potential.

Postmodern feminism	Postmodernist theory, especially as it relates to issues of power	Postmodernist analyses of power recognize that it is not operated in any simply way; that women have certain kinds of power (for example, over children) and that other 'others' (such as women who are disabled, transsexuals) are also discriminated against, excluded and oppressed.	Analyses of power must go beyond a preoccupation with gender. Any feminist analysis must also acknowledge other systems of oppression.
Cultural feminism	Theories which view women as essentially different from – and better than – men	Male qualities of dominance, violence and a preoccupation with technological 'fixes' which destroy nature.	A change to a society in which women hold the power, so that their qualities of human warmth, co-operation, mutual support and empathy with nature can make the world a better place.
Post feminism	Postmodernism's denial of all 'explain-all' theorization, plus the recognition that in the 1990s many women fail to identify with feminism	Critical of feminism's preoccupation with women's oppression in a world where there are many other forms of oppression. Also challenges the way that conventional feminist theory presents women as victims.	A call to move beyond feminism and relocate the struggle against discrimination and oppression. Also argues that women must stop being 'victims' and recognize the power that many of them have.
Psychoanalytic feminism	Psychoanalytic theory, particularly that originating from Lacan	The focus here is on the unconscious, and some feminists have drawn on traditional Freudian notions such as scopophilia. Most, though, draw on Lacan's concept of the symbolic order, which is seen to operate at an unconscious level (for example, through desire). Constructed in a male-centred way, it is this which is seen to oppress, exclude and marginalize women.	Change needs to be made at the level of the symbolic order – for example, by feminist film-makers and artists creating works which challenge it.
Libertarian feminism	Libertarianism	Although libertarian feminists wish to challenge sexism, they oppose regulation or control, either by the state (for example, laws for positive discrimination; censorship) or through social forces (for example, 'political correctness').	Women should be liberated and empowered by individual and small-scale collective action. Some libertarian feminists support forms of 'in-your-face' subversion, such as engagement in sado-masochism.

socialization – how to raise gender-aschematic children in a gender-schematic world (see Chapter 2).

Marxist feminism

Marxist feminists are also first wave in their concerns. They work from Marxist theorizing about the centrality of capitalism and also use Marxist analytics such as dialectic reasoning. In this perspective, capitalism uses women in two main ways: to maintain the workforce by servicing men; and to renew the workforce by giving birth to and rearing children. Hence, capitalism is viewed as the machine that grounds the oppression of women – and so it is capitalism which must be overthrown (or at least fundamentally changed) if women are to be liberated from their oppression. Theoretically, in a Marxist state women would cease to be oppressed because they would cease to be obliged to care for their male partners or their children.

Radical feminism

Radical feminism is something of a portmanteau term, used to encapsulate the many different strands of second-wave feminism. For radical feminists, women's oppression is ubiquitous, outside of class, ethnicity, time or social system, and brought about through patriarchy. The idea that 'the personal is the political' is central, and from this arises a concern with the 'micro-politics of power'.

Socialist feminism

Socialist feminism is informed by liberal, Marxist and radical theorization. It is concerned about the way that the economic system and the system of gender relations conspire together to oppress women. Central to it are issues of heterosexual coupledom and families as sites of gender and economic tensions. At the same time it has broader alliances with politics of the Left, seeing political action (such as the provision of welfare benefits) as an important means to counter the ways in which women are exploited and disadvantaged. Socialist feminism has its roots in the hard-left politics of the 1960s.

Separatist feminism/political lesbianism

The theory-base of separatist feminism is the idea of compulsory heterosexuality or what Butler (1990) calls the '**heterosexual matrix**', in which patriarchal social conventions and organization create the conditions in which women are led to assume that heterosexuality is both normal and desirable. It is this 'compulsory heterosexuality' which is viewed as maintaining male power over women. Consequently separatists argue that women should cease 'sleeping with the enemy' (since to do so is collusive) and should adopt the identity of a 'political lesbian' (that is, a political woman-centredness which does not necessarily imply anything to do with sexuality).

This dialect has developed directly from radical feminism. Often there is an uncomfortable alliance between separatist feminists and other radical feminists who do not accept the separatist argument. Given that they have many concerns in common, they often work together while still hotly debating their differences. For example, these two groups co-operated to set up Women in Psychology and to form the Psychology of Women Section of the British Psychological Society, although this has not been done without conflict (see Burns and Wilkinson 1990 for more details).

Cultural feminism

Cultural feminism arose out of the second wave theorization about women being different from men, but goes further – it sees the feminine as *better* than the masculine. It contrasts male qualities of dominance, violence and a preoccupation with technological 'fixes' which destroy nature, with female qualities of peacefulness, nurturance, sensitivity and empathy with nature. For some feminists this difference is an essential biological one; for others it is more a socio-cultural product. A good (and witty) example of its development is provided by Daly and Caputi's *Wickedary*, in which, for example, they redefine the term 'prude' thus:

> Good, capable, brave woman endowed with Practical/Passionale wisdom; one who has acquired the E-motional habit of Wild Wisdom, enabling her to perform Acts which, by the standards of phallicism, are Extreme: Lusty Woman who insists upon Self-esteem, and Pride of her sex; Shrewd woman who sees through the patriarchal norms of 'good' and 'evil', constantly Re-membering the Good.
>
> (Daly with Caputi 1988: 157)

Much writing within this perspective is highly poetic and playful, taking pleasure in reversing the reversals of **phallocentric** language to celebrate female qualities and drawing on what is seen as pre-patriarchal women's wisdom and power. Cultural feminists seek to create a society in which women hold the power, so that their qualities of human warmth, co-operation, mutual support and empathy with nature can make the world a better place.

Postmodern feminism

In many ways postmodern feminism is the opposite of cultural feminism. It challenges the dualistic categorization that portrays men and women as inherently and essentially different. From a postmodern perspective, the distinction is not a matter of biology but of human meaning-making.

Zimmerman, writing in the context of queer theory and drawing in particular on the work of Butler (1990, 1993), describes the distinction like this:

> For classic feminism, sex refers to the biological sub-stratum (nature, the real) upon which gender roles (society or culture, the representational) are built. Sex (male and female chromosomes, hormones, bodies) is the origin or base upon which a particular culture constructs an edifice of roles, behaviours, images and expectations which are transmitted through education, socialization, media and so forth. Sexual difference cannot be changed, but gender must. . . . For Butler, gender is a system of representation that makes sex possible. In other words, gender is the origin of sex (insofar as it is meaningful to even talk about origins) rather than the other way around. . . . One solution, insofar as there are any, may be to undermine naturalistic assumptions about sex and gender – that a particular gender 'belongs' to a particular sex, that any particular constructions of gender are natural or necessary – through inversion, parody and play.
>
> (Zimmerman 1997: 152–3)

Butler's theorizing is discussed in more detail in Chapter 9. More generally, postmodern feminism applies the analytic of deconstruction to feminism. Burman (1998) stresses that this has less to do with discontents directed towards feminism, and is more about what its presence allows and disallows. She views deconstruction as opening up a number of crucial questions:

> What work does this arena perform for the discipline of psychology? What does this do for the existing social order, including gender, cultural and sexual hierarchies [that] psychology informs and maintains? What forms of political engagement and intervention does it promote, both in relation to the rest of psychology and in connection with feminist movements and campaigns elsewhere? What does it speak for, and to?
>
> (Burman 1998: 1–2)

We will be looking at these kinds of question in more detail when we come on to consider postmodern challenges in the next chapter.

Black feminism

A black women's collective was set up in 1974 in the USA, calling itself the Combahee River Collective as a tribute to a battle in 1863 which freed more than 750 slaves. They wanted to contest the way white women had presumed to speak for all women and their statement expresses their argument cogently:

> We believe that sexual politics under patriarchy is as pervasive in Black women's lives as are the politics of class and race. We also often find it difficult to separate race from class from sex oppression because in our lives they are most often experienced simultaneously. We know that there is such a thing as racial-sexual oppression which is neither solely racial nor solely sexual, e.g., the history of rape of Black women by white men as a weapon of political repression.
>
> Although we are feminists and lesbians, we feel solidarity with progressive Black men and do not advocate the fractionalization that white women who are separatists demand. Our situation as Black people necessitates that we have solidarity around the fact of race, which white women do not of course need to have with white men, unless it is their negative solidarity as racial oppressors. We struggle together with Black men against racism, while we also struggle with Black men about sexism.
>
> (The Combahee River Collective, as quoted in Humm 1992: 135)

Collins (1990) reminds us that black women were early contributors to first-wave feminism. Black feminists contest the way that their contributions have been ignored or made invisible, and challenge the way in which they continue to be oppressed by other women. To give just one illustration, the Brent Asian Women's Refuge and Resource Centre was set up as an alternative to the women's refuges that were run by white women. They made the point that '[t]he last thing a woman wants when she seeks shelter in a refuge is to have her cultural traditions and values attacked by women who feel they know and understand what is best for her' (cited in Williams 1989: 71).

Psychodynamic feminism

Although traditional (Freudian) psychoanalysis is widely viewed as patriarchal by feminists, a strand of feminism has taken up the new forms of psychoanalytic theorization which emerged in second-wave feminism (described above). This theorization has been used to inform, in particular, feminist-informed therapy and counselling.

Post-feminism

For many feminists this is a term of abuse, describing attempts to mute or play down the continued importance of the feminist agenda. However, to others, it is an attempt to take two things seriously:

- the continued 'failure' of most women to identify with feminism, although they may appreciate the achievement of some feminist goals – which is, clearly, a significant research (and political) issue; and

- the changes that have occurred since the 1960s, both in terms of women's social, economic, interpersonal and civil conditions, and in the new forms of analysis that are now available for those examining these conditions – particularly those coming from post-structural and postmodern theory.

We will come back to this in the final chapter of this book.

Libertarian feminism

Libertarianism is based on a profound distrust of the power of the state and of any form of central regulation or control, including that wielded by big business and the multinationals. Libertarians of the Left look to anarchistic social arrangements. Today they are mainly found in green politics, 'eco-warriors' who are prepared to take direct action in protests over road-building. The 'Mc-libel' case is another example. It is, however, libertarians of the Right who have tended to become involved in challenging the right of the state to control sexuality. They are opposed to any form of censorship, and any laws that seek to proscribe sexual conduct. Individual or small-scale collective agency is highlighted. Libertarian feminists are likely to be anti-censorship and opposed to other regulatory practices (for example, political correctness) on the grounds that they debilitate rather than help women.

Feminist psychology

If you recall, in the Introduction to this book we wrote about the study by Broverman *et al.* (1972) in which health professionals were found to assume that to be a mentally healthy man is to be a mentally healthy adult. But for a woman to be viewed as mentally healthy, she needed to be 'feminine'. If she was assertive, a bit emotionally 'hard', and not very interested in her appearance (that is, a bit masculine), then she had to be a false eyelash or two short of a 'real woman'.

This study exposed the sexism underlying the practice of psychology. Moreover, it exposed it in a form that was difficult for psychologists to ignore – hard data. Such work was very much in the mould of first-wave feminism, challenging psychology's 'mistaken social knowledge' (Humm 1992) which treated women as inferior to men (see Sayers 1982 for a review). Psychology was exposed as androcentric – preoccupied with male experience and with male issues, and conducted from a male point of view. Burr (1998) offers as an example work carried out by Levinson and his colleagues (Levinson *et al.* 1978) on life-span development, based entirely on interviews with men. Typical of its time, the book was entitled *The Seasons of Man's Life*. The convention of using the term man as a generic for people obscured the exclusion of women – but in this case it really did mean 'man'. Other examples were highlighted in Chapter 2, such as the way in which the Mf subscale of the MMPI was based only on men's responses and the female pole was 'validated' through responses from male homosexuals; and in Chapter 3, where Kohlberg established his norms for moral development in studies that included only male subjects.

The obvious initial solution was to expand the framework to include women. However, it soon became clear that this would not work, because not only did the androcentric approach concentrate on men's experience, it was couched in a masculine conceptual framework. This did not easily accommodate the inclusion of women. Its preoccupation with men's concerns (such as achievement-motivation and leadership) also excluded many topics that are important to women. Ussher (1989), for example, has commented on how her research into menstruation was not regarded as 'real psychology' by her male colleagues. One factor in this andocentrism had to do with how research was funded. Sherif (1987) has pointed out that a vast amount of research money was provided by the military in the USA during the cold war years – and, as you can imagine, such funding was not given to topics such as menstruation. Another factor was that up until recently editorial decisions about what got published were an almost exclusively male preserve (Spender 1981).

It became apparent that simply tinkering with psychology to make it more woman-friendly and woman-inclusive would not do. Something more radical was needed. The impetus for a more fundamental challenge was provided by second-wave feminism, especially its analytics of power and difference. Specifically, women's 'new ways of knowing' were given centre stage, opening up a much broader set of challenges to psychology. Although a simplification, it can be helpful to think in terms of three main kinds of challenge:

- challenges to psychology's *epistemology* – its assumption about what constitutes knowledge;
- challenges to psychology's *modes of enquiry* – the methods and approaches psychologists use to gain empirical evidence; and
- challenges to psychology's *subject-matter* – the topics and issues it studies.

More broadly, feminist psychology has pursued the political objectives of feminism. This has not been easy, since psychology's academic and professional organizations in the English-speaking world have strenuously opposed the formation of groupings based on feminism (Wilkinson 1997). Unger and Crawford (1992) have identified two common themes in feminist psychology: valuing women's experience and treating it as worth studying in its own right; and a commitment to countering the exclusion, prejudice and oppression which women continue to face under patriarchy.

Challenges to psychology's epistemology

Over the past 10 or so years a number of feminist psychologists have called into question the knowledge-base on which psychology has constructed its theories about gender. In 1990 Morawski complained, for example, that:

> Psychological knowledge about gender continues to depend upon core axioms of socialization, role acquisition, stereotypes, femininity and masculinity. . . . In the face of the tremendous personal and intellectual challenges of feminism, the psychological perspective on and analysis of gender have remained unchanged, as have the foundational metatheory and epistemology. . . . Can a feminist psychology of gender thus proceed on the preexisting epistemological edifice?
>
> (Morawski 1990: 150)

Drawing on the work of Harding (1986), she answers by suggesting that there are three different routes out of the impasse: to create a feminist empiricism; to move to a feminist postmodernism; and to develop a new epistemology based on a feminist standpoint.

Creating a feminist empiricism

The first of these – creating a feminist empiricism – stays in the mainstream positivism of established psychology, but seeks to redress its androcentrism, especially by concentrating on work which pursues a political agenda. Although, as we have already noted, this poses some problems, it is defended by many feminist psychologists for pragmatic reasons. It allows, for example, exploration of women's 'different voice' (see, for example, Taylor *et al.* 1996). And as Eagly points out, 'evidence of women's oppression (e.g. statistics showing victimisation and discrimination) can be deployed to attract attention to women's plight and to galvanise people into action' (Eagly 1996: 159).

Adopting a postmodern 'take' on epistemology

The second solution – adopting a postmodern 'take' on epistemology – is a relativist position in which all knowledge is seen to be constructed:

> Perhaps the chief feature [of this approach] is a general disclaiming of the search for enduring, absolute, or universal truths; these dubitable truths include the existence of a stable, autonomous knower, the possibilities of objective, disinterested knowledge, the existence of logic, rationality, or reason that is independent of a social system endorsing these mental processes, and the feasibility of referential language to describe reality.
>
> (Morawski 1990: 172)

For many feminists the relativism of this approach makes it highly problematic (see, for example, Wilkinson 1997; Burman 1998). This is because they see it as detracting from the political agenda, failing to accept the very real impact of patriarchy, and deprioritizing feminist analyses. This concern is captured well by Weissenstein when she argues against post-modernism: 'Sometimes I think that when the fashion passes, we will find many bodies, drowned in their own wordy words. Like the Druids in the bogs. Meanwhile, the patriarchy continues to prosper' (Weissenstein 1993: 244). We will take up this argument in the next chapter.

Developing a feminist standpoint epistemology

Many feminist psychologists have taken the third option – the development of a feminist standpoint epistemology. Vickers (1982) suggests that within this standpoint there are five main 'rebellions'. Three have to do with the philosophy that informs the methods of enquiry adopted by the malestream (a deliberate play on the word 'mainstream'). The first is *against decontextualization*. This is a battle against the **physics envy** of social scientists who, in their desire to make their research as scientific as possible, strip away all the contextual elements in their studies. They try to study 'the social' in laboratory settings, treating subjects as isolated, private entities. This makes it impossible to study issues (such as rape, sexual harassment or, as we have noted, the effects of pornography) which are not amenable to laboratory modelling. It limits psychology's knowledge base in two ways: it makes it highly selective in its coverage and it limits what can be 'known' to just that which can be measured.

The second of these rebellions is *against objectivity* – treating the people being studied as objects and leaching ethical concerns out of the accounts of their experiences. In malestream research, objectivity implies a set of rules for communicating in the scientific community so that research findings and the controls required to produce them (for example, reliability and validity) can be replicated and established. Feminists frequently reject both the view of knowledge built into that framework and the view of the dehumanized human 'being' it glorifies.

Third, there is the rebellion *against linearity, lawfulness and inevitability*. Malestream social science assumes that 'laws of human nature' can be derived from empirical research in the same way that 'laws of natural science' can be derived from experiments in physics and chemistry. But this presupposes that at some fundamental level people are all constituted in a similar way, just as molecules of salt are all made from the interaction of sodium and chlorine. People's behaviour and experience, it is argued, cannot be explained in the same simple, linear terms that work for a chemical reaction. The assumptions of linearity and lawfulness obscure two things – important differences between people's experiences and the complex nature of the phenomena and processes that are being expressed as lawfully related.

Theories of child development are good examples. Burman (1994) has drawn attention to the way that these theories are presented as universal, but, in fact, implicitly assume it is a male, white, middle-class child who is developing. Such theories conceal the enormous differences to be found between the experiences and socialization of boys and girls; between, say, a child growing up in Cheltenham and a street child working as a prostitute in Manila. Furthermore, there is a tendency to assume that regularity implies inevitability. Just because in virtually every society it is women who take on the bulk of childcare responsibilities does not mean that only women can do this job – although Bowlby's theory of 'maternal deprivation' certainly implied this. Just because men tend not to do the ironing does not mean that men can't iron.

Vickers' other two rebellions concern the way that language is used in malestream social science. Both have to do with the way that certain kinds of language obscure *agency* – that is, the actions taken by particular people or groups of people. Her fourth rebellion is against the way that certain kinds of language (such as mathematics and the conventions of writing scientific papers) are so abstract that they lead to a *denial of agency*. Vickers draws heavily here on the work of Daly: 'the point is that no agent is named – only abstractions' (Daly 1978: 29). Daly works from the example of the practice of suttee (where a Hindu widow is expected to throw herself on her husband's funeral pyre). This, she points out, is written about in malestream academic literature as 'a custom'. It is treated as if it happens through some abstract force of culture rather than as a result of the actions of people. Daly brings home her point by saying how shocked we would be if someone wrote an academic paper about the 'custom' of genocide. Yet when male anthropologists wrote academic papers about suttee they described it as a Hindu rite which spared widows from the temptation of impurity, with no acknowledgement of the human agency involved.

Psychology is replete with this kind of abstraction. 'Variables', such as socio-economic status and gender, are described as influencing other 'variables', such as school performance or career choice. The impression given is of a process going on in some kind of psychic ether, quite separate from all sorts of actions that people take. Consider, for example, Walkerdine's (1997) work on girls' and boys' mathematics performance in school. She contrasted the ways a teacher described a girl who was performing well and a boy who was performing badly:

> *Girl performing well*: 'Very, very hard worker. Not a particularly bright girl . . . her hard work gets her to her standards.'
>
> *Boy performing badly*: 'can just about write his own name . . . not because he's not clever, not because he's not capable, but because he can't sit still, he's got no concentration . . . very disruptive . . . but quite bright.'
>
> (Walkerdine 1997: 173)

Are we to assume that this kind of attribution by the teacher has no effect? That it is simply gender – an abstract entity – which was causing the girls to do worse at maths than the boys? What about other kinds of agency – the talk and expectations of parents, the children themselves, a girl's own self-perceptions measured against her concept of femininity, and the ways in which femininity is portrayed in the media? With hindsight it is easier to detect the lie, given that even in the 'masculine' subject of mathematics girls had, by the late 1990s, overtaken boys in their performance at GCSE (see Chapter 11).

Vickers made her most vociferous attack, however, on the use of language *to reverse agency*, arguing that reversal is 'the worst kind of context stripping in which academics engage'. To see what she was getting at, consider this statement cited by Daly, from a textbook about Hinduism: 'At first, *suttee* was restricted to the wives of princes and warriors . . . but in the course of time the widows of weavers, masons, barbers and others of the lower caste *adopted the practice*' (Walker cited in Daly 1978: 117; emphasis added by Daly). Vickers responded:

> Given the fact that widows were dragged from hiding places and heavily drugged before being flung on the pyre, often by their sons, this is like saying that although the practice of being burned in gas ovens was at first restricted to political dissidents, eventually millions of Jews *adopted* the practice.
>
> (Vickers 1982: 39; original emphasis)

Vickers described reversal as a 'grammatical, theoretical and methodological trick' that beguiles the reader or listener into misattributing agency. An example from psychology is the research that was carried out into the effects on male subjects' 'sexual arousal' of photographs of 'attractive female nudes' (see, for instance, Clark 1952). The implication in research of this kind is that it is something in the photographs themselves which is causing the arousal, as if the arrangement of light and shade in the pictures can act as a 'cause' in this situation and the cause is nothing to do with male socialization, expectation or predeliction. If you find this argument difficult to grasp, think about the way that some people are prepared to pay a great deal for clothes that have certain labels. It is not the labels themselves that are causing these people to spend their money; it is what the labels mean that give them their value. And meaning is something that people *do*. Without the active thinking and 'making sense' that goes on when somebody recognizes a label, it would have no meaning and hence no value.

A challenge to established research methods

From a more or less non-existent academic presence before the 1960s (although earlier work is now being 'reclaimed') feminist research today is a diverse and vital field. This is a tribute to at least two things: the sheer energy that feminist psychologists have devoted to opening up alternative methods; and the ability to say and do new things in the social disciplines that these new methods have opened up. By the early 1990s the emergent challenge to the malestream was established enough for a number of books to be devoted to feminist methods, including Roberts (1981), Harding (1987), Fine (1992) and Reinharz (1992).

There are a number of key features running through feminist research methods. These include:

- Research is carried out into topics that relate to women's interests, concerns and priorities. Sometimes this reflects experiences that are unique to women (such as menstruation, childbirth and menopause). Sometimes the topics are chosen because the results obtained can be used politically (the Broverman *et al.* study mentioned at the beginning of this section is a good example). Sometimes the issues studied are important to women's lives, such as 'date rape', sexual abuse, domestic violence and inequalities in the workplace.
- Research is informed by feminist theory in its planning, in how it is carried out and, particularly, in the interpretation of the data obtained and how this is disseminated.
- Researchers strive to be reflexive, acknowledging their own engagement with and investment in the topic under study, and reporting on their experiences during the research and its impact on them.
- The way in which research is carried out is informed by feminist ethics. In particular feminist researchers strive to acknowledge and address the power relationship between themselves as researchers and those with whom the research is conducted, treating them as participants in rather than subjects of the process. They avoid 'tricking' or deceiving the participants and seek to engage them in the research process, including its planning and execution. They negotiate with participants about what is done with the data, giving them a degree of control over what is reported and how it is interpreted. Some researchers, in addition, use advisers drawn from the researched group, with whom they consult at all stages in the process.
- Feminist research uses a multiplicity of methods, and often combines several methods in a single study. It is open to being transdisciplinary – to breaking down the barriers between disciplines. Thus methods are drawn from disciplines such as anthropology, sociology and social geography and adapted for use in psychological research (and vice versa).
- Much feminist research seeks to create social change, and to pursue the political agenda of feminism. For this reason the methods and approaches that are used are chosen tactically – not because of their methodological benefits and drawbacks but for their potential to make an impact.

- Most feminist methods recognize diversity – they seek to explore and gain insight into variability rather than to try to 'iron it out'. Feminist research also aims to be sensitive to culture and context, striving to make sense of the topic under study with the aim of giving a voice to those whose views or opinions may not otherwise be heard.

Table 5.2 summarizes the main feminist methods that are being used in psychology. It has been amended from Reinharz (1992).

Many of these principles and methods are also found in **critical psychology** (see also Fox and Prilleltensky 1997; Ibáñez and Íñiguez 1997), and we will examine them further in the next chapter. However, feminist research is distinctive in two main ways. First, it prioritizes feminist theory and the feminist standpoint, especially in its interpretation of the results it gains. Second, it has an explicitly feminist political agenda. Feminist research is done in order to challenge the oppression and exclusion of women, and to stimulate (and sometimes to actually contribute to, directly) social change in ways which emancipate women and counter patriarchy (including patriarchal modes of thinking).

A challenge to the subjects and topics that psychology studies

We have already mentioned that funding agencies have tended to be more willing to support research conceptualized from male concerns – which is not surprising, given that up until recently the vast majority of those who held the research funding purse-strings were men (and even today they are still in a majority, although this is slowly changing). Topics such as menstruation are not easily funded from defence budgets.

Despite this, the past few years have seen a proliferation of feminist-inspired work on topics of relevance to women. The types of issues identified as important by second-wave feminism – reproduction, sexuality, sexual and domestic violence, sexual and gender stereotyping and the objectification of women's bodies – have all recently been opened up as topics for research. Examples include Malson's (1997) study of anorexia nervosa, Boyle's (1997) work on abortion and Nicholson's (1998) investigation of postnatal depression.

Another challenge that feminism has presented to psychology stems from its identification of otherness as a crucial analytic of difference. This has led to the opening up of theorization and research about topics such as masculinity and heterosexuality. The idea here is that psychology has conventionally taken these for granted as the norm – and hence not in need of study. The preconception is that only deviations from the norm – otherness – need to be explained, and hence need to be investigated. Feminist psychologists have challenged this preconception, arguing that such norms require as much explanation and hence merit investigation just as much.

Probably the most influential work here is Wilkinson and Kitzinger's *Heterosexuality: A Feminism & Psychology Reader* (1993) in which they

Table 5.2 Feminist research methods

Method		*What makes it feminist*	*Examples*
Feminist interview research	Interviews may be unstructured, semi-structured or structured. Includes both individual and group (focus group) interviews.	Giving interviewees some control over the agenda and how the data are used, recognizing and doing something about the impact of the process on the interviewees.	Ussher's (1989) study of women's experiences of menstruation.
Feminist ethnography	Observation carried out in naturalistic settings; often includes some degree of participant observation.	Openness about the study and its purpose, seeking to involve those being studied in the research process, including the use made of the data. Attempting to 'give something back' – seeking to ensure that the study contributes something positive to the community or group being studied.	Walkerdine's (1989) study of gender issues in the teaching and learning of mathematics in schools.
Feminist survey research and other statistical research formats	Apart from surveys *per se*, it covers secondary analysis of existing databases.	Through the political use of results.	Mahstedt and Keeny's (1993) study of the frequency and types of 'dating violence'.
Q methodology	Derived from Stephenson (1967), adapted for use within a critical perspective.	Through the political use of the results.	Kitzinger's (1987) study of lesbian identities.

Feminist experimental research	'Experimental' here is not only psychological.	By a frequent challenging of its place in feminism, and its tactical use for a political purpose.	Much of Bem's work on androgyny was laboratory-based (see Chapter 3)
Feminist cross-cultural research	May use qualitative, quantitative, or both methodologies in contrasted cultural sites.	A heightened sensitivity to ethnocentrism.	Marcos (1987): popular (folk) medicine used by Mexican women rather as self-help groups are used in USA.
Feminist oral history	Collecting life stories: a transdisciplinary methodology *par excellence*.	Listening to women. Through themes and experiences explored.	Russell (1989): South African women.
Feminist case studies	Can be single issue as well as single case.	May be taken from within feminist experience/history. Gender/power focus.	Mackinnon (1979) on the sexual harassment of women in the workplace.
Feminist action research	'Applied' rather than 'pure' research with the focus on changing something.	The site of research and the change sought fit feminist agendas.	Mies (1984) on the abuse of women in the family and the setting up of a refuge.
Feminist multiple methods research	Typically, this combines qualitative and quantitative methodologies and seeks to 'triangulate' the results between them.	Topics and principles	Chesler (1972): women and madness.
Original feminist research methods	Mostly, creative variations on received methods.	Meeting the researcher's feminist criteria.	MacKinnon (1983) claims originality for consciousness-raising.

invited a number of heterosexual feminists to contribute chapters on the topic. A more recent book *Theorising Heterosexuality* (Richardson 1996) is more broadly based, drawing on sociology, social policy, queer theory, women's studies and health studies. Richardson specifically makes the point that:

> little attention has traditionally been given to theorising heterosexuality. Although it is deeply embedded in accounts of social and political participation, and our understandings of ourselves and the world we inhabit, heterosexuality is rarely acknowledged or, even less likely, problematised. . . . Where sexuality is acknowledged as a significant category for social analysis it has been primarily in the context of theorising the 'sexual other', defined in relation to a normative heterosexuality.
>
> (Richardson 1996: 1)

Equally, until recently in psychology it has been femininity that has been researched and theorized whereas masculinity has been taken for granted. Anthropologists got into investigating masculinity earlier, in relation to 'exotic others' at least. But more recently a number of psychology texts have been written on the topic, such as Mac an Ghail's (1996) *Understanding Masculinities*.

Summary box Feminist psychology

Feminist psychology offers three main challenges to the mainstream:

- It challenges traditional psychology's epistemology, arguing that there are other forms of knowledge which are worth pursuing. Three possible solutions are offered: developing a feminist empiricism (Gilligan's 'different voice', as outlined in Chapter 3, is a good example); adopting a postmodern, relativist approach to knowledge; and developing a feminist standpoint epistemology.
- It challenges psychology's usual modes of enquiry, suggesting new methods and new ways of approaching research.
- It challenges the topics and subjects that psychology has traditionally addressed.

Chapter review

We have used this chapter to set out the main elements of feminism, including its history, its theorization and its approach to research methods. We believe that these are essential starting-points to understanding why feminist psychologists have challenged mainstream psychology's treatment of gender and sexuality, and what it is they are seeking to achieve: or rather, we should say what are the *different things* that feminist psychologists are seeking to achieve. This chapter has made it clear that feminism is in no way a single, homogenized approach, and that there are, indeed, strong conflicts between the various forms of feminism. When you come on to Part III you will find feminist theorizing, analysis and research woven into the chapters there. The chapters in Part III also incorporate postmodern and social constructionist theorizing and analysis (and indeed, there is considerable interplay between feminist and postmodern/social constructionist approaches). This is what we move on to next.

Further reading

Burman, E. (1996) *Challenging Women: Psychology's Exclusions, Feminist Possibilities*. Buckingham: Open University Press.

Crawford, M. (1995) *Talking Difference: On Gender and Language*. London: Sage.

Henwood, K., Griffin, C. and Phoenix, A. (eds) (1998) *Standpoints and Differences: Essays in the Practice of Feminist Psychology*. London: Sage.

Howard, J. and Hollander, J. (1996) *Gendered Situations, Gendered Selves: A Gender Lens on Social Psychology*. London: Sage.

Letherby, G. (1999) *Feminist Research in Theory and Practice*. Buckingham: Open University Press.

Reinharz, S. (1992) *Feminist Methods in Social Research*. Oxford: Oxford University Press.

Sawiki, J. (1991) *Disciplining Foucault: Feminism, Power and the Body*. London: Routledge.

Unger, R. (1998) *Resisting Gender: Twenty Years of Feminist Psychology*. London: Sage.

Wilkinson, S. (1997) Prioritizing the Political: Feminist Psychology, in T. Ibáñez and L. Íñiguez (eds) *Critical Social Psychology*. London: Sage.

6 Postmodern challenges

Sexuality must not be thought of as a kind of natural given, which power tries to hold in check, or as an obscure domain which knowledge tries gradually to uncover. It is the name given to a historical construct; not a furtive reality that is difficult to grasp, but a great surface network in which the stimulation of bodies, the intensification of pleasures, the incitement to discourse, the formation of special knowledges, the strengthening of controls and resistances, are linked to one another, in accordance with a few major strategies of knowledge and power.

(Foucault 1976/90: 105–6)

If ideas like this are new to you, you may be asking yourself what on earth knowledge, power and discourse have to do with sexuality. What did Foucault mean when he argued that sexuality is not 'a kind of natural given' but rather 'a historical construct'? What has history got to do with it? Foucault was saying here that however much it may seem to you that your sexuality is simply something you 'are' – gay, straight or bisexual; highly sexed or celibate – this is not a natural reality, nor is it in any way simple. It is important to understand what he was *not* saying. He was not suggesting that sexuality is simply a matter of choice that can be changed at will, that it is 'all in the mind' or that it is anything other than powerfully real in its effects. Rather, his point was that concepts such as 'being gay' or 'being highly sexed' are cultural and historical consequences of people constructing them to be significant and to mean something; and that the significance and meaning we accord to them is part of a 'great surface network' by which power is strategically deployed.

An example might help here. Think of a container of milk turning sour through the action of bacteria. What is it when it has 'turned'? Well, it all depends on your **standpoint** – your intentions for the milk. If you were planning to pour it in your coffee, then it is sour milk and good only for tipping away. But if you were making yoghurt, then (as long as the bacteria doing the souring are the right ones) everything would be fine and dandy. It is yoghurt-in-the-making, to be carefully nurtured while it matures. The sour milk could be the same in either situation. What is different is what it *means and signifies*. Now, to go back to the concept of being 'gay'. What does this mean – an identity, a form of mental illness, a sin against God, an aberration of nature, a life choice, a role to play in certain situations, a political position to adopt? Or none of these but something else entirely? It all depends on your standpoint.

But what does standpoint mean? Again, it is important to understand what it does *not* mean. It is not just a question of different people having different points of view. It is much 'bigger' and more complicated, much more fundamental than that. Try a different tack. Was William Shakespeare gay? There is evidence that he had sexual relationships with men – certainly many of his poems and plays have homoerotic themes. Does that make him a homosexual? Mary McIntosh (1968) argued not, for the reason that in Shakespeare's time homosexuality was something a person 'did' or 'felt', not what they 'were'. She argued that viewing sexuality as an identity is a fairly recent idea. And it works for us only because a person's sexuality has come to matter enormously at this particular time and place of contemporary Western society.

Think about it – we don't have clubs and bars especially for people who bite their nails. People do not anguish themselves over 'coming out' as a snowboarder or an Abba fan in the same way as many gay people do over being homosexual. Other identities – such as being a *Guardian* reader, a 'crustie' or a single parent – may be positively or negatively valued, depending on your perspective, but they generally do not have the same significance as being 'gay'. But at another time, or in another place, other identities would be much more significant and meaningful. As we noted in Chapter 4, being 'a woman of good character' mattered a lot a hundred years ago. It had an enormous impact on how a woman was treated, what she was allowed to do, where she would be made welcome, whom she could marry, and so on. A woman could lose her good character very easily, simply by spending time alone with a man in a setting that was not socially sanctioned. This was even more true if she had sex outside of marriage. Yet the same is not the case today, when having a sexual affair outside of marriage is commonplace. The contrast between John Fowles' book *The French Lieutenant's Woman* and the film of the book captures this historical shift very effectively.

This observation takes us closer to understanding what Foucault meant when he wrote that '[s]exuality . . . is the name given to a historical construct . . . a great surface network in which . . . the strengthening of controls and resistances . . . are linked to one another . . . in accordance with a few major strategies of knowledge and power'. Fowles' French lieutenant's woman was subjected to a strategy of power which significantly controlled her actions, and which determined her place in society and how people viewed her. At the same time, she found a way to resist these controls by allying herself to a group of liberal thinkers who contested the conservative ideology of the time. The film version of the book deliberately played on the contrast between historical and contemporary sexual mores by interweaving the story of the actors playing the characters in the book into the historical narrative. In so doing it vividly highlighted the way in which sexuality *means* something different and has a different significance at different historical times.

Standpoint, then, has more to do with time and place, history and culture, than it has to do with any individual's point of view or perspective. This was the central idea that Foucault was trying to get across. His book *The History of Sexuality: Volume I*, from which the quotation was taken, was the first in a three-volume set. In these books he developed a detailed analysis of the 'strategies of knowledge and power' that operate around sexuality in contemporary Western culture. Foucault was, if not the first, certainly the most influential advocate for a postmodern analysis of sexuality, and we will come back to look at this later in the chapter.

Social constructionism

For psychology one of the best-known aspects of the 'climate of perturbation' (described in the Introduction to Part II) is **social constructionism**. Its roots can be traced to new ideas in the 'climate of perturbation' coming from the sociology of knowledge, especially a book by Berger and Luckmann (1966) entitled *The Social Construction of Reality*.

There are a number of parallels between Foucault's concerns and those of Berger and Luckmann. Both, for example, were interested in historical shifts in the mechanisms of identity, and in how power operates. Similarly, there is a resonance between Foucault's ideas about subjugation and Berger and Luckmann's suggestion that reality is constructed through three 'moments': **externalization**, **objectification** and **internalization.**

Externalization

This refers to the way that cultures, societies and social groups of different kinds make sense of – and therefore 'make' – their social worlds, including a whole range of social institutions and constructs.

Objectification

This is how those constructs and social institutions are then perceived as being 'out there', just as 'nature' is 'out there'. An uglier but in some ways more transparent term is **thingification** – the process whereby a whole set of coincidental events and occurrences get turned into a 'thing'. A good example is premenstrual syndrome, which is covered in Chapter 1. If you recall, it comprises a whole list of symptoms. By associating them together as a 'thing', it has become objectified.

Internalization

This is where the objectified social world becomes known, understood and made familiar through processes of socialization and **enculturation**. Gender is a prime example (as we saw from Chapters 2 and 3). Children, as they grow up, learn that 'male' and 'female' are distinct and important categories, and internalize this knowledge to the point that it becomes completely self-evident and taken for granted. Depending on their culture and on other factors (such as their own gender) they internalize particular knowledge about the different qualities of male and female. This knowledge that is acquired in childhood is not fixed – internalization is an ongoing process. For example, for many women, gaining an understanding of feminism has profoundly changed the way they see themselves *as* women and has transformed their ideas about masculinity and femininity.

The main elements of social constructionism

Burr (1995) provides a readable and useful introduction to social constructionism. She makes the point that it is not possible to offer a single definition, since there are now many different versions. But she lists a set of four main 'things you would absolutely have to believe in order to be a social constructionist' (Burr 1995: 3). These are (somewhat modified): taking a critical stance towards knowledge; seeing knowledge as history-, culture- and domain-specific; viewing knowledge as created and sustained by social processes; and recognizing that knowledge implicates action.

Taking a critical stance towards knowledge

According to social constructionism, what we know about the world does not simply 'mirror' its reality. Our knowledge is always constructed through the 'lens' of our interpretation and understanding. This is not just a matter of different individuals having different points of view or perspectives. Our understanding and interpretation are based on our internalization of our culture's constructed knowledge. Consequently, we need to be cautious about knowledge. Given that it is a human product, we need to ask ourselves '*who* made this knowledge, and *for what purpose*?'

As you saw in the previous chapter, feminists have drawn attention to the way that 'man-made' language permeates the symbolic order, constructing knowledge in ways that exclude and/or discriminate against women. For example, the term 'emasculate' is often used to describe somebody or something that has lost (or had taken away) its power and potency.

But it works only if applied to a man or certain kinds of thing. To say that a woman has been 'emasculated' is paradoxical and odd. And as we cannot really say it, it is harder to think it. And because it is hard to think it, it is less easy to see women as capable of being powerful. Indeed, to talk about a 'powerful woman' does not give at all the same impression as talking about a 'powerful man' (she comes across as pushy, bossy and unfeminine).

Sometimes it is obvious that somebody is deliberately constructing reality in a particular way. During the Gulf War, official reports spoke about bombs causing 'collateral damage', when what they really meant were civilian casualties. And what 'civilian casualties' means is that 'people are getting killed and injured'. Or we could talk about them as 'innocent little children with their heads blown off, their eyes gouged out, their tiny limbs brutally twisted'. All four terms refer to the same set of circumstances, yet each one encourages us to view what happened in a different way. In particular, the first and last are *intended* to generate a different reaction. The official reports wanted to downplay the human pain and suffering, whereas the last description (which we made up) is just the kind of language a lobbying campaign would use.

Cranston (1953) uses the terms **boo-word** and **hurrah-word** to highlight the way that language can be used strategically, not just to describe but deliberately to indicate the required response from the reader. As we will see in Chapter 9, 'female genital mutilation' is an obvious example of a boo-word; so too is child abuse (Archard 1998). Terms such as liberation (as in sexual liberation) and freedom (as in freedom fighters) are equally obviously hurrah-words. Both, of course, are nowhere near as obvious as they seem.

Considering language strategies such as these allows us to recognize that often our knowledge has become so familiar to us that we take it for granted. Gender itself is a good example. The idea that humankind is divided into two genders – men and women – is so self-evidently true, so obviously natural, that it is almost impossible to see that it is a category that is socially constructed. So deeply sedimented is our knowledge of gender, so much is gender woven into our world-view, that to suggest that males and females are anything but naturally occurring, distinctly different kinds of person comes across as bizarre and stupid. The same is true for other categories that seem obvious to us, such as race. There was one episode of *Star Trek* that dealt with this issue. The *Enterprise* came across a race of beings divided into two groups. In one group the right-hand side of their faces was black and the left was white; and in the other group the left-hand side of their faces was black and the right was white. To these beings the difference was obvious, and fully justified the antagonism acted out between the two races. Yet to the crew of the *Enterprise* the difference seemed contrived and irrelevant. Science fiction can be a useful way of speculating about the social construction of knowledge, and we will take up this idea again in Chapter 9.

Just because it is possible to make a category discrimination does not mean that the difference is 'out there' in nature. People differ in lots of ways – some have earlobes, others do not; some have brown eyes, others have grey, green or blue; some people can naturally sing in tune, others cannot. Yet we barely distinguish between them, except in circumstances where these characteristics matter (auditioning people to join a choir, for example). So why do gender and race (but not these other distinctions) seem to us to be crucial categories that mark out a real and meaningful difference? The answer is that they *are* meaningful, and the reason they are meaningful is that humankind has *made* them meaningful. Meaning is *something people do* – people make it; people socially construct it.

Seeing knowledge as history-, culture- and domain-specific

Given that knowledge is a human product, gained through our effort-after-meaning, it follows that knowledge is meaningful and useful only in the historical time and the culture in which it was/is created and maintained. Take the example we considered earlier of the quality of 'being of good character', which was so important in the time and place in which *The French Lieutenant's Woman* was set. People there and then would have regarded it as obvious and self-evidently true. In the dominant culture of Britain today, being of good character still has meaning, although its meaning has mutated. Whereas in the past its focus was on sexual virtue, these days it tends to refer to trustworthiness, reliability (for example, over money matters) and dependability over keeping one's word. But it has much less significance and impact – losing one's 'good character' no longer results in social ostracism. Yet in some cultural settings today a woman's sexual virtue is regarded as crucial, and is protected by segregation, chaperonage and, in some cultures, by the veil (see Abu Odeh 1997 for a detailed discussion).

Some knowledge is even more localized. Religious creeds, for instance, consist of bodies of knowledge and beliefs which are internally coherent and consistent, but which 'work' only in their own belief system. Science is another example. It is based on a particular philosophy of knowledge, and in its theorization and practice certain truths are regarded as self-evidently valid and real. Berger and Luckmann wrote of 'socially segregated sub-universes of meaning', although a more common term these days is discourses. We will be doing more with this concept later in the chapter.

There is one thing we need to be wary about. It can be easy to fall into the trap of thinking that one's own time and culture are somehow superior, and hence that the knowledge *we* have is better and more accurate than that of other times, cultures and social groups. Said (1995), for example, has drawn attention to the **Orientalism** of Western thinking. By this Said was exposing the extent to which the dominant culture of the West views its own knowledge as 'the norm' and treats other forms of knowledge (such as that coming from the East – the Orient and the Arab world) as 'exotic' and other.

Young, an anthropologist, has made a similar point in respect to the knowledge of biomedicine, which is based on certain fundamental beliefs about how human bodies work, what constitutes illness and how cures are to be effected: 'These beliefs appear to the people who use them . . . to merely reflect "empirically observed" facts of nature . . . taken for granted, commonsensical, and admitted without argument: they attract no epistemological scrutiny and receive no formal codification' (Young 1980: 136). Taussig (1980) went further, accusing biomedicine of 'reproduc[ing] a political ideology in the guise of a science of (apparently) "real things"' (Taussig 1980).

Viewing knowledge as created and sustained by social processes

This accusation takes us into the next tenet of social constructionism – that knowledge is made through and sustained by social processes. Burr expresses this succinctly:

> It is through the daily interactions between people in the course of social life that our versions of knowledge become fabricated. Therefore social interaction of all kinds, and particularly language, is of great interest to social constructionists. The goings-on between people in the course of their everyday lives are seen as the practices during which our shared versions of knowledge are constructed. Therefore what we regard as 'truth' (which of course varies historically and cross-culturally) i.e. our current accepted ways of understanding the world, is a product not of objective observation of the world, but of social processes and interactions in which people are constantly engaged with each other.
>
> (Burr 1995: 4)

Szasz, an anti-psychiatrist who has argued that mental illness is socially constructed, brings this point home in a review of Raymond's *The Transsexual Empire* (1980). Reprinted in the frontispiece to this book, Szasz has this to say about transsexuality:

> The transsexual male is indistinguishable from other males, save by his desire to be a woman. ('He is a woman trapped in a man's body' is the standard rhetorical form of this claim.) If such a desire qualifies as a disease, transforming the desiring agent into a 'transsexual', then the . . . poor person who wants to be rich is a 'transeconomical'. . . . Clearly not all desires in our society are authenticated as diseases.
>
> (Szasz 1980)

The point Szasz is making is that biomedicine, in this case, treats some things as diseases to be treated but not others. So, whereas it is possible for a transsexual to get medical treatment to rectify 'being trapped in the wrong body' (because biomedicine recognizes as 'real' the medical-condition-to-be-treated of transsexualism), it does not offer treatment to rectify 'being trapped with the wrong bank-balance'. Being a poor person who powerfully wants to be rich is not constituted as a medical condition, hence the issue of medical treatment does not arise.

Samuel Butler played on this distinction specifically in his novel *Erewhon* (Butler 1872). In the mythical country Erewhon, illness and crime are treated in the reverse manner to how we treat them in our world. When a man 'suffers from fraud' in Erewhon, his friends visit to offer condolences and express their hope that he will soon get better. But there is a complex schedule of punishments for different illnesses, with a minor cold meriting only a fine, whereas a prison sentence must be served for mumps or measles. In *Erewhon Revisited* (Butler 1901) Butler took this kind of transposition further. For instance, he described a practice of 'Spiritual Athletics' in which people seek treatment for their moral failings through the use of 'moral try-your-strengths, suitable for every kind of temptation' (Butler 1901: 78). The services offered included those of 'Mrs Tantrums, Nagger, certificated by the College of Spiritual Athletics. Terms for ordinary nagging, two shillings and sixpence per hour. Hysterics extra'. Her work received the following testimonial:

> Dear Mrs. Tantrums – I have for several years been tortured with a husband of unusually peevish, irritable temper, who made my life so intolerable that I sometimes answered him in a way that led to his using personal violence towards me. After taking a course of twelve sittings from you, I found my husband's temper comparatively angelic, and we have ever since lived together in complete harmony.
>
> (Butler 1901: 79)

Notice what is going on here. Butler is ironizing the usual assumption that the person who is morally at fault is the one with the 'peevish, irritable temper'. It is the *wife* who seeks the services of Mrs Tantrums, in order to inure herself against her husband's ill humour. And yet, how ironic is this? Butler is using the story to highlight the kind of reversal that we considered in Chapter 5. If you recall, Vickers wrote about reversal as the 'grammatical, theoretical and methodological trick' that beguiles the reader or listener into misattributing agency. Even today women who suffer domestic violence still often see themselves as responsible, and feel that if they could only behave differently they could stop it happening. Some theorists – most notably Erin Pizzey, who set up the first women's refuge – locate (at least some of) the blame for domestic violence in the actions of the woman (Pizzey and Shapiro 1982). As Dobash *et al.* have noted, in their writing in the 1980s about the treatment of battered women by social and medical agencies:

> contact with a psychiatrist is likely to entail implicit, sometimes explicit notions that 'the problem' probably resides in the woman's personality and/or behaviour. The long standing psychiatric theories and professional ideologies that emphasize the provoking, masochistic and violence-seeking nature of women often result in victim blaming.
>
> (Dobash *et al.* 1982: 159)

Butler's story is worth spending some time on because it demonstrates that the ideas of feminist and social constructionist theorizing are not new. Butler was expressing them some 100 years ago, albeit in literary form. His *Erewhon* novels were intended to raise precisely the issue that is so central to social constructionism – that of the social and cultural construction of 'reality'. The central point here, then as now, is that, as a product of social processes, knowledge can and does differ according to its social and cultural context.

This raises important questions about knowledge. It means that we always need to be suspicious about it. We need to ask *whose* knowledge it is – *who* made it? Why has it been made in this way – whose interests is it serving? Who benefits from it and who loses? What happens because of it? And what would happen if a different knowledge were accepted as true instead?

Recognizing that knowledge implicates action

These questions lead us into the fourth and final tenet of social constructionism, which is that knowledge often carries with it a mandate or warrant for action. Butler's ironic world reverses the usual expectation that it is the bad-tempered, violent husband who needs to change his behaviour, and places the responsibility for change on to the wife. This particular social reality locates blame and responsibility in one person (the wife) rather than another (the husband) and hence that she needs to take action to 'resolve' the problem.

Now compare this with the explanation offered by Eysenck for why women are much more likely than men to report having engaged in sexual behaviour that they disliked. You met this in Chapter 3. Eysenck attributes the 'problem' to women's greater prudery and sexual shyness. So, by implication, women need to solve their 'problem' (of engaging in sexual activities they don't enjoy) by overcoming their shyness and prudery – perhaps by getting therapy. This has often been precisely what lesbians and women sexual abuse survivors have been urged to do, to help them to overcome their aversion to engaging in sex with men.

Kitzinger and Perkins (1993), in a book about lesbian feminism and psychology, write about the 'tyranny of the "should" ', and the way that therapy can 'privatise pain'. They relate these ideas to the construction of the 'knowledge' that mature women *should* enjoy sex with men (which is what, if you recall from Chapter 3, Freud advocated). This carries with it the requirement that women who do not enjoy sex with men *should* do something about it. Their pain is privatized – it becomes their own personal, private problem. But replace this 'knowledge' by another 'knowledge' – the knowledge of lesbian feminism – and the 'problem' ceases to be private. It becomes a matter of public concern. Kitzinger and Perkins place the blame squarely upon 'heteropatriarchal oppression':

> The oppression of lesbians causes suffering. Anti-lesbianism can mean rejection by a mother, daughter or sister. It can mean losing our jobs, or our children. It can mean being mocked, ridiculed and physically assaulted. All these experiences can cause immense pain and distress to individual lesbians. Most of us feel, to varying degrees at different times, angry, hurt, rejected and lonely because we do not fit into heterosexual society.
>
> (Kitzinger and Perkins 1993: 77)

Within this 'knowledge', what needs doing is to counter anti-lesbianism. It is society which needs to change, both at an institutional level (for example, by the legal system ceasing to view lesbianism as incompatible with being a good and capable mother) and in terms of public attitudes (by people stopping mocking and ridiculing lesbians, excluding and rejecting them). It is homophobia that needs to be tackled, not individual women who need to change.

Knowledge is not just made. The *form* in which it is made (that is, what it 'says') carries implications for people's lives, livelihoods and life opportunities. Sometimes it can mean the difference, quite literally, between life and death. Constituting having sexual intercourse with the King's wife as 'treason' can lead to execution; so too can constituting buggery as a capital offence. Constituting a set of behaviours and/or bodily experiences and manifestations as a 'medical condition' implies that 'it' is something that can be treated, and then it is but a short step to assuming that it *should* be treated. Before 1976 this is what happened to many homosexuals (and still happens to sexual offenders in our prisons and mental hospitals). At a time when masturbation was considered a 'medical condition', a variety of quite horrifying **anti-masturbatory devices** were used to treat it, and when these failed to 'cure', **clitorectomy** was used (Stainton Rogers and Stainton Rogers 1992).

Summary box Social constructionism

Berger and Luckmann's (1966) *The Social Construction of Reality* was probably the most influential text in introducing the notion of social construction to the social sciences. They suggested that reality is constructed through three main 'moments': *externalization* (whereby societies and cultures create particular versions of reality); *objectification* (whereby those constructed realities are made to seem really real – as if they occur naturally, are 'out there' waiting to be discovered); and *internalization* (whereby, through socialization and enculturation, individuals incorporate this socially constructed reality into their understanding of the world).

- The main elements of social construction are:
  - taking a critical stance towards knowledge;
  - seeing knowledge as historical time-, culture- and domain-specific;
  - viewing knowledge as created and sustained by social processes; and
  - recognizing that knowledge implicates action.
- *Taking a critical stance towards knowledge* accepts that since knowledge is socially constructed, it can be and is deployed strategically. This is evident in the way that language is used. We can see this in the way that certain terms operate as boo-words whereas others operate as hurrah-words. Calling a group of people 'terrorists' or 'freedom-fighters' is a good example.
- *Seeing knowledge as historical time-, culture- and domain-specific* means recognizing that any kind of knowledge works only in certain domains and places and at certain times. This stance thus denies that there can ever be a single, *true* knowledge: truth is always relative.
- *Viewing knowledge as created and sustained by social processes* highlights the agency of human meaning-making. Another way of putting this is that knowledge is 'discoursed into being' and is maintained through 'discursive labour'. Accepting that constructive processes are involved in the creation and maintenance of knowledge raises some key questions – why *this* knowledge, why *here* and why *now*?
- *Recognizing that knowledge implicates action* directs us to look at the consequences of knowledge being constructed in a certain way. What action does it warrant? What does it prevent? Who gains and who loses? It reminds us that constituting knowledge in a certain way can have a profound impact on people's lives and life opportunities.

The 'psy' complex

Psychology is especially implicated in all this, because psychology is a major site within which the knowledge dominant in the English-speaking world is made, maintained and mongered. As Rose says: 'Since the end of the Second World War, psychological expertise has been increasingly deployed around a range of practical problems and within a large number of administrative and reformatory practices' (Rose 1985: 1). In so doing it has 'taken up and transformed problems offered by political, economic, and moral strategies and concerns . . . and [has] made these problems thinkable in new ways and governable by new techniques' (Rose 1990: ix). And as a consequence:

> Psychological expertise now holds out the promise not just of curing pathology but *reshaping subjectivity*. On every subject from sexual satisfaction to career promotion, psychologists offer their advice and assistance both privately and through the press, radio and television.

> The apostles of these techniques proffer images of what we could become, and we are urged to seek them out and help fulfil the dream of realigning what we are and what we want to be. Our selves are defined and constructed and governed in psychological terms, constantly subject to psychologically inspired techniques of self-inspection and self-examination. And the problems of living a good life have been transposed from an ethical to a psychological register.
> (Rose 1990: xiii; our emphasis)

Life, in the English-speaking world at least (and particularly in the USA), has been psychologized. Rose (and others, such as Ingleby 1985) has adopted the term the **psy complex** to describe that set of institutions and professions (such as psychiatry, counselling and social work) which draw on psychological theory and methods to intervene in people's lives across a whole range of domains. Our working and family lives, our intimate and social relationships, what and how we eat, our purchases and consumer preferences, our engagement with institutions such as education and the law – psychology has infiltrated all of these and more. If done 'in excess', almost any human activity – from shopping to exercise, from work to eating chocolate – has been defined as a 'syndrome', turning us into shopaholics, exercise-addicts, chocoholics and workaholics. And nowhere is this more prevalent than in the domains of gender relationships and sexuality.

Popular psychology constructing subjectivity

Take the books lined up on the shelves in the psychology section of your local bookshop. Here is just one example:

> ⋆ Is having 'somebody to love' the most important thing in your life?
> ⋆ Do you constantly believe that with 'the right man' you would no longer feel depressed or lonely?
> ⋆ When you meet a man who is distant, moody or unpredictable, do you find him exciting and attractive?
>
> If being in love means being *in pain*, this book was written for you. Therapist Robin Norwood, M.A., describes loving *too much* as a pattern of behaviour developed as a response to problems from childhood. Many women find themselves repeatedly drawn into unhappy and destructive relationships with men.
>
> This bestselling book takes a hard look at how powerfully addicting these unhealthy relationships are – but also gives a very specific programme for recovery from the *disease* of loving too much.
>
> (Back cover blurb from *Women Who Love Too Much*, Norwood 1986; emphases in the original)

Another example you have met already – John Gray's (1993) *Men are from Mars, Women are from Venus* ('a fascinating book that offers hope and insight into having whole and healed relationships', according to Gerald Jampolsky on the back cover). Then there is Gael Lindenfield's *The Positive Woman* (Lindenfield 1992), which offers a complete course for women on 'developing an optimistic outlook, improving relationships, self-motivation, becoming happier, initiating change, getting out of a rut'; Ellen Bass and Laura Davis' *The Courage to Heal* (Bass and Davis 1988), which 'offers hope and encouragement to every woman who was sexually abused as a child'; and, our favourite, Dr Dan Kiley's *The Wendy Dilemma: Do you Mother your Man?* (Kiley 1985), in which he offers an ' "adult love script" [in which] he presents an exciting new role for women – no longer based on the traditional mother figure but the far more fulfilling alternative model of independent but cherished companion'. (All of the quotations are from the books' cover blurbs.)

This is what Rose meant when he asserted that: 'Psychological expertise now holds out the promise not just of curing pathology but *reshaping subjectivity*' (Rose 1990; our emphasis). In the English-speaking world, women especially are constantly bombarded with advice and exhortations to improve themselves through, as Lindenfield puts it, 'positive thinking'. Mary Crawford (1995) has written of an 'assertiveness bandwagon', which, she argues, 'grew to monumental proportions' in the USA between the 1970s and 1980s. Ruben (1985) counted 1672 works on the topic published between 1973 and 1983. Crawford sees these texts as conveying a number of messages to women:

- Assertiveness is a quality in the individual. If an individual cannot get their wishes heard and respected, it is because they lack assertiveness (and not because of situational or structural constraints).
- Women lack assertiveness compared with men and need to do something to resolve this lack.
- They should become more assertive. This involves pursuing their own self-interest and downplaying their interconnectedness with (and responsibilities towards) others.

This is a prime example of seeking to 'reshape subjectivity'. In psychological terminology it is usually called cognitive restructuring. It is the direct application of psychological ideas and theories to intervening in people's – mainly women's – lives. Kiley's book is full of psychological terminology – he writes about 'psychological distance', 'reading cues', 'loss of identity', 'denial', 'false self-esteem', 'nonverbal spanking' (no, we didn't make that one up) and 'aversive conditioning'. But hope is at hand, he claims: all you have to do is *change the way you think* – cognitive restructuring again, in all but name.

Summary box The 'psy' complex

- Psychology, in the English-speaking world particularly, is a potent force in creating knowledge and thereby shaping people's subjectivity. This, and its institutionalization in professions such as counselling and social work, has been termed the 'psy' complex.
- Its effects have been to psychologize our selves, our lives, our experiences and our relationships. We understand the world through the 'lens' of psychology – and so it affects what we feel, think and do.
- This is manifested, for instance, in the burgeoning of self-help and other 'popular' psychology books.
- Running through these books – and television programmes, magazine articles and so on – is a dominant discourse that constructs men and women differently. Women, for example, are located as powerless because they lack assertiveness. The onus is placed on them to tackle their lack of power by becoming more assertive.

Postmodernism

In the 'climate of perturbation', postmodernism is a much more transdisciplinary term than social constructionism, although it shares much of its assumptions. As its name implies, it can be thought of as a system of thought that transcends Modernism, although (as in much of post-Modernism) things are rather more complicated than that. A central tenet of Modernism is that it represents the end-state in a three-stage developmental theory of civilization, namely:

first of all there was	a *primitive world* understood in terms of a belief in magic and superstition;
this was superseded by	a *pre-modern world* understood by way of religious belief, where an all-knowing God was viewed as the sole authority of what constitutes true knowledge;
which was itself then superseded by	a *modern world* understood through science and rationality, where science is held to be the sole source of objective, empirical knowledge.

This 'up the mountain' tale of human progress (see Kitzinger 1987) thus prioritizes science as a superior form of knowledge. All other forms (such as magic, religion and traditional folklore) are (within Modernism) regarded as invalid – not really knowledge at all, merely beliefs and myths.

But in its own theorizing it is wrong to think of postmodernism as simply a further, fourth stage in the progression – although, at first sight, this is what the term seems to imply. However, it does challenge the central claim of Modernism to have access to a single, coherent, real world of nature which lies 'out there' waiting to be discovered; and it denies that science is the sole authority over what constitutes knowledge. Postmodernists contend, instead, that there are multiple alternative realities, each one of which is made – and made real – by way of human meaning-making. Another way of putting this is that our realities are the products of 'representational labour'. The parallels with social constructionism are clear.

Where **postmodernism** differs from social constructionism, other than its greater ubiquity, is that it offers not just a challenge to the positivistic approach to knowledge, but an extensive and elaborate body of theorization about the processes involved in the making, maintenance and mongering of knowledge. Its best-known theorist is Michel Foucault, and his theorizing around sexuality is a good way to begin to get to grips with what postmodernism has to offer. We will look at this next. Postmodernism is also notable for the way it has profoundly influenced analysis and enquiry. Since it asks different questions from those investigated through scientific method, it has engendered and encouraged an array of innovative methods and analytics, and we will move on to these at the end of the chapter.

Summary box Postmodernism

- Postmodernism is sometimes seen as the latest stage in a progression that began with primitive thought (based on superstition), moved to pre-modern thought (based on religion), and then on to Modernism (based on science and rationality). But postmodernists would generally say this is an over-simplification.
- Postmodernism accepts the tenets of social constructionism, but also offers an extensive body of theorization about the processes of making, maintaining and mongering of knowledge.

Foucault on sexuality

Foucault has a number of claims on our attention: as a theorist of sexuality; as a crucial figure in the emergence of discourse analysis; as an analyst of social change; for his unique take on 'power'; and for his treatment of the 'subject'. Foucault was a demanding writer whose interests, analytic language, aims and objectives shifted over his life. You have been warned!

Foucault was gay, and adventurously so, according to his biographers (see, for example, Macey 1993). At one level, his final project – an uncompleted *History of Sexuality* – reflects Foucault's own interests, especially in homosexuality. As we saw at the beginning of the chapter, what Foucault asks the reader to consider is why we think of sexuality as we do: as something that was (in Western Europe and North America) first 'repressed' and then 'liberated' over the course of the past three centuries; as something that each one of us 'has'; as a significant (central even) part of who we 'are'; and as a pivotal vehicle of power-relations.

It is probably easiest to work through Foucault's account of the last three points first. His approach relies on the argument that sexuality is not a 'thing' at all. Rather, it has been culturally constituted out of the pleasurable possibilities of our embodiment (for ourselves and for others) and discourse (in the sense of that which creates knowledge and order). Now to turn to the last point, what then happens in any quest for liberation? Only that we become ever more embroiled in the very network of powers from which liberation purports to free us.

Thus, for Foucault, the more we learn of sexuality, the more sexually educated we become, the more we are controlled under a regime of 'bio-power'. By the way, this idea of the body as a machine to be regulated, fine-tuned and put to work and play, covers not only sexuality *per se* but issues of health promotion, weight regulation, dietary fads, the cultural valorization of sport and the pursuit of martial arts, yoga and so on – in fact, the bulk of the stuff with which people in modern societies fill their lives. Also, according to Foucault, we should talk not of sexuality but of sexualities, since everyone is drawn into the discursive net: children, gays and lesbians, the disabled, the old, the celibate. All have a sexuality that can be studied, liberated/regulated and subjugated – we are all sexual subjects now.

Strategies to regulate sexuality

Foucault (1976/80) began his *History of Sexuality* by observing that it is commonly assumed in Western culture that there has been a sequence of transformations of sexuality. According to this story, in the seventeenth century sexuality was relatively openly and freely acted out and discussed. By the nineteenth century sexuality had become repressed – regulated, censored and hidden away. Now it is supposed that we have sexual liberation – a reaction against the old hypocrisy and prudery and an opening up of sexuality. Foucault argues that although there is some truth in this perception, it is only one of the stories that can be told. A counter-argument is that, far from being repressed, over time sexuality increasingly became something that mattered – it became a site of power, a means of regulation and a source of knowledge. The task Foucault set himself was therefore to 'define the regimes of power-knowledge-pleasure that sustain the discourse on human sexuality' (1980: 11). He proposed that four main strategies have been used to regulate sexuality:

- the socialization of procreative behaviour;
- the hystericization of women's bodies;
- the pedagogization of children's sexuality; and
- the psychiatrization of perverse desire

The socialization of procreative behaviour

This strategy involves restricting legitimate sexuality to long-term relationships between heterosexual couples, and making these couples responsible for procreative sex and the rearing of the children. In this way legitimate sexuality gets doubly 'contained'. First, it gets neatly cordoned off in the confines of the normative family. And then, in the family, it gets hidden away behind the parental bedroom door. This strategy warrants what Foucault calls the 'alliance of the family' – the creation of a powerful interpersonal alliance between family members, who are seen (and see themselves) as entitled to privacy and immunity from external intervention. This acts as a normalizing force, which privatizes fertility control and childrearing.

The hystericization of women's bodies

In this strategy women's sexuality is constituted as central to their identity – they *are* their biology, and sexuality is at the core of their biology. In this context 'sexuality' is not just about 'having sex' but incorporates experiences such as menstruation, pregnancy, childbirth and menopause. What Foucault is implying here is that women get to be treated as 'walking wombs' (given that *hustera* is the Greek word for womb). This 'hystericization' then warrants the regulation of women, making them the legitimate objects of medical and psychological scrutiny and intervention.

The pedagogization of children's sexuality

This strategy can be seen both as problematizing (turning into a problem) and seeking to regulate children's sexuality. These can be viewed as responses to the potential of childhood sexuality to act as a site of resistance to adult power. Foucault writes of the 'precious and perilous, dangerous and endangered potential' (1990: 104) of childhood sexuality which, being both 'natural' and at the same time 'contrary to nature', 'poses physical and moral, individual and collective dangers'. Consequently, he argues: '[t]he sex of children has become, since the eighteenth century, an important area of contention around which innumerable institutional devices and discursive strategies have been deployed' (Foucault 1990: 30). Foucault asserted that we can see this manifested, for instance, in the architecture of schools, designed to expose children to constant and vigilant scrutiny. More generally, the strategy places all those in authority over children in a state of perpetual alert, and exhorts them to control the sexuality of the children in their care.

This shows how our society has – Foucault argues, for the first time in history – assembled a machinery for 'speechifying, analysing and investigating' children's sexual activity, casting sexuality in childhood as precocious and perilous, and children as simultaneously dangerous and endangered by their sexual potential.

The psychiatrization of perverse desire

This strategy works by pathologizing – turning into an illness – all deviations from 'normal sexuality'. Foucault was particularly concerned about homosexuality – which is not surprising, given that he was gay. (Remember that in the 1970s, when Foucault was writing, homosexuality was generally regarded as a form of 'mental illness', and indeed was defined as such in the US manual DSM-III.) Foucault's label highlights the particular warrant this gave psychiatry to intervene in and control homosexuality, by using a range of corrective technologies including different kinds of medical treatment: drugs to reduce libido, aversion therapy and psychoanalysis. But Foucault was also active in arguing against the controls on sex between adults and children (paedophilia).

How the strategies work

Foucault suggested that these strategies, acting in concert, do not, however, just act on sexuality to regulate it. They use this regulation of sexuality as the 'glue' to hold together a normalized/normalizing social structure. This is a theoretical position that goes far beyond the usual way in which sexuality is perceived. It suggests that sexuality is a potent site of power that operates across the variety of human action and experience. Sexuality, according to Foucault, functions as 'a unique signifier and as a universal signified' (Foucault 1980: 154). It allows a host of different things – anatomical elements, biological functions, conducts, sensations and pleasures – to be linked together as a single 'whole'. Thus the purpose of regulation, according to Foucault, was not simply to repress the sexuality of the governed – to force them to hide it away and to deny it. This may seem on the surface to be what is going on, but it is only one manifestation of regulation. Rather, the main goal was to promote:

> the body, the vigour, the longevity, progeniture and descent of the classes that 'ruled'. This was the purpose for which the deployment of sexuality was first established, as a new distribution of pleasures, discourses, truths and powers . . . a defense, a protection, and an exaltation . . . a means of social control and political subjugation.
>
> (Foucault 1980: 123)

But the important point Foucault makes is that this is not just a one-way process. As a site of power, sexuality is as much a locus for **resistance** (that is, the resisting of power) as for control. Foucault tended to be preoccupied with homosexuality and to somewhat ignore the issue of women's sexuality (see Sawicki 1991; and Bell 1993 for more detailed examinations of this facet of his work). Yet we can include here the 'power' that sex can accord women. More generally, 'deviant' sexuality (that is, anything outside of the privacy of the heterosexual married couple) is often used to undermine those in an otherwise powerful position – as, for instance, US president Bill Clinton found to his cost.

Foucault's formulations can be viewed as just as self-serving and self-justifying as any other theorizing we have criticized in this book. In arguing that sexual 'deviance' is not just a lifestyle choice or a predeliction, and that homosexuality – and indeed other forms of 'perverse pleasure' (such as fetishism) – are potent means of political action, Foucault can be seen to be warranting his own sexuality as a form of resistance against power. In Foucaultian terms *all* theorization (as a form of discourse) is a strategic use of power to produce knowledge. Foucault would never have claimed that his own discourse was immune to such a reading. At the same time, Foucault's (sadly unfinished) exploration of the topic dramatically changed the way we can 'make sense' of sexuality. Far from being a biological 'given', or even an isolated and limited aspect of human experience, he opened up for us the possibility that sexuality is 'an important area of contention around which innumerable institutional devices and discursive strategies have been employed' (1980: 30). As a consequence, sexuality has become one of the major preoccupations of our times:

> From the singular imperialism that compels everyone to transform their sexuality into a perpetual discourse, to the manifold of mechanisms which, in the areas of economy, medicine and justice, incite, extract, distribute and institutionalize the sexual discourse, an immense verbosity is what our civilization has required and organized.
>
> (Foucault 1980: 33)

Summary box Foucault on sexuality

- Foucault argued that in the Western world sexuality is not a 'natural given' but a form of socially and culturally constructed knowledge that is specific to its time and place. Moreover, he claimed that the form in which it has been 'knowledged into being' operates as a form of social control over people's behaviour.

- Foucault suggested that there are four main strategies by which this social control is enforced: the socialization of procreative behaviour; the hystericization of women's bodies; the pedagogization of children's sexuality; and the psychiatrization of perverse desire.
- *The socialization of procreative behaviour* restricts legitimate sexuality to procreative sex within long-term, heterosexual, couple relationships. It is thus doubly contained – contained in the family and contained in the parental bedroom. All other forms of sexuality are thereby treated as, if not deviant, then less legitimate and less meaningful and worthwhile.
- *The hystericization of women's bodies* constitutes women's sexuality as central to their identity – it treats them as if their biology were their identity. Another way of putting this is that women are treated as 'walking wombs'. This allows women to be regulated and controlled, especially by the medical profession.
- *The pedagogization of children's sexuality* places children 'off limits' with regard to sex, because of the dangerous potential of their sexuality to threaten adult power. This warrants the surveillance and control of children's sexuality.
- *The psychiatrization of perverse desire* pathologizes all deviations from 'normal sexuality'. This provides a justification for the regulation of what is considered 'deviant' sexuality.
- Foucault saw sexuality as a potent site of power, and hence the regulation of sexuality as being crucial to the way that those in power exert and maintain their control over the rest of society.
- However, Foucault pointed out that sexuality is also a powerful means of resistance to this elite power.

A new standpoint on research

Postmodernism is profoundly suspicious about the importation of scientific method into disciplines such as psychology. Psychology is beset by **methodolatry** – the worship of method (Curt 1994) – where, however inane and naive the idea explored (such as investigating whether men can be conditioned to be aroused by thigh-length boots), it will pass as 'scientific knowledge' as long as the study is methodologically sound. Moreover, statistics generally, and statistical significance in particular, are treated like religious talismans – unless you have them in your study, it simply will not pass as serious scientific research.

At a more profound level, methodolatry rests on a basic error – that evidence (derived from averaged responses) of an association between measures (for example, between introversion and a preference for women with larger breasts, see Wiggins *et al.* 1968), or between measures and indices (such as between *Playboy* readership and a preference for large breasts, see also Wiggins *et al.* 1968), contributes to psychological knowledge. It does not. What such studies actually offer is evidence of a relationship between measures. As Brown (1980) has pointed out, this is just like going around your house, looking at all the clocks and discovering that the time each one shows is roughly the same – and then claiming to have 'measured time'. All you have done is find out something entirely obvious and trivial about the conventions of setting clocks.

A mainstream psychologist might, of course, counter that it is not really the measures (that is, the tests, inventories and responses) that matter, but the psychological states and traits they index. The trouble is that any statement that social psychology might make about someone (such as labelling them 'a *Playboy* reader') can be understood in a variety of different ways. For example, does it index some trait that can be regarded as a cause, impelling people to prefer women with large breasts? Or is it an effect of some earlier life experience (perhaps during the oral stage) that results in a tendency to read *Playboy*? These purported causes and effects are not, however, like causes and effects in the physical world. We cannot say to a piece of ordinary, unmagnetized steel, 'I would like you to role-play a magnet', and then provide some iron filings and expect to find a pattern appearing that indicates a magnetic field. But we *can* say to participants in a study who have never opened the covers of *Playboy*, 'I would like you to role-play the kind of person who reads *Playboy*', provide them with some silhouette pictures of women, and expect them to say that they like best the ones with big breasts.

From a postmodern perspective, mainstream social psychological experiments can be thought of as standardized interrogations in which answers to certain questions are asked. The point is that those research questions do not emerge in a vacuum but from within a particular view of the world – within a particular constitution of reality. The reality in which mainstream social psychology has interrogated sexuality and gender has been a very specific one. It is largely located in the USA and – in the case of experimental social psychology – is largely restricted to experimentation on undergraduates on university campuses. This raises profound issues when, as recent anthropological work on gender and sexuality suggests:

> What gender is, what men and women are, what sorts of relations do or should obtain between them – all of the notions do not simply reflect . . . upon biological 'givens', but are largely the product of social and cultural processes.
>
> (Ortner and Whitehead 1981: 1)

If we accept the postmodern case that cultural knowledge of gender and sexuality is central to constructing our identities, and if we accept that the studies being carried out are also the main source of psychological 'knowledge' about gender and sexuality, then we have to conclude that there is a self-fulfilling prophecy in operation. Interrogative research simply reaps what it has sown. The knowledge that psychologists 'discover' in their research is not about (as it purports to be) 'universal laws of human behaviour' in relation to gender and sexuality. It is simply an account of the historically and culturally specific conventions, expectations and assumptions that operate about gender and sexuality, within the domain psychologists study (that is, primarily the life-world of US college students).

If this were all that was at stake, perhaps it would not be too bad. We could just pass it off as poor scholarship, or, perhaps, as anthropology masquerading as psychology. But there is a more serious problem. The psychological research sustained by methodolatry produces a certain kind of knowledge – and it is this knowledge which feeds into and sustains the 'psy complex'. It is this knowledge, for example, which provides the mandate for the 'assertiveness bandwagon' which tells people how to behave, what to believe and what to think. If we return to the four main tenets of social constructionism then we can see that adopting a social constructionist and/or postmodern standpoint on research involves asking different research questions.

Mainstream psychological research is based on the principles of hypothetico-deductive logic. Researchers generate hypotheses, from these make predictions, and then seek to test whether the predictions work. Experiments that compare experimental and control conditions are generally regarded as the best way to do this, although other methods (such as conducting surveys) are also used. Part I of this book is packed with research of this kind. The sorts of questions asked included: Is male aggression caused by testosterone (Chapter 1)? Do parental attitudes influence the degree to which children acquire gender stereotypes (Chapter 2)? Are extraverts more sexually adventurous than introverts (Chapter 3)? We have already, as we moved through this work, raised questions about the methodological adequacy of many of these studies.

Research from a social constructionist/postmodern perspective regards **hypothetico-deductive method** as completely incapable of investigating topics such as these. It views the products of such studies (the data they yield) not as facts-that-have-been-discovered, but as *arte*facts-that-have-been-constructed-into-being. This is because the topics under scrutiny – aggression, gender stereotypes, sexual adventurousness and so on – are not things that can be objectively defined, but the thingified products of human meaning-making; so too are the variables being manipulated. Hence the questions being asked are seen as unanswerable, since the only answers that can be obtained are yet more constructions. The whole enterprise is enmeshed in a dense, interconnected network of constructed knowledge. Moreover, this knowledge is always constructed ideologically – *by* people and *for* people's purposes, to achieve certain ends. The resolution of this is to turn the dilemma on its head and ask questions about the constitution of knowledge: *Whose* knowledge is it – *who* made it? Why has it been made in this way – whose interests is it serving? Who benefits from it and who loses? What happens because of it? And what would happen if a different knowledge were accepted as true instead?

We have also been critical throughout this book of theorizing which is speculative – which is not based on experimental evidence at all, but deduced through logical interpretation, such as the sociobiological theorizing (Chapter 1) which claims that men's biology drives them to be promiscuous, even though there is no way of subjecting this claim to empirical test, even within the conventions of hypothetico-deductive method. It is towards this kind of knowledge, in particular, that these 'climate of perturbation' questions are directed. Who stands to benefit from the claim that men have a natural propensity for promiscuity, and so 'can't help being unfaithful'? And what would be the implication if a different knowledge were accepted as true instead? It would be that men could no longer use their biological drives as an excuse for being unfaithful in their relationships (always, accepting, of course, that the notions of promiscuity, unfaithfulness and even biological drives are constructions, articulating their own particular ideology). The result is a very different kind of endeavour, of which Foucault's work is such a good example. It is an endeavour centrally concerned with issues of power and ideology and how constructing knowledge in particular ways can be used strategically to bring about particular outcomes.

Summary box Postmodernism's new standpoint on research

- Postmodernists are highly critical of the conventional approaches that psychology has taken to research. These criticisms include the following:
  (a) Because of its conviction that it must use hypothetico-deductive method, conventional psychological research asks only a limited set of questions – those that are amenable to such methods.
  (b) Often these kinds of studies simply show an association between measures, which in fact indicate only quite trivial linkages and tell us nothing about cause and effect.
  (c) Research tends to be driven by pragmatics. Especially in the USA (where most psychological research is done) but increasingly in the UK too, psychologists use their students as the subjects of their studies. So the data produced tell us only about the conventions, expectations and assumptions of students – not about people in general.
  (d) The 'results' of such studies then feed into the 'psy' complex, and thereby have consequences for the way people live their lives. For example, they set up expectations about how people *should* behave.

- Postmodernists are also critical of theorizing (such as sociobiology) which is speculative – where its claims cannot be tested.
- Postmodernists therefore ask different research questions about the constitution of knowledge. These include:
  (a) Whose knowledge is it? Who made it?
  (b) Why has it been made in this way – whose interests is it serving?
  (c) Who benefits from it and who loses?
  (d) What happens because of it? And what would happen if different knowledge were accepted as true instead?

Chapter review

It has been possible in this chapter to touch only briefly on what is a vast body of postmodern theory and critique. Indeed, a good reason for keeping the chapter (relatively) short is that once you get into this work, it soon gets very complicated indeed. Postmodern theorists would generally prefer people to *fail* to understand them than to be misunderstood. (Actually, they usually manage to do both.) Rather than weighing you down with vast amounts of theory, we decided to design the book with a three-part structure, in which the last section takes up 'climate of perturbation' ideas and analytics that we have described here and in the previous chapter, and puts them to work on topics that affect and interest you.

Further reading

Curt, B. (1994) *Textuality and Tectonics: Troubling Social and Psychological Science*. Buckingham: Open University Press.

Foucault, M. (1980 [1976]) *The History of Sexuality, Volume I*. Harmondsworth: Penguin.

Gergen, M. and Davis, S.N. (eds) (1997) *Toward a New Psychology of Gender: A Reader*. London: Routledge.

Kitzinger, C. (1987) *The Social Construction of Lesbianism*. London: Sage.

Kvale, S. (ed.) (1992) *Psychology and Postmodernism*. London: Sage.

Stainton Rogers, R., Stenner, P., Gleeson, K. and Stainton Rogers, W. (1995) *Social Psychology: A Critical Agenda*. Cambridge: Polity. Particularly Chapter 10: Pomosexualities: Challenging the Missionary Position.

Wodak, R. (ed.) (1997) *Gender and Discourse*. London: Sage.

Part III

Applications of a critical approach

7 Where's the action?

Clear age-related patterns emerge from the data on sexual orientation. . . . In terms of life-time experience, the age-related pattern differs markedly for men and women.

(Wellings *et al.* 1994: 195)

What I can't stand is quiet sex . . . If I'm with a guy and he won't say anything, just breathes, and I'm too timid to start up all the heavy moaning that really turns me on, I fantasize. I remember the first time I ever heard people fucking, and remembering it, well, it releases me. I was only about eleven when this happened. We were all living in a big block of flats with a centre courtyard. All the bedroom windows opened onto this court, and sometimes in the middle of the night in that building it sounded like a mass orgy. I may have been only eleven but no one had to tell me what all that moaning and yelling was about. I'd lie mesmerized – that's when I began masturbating, I think – listening to the first couple. Invariably, they'd wake up other couples. And like some chain reaction within minutes the whole building was fucking. I mean, have you ever heard other people fucking, really enjoying it? It's a marvellous sound . . . not like in the movies . . . but when it's real. It's such a happy, exciting sound.

('June', quoted in Friday 1975: 202)

In this chapter we look at how people act out their sexuality – who is doing what with whom, where and when. We begin by reporting information from surveys, and then move on to look at what reports like this tell us – and, crucially, what they do not tell us and what they obscure and cover up.

Sex is sexy

Academics often use the adjective 'sexy' to describe research which is 'topical', 'easily fundable' and 'hot' – as in 'X is a really "sexy" topic right now'. Whether you are talking about Madonna or Prince (the historical 'formerly known as' character, of course), film or fiction (or even research), sex is undoubtedly sexy. Appetites for sexual stories, sexual jokes, sexual gossip and the sexually unusual seem culturally universal and as old as recorded civilization. *How* they get relayed and retold, is, of course, historically and culturally specific. One thing is for sure – the sexual grips us. It is eternally fascinating and deeply embarrassing. Sexy jokes are often hilariously funny. Yet descriptions or portrayals of sexual practices can both disgust and excite (see Chapter 4). So it is intriguing just how dry sex becomes when taken on by survey researchers.

Sexual conduct

Usually, information about what people do, sexually, is gained from survey data. Either they are asked to fill in questionnaires, or they are interviewed. In this section we will briefly review some of these data. We have been very selective (there are a lot of these data around) and have simply summarized enough to give you a general picture of who is doing what with whom, and how often.

First sexual experiences

Kinsey and colleagues, in their massive researches into sexual behaviour (*The Sexual Behavior of the Human Male*, 1948; and *The Sexual Behavior of the Human Female*, 1953), suggested that at that time (that is, in the 1940s and 1950s) about 30 per cent of girls had had some heterosexual experience by the age of 13. Within that 30 per cent, 17 per cent reported attempted intercourse (that is, about 5 per cent overall). For young men the comparable figures were 40 per cent with some heterosexual sexual experience by age 13 and, within that group, 55 per cent reported attempted intercourse (that is, about 22 per cent overall). Homosexual sexual experience was reported at similar levels of incidence.

Research contemporary with Kinsey's gives us a somewhat broader picture of what was going on at that time. Ellis (1949) reported that among young women at college in the USA, 57 per cent recollected at least one 'infatuation' before the age of 12 and 11 per cent recalled at least one experience of 'being in love'. Burgess and Wallin (1953), also working in the USA, reported that about 15 per cent of boys and girls started dating before the age of 14, and these figures match quite well with those in another USA study (Hollingshead 1949). These data provide evidence that in the USA in the immediate post-war period a substantial minority of young teenagers had begun to engage in sexual relationships, but typically these progressed no further than what was, at the time, called 'necking'.

More recent data from both the USA and the UK suggest that there has been a marked shift over the past 50 or so years in young people's first sexual experiences. It seems that more young people, proportionately, now get into sex before they are 16, and their conduct has increasingly come to encompass 'heavy petting' and sexual intercourse (Masters *et al.* 1994; Wellings *et al.* 1994). One UK source, Bremner and Hillin (1994), estimates that in Britain about 48 per cent of girls and 36 per cent of boys have had penetrative sex before the age of 16. However, Wellings *et al.* (1994), in a report based on the *National Survey of Sexual Attitudes and Lifestyles*, give a lower estimate of 18.7 per cent of girls and 27.6 per cent of boys having experienced heterosexual intercourse before the legal age of consent (16). By comparison, in this survey 4.3 per cent of young men and 3.0 per cent of young women reported having had some homosexual experience. (Differences in research procedures make these data incommensurable with the higher rates in the Kinsey data.) About half those numbers claimed such experiences before the age of 16. One of the most compelling findings in the Wellings *et al.* data is that the younger the person interviewed in the survey overall, the more likely they were to have engaged in sexual intercourse before they were 16, as shown in Table 7.1.

These data, together with a similar pattern showing that in general the younger cohorts began having sex earlier overall and were more likely to have more partners than older cohorts, do suggest that there has been a systematic shift in sexual behaviour among the young.

Table 7.1 Percentages reporting first sexual intercourse before the age of 16, in relation to age at interview

Age at interview	*Women*	*Men*
16–19	18.7	27.6
20–24	14.7	23.8
25–29	10.0	23.8
30–34	8.6	23.2
35–39	5.8	18.4
40–44	4.3	14.5
45–49	3.4	13.9
50–54	1.4	8.9
55–59	0.8	5.8

Source: Data from Wellings *et al.* 1994

Adult sexual experience

Experience of vaginal intercourse is near universal for both men and women. Between the ages of 16 and 59, more than 90 per cent of adults have engaged in this form of sex at some time in their lives. To get into a bit more detail, the respondents interviewed by Wellings *et al.* who were identified as heterosexual provided the data about their sexual conduct shown in Table 7.2.

Table 7.2 Percentages reporting different kinds of sexual activity

	Have had vaginal intercourse		*Have engaged in oral sex (cunnilingus and/or fellatio)*		*Have engaged in anal sex*		*Have had non-penetrative sex*	
	In the past year	*Ever*	*In the past year*	*Ever*	*In the past year*	*Ever*	*In the past year*	*Ever*
Men	85.5	92.7	62.4	75.2	6.5	13.9	65.5	80.1
Women	84.7	95.7	56.3	69.2	5.9	12.9	60.2	75.0

Source: Data from Wellings *et al.* 1994

Again age differences are apparent. Oral sex, in particular, tends to be more common among younger people. For example, whereas more than 60 per cent of men and women aged 18–44 reported having engaged in oral sex in the past year, this declined to less than 30 per cent of women and 42 per cent of men aged 45–59. Wellings *et al.* conclude that 'there are generational changes in the practice of oral sex and . . . this has become an increasingly common practice in recent decades' (Wellings *et al.* 1994: 156). There are likely to be a number of influences. One Wellings *et al.* suggest is the move to a more secular society. Many religions teach that sex is a matter of reproductive responsibility and/or place strict limits on what is acceptable. As religion has lost its influence over most people (see, for example, Wilkinson and Mulgan 1995) sex has come to be seen much more as a route to personal fulfilment, satisfaction and pleasure. Hence non-procreative and otherwise 'aberrant' practices are likely to become more popular. Another influence is likely to be the threat posed by AIDS and a shift to 'safer sex'. Wellings *et al.* found some evidence of people (especially younger men) engaging only in non-penetrative sex. Other factors that were shown by the survey to affect sexual conduct included social class (those from higher socio-economic classes tended to engage in more sex than those from lower classes). However, the differences were small.

In terms of frequency of having vaginal sex, this tended to be highest (an average of about five times a month) among women aged 20–29 and men aged 25–34, thereafter decreasing. More than 50 per cent of women aged 55–59 reported having had no sex in the past month. Not surprisingly, people who were married or cohabiting reported having sex more frequently than people who were not. More than 50 per cent of single people and more than 75 per cent of widows and widowers reported not having had sex in the past month. Again, there was a small influence of social class, with those people from higher social classes reporting slightly higher rates than those from lower social classes. In terms of numbers of sexual partners, the data reported are summarized in Table 7.3.

Table 7.3 Percentages reporting different numbers of sexual partners

	Men			*Women*		
Number of sexual partners	*Over their lifetime*	*In the past 5 years*	*In the past year*	*Over their lifetime*	*In the past 5 years*	*In the past year*
0	6.6	8.7	13.1	5.7	9.1	13.9
1	20.6	56.5	73.0	39.3	67.4	79.4
2	10.6	10.0	8.2	16.9	11.0	4.8
3–4	18.4	12.0	4.1	18.2	8.1	1.6
5–9	19.4	7.9	1.5 (5+)	13.0	3.6	0.4 (5+)
10+	24.4	4.8		6.8	0.8	

Source: Data from Wellings *et al.* 1994

All these data based on averages, however, obscure enormous diversity. For example, a small number of people reported having had sex more than 100 times in the past four weeks. Equally, a small number of people reported having had more than 100 sexual partners.

Homosexual experience

In the sample in Wellings *et al.*'s (1994) survey, covering all ages, was a group of 6.1 per cent of the men and 3.4 per cent of the women who reported that they had had same-sex experience over their lifetime. These figures for homosexual experience almost doubled for respondents in London, suggesting selective migration to the capital. Two further factors were associated with homosexual experience: higher social class and attendance at boarding school. However, having same-sex experience does not mean, in the conventional sense, that a person is 'gay', as shown in Table 7.4.

Thus, only 1 per cent of men and 0.8 per cent of women in the sample said that their sexual attraction was mostly or only homosexual.

Table 7.4 Percentages of men and women reporting different kinds of sexual attraction and sexual experience

	Sexual attraction		*Sexual experience*	
	Men	*Women*	*Men*	*Women*
Only heterosexual	93.3	93.6	92.3	95.1
Mostly heterosexual	4.0	3.8	3.9	2.2
Both heterosexual and homosexual	0.5	0.2	0.3	0.1
Mostly homosexual	0.5	0.2	0.6	0.2
Only homosexual	0.5	0.3	0.4	0.1
None	0.8	1.2	2.0	1.6
Refused to answer	0.5	0.7	0.6	0.7

Source: Data from Wellings *et al.* 1994

Male homosexual experience

Wellings *et al.* (1994) report that of those men who have had some same-sex experience, nearly 90 per cent said that they have had non-penetrative sex (mainly mutual masturbation and/or oral sex); 33.7 per cent say they have had insertive anal sex; and 35.4 per cent say they have had receptive anal sex. Having experienced both receptive and penetrative sex is more common than having experienced one of these practices alone. As might be expected, these figures, drawn from a sub-set of a random sample, reflect less activity than has been found in studies of men who identify themselves as gay (for example, the Project Sigma data, Hunt *et al.* 1991). Nevertheless, to put gay sex in perspective, 'the prevalence of penetrative sex is lower in homosexual than in heterosexual relationships' (Wellings *et al.* 1994: 223).

The distinction between men who report homosexual experiences and self-identified gay men is important when we look to the number and gender of their partners. The former, not surprisingly, are more likely to report female partners as well (in more than 90 per cent of cases). Among self-identified gay men, other research (summarized by Wellings *et al.*) suggests that about 60 per cent have heterosexual experience. In others words, bisexual experience is commonplace. In the male population as a whole, about half of all homosexual experiences are with just one partner. However, 3.9 per cent reported more than 100 partners. Despite some high-profile reporting in the media, the 'promiscuous' gay man seems to be the exception rather than the rule. Over a lifetime, Project Sigma (Hunt *et al.* 1991) suggested a median of seven penetrative partners among self-identified gay men. This sort of figure is not unusual among straight men.

Female homosexual experience

Drawing again on Wellings *et al.*, slightly more women (95.1 per cent) than men reported exclusively heterosexual experiences. About 3.4 per cent reported at least one homosexual experience ever, and half that percentage reported a homosexual experience involving genital contact. These levels varied little by age but were higher for women who had attended boarding school. What we might call a lesbian pattern of sexual experience (that is, mostly or exclusively with other women) was reported by less than 0.25 per cent of women in the Wellings *et al.* sample. (A broadly similar rate has been found in a survey conducted in Norway; ACSF Investigators 1992). Homosexual experience for women was higher in London, but the capital city effect was lower than for male homosexual experience. Another distinctive feature of female homosexual experience was that (in the sometimes arch prose of Wellings *et al.*): 'For women the chances of making a homosexual début are remarkably constant, up to the fifth decade' (Wellings *et al.* 1994: 198). By contrast, once past their early thirties, men showed a marked decline in their probability of having a first homosexual experience. Lesbian women reported having had fewer sexual partners.

Bisexual conduct

As the research just reviewed revealed, a small number of men (0.5 per cent) and women (0.2 per cent) reported an attraction to both men and women, and about half those numbers also report sexual experience with both men and women. Little research exists about bisexuality, but there has been some (Weinberg *et al.* 1994). This research is constrained in two ways, by location (San Francisco) and by sample (relatively small numbers of self-identified bisexuals: 49 men and 44 women in their 1983 study). Bisexuals of both sexes seem to have large numbers of sexual partners over their lifetimes, with both male and female bisexuals more likely to take up with men. The range of sexual activities engaged in was considerable. It included not only the most obvious but also anal stimulation with fingers (roughly half reported having this experience in the previous year), oral-anal stimulation and dominant-submissive **sadomasochism** (about a quarter), **urine play** (about 10 per cent) and **anal fisting** (about 11 per cent for males and about 4.5 per cent for females).

In 1984/85, the same researchers conducted a postal questionnaire study that obtained usable responses from 682 people, very roughly equally divided among male and female homosexuals, bisexuals and heterosexuals. All were members of organizations in the Bay Area in San Francisco (an area known for its culture of 'sexual freedom'). In other words, we should expect there to be a more sexually active set of control group heterosexuals than in a random sample. The median numbers of sexual partners here offer interesting comparisons by sexual preference. The comparison is shown in Table 7.5.

Table 7.5 Percentages of hetero-, homo- and bisexual respondents reporting other/same-sex partners

	Heterosexuals		*Bisexuals*		*Homosexuals*	
	Men	*Women*	*Men*	*Women*	*Men*	*Women*
Other-sex	20	25	20	30	2	10
Same-sex	0	1	30	7	100	10

Source: Data from Weinberg *et al.* 1984

These data supported findings in their earlier study, suggesting that bisexuals of both sexes tend to have had more male partners. The self-declared heterosexuals were, unsurprisingly, heterosexual in their choice of partner, with a higher median number of partners than would be expected in a random sample. The self-identified gay men were just as clear in their partner choices and again had a markedly higher number of partners over life than a random sample would yield. Finally, the lesbians were less clearly homosexual in partner choice than might be expected given the research context.

Bisexuals and their response to the emergence of HIV

Weinberg and colleagues' final study in 1988 also included fieldwork in San Francisco. To put the research in context, the HIV virus was first isolated in 1983, and by 1989 it was estimated that more than one million US residents were infected. We are, in other words, looking at what may well have been a uniquely rapid episode of change in sexual conduct. As the authors note, the 'scene' was transformed:

> The gay bath houses in San Francisco had also closed down [along with] the 'piss and fist' club frequented by some of the bisexuals in 1983 . . . group-sex parties, which were commonplace in 1983, had been transformed into what were called 'Jack-and-Jill-off' parties – gatherings of men and women who participated together in masturbating themselves or others. Some of the institutions of the sexual underground . . . remained intact, but none had escaped the biggest change of all – the alteration of the meaning of sex in the face of the AIDS epidemic. Gone was the hedonistic flavor of the early 80s when sex was celebrated and explored. Now sex could hardly be discussed without reference to the fear of contracting the AIDS virus. San Francisco, with its concentration of homosexuals and bisexuals, had suffered from the onslaught of the disease and was a very different place.
>
> (Weinberg *et al.* 1994: 208)

This pen picture was supported by follow-up study data which was both closed-ended and open-ended. This was reflected both in reported shifts towards 'safe sex' practices and in a tendency to avoid men (particularly bisexual men) as partners.

Taking a critical stance

The two quotations with which we began this chapter give very different impressions of what goes on in sexual conduct. The first, typical of the kind of account given so far, comes across as highly authoritative and objective. The second, a quote from a book on sexual fantasies, is much more alive, but at the same time is clearly much more impressionistic. Actually the fantasy quoted is one of the milder and least bizarre of the women's sexual fantasies collected together by Nancy Friday in *My Secret Garden* (Friday 1975). (If you doubt our judgement, then check it out for yourself.)

When we watch, read or hear descriptive accounts or depictions of sex in movies, magazines and books (even textbooks!), then we know that there is *somebody* (or some people) doing the describing and/or depicting. Even when we get carried away by the story to the extent that it gains a potent sense of reality, we still know that there is human agency involved. Someone is 'conjuring up' the story for us. But when we are presented with quantitative data, the human agency slips out of sight. We face a barrage of statements like: 'the figures almost doubled' (as if the figures themselves were involved in an orgy of reproduction); 'the data suggest' (as if they were doing the talking – shades of *Star Trek* again); 'clear age-related patterns emerge from the data' (sounds like something nasty in the woodshed); 'oral sex tends to become more common' (as if it had agency in itself – it is almost as though Cunnilingus and Fellatio have become characters in a bad Italian Soap).

But this is not the only problem. We were highly selective in the data we presented to you – we aimed to report just enough to give a sense of overview. But what about all the things we left out? For example, there was nothing on sexuality in childhood. And yet, as raised in Chapter 6, the sexuality (or lack of it) of children is a serious issue today. And did you notice that it was only when we got to San Francisco that we mentioned oral-anal stimulation, dominant-submissive sadomasochism, urine play and anal fisting? None of these is even mentioned in the index of Wellings *et al.* We did not write about them because the survey did not specifically ask about them. But think, for a minute, what impression that left you with.

Reporting data is always constrained by the questions that were asked and the categories that were used for analysis. Look back at the first section and you will find, repeatedly, that the following categories were used: gender (male/female), age, social class, heterosexual/homosexual/bisexual. By using these categories to carve up the data (and feeding them into the data by the questions asked) the original research and our account of it are contributing to the objectification of these categories as real things. And the lack of mention of other categories (such as transsexuals or political lesbians) tends to make these categories more invisible.

And finally, it is all too easy to gain a misleading impression from how the data themselves are crafted and described. For example, Kinsey and his colleagues reported data about first sexual experience in terms of the age at which something first happened. Hence, when they reported that by age 13 about 30 per cent of young women had had some heterosexual experience, this simply means that at some time from birth to the age of 13 something sexual happened to them. It could have been just one incident (say of being fondled at age 10). In this form of reporting the experience never goes away from the data. The girl might have had no further heterosexual experiences (that is, none after the age of 10). Data like these are often misleading. They tell us *something* about what it was like to be young in the 1940s and 1950s in the USA – that at that time a fair proportion of teenagers had experienced at least one sexual encounter of some sort. But that is *all* it tells us.

It gives no clues, for example, about how many of these teenagers were regularly 'petting' with someone of their own age, compared with how many had had just one isolated sexual encounter. The same data could have manifested at least three very different situations. We could be looking at a USA in the 1940s and 1950s that was riddled with sexual abuse. Or we could be looking simply at a situation in which many 11- and 12-year-olds were dating. Or it could be that these individuals had played a lot of 'doctors and nurses' when they were little. We simply do not know which one, which combination of these, or what else may have been happening. This effect is even more marked when data reporting is interspersed with more open-ended commentary. Such commentary tends, not surprisingly, to draw on the writer's own experiences and speculations, and on what already published work is available to them. So, for example, two explanations were offered for the more frequent reports of oral sex coming from younger respondents – the secularization of society, and the threat of AIDS. Other possibilities were not mentioned. A feminist-informed commentator might well have focused on other possibilities, such as growing assertiveness among women about their sexual preferences. Or somebody who admitted to reading magazines such as *Cosmopolitan* might simply point out that unlike editions even 10 years ago, they now offer explicit advice on 'how to give good head' and 'how not to swallow'. The media can have a powerful effect. By giving this kind of advice, magazines such as *Cosmo* are not only telling their readers how to have a more satisfying sex life, they are also telling them, by implication, that fellatio is a normal sexual practice.

Data or creata?

Andersen (1994) invented a rather lovely neologism – **creata**. By this term he drew attention to the way that data are not – as they are usually seen to be – real things but constructions. As we argued in Chapter 6, they are created out of processes of interrogation, in which certain questions are asked, in certain specific ways, of certain people. To give just one example, Kinsey and his colleagues did not ask people the question 'Have you ever had X kind of sex?' (for example, sex with an animal). Instead they asked questions such as 'When did you first have X kind of sex?' or 'When was the last time you had X kind of sex?' Their rationale was that they would be more likely to get positive responses from the wording they adopted. But this immediately opens up the question, how far can we trust data that are dependent on small nuances of the wording used in questions? Given the 'grip' of sex, its potential to embarrass and strong conventions about its 'private' nature, sex is probably the most difficult research topic to pursue. It is impossible to know to what extent people are being honest in their replies. Crucially, we do not know who is being honest and who is being 'economical with the truth'.

Research like this can work only if you make the assumption that everybody taking part is responding in broadly the same way. But it is quite possible (even probable) that they are not, because the questions will have different meanings and different significance for different people, and so too will their replies. For instance, running through the data were differences between the responses of men and women. Both gay and straight women, for example, tended, on average, to report having had fewer sexual partners than men. Now, was that because they actually did have fewer partners? Or was it because the double standard (in which women who 'sleep around' are 'slags', whereas men who have lots of partners are 'studs') led women to underreport and led men to overreport? Or, again, some combination of the two, or something else entirely?

What gets researched and what does not

There is considerable concern at present about whether children are sexual or asexual. Early sexological research (Townsend 1896; Bell 1902) established that most people gain their first sexual experience – masturbation – in childhood. So too did Kinsey *et al.* (1948, 1953). They confirmed that children generally engage in a range of sexual activities, from masturbation through to attempted and successful coitus. Mostly, though, we tend to regard children as not so much sexual as 'playing' at sex. As we have discussed in more detail elsewhere (Stainton Rogers and Stainton Rogers 1992, 1998), childhood (and indeed adult) masturbation gave rise to a considerable moral panic in the nineteenth century. Today, the act *per se* (provided it is solitary) has been more or less accepted as normal and natural. However, research into childhood sexuality – including masturbation – is another matter altogether. Society today is highly sensitized to any hint of child sexual abuse. It would be hard today even to hang around and play marbles with children (as Piaget did, see Chapter 3) without raising eyebrows and concerns about ulterior motives.

To emphasize how the cultural climate has changed, it is worth observing that Kinsey and colleagues (1948) engaged a number of **paedophiles** as researchers, and included considerable amounts of data based on the records these men kept of their sexual encounters with children. For example, their data include information about the time that it took boys to reach orgasm when masturbated. However, by 1966 Broderick made it clear that issues about the early (even 'innate') sexuality of children had become unresearchable. He commented: 'Given the present societal values concerning the sexual stimulation of children it is clear that this question can never be answered for any representative sample of children' (cited in Juhasz 1973: 28–9). Today, the range of issues concerned with children's and young people's sexuality that is regarded as unresearchable has widened further. For example, it is virtually impossible to get ethics committee approval for any questioning of children about sexual matters, and it is notoriously difficult to get research funding for this topic, even where no children are involved at all. The impact of this is that there is an enormous gap in our knowledge, and this lack can come across as suggesting that children are asexual because we know virtually nothing about their sexuality.

By contrast, some topics receive extensive attention by researchers. In the 1950s and 1960s there was a focus on finding out about young people who were engaging in sexual intercourse. Intercourse was a social concern at that time, in part because of a residual puritan regulatory morality. It was also a social concern because it was seen as behaviour which had serious potential outcomes: sexually transmitted diseases and particularly 'unwanted' pregnancies (at a time when both contraception and abortion were difficult to obtain, and considerable stigma was attached to 'having a child out of wedlock'). These days it is AIDS that provides the strongest impetus for research into sexual conduct. Hence Welling *et al.*'s survey concentrated on activities that posed particular risks, and there were even questions about injecting drugs. Female–female sex is generally regarded as 'safer sex' and is far less researched than any other coupling. One consequence of this is that sex between women is made even more invisible – it is already a lot less visible than sex between men, given the differential treatment in law.

This issue of what is made visible by research and what tends to get obscured is not just a matter of arcane postmodern critique. It has very real consequences for people's quality of life and happiness. For example, a recent book entitled *Ageing and Male Sexuality* (Schiavi 1999) is concerned solely with older men's ability to get erections, the problems they face when unable to do so – and hence in engaging in penetrative sex – and advice about how to treat this problem. But there is, for example, no mention at all of oral sex, or, indeed, any other means by which sexual pleasure may be given or obtained. Not only does this reinforce the stereotypical idea that penetrative, vaginal, heterosexual intercourse is the only sex worth having, it, as a result, contributes to creating the problem for which it purports to offer a solution. Think, for a moment, about the consequences of this constrained approach – not least for the sexual partners of these older men. And think about what could be made possible (both for women and for men) if, for example, a man's ability and willingness to give a woman sexual pleasure via cunnilingus were accorded as much value as his capacity to engage in penetration.

Science as storytelling

All of these concerns about the way such data are created and re-created in their telling should, we hope, have alerted you to the possibility that there is much less of a distinction between fact and fiction than scientists would have us believe. Research reports are the products of human meaning-making, as much as are films, fiction and fantasies. The sociologist of science, Michael Mulkay, expresses this cogently:

> If you accept, as I do, that every 'social action' and every 'cultural product' or 'text' has to be treated as a source or as an opportunity for creating multiple meanings, or further texts . . . then forms of analytical discourse which are designed to depict the singular, authoritative, supposedly scientific meanings of social phenomena can never be entirely satisfactory.
>
> (Mulkay 1985: 9–10)

Haraway goes even further, claiming that the practice of science is a storytelling craft:

> The story quality of the sciences . . . is not some pollutant that can be leached out by better methods, say by finer measures and more careful standards of field experiment. . . . The struggle to construct good stories is a major part of the craft.
>
> (Haraway 1984: 79–80)

In other words, the ability to 'tell a good story' about your data is a crucial practitioner skill that psychologists need to learn, and over which they (you?) spend many hours labouring to learn. Much of the trick is to mould one's prose so craftily that it can beguile the reader into assuming that 'the facts speak for themselves'. We will let you into a well-kept secret – facts cannot speak; only people can.

Reports of data are presented as 'telling it like it is', but underneath the glossy surface of objectivity they tell us a partial and selective story. A good illustration of this is the way in which data are used in debates about homosexuality. You may have been surprised by Wellings *et al.*'s low estimates of the proportion of people who are homosexual. In their survey only 6.1 per cent of men and 3.4 per cent of women reported having had *any* same-sex sexual contact, and of these only 1 per cent of men and 0.8 per cent of women said their sexual attraction was mostly or only homosexual. This differs markedly from the usual estimate of about 10 per cent. Diamond (1993) argues that '10 per cent is a political figure', used by gay lobbyists to promote the view that homosexuality is widespread. Moir and Moir (1998) take up the debate mainly around the issue of what they see as the myth of bisexuality – the claim that sexuality is not fixed and that all of us have the capacity to be gay:

> To tolerate something is to put up with what you do not like and gays, of course, want more than toleration; they want acceptance, and believe that the rest of us must give that acceptance. They think we will do so more easily once we recognise that we are all gay – or at least, that all of us are bisexual and so have the capacity for gayness in us.
>
> (Moir and Moir 1998: 34)

From an earlier quote, it is quite clear where Bill Moir is coming from when he makes this argument:

> . . . I don't want them [homosexuals] anywhere near my private space. My private space is you and I, and I don't want a third person in there telling me that with a little gender-bending I could enjoy lifting his shirt.
>
> (Bill Moir, quoting himself in conversation with Anne, in Moir and Moir 1998: 34)

We could say that the 1 per cent figure the Moirs are quoting is also political. But that is the point – in the storytelling of data reporting, all figures are used politically (in the micropolitics-of-power sense of the word, see Chapter 5).

Damn lies?

People are far from naive about the use of statistics by government or other groups which clearly have 'an axe to grind'. We know that we need to be suspicious in circumstances like these. But we are more likely to assume that scientists are cool-headed, apolitical and objective, and that their reports of data can be trusted. In some ways, then, it is all the more important to resist the enchantments that they weave, given that they can wrap them up in a cloak of scientific credibility and respectability. To be fair to the Moirs, although they make extensive use of scientific research to legitimate their claims, they write in a way that is up-front about its polemics (even though they do say 'our aim is to explain, not to campaign', p. 14). You know where you are with them. It is books such as Wellings *et al.*'s that we need to be wary about, for its politics are hidden (and almost certainly its authors would claim that it has none).

This is not to say that such survey work has no value, or that we can learn nothing from it. As feminist psychologists such as Sue Wilkinson (1997) argue strongly, survey data can be useful in, for example, informing the police, the courts and policy makers about the mistreatment of women. As we describe in Chapter 10, such data have been used to challenge myths about rape, and have had a positive impact on the way, for example, the police treat women who report rape. Equally, we would not contest the pragmatic need to, for instance, find out about sexual practices if you want to devise a well-informed policy initiative to reduce the risks posed by AIDS.

Nevertheless, the purpose of this chapter has been to bring home the need to treat survey research with at least as much suspicion when it is couched within the realm of science as it is treated when coming from any other source. As Haraway so eloquently puts it: 'facts are theory-laden, theories are value-laden, values are story-laden' and all of these add up to a highly potent cocktail. And like most cocktails, it has more of a kick than you sometimes realize – treat it with the same degree of caution.

Implications for psychology

- Data are always 'creata' – they are constructed by people, and reflect those people's concerns and interests.
- Reports of data may come across as factual, but they are always 'storied into being'. They categorize the world in particular ways. They highlight some things, make them 'real' to us, and bring these 'real things' to our attention. They also ignore and omit some things, and so obscure them.
- Research into sexual conduct has tended to portray particular versions of gender and sexuality. Alternative understandings are possible.

Further reading

Curt, B. (1994) *Textuality and Tectonics: Troubling Social and Psychological Science*, particularly Chapter 5 'Crafty Dodges: The question and questioning of methods'. Buckingham: Open University Press.

8 Aliens and others

Cyborg monsters in feminist science fiction define quite different political possibilities and limits from those proposed by the mundane fiction of Man and Woman.

(Haraway 1991: 180)

Human creativity has long drawn on the imaginal and the material sexual possibilities provided by the diversity of living creatures. For instance, myth, magic, images and erotic literature are full of human–animal liaisons – possibly the most famous is Leda and the swan (Zeus in disguise). Yet even the most mundane aspects of human experience can hide in their names a history of the mysterious. Take nightmares, for example. This term comes from the Old English *mare* – an evil spirit. A nightmare is, etymologically, an evil spirit that troubles or suffocates the sleeper. In the altered states of consciousness known as the parasomnias we may sleepwalk and/or experience 'night terrors'. Parasomnia is an accepted psychiatric diagnosis (it has even been used as a successful defence against a charge of murder). The alternative word for the demonic sense of nightmare is incubus, a term also used for a male demon who has exhausting sex – for his partners that is – with sleeping women. A succubus, a female demon with similar proclivities, can visit men.

Historically, in psychology it is probably Jungian analytical psychology that has been most drawn to the study of humans, myth and magic (probably the easiest introduction is Jung 1964). But in the present day such myths are usually told as science fiction and science fantasy. In this chapter we will examine some of the ways in which science fiction and fantasy, as literary genres, allow us to explore alternative versions of gender and sexuality – and the issues and questions these explorations open up our understanding of them. We will be using science fiction as an interesting and powerful route to deconstructing our preconceptions about gender and sexuality.

Deconstruction is a common method of analysis in critical work. Erica Burman, writing about her own critical work directed towards developmental psychology, defines deconstruction thus:

> I use the term 'deconstruction' in the sense of laying bare, of bringing under scrutiny, the coherent moral-political themes that developmental psychology elaborates, and to look beyond current frameworks within which developmental psychological investigation has been formulated to take up the broader questions of where these themes fit into the social practices in which psychology functions.
>
> (Burman 1994: 1)

The most usual methods of deconstruction are to examine particular phenomena or praxes either through historical or cultural comparison – Burman uses both. For example, by tracing the origins of developmental psychology she is able to demonstrate that as a discipline it is not – as it is often purported to be – merely the recounting of a set of naturally occurring 'facts' that have been discovered about the ways in which children develop. Rather it is an enterprise that was established by a quite specific group of people (mainly middle-class, white men), which served to meet the demands of the social anxieties that prevailed at the time it was established. Primarily these were concerns about eugenics and fears that 'overbreeding' among the poorer classes was leading to a depletion of the 'stock' of the population. In this way Burman was able to demonstrate that far from the ideologically neutral endeavour that it is presented as being in mainstream psychological texts, the setting up of developmental psychology as a discipline in its own right was a highly political enterprise – it served a particular political agenda.

Science fiction can be used in a similar way as a deconstructive device. As de Lauretis *et al.* (1980) has suggested, science fiction is:

> potentially creative of new forms of social imagination, creative in the sense of mapping out areas where cultural change could take place, of envisioning a different order of relationships between people and between people and things, a different conceptualization of social existence, inclusive of physical and material existence.
>
> (de Lauretis *et al.* 1980: 161)

In other words, science fiction can be made to operate as a potent technique for asking 'what if' questions – What if the world were different? What if there were no sexes and everybody was androgynous? What if there were three sexes rather than two? What if society was dominated by a matriarchy rather than by a patriarchy? What would be the consequences – for men, for women, for the kinds of people we are, for our relationships with each other, for the way we live our lives, for how we would rear our children, for the language we would use and the possible futures to which we might aspire?

You have already met this kind of 'literature-as-thought-experiment' in Chapter 6, where we used an illustration from Samuel Butler's *Erewhon Revisited* (Butler 1901) to gain insight into the way that particular assumptions (in that case about responsibility for interpersonal conflict) can be challenged. Butler ironized the usual assumption that it is a violent husband who should be held responsible for his aggression towards his wife. Instead, in his fantasy world – Erewhon – it is the wife who sees herself as to blame (because she was intolerant of his 'unusually peevish, irritable temper') and hence she sees *herself* as needing to take action (learning to become more tolerant). By drawing parallels with the way in which battered wives may see themselves and are often seen by others as 'asking for it', we were able to expose the reversal of agency (discussed in Chapter 5) operating in this kind of 'victim blaming' thinking.

Science fiction as a deconstructive device

This kind of 'what if' speculation is the basis of much science fiction/ fantasy writing. Sexuality and/or gender have often been targeted for such treatment, especially in the sub-genre of feminist science fiction (see Lefanu 1988 for a detailed treatment). Of course, they are more often not targeted. Science fiction is very much a male-dominated field, both in its authorship and readership. Its mainstream plays around mainly with the technical possibilities opened up by speculative innovations that make, say, space travel possible over immense distances and hence allow contact between humans and aliens from other worlds. In such stories the masculinities and femininities of 'our' world (that is, the world of the USA of the twentieth and twenty-first century – and, to a lesser extent, other Western culture) are usually simply transported into the future without being questioned. From *Star Wars* (almost any episode you care to choose) to *Dune* to *Blade Runner*, women (human or alien) tend to be the 'damsels in distress' – often exotic, sometimes powerful – but who still need to be rescued by the male heroes.

Where science fiction has played around with sexuality and gender it has tended to make use of notions of 'the alien' and 'the other' in order to expose to scrutiny our own taken-for-granted modes. Probably the best-known exponent of this kind of science fiction writing is Ursula Le Guin, particularly in her books *The Left Hand of Darkness* (1969) and *The Dispossessed* (1974).

The Left Hand of Darkness is set on the planet Gethen. In it Le Guin explores what life might be like in a world lacking in sexual difference – and hence sexual desire and sexual repression. Physiologically, most of the time, Gethenians are asexual and androgynous – neither male nor female. However, periodically they cycle into 'kemmer' and emerge, unpredictably, as temporary males or females. The concept is powerful and clearly appealed to women readers and more 'liberal' men of the time (see Lefanu 1988: 131). Another version of androgyny featured in Mary Gentle's two books, *Golden Witchbreed* (1983) and *Ancient Light* (1987). In these novels, the alien Orthians are neuter until adolescence. By consequence, children in this society are socialized and educated in a gender-neutral manner.

Language games

Embarrassingly, to current ears, the Gethenian protagonist in *The Left Hand of Darkness* is always referred to as 'he'. There have been several resolutions of the gendered personal pronoun tried out in science fiction. Probably the neatest linguistic solution is that employed by Marge Piercy in *Woman on the Edge of Time* (1976): per. Per is perturbating – it does some of the work to be found in the current popular use of 'partner'. We can put the two neatly together to illustrate the effects and the distinction.

Contemporary new speaker: Do you want to bring your partner along to the party too?
Gethenian time traveller: I don't know, I'll ask per.

For us (and presumably for the contemporary new speaker), the sex marker matters because it reveals whether you are talking to someone who is heterosexual or homosexual. An answer of either 'I'll ask him' or 'I'll ask her' allows us to tell this in a way that 'I'll ask per' does not. The Gethenian answer dissolves the possibility that anything that matters is at issue. The point such an exchange makes is that because in such a life-world both the nature of the relationship to and the gender of the person concerned are not revealed, our preconceptions about gender and about the significance of particular kinds of relationship are rendered 'unsayable' and hence become effectively unthinkable. The effect of gendering a person's partner is, if not removed, at least muted.

Indeed, a similar effect was deliberately gained when feminists introduced the title Ms to replace Miss or Mrs in the 1970s. They did so in order to give adult women the same opacity that men had always had when called Mr – you cannot tell, from this title, whether or not a man is or has been married. And, presumably, this is why the term Ms aroused such hostility when it first came into common parlance – certainly most times when a woman tried to use it at that time, it brought forth sneers and accusations of being a bra-burning feminist.

Alternative sexualities, alternative genders

This is one of the advantages of exploring gender through science fiction. It allows us to contemplate what is possible, simply by changing social and linguistic conventions. Once we see that there are alternative realities to our own, then we can get a better understanding of just how much our own realities are set by convention rather than being 'naturally occurring', and hence how much they are open to change.

Much of *Woman on the Edge of Time* fits better in our category of alternative cultures. However, within Piercy's future Utopia (Mattapoisett) we would note here that the ironing out of gender difference, far beyond linguistics, is a crucial element. Another, and earlier, female 'chameleon' in science fiction was C.L. Moore. We have taken the term 'chameleon' from Pearson, who sees it as common mode for women writers: 'female writers show their usual chameleon ability to accommodate themselves to traditional androcentric models, and yet simultaneously to subvert these modes from within' (Pearson 1990: 11).

Pearson argues that Moore frequently used a narrative structure in which the 'battle of the sexes' was hyperbolized into human (male)/alien female encounters. In these encounters, the initial meeting is often cast as a received androcentric rescue of the alien 'victim' by the male 'hero'. However, in what follows, the purported hero becomes a victim of the more powerful, more sexual alien. Beyond displaced reworkings of the 'war between the sexes' science fiction is also a major site for exploring non-heterosexual relationships and accounts of temporary and permanent sex changes and exchanges. One of most versatile is provided by Samuel Delany, in *Triton* (1977). Delany is one of the few male writers sometimes taken seriously (as opposed to being deconstructed) in feminist-informed writers in the genre.

In the 1950s, the realities of nuclear politics opposed order and chaos. The potential of a 'new order' led to a whole genre of survivalist post-nuclear holocaust stories. Concern with its potential for chaos spawned the mutant narrative and the monster ant (and so on) horror movies of the time. Mutants and hybrids are frequently sterile and/or asexual. As such they can stand in for other powers, like the psychic and tyrannical Mule of Asimov's *Second Foundation* (1964).

By the 1960s science fiction had become responsive to the sexually liberatory possibilities permitted by the emerging climate of permissiveness. For example, the future-woman warrior Barbarella made the transit from strip cartoon to the movies in 1968. Barbarella (albeit in the hardly feminist-identified shape of Jane Fonda) proved her liberation by defeating 'torture' in the Orgasmatron – her ability to be subjected to orgasmic overload and survive. But in the movie, Barbarella, like the other 'liberated chicks' of the time, is still conquered by the 'true love' of a 'real' man. We might question how far she was a serious icon of liberated female sexuality, and how far she simply fed into the male fantasies of that period – of a woman with a voracious sexual appetite but who is none the less helpless when she finds a man who can satisfy her.

The idea being worked here is that far from the pious, pure and submissive shrinking violet of Victorian 'true womanhood', the modern woman is sexy, experienced and dominant – although how new this is, given the turn-on 'Miss Whiplash' can be for many men, is debatable. But at the same time the women's liberation movement of the 1960s and 1970s clearly also exposed major male anxieties. The possibilities of an interventional male backlash were cleverly picked up by author Ira Levin (also responsible for *Rosemary's Baby*) in a theme which became a catch-phrase for androcentric female socialization, *The Stepford Wives* (1972). In this book (and its subsequent movie) the men of Stepford replace their 'uppity' wives – wives who were getting too far into women's liberation for comfort – with android versions who are appropriately docile and subservient. Levin's portrayal of robot-like acquiescence provided a powerfully ironizing image of femininity – one where obedience is valued more than the ability to think. In so doing it brought into sharp focus the 'war of the sexes' going on at the time. The electronic, prosthetic, alien-human and even humorous aspects of sexual encounters were widely explored in 1970s science fiction. A collection of exemplary short stories of varied quality was put together by Hill (1978) under the (possibly ironic) title *The Shape of Sex to Come.*

What can we learn from the ler?

At the same time, genomic unravelling had reached the point where the theme of super-people could be given a new credibility. A good illustration here is the way that M.(ichael) A. Foster offers an elaborate construction of a deliberately modified new species: the *ler*. In his book *The Gameplayers of Zan* (1979b) he portrays the *ler* as based on human stock, but as, in many ways, 'superior' to humans. They therefore choose a 'separatist' existence from their human creators. How a 'mere' human male encounters a female *ler* during her sexually insatiable but sterile adolescence is a subtheme of his second book *The Warriors of Dawn* (1979a).

The books make interesting reading in particular because of the way that Foster invests the *ler* with identities in which gender is not significant. Here is how a *ler* sociologist, Fellirian, explains *ler* characteristics:

> 'The Four Determinants of a person are these: Aspect, Phase, Class, Position'. She added fastidiously 'Gender is not a determinant. So, then, if one of us knows all four determinants of another person, we are thereby able to predict, with reasonable accuracy, what that person will do in various circumstances.'
>
> (Foster 1979: 40)

Foster invents for the *ler* a quite different set of conventions for family relationships from those of humans – a four-person 'braiding' – and identities which relate to an individual's position in the braid: *Zerh* ('extra'), *Thes* (younger outsibling), *Nerh* (elder outsibling) and *Toorh* (insibling). Braiding consists of a complex sequence of relationships between successive generations. A *Toorh* and a *Zerh*, one male and one female and coming from different families, mate and produce a child, who is the *Nerh*.

Subsequently the *Toorh* and *Zerh* choose a partner for each other (one *Thes* and one *Nerh*), and each of them mate, producing a child each: insiblings – one *Zerh* and one *Toorh*. Finally, the *Thes* and *Nerh* mate and produce a *Nerh*. Thus each braiding involves four adults who, between them, produce four children. The braid maintains continuity by the *Toorh* child staying with the family and, in time, becoming the parent of the next generation. The *Zerh* child, when s/he reaches sexual maturity, moves to another family and pairs with its *Toorh*.

If you are having trouble understanding all this, do not worry – it is complicated and its details do not really matter. What does matter is the *what if?* speculation about the impact of such a family structure – what do you suppose would be the consequences of such an arrangement? One that Foster explores is what kinds of sibling relationships it produces. He does this through the device of the human – Vance – contemplating Fellirian's relationship with her Insibling:

> This bothered Vance . . . in some unconscious manner he could not quite fathom; the insiblings did not have common biological parents, yet they were raised together. They were always close in age, separations of more than a year being so rare as not to be worth mentioning. In some ways, closer than a brother and sister in the human analogue. Indeed closer, since the ler had no incest taboo. This circumstance took the ancient argument of nature versus nurture, genetics against culture, and brought it head-on into direct opposition. The insiblings were alike and different, all at the same time.
>
> (Foster 1979: 48)

The combination of a family producing children who were genetically unrelated but none the less siblings in their upbringing and affiliations and the lack of incest taboo does some things to family relationships that are very strange to us. For a start, it brings sex into the family – the implication is clear that insiblings sometimes have sex with each other. Indeed elsewhere in the book we discover that *ler* adolescents are highly sexed yet sterile. They take casual sex partners as sexual recreation with the full approval of their parents and there is even a *ler* word for this – *didhosi*.

If you recall from Chapters 5 and 6, critical approaches make much of the power of language to construct reality. The concept of recreational sex, with no claim to it being anything to do with love, as an accepted and expected part of growing up fundamentally changes what a 'casual sex partner' means. Taking a *didhosi* for recreational sex is seen as a positive thing to do rather than something to be ashamed of. Imagine a world in which adolescents were free – through both biology and custom – and even expected to regularly have recreational sex with a variety of *didhosi* before settling down to their childbearing responsibilities to their braid in adulthood. At a stroke, many of what we see as 'adolescent problems' with regard to sexuality – promiscuity, teenage pregnancy, a girl getting a bad reputation or settling down too young – are eradicated. So too is divorce, since sexuality and procreation are largely detached from one another. In some ways the *ler* arrangements for having and raising children are similar to arranged marriages in our culture – save that both young men *and* young women are free to 'sow their wild oats' without any expectation that love is involved, or that having sex with someone could lead to 'falling in love'. In the 1970s these were very radical possibilities indeed in US culture, and even today (if in a more subtle way) go against our expectations of what sex means.

Utopias and dystopias

Utopias and dystopias, by painting exaggerated images of the-world-as-it-could-be, have long been used to raise questions about the-world-as-it-is. They are, in other words, political devices in other clothes – and highly salient to our purposes here. The rights of women and their current oppression in a gendered culture became a key issue at the start of modernism (the late eighteenth-century). Pearson (1990) disinters an interesting example from a male author, James Lawrence: *The Empire of the Nairs: or the Rights of Women, An Utopian Romance* (*c.* 1800). In this book a sexually egalitarian culture is outlined. In their recovery of 'roots', feminists often turn to Mary Bradley Lane's *Mizora* ([1890] 2000) and Charlotte Perkins Gilman's *Herland* (1915). These first-wave feminist texts very much reflect the political concerns of the feminism of their time and place. The theme of separatism was strong, and was presented as a necessary condition for other changes to the social order. Early feminist utopias tend to be egalitarian communes operating agricultural or 'mixed' economies with a sexual permissiveness that challenges received notions of 'compulsory monogamy'. They have considerable resonance with the utopian thinking of the early kibbutz movement.

By contrast, the recent feminisms are plural, exploring many possibilities. So too are their grounding horrors – from the present-awful of *Woman on the Edge of Time* (see earlier), through the near-present drear of Zoë Fairburns' *Benefits* (1979) to the dystopian patriarchy of Margaret Atwood's *The Handmaid's Tale* (1986). However, whereas dystopian writing can often 'get away with' (say, by the very taken-for-grantedness of its assumed mechanisms of emergence) its assumptive reality, utopian writing often wants to proselytize, even to celebrate, its 'roads to freedom'. In the modern feminisms these are multiple and include:

- human agency (particularly those employing women's particular strengths, for example in language), for example Elgin, *Native Tongue* (1985);
- technology (particularly as applied to reproduction), for example Piercy, *Woman on the Edge of Time* (1976);
- mysticism and magic (as especially, and separately, women's), for example Gearheart's *The Wanderground* (1985); and

- the forging of disparate communities, occupied by 'real' and diverse characters none of whom is male, for example the 'Riding Women' and 'Free-Fems' of Charnas' *Motherlines* (1980).

(For more details of these texts and themes, although not as structured here, see Lefanu 1988.)

Alternative analytics and the challenge for psychology

In conceptual as well as literal terms, what we perceive is a function of our viewpoint. Even in mainstream psychology it is recognized that viewpoint does not imply only a position in physical space but the condition of the viewer. For example, in social psychology, the concept of gender schema (see Chapter 3) has been used to explain individual differences in the processing of gender-related information. However, the limits of our theories tend to be set by the limits of our realities. The realities of psychology have in the past been (and to a large extent still are) bounded by who psychologists *are* in terms of:

- their *gender*: psychology was originally a largely male preserve. Although it is now moving towards a predominantly female student intake, much of its status positions and power remain male-dominated;
- their *social class*: although more open to 'alternative entry' than, say, mathematics, psychology still recruits its students most heavily from better-educated, better-paid backgrounds;
- their *ethnic and national origins*: psychology was largely shaped in the USA, Northern Europe and the English-speaking British Commonwealth. Wherever it operates, disadvantaged minorities are markedly under-represented;
- their *politics*: the discipline is broadly liberal-humanistic in posture, with a strong investment in regulation (the governmentality of the self). Radical politics are generally marginalized;
- their *sexuality/gender orientation*: medical psychology gave the discipline a pathologizing stance on anything other than heterosexuality. Notions of normality and adjustment did the same for personality theory and developmental psychology. Only recently has sexual politics been given academic recognition in psychology (notably in, and through, feminist psychology).

In other words, psychology has been, and still is, very limited in its world-view. It is severely underinformed by views from the margins, and indeed treats those who occupy marginal status as 'alien' and/or 'other'. But things are changing, both within psychology and outwith it.

Challenges from within include the feminist and postmodern/social constructionist approaches we outlined in Chapters 5 and 6. Challenges from the outside come from many quarters. Possibly the one that will have most effect is a practical one – the emergence of cybersex activity on the internet (Wakeford 1997). It is now possible for anyone with access to the internet to explore – and to participate in – 'alternative sexualities' in a medium that is less a '*What if*' speculation than a '*What if*' praxis, whereby new and innovative cyber-sexualities become possible. Not only can men pass as women on the internet and vice versa, but a person who purports to be lesbian could be a man, or a person who purports to be gay could be straight – it is now easy to engage in 'gender tourism', in other words. The internet is clearly capable of being perturbating, not just experientially but because it raises both new possibilities (cyber-sex as the ultimate 'safe sex') and new dilemmas (are you 'cheating' on your partner-in-actuality if you indulge in cyber-sex with another?).

Equally the activities of the alien and the other take many forms more broadly in culture, for example:

- as an influence on design, including body design (for example, piercing);
- as an impact on popular culture (for example, in music, dance and film-making); and
- as a stimulant both to slang and to ordinary spoken language.

However, it is unusual for the alien and the other to formally theorize (that is, theorize in ways that the centre recognizes) themselves, and even more unusual for them to do so, in part, from within the mainstream as academics. It is worth noting, though, that there are established precedents. The role of Jewish academics is the most obvious example. In the domain of gender and sexuality, they have been far from marginalized – Freud, as we saw in Chapter 3, is a good case in point. However, this is changing with the introduction of the new disciplines of gay and queer theory.

Gay and queer theory

In the form of gay and queer theory, the alien and other has both placed itself as a voice in the centre and, sometimes, been listened to. This can be primarily a challenge – as when the paucity of theorization on heterosexuality was thrown back at heterosexual feminists (see Chapter 5). But, perhaps more crucially, there has also been a major effort in first-order theorizing (see, for example, Medhurst and Hunt 1997; Nardi and Schneider 1998). At the heart of this theorizing has been a troubling of the very concepts around which this book is cast: gender and sexuality. Yet their very linking can be problematic, as Pringle notes, for in their academic life theorists much of the time 'ignore each other completely, with the result that there is a large literature which treats sexuality as if gender barely exists and another literature on gender that ignores or marginalizes sexuality' (Pringle, 1992: 72–3).

Following Pringle's argument this is, in part, the result of a muted third player – sex. For example, if sexuality is construed as matter of some entity such as libido or sexual drive, then men's sexuality and women's sexuality are basically alike (rather like we tend to assume that hunger and thirst are asexual). This gives a theoretical simplicity, but at the price, feminists might argue, of a sexuality constructed largely by male researchers and in implicit male terms. Or, as gay theorists might argue, of a sexuality constructed largely by heterosexual theorists and in more explicitly heterosexual terms. A muted fourth player now enters the analysis – power.

Through Reich (see Chapter 4), liberatory theorists such as Marcuse (1955) bestowed on the New Left of the late 1960s to early 1970s a view of sexuality as a force antithetical to power (see also Weeks 1986). This became a significant focus of critique for feminists of this period, who argued that it was opaque as to the different positioning in relation to sexuality of gays and straights, men and women. Indeed, liberation was seen as part of the problem rather than part of the solution. Sex, in a patriarchy, was, in some ways, power. Sexual power was the key to domination (as the slogan had it: 'every man is a potential rapist'). With men (and sex with men, 'sleeping with the enemy') now problematized, women's sexuality could then be retheorized as 'different' and lesbianism valorized.

These, however, were not the central concerns for gay theorists. Foucault was a dominant influence here (Probyn 1997) and they were more concerned with challenging dominant, normative theories of sexual identity that positioned them as deviant. Associations with effeminacy were challenged by gay machismo – gender, in other words, decoupled from sexuality. The same could be argued of sado-masochism subculture. In the context of a recognition of the contrasts in theoretical agendas between the gay and feminist-lesbian communities, the term 'homosexual' itself became open to deconstruction as gender-opaque. This has, understandably, concerned feminist-lesbian theory much more than gay theory. Indeed, as a generality, gay theory tends to see man/woman similarities, whereas some feminist theory tends to highlight difference – indeed, to use it as an analytic (in Pringle's (1992: 76) terminology, 'sexual difference theory').

Poststructuralism added one further complication to theorization: discourse (see Chapter 6). Discourse became a key analytic, seen as having massive formative and pre-formative powers. Reading Foucault that way leaves us with discourses on sexuality that shape the only sex (and non-sex) we can know. Similarly, Butler (1990: 7) talks of 'the apparatuses of gender' as productive of naturalized sex. Of course, a biology that is itself socially constructed allows a sex that is no longer essentialized. We could, in that sense, have written this book around the themes of sex and sexuality instead of gender and sexuality. It was largely to avoid the whiff of essentialism, both for our own comfort and to achieve the catchment we had intended, that we did not.

Implications for psychology

- From their beginnings, literature and art have often explored alternative constructions of gender and sexuality, demonstrating just how 'fixed' conventional psychological ideas are.
- Science fiction is a particularly fertile genre for considering alternative worlds, in which gender and sexuality operate in quite different ways from our own. Psychologists can learn a lot from the possibilities this opens up.
- More recently, both within psychology (for example, feminist psychology) and outwith it (such as gay and women's studies), academics have begun to challenge the dominant malestream standpoint of conventional psychology. Not only do they offer different understandings, they also provide the theory with which to change the material conditions of life for those constructed as alien and other.

Further reading

Gordo-Lopez, A. and Parker, I. (eds) (1999) *Cyberpsychology*. Basingstoke: Macmillan.

Lefanu, S. (1988) *In the Chinks of the World Machine*. London: The Women's Press.

9 Bodies

When a cat wants to eat her kittens, she calls them mice.

(Old Turkish Proverb)

Everywhere you look there seems to be a fascination with the body. Newspapers, magazines and television deluge us with articles, adverts and programmes about body image, eating disorders, plastic surgery; how to make bodies attractive and beautiful and/or healthy and fit; how to lose weight, firm up, dry out, chill out, get rid of cellulite. Going to the gym or exercise class, therapies from massage to reflexology, Alexander technique to chiropractic – it can feel as though we have become obsessed with our bodies.

Bodies are also becoming a preoccupation for academics throughout the social sciences, with a number of dedicated journals and a proliferation of texts (see, for example, Lupton 1996; Turner 1996; Ussher 1997; Bayer and Shotter 1998; Nettleton and Watson 1998; Sagara 1998; Stam 1998). In this chapter we cannot begin to do justice to all this theorizing, and so we have been highly selective in our focus. The idea is to give you just a taster which, hopefully, will whet your appetite for more.

The body exposed

In the social sciences one of the earliest targets for studies of the body was the situation where the normally hidden body is exposed – the medical examination. Henslin and Biggs (1971), a dramaturgical sociologist and an obstetrical nurse, carried out an analysis of vaginal examinations in medical settings. Their conclusion was that a complex ritual was being performed. During the examination the patient was transformed from a 'person' to a 'pelvis'. The paper assumes that there is a male gynaecologist (statistically highly likely in the USA at that time) who absents himself while the patient removes her underwear and a nurse places a drape over her hips. In this way, when the gynaecologist returns, he faces just her pelvis. No eye contact is possible with the patient. From his point of view it is not she who is exposed but just her pelvis. From her point of view she is dressed (that is, all she can see is the drape). In this way, the authors suggest, a complex set of rules is played out by the actors, which enables a sacred and private part of the body to be approached without the usual taboos being breached.

Clearly, from a feminist perspective, there is something missing from this research – the woman's understanding of what was going on. A powerful treatment of that theme has been provided by Emily Martin, a US anthropologist turning inward to study her own, strange tribe of Americans. Although her book is quite old now, it still offers, we believe, the best starting-point into the way that social scientists have approached the study of women's bodies. Martin (1987) reports on the outcome of 165 interviews conducted with women who were diverse in age, social class and ethnicity. The interviews covered three important domains of women's bodily experiences: menstruation, childbirth and menopause. Martin's approach to research was feminist-informed (Chapter 5). Her book is rich in women's accounts and is impossible to summarize with justice (sometimes you just have to read things in the original), but one paragraph captures the spirit of her argument:

> What I would like to suggest . . . is that the seemingly abstract code of medical science in fact tells a very concrete story rooted in our own particular form of social hierarchy and control. Usually we do not hear the story, we only hear the 'facts' and that is what makes science so powerful. But women – whose bodily experience is denigrated and demolished by models implying failed production, waste, decay and breakdown – have it literally within them to confront the story science tells with another story, based on their own experience.
>
> (Martin 1987: 197)

Martin's refusal to accept the absolute separation of science and storytelling (fact and fiction) is part of the challenge that both feminist and critical human scientists have put to their mainstream disciplines, as we saw in Haraway's work (see Chapters 7 and 8). The first part, at least, of the quotation could be made about any human science and certainly about psychology. Such a critique is not denying the body, but rather arguing that all knowledge of the body (that is, both ordinary and professional) is constructed. If we become, or are rendered, singularized around one representation, then we become its plaything (and the plaything of its promoters). For example, premenstrual syndrome (see Chapter 1) does not become the only story around by virtue of being a 'syndrome' – unless we let it.

Another excellent starting-point is a book chapter which has one of our favourite titles in the whole literature: 'A funny thing happened on the way to the orifice: Women in gynaecology textbooks' (Scully and Bart 1980). It comprises a content analysis of 28 gynaecology textbooks, and uses this to explore how the knowledge of women's bodies was constructed by medical men, and some of the implications of the way this knowledge was formed and used.

The rebellious body

One of the attractions of studying the body is its materiality. It provides a site of study where theorists are forced to examine the interplay between the material world of real things and the constructed world of knowledge – what Mulkay (1985) calls 'the World and the Word'. As we saw in Chapter 1, gender and sexuality can be strongly influenced by the workings of the body. Sometimes the impact of its materiality can be very real indeed:

> A girl entered hospital complaining of vague abdominal and other symptoms . . . the indications were too vague for anything except an 'expectant' policy, so the girl was discharged and told to come back again should there be any marked change. This she did some months later. The change was marked indeed. Her auburn hair seemed to have invaded her cheeks and chin – in fact, she had begun to develop a red beard. The voice had deepened and become more masculine. In the abdomen a distinct growth could be felt and consequently an exploratory operation was undertaken. A benign tumour was discovered pressing upon one of the suprarenal glands and was removed. The sequel was remarkable. Within a short time the bronze beard was shed and the voice resumed its feminine pitch and timbre. The superficial signs of masculinity disappeared.
>
> (Mottram 1952: 89–90)

Cortico-steroid abnormalities (of which this is an example) give rise to dramatic physical effects on a person's gendered body characteristics and sexual behaviour. Mottram also describes the parallel case of a man whose tumour led to breast development, putting on weight and reduction in sex drive and potency in the man concerned – also simply and effectively treated by the removal of the tumour. Other similar syndromes include the effects of an underactive thyroid gland. This results in mental lethargy, sterility and male impotence as well as hairlessness and skin degeneration. These symptoms disappear when the person is given carefully controlled maintenance doses of thyroxin.

In cases like these we take it for granted that the sufferer is entitled to medical treatment which will reinstate 'normal' function. The same is true when a problem arises from a birth defect or injury. For example, women born without a vagina and boys whose testicles do not descend into the scrotum will be offered restorative surgery as a matter of course. However, the situation over domains such as genital and breast restructuring through *cosmetic* plastic surgery, infertility treatments and, most recently, the 'anti-impotence' drug Viagra, is much more troublesome. So too are surgical interventions such as the reconstruction of a woman's hymen. What *can* be done to the body does not necessarily warrant what *should* be done. Female circumcision is an obvious extreme example, although male circumcision is also now being called into question (Katz 1998).

Material practices: circumcision

Circumcision is a good example of what is at issue here, since it is so self-evidently an issue of *culture* and so bound up in what it *means and signifies* to be circumcised or not. Katz describes male circumcision from the standpoint of a secular Jewish man: 'I was quite proud to circumcise my sons, and saw their circumcision as a slightly risky but inevitable duty which needed to be undertaken if they were to take their places in the community' (Katz 1998: 92). Nelson Mandela received his own circumcision in adolescence, as part of his rite of passage into adulthood, and thus could give a first-hand account. For Mandela it was an incredibly painful experience, but also very exciting and enormously significant:

> There was excitement in the crowd, and I shuddered slightly, knowing that the ritual was about to begin. . . . The old man would use his assegai to change us from boys to men with a single blow. . . . Without a word he took my foreskin, pulled it forward, and then, in a single motion, brought down his assegai. I felt as if fire was shooting through my veins; the pain was so intense I buried my chin in my chest. Many seconds seemed to pass before I remembered the cry, and then I recovered and I called out 'Ndiyindonda' (I am a man).
> (Mandela 1994: 25–6)

Although they each acknowledge the pain and risks of male circumcision, both of these descriptions, coming from quite different cultures, are couched in positive terms. Male circumcision in both cases 'inscribes on the body' a critical transition for the individual – into inclusion in a cultural community in the case of a secular Jew; from boyhood to manhood for an African in the setting in which Mandela's circumcision took place. Contrast this with the term more commonly used in the West to describe female circumcision – female genital mutilation, a boo-word if there ever was one (see Cranston 1953, also described in Chapter 6). Yet it is as culturally embedded as male circumcision, is also practised in many cultures, and has the same long history (Lightfoot-Klein 1989; Dorkenoo and Elworthy 1992).

Katz (1998) contrasts the very different ways in which these two practices are treated in the UK. *All* forms of female genital mutilation are proscribed in law (by the Prohibition of Female Circumcision Act 1985), whereas *no* form of male circumcision is legally proscribed. Male circumcision is almost universally regarded as normal and acceptable, whereas female genital mutilation is almost universally seen as barbaric and totally unacceptable. In part, Katz argues, this is because the physical consequences and risks are different. Female circumcision varies in its form, but it usually involves the excision of the clitoris and may include the surgical closure (for example, with thorns) of the vagina in a way that leaves only a very small opening. There is a high risk of infection, both from the practice itself and from its aftermath (for example, where the vagina has been closed, it has to be opened to allow sexual intercourse – often with a knife). But Katz also comments that female circumcision is also much more 'other' to Western sensibilities, and those who practise it (mainly rural African refugees) are a less powerful group to confront than the Jewish and Muslim communities. And crucially, he observes, female circumcision 'has become part of the global struggle for women's rights', not surprising given both its symbolic meaning and its strategic use (that is, to de-sex women and forcibly impose virginity and fidelity).

We might add another reason why male and female circumcision are viewed differently: they have different implications for the person's sexuality and are done for different reasons. Male circumcision is often justified as having benefits for hygiene – the removal of the foreskin makes the head of the penis easier to keep clean. There are also claims that it has benefits for the man's sexual response. By contrast, female circumcision, where the clitoris is excised, reduces a woman's capacity for sexual response (although orgasm is still possible with a skilled lover). Where the vagina is closed up, this prevents a woman from having penetrative sex unless and until the vagina is opened up again. It is not hard to see these as regulatory practices, intended to control a woman's sexuality.

Body politics

The rights that people have over their own bodies, over the bodies of those for whom they have responsibility, and over the bodies of others – all these have generated intense debate both in feminism and more generally. Many of these issues relate to gender and sexuality. Whether a foetus is a person in its own right, a parasite in a woman's body or a simple biological entity; whether penises 'invade' or 'penetrate' vaginas or whether vaginas 'engulf' or 'absorb' penises; whether face-lifts and breast enhancements are forms of beautification or mutilation – these are not just matters of linguistic construction, of boo-words and hurrah-words, they exemplify a whole new area of concern: the politics of the body.

One of the greatest achievements of the climate of perturbation was to erode faith in the reasonableness and self-evidently obviousness of the taken-for-granted world, and to bring to our attention the practical and moral consequences of 'what passes for knowledge' (Berger and Luckmann 1966). And, as the examples above show, nowhere is this more relevant than in performances and manifestations of gender and sexuality.

Abortion

The issue of abortion illustrates this well. The Turkish proverb with which we began this chapter is instructive here. Each different understanding of the nature of the foetus carries with it a different warrant for action. If a foetus is a 'person in its own right' from the moment of conception – a person with a soul (in religious terms) or full human rights (in liberal-humanistic terms) – then he or she is entitled to the full protection of the law against being aborted. Since the foetus is a person, this would be murder. If, by contrast, the foetus is a parasite, where its presence in a woman's body is debilitating at best and potentially lethal at worst, then the woman is fully entitled to have it surgically removed to protect her own health. Yet again, if the foetus is no more than a biological entity – simply a bundle of cells in the process of development – then its fate is a matter for the woman to choose. She may well consult with others (for example, with her partner about whether they can afford to have a baby, or with a doctor about the chances of congenital deformity). But in the end it is she who is entitled to make the cost–benefit analysis between 'keeping the baby' (that is, according the foetus the potential to become a child) and 'having an abortion' (that is, refusing the foetus the potential to become a child).

This illustration demonstrates three things clearly. First, it shows that the 'knowledge' that people have about the body differs markedly according to who they are and where they are coming from. It brings home the argument made in Chapter 6 that knowledge is always contingent on the time and cultural location in which it has been made and is maintained and mongered. If you are a devout Roman Catholic, for example, there is no doubt which one of these knowledges will be powerfully true for you. Second, it shows that knowledge can never be separated from issues of ideology. It brings home the argument made in Chapter 7 that 'facts are theory-laden, theories are value-laden' (Haraway 1984: 79). Third, it shows that knowledge usually implies consequences, and hence can be (and often is) used to warrant action.

Warranting action

The philosopher Toulmin carried out a detailed analysis of how argument works. He drew a distinction between 'the *claim* or conclusion whose merits we are seeking to establish (C) and the facts we appeal to as a foundation for the claim – what I shall refer to as our *data* (D)' (Toulmin 1958: 97; emphasis in the original). The link between D (data) and C (claim) can, he suggested, be established only by drawing on a third kind of proposition – **warrants** (W) 'which can act as bridges, and authorise the sort of step to which our particular argument commits us' (p. 98). We can think of the basic structure of the argument like this:

D ———————— (since W) ————————→ So C

If we apply this to the arguments about abortion, we can see that in the 'pro-life' argument, the datum (the woman is pregnant) is seen to lead to the claim or conclusion that she should keep the baby through the warrant that the foetus is a person – an unborn child, and children (whether born or unborn), merit protection. Equally, the 'pro-choice' argument also works through a warrant – albeit a very different one. The datum (the woman is pregnant) is seen to lead to the claim or conclusion that she has a right to choose to have an abortion through the warrant that she has a right to control her own body, including having control over the biological entity which is the foetus.

In each case it is the warrant which legitimates the claim or conclusion. Warrants are thus rhetorical devices, whereby language is used strategically to justify taking (or not taking) certain kinds of actions. Notice too that the labels used to describe the arguments – pro-life and pro-choice – are also rhetorical devices being used strategically. Both are very much hurrah-terms, inviting agreement – who would want to be either anti-life or anti-choice?

Harm warranting

O'Dell (1997, 1998) has carried out a detailed theoretical and empirical analysis of a particular form of warranting in which psychology is strongly implicated – **harm warrants.** She argues that 'harm warranting' is frequently used to justify intervention (governmentality in Foucaultian terms). Concern over female circumcision is a good example of what she means. Most of the arguments against this practice make use of its harmfulness to warrant its prohibition:

D ————————	(since W) ————————→	So C
female circumcision	carries a high risk of injury and infection	so it should be banned

However, the harm here is physical; it is clearly observable on the body. Like the physical abuse and neglect of children, the harm is 'obvious', and so it is 'obviously' necessary to intervene to protect children from harm. Psychology (and the 'psy' complex more generally, see Chapter 6) has provided the knowledge to massively extend the harm warrant beyond harm done to the physical body to psychological and emotional harm. This is the main justification for intervention in situations where child sexual abuse is suspected. The argument goes like this:

D ————————	(since W) ————————→	So C
child sexual abuse	carries a high risk of psychological and and emotional harm	so intervention is to stop it and prevent and stop it

The 'psy' complex achieves this warrant in two ways. First it does so by making links between the experience of sexual abuse and behaviour. Children who have been sexually abused are seen, for example, as likely to become 'sexualized' in the way they behave towards adults. This makes them more vulnerable to being sexually abused again (either by the same perpetrator or by others). Second, it does so by recourse to psychodynamic theory (see Chapter 3). Psychodynamic theory views experiences of trauma in childhood as causing severe psychic disruption, with massively negative consequences for adult mental health. Sexual abuse in childhood is seen as causing a whole host of psychological problems: eating disorders, multiple personality, depression, suicide, sexual dysfunction – it is a long list (see O'Dell 1998 for a detailed examination of these). The psychological harm warrant is by far the most influential (see, for example, Miller 1986).

The psychological harm warrant embodies harm through the psychodynamic process of somatization. This is where psychological reactions to trauma (unpleasant life events, relationship problems and so on) are seen to become manifested in bodily reactions. Stress is a prime example. External stressors are held to give rise, through psychodynamic forces, to a whole host of bodily reactions – increases in adrenaline, disruption of digestion, lowering of immune reactions and so on – which then have a direct detrimental impact on bodily health and well-being. These include raising blood pressure, causing stomach ulcers and increasing susceptibility to disease (see Stainton Rogers 1991; Brown 1997 for more detailed expositions of these arguments).

O'Dell carried out a meticulous analysis of the scientific evidence for the emotional and psychological damage done by the sexual abuse of children. She worked from two of the best-known **symptomologies** (that is, lists of symptoms associated with child sexual abuse, together with the scientific evidence cited to support each one). Her analysis showed that this 'evidence' is far from satisfactory, even when judged against basic standards of empirical science. Much of the evidence derived from clinical observations, opinions expressed by clinicians and therapists, and first-hand accounts in books and stories written by abuse survivors. A number of the empirical studies are misquoted, and even those that derived from systematic survey data were often far from satisfactory. Many studies had no control group and, of these, a significant proportion were extrapolated from studies on another topic and then converted into a 'consequence'.

For example, Mrazek and Mrazek (1981) included a category of 'conceiving illegitimate children' in their symptomology of the harmful effects of child sexual abuse. They cited a study by Malmquist *et al.* (1966) as the supporting evidence for this claim. But the study by Malmquist *et al.* was carried out to explore the personality characteristics of women who had 'repeatedly had children outside of marriage'. That five of the 20 women studied reported having had 'incestuous relationships' was simply a comment made in the paper. Almost as if by magic, 'conceiving illegitimate children' then gets turned into an *effect* of child sexual abuse.

Overclaiming was also very common. Wachtel and Scott (1991) included 'somatic problems' in their list of effects of child sexual abuse. They cited an article by Goodwin and DiVasto (1979) as supporting evidence. Yet examination of the Goodwin and DiVasto article reveals only two passing references to somatic problems: both women who had suffered from headaches. The sheer scope of the errors, distortions and obfuscation in this research is highly disturbing. O'Dell does not suggest in any way that there is no harm done to children by being sexually assaulted. But she does assert that the claims made for *psychological* harm being a serious consequence of child sexual abuse fail to stand up to the normal scrutiny that is applied to evidence in the social sciences. She argues that the whole enterprise of 'harm warranting' merits careful scrutiny. She points especially to the way that the dominant discourse operating in this field acts to regulate sexuality. For example, it constructs heterosexuality as the norm, with both homosexuality and bisexuality rendered deviant by being seen as harmful effects of child sexual abuse.

O'Dell's work is an excellent example of the application of postmodern theorizing to real life issues and problems. By opening up questions about what the 'harm warrant' is *doing*, she challenges the often rather cosy assumptions that are made among professionals who work in the field of child protection. 'Protection' is another hurrah-word – who would want to deny protection to innocent and vulnerable children? Yet O'Dell's work powerfully points out that, for all the well-meaning motives of child protection practitioners and policies, protection from sexual abuse can have serious adverse consequences for children (we have explored these issues ourselves in Stainton Rogers and Stainton Rogers 1992, 1998).

Attractiveness

> How beautiful are thy feet with shoes O prince's daughter! The joints of thy thighs are like jewels, the work of the hands of a cunning workman. Thy navel is like a round goblet, which wanteth not liquor: thy belly is like a heap of wheat set about with lilies. Thy two breasts are like two young roes that are twins. Thy neck is as a tower of ivory.
>
> (The Song of Solomon in the Authorised Translation 7: 1–4)

Delight and pleasure in beauty is nothing new. Yet despite the cliché that 'beauty is in the eye of the beholder', conventional psychology, true to form, has approached attractiveness as though it was an objective manifestation of the body. Having objectified 'attractiveness', psychologists then investigated its impact on human behaviour and experience. For example, there have been numerous studies on the way that a person's physical appearance affects their interpersonal encounters (see, for example, Argyle *et al.* 1985; Duck 1988; Brehm 1992). Mostly these kinds of studies show that the more attractive a person is, the more other people like them and perceive them positively. One study even showed that attractiveness was the *only* significant variable (well, the only one they measured) that affected whether or not the person was liked on an initial encounter (Walster *et al.* 1966).

Sociobiological explanations of attractiveness

It will come as no surprise to you after reading Chapter 1 that psychologists working from a biological orientation assume that attractiveness has an evolutionary basis, especially in women. Theorists such as Morris (1971) and Wilson and Nias (1976) have argued that attractiveness relates to reproductive potential – attractive women are those whose bodies are best suited to reproduction and childcare. Ideal mates, reproductively speaking, are women who are young and healthy, and who have large hips for easy childbirth and big breasts for suckling infants. These qualities are seen to make a woman 'beautiful'.

Hence, goes this argument, women are right to 'suffer to be beautiful', since the more beautiful a woman is, the more likely she will be desired, and hence the more likely it is that her 'selfish genes' will be replicated. All the dieting, the hours in the gym, the liposuction, the face-lift and the anti-wrinkle creams will be worth it if she can look younger and fitter. If human beings are, fundamentally, naked apes and/or gene machines (as sociobiologists maintain), then anything they can do to up the odds in terms of reproductive mate selection is going to be a sensible strategy, evolutionarily speaking.

In general, this tradition of work derives from the time before psychology (largely, in this context, US psychology) acquired institutional gender sensitivity (for example, before gendered writing became an issue). What its research 'revealed' was that the attractive person (generally the 'attractive woman') was better adjusted, happier and had a more positive self-concept. The converse also held. Psychiatric patients who were physically unattractive tended to be hospitalized for longer (Farina *et al.* 1977). The attractiveness effect proved strong and consistent. Or, at least, it did so for the young. On reaching middle age, attractive women became less happy and less well adjusted than their less attractive peers (Berscheid and Walster 1974).

Warranting intervention

This phenomenon was even elevated to the status of a syndrome (we kid you not) – the **ageing actress syndrome** – by Wilson and Nias (1976). In more recent years, the issue has emerged again, repackaged and pathologized as **Body Dysmorphic Disorder** (Phillips 1996). Among its purported signs are overuse of or avoidance of mirrors, frequent and prolonged grooming, and feeling bad because of how you look. In extreme cases, some people's dislike of their body goes as far as self-harm and wanting amputations. Again we can see psychology acting as a pathologizing force, objectifying men and women's dissatisfaction with how they look into syndromes and disorders and hence, in the USA in particular, constructing a warrant for therapy:

D ———————	(since W) ——————→	So C
women see themselves as unattractive	this is a syndrome or disorder	so they 'need' therapy to help them overcome this disorder

Which all, as one might cynically say, makes work for psychologists to do. The more syndromes and disorders that psychology can construct, the more need there is for therapy, and the more need there is, therefore, for therapists. It is worth noting in this regard that most psychologists in the USA are in private practice – therapy and counselling are how most of them make their living. So the more Body Dysmorphic Disorders there are around, the more eating disorders, the more gender dysphorias, the wider and more lucrative the market becomes.

Attractiveness as a situated variable

Social psychologists have made their contribution to opening up this market. More recent work in this field has looked at 'attractiveness' as a situated variable. Women as well as men have been found in these studies to be strongly interested in physical attractiveness. This showed up both in laboratory studies and in studies of commercial dating services (Woll 1986). Other research has shown that both men and women have an attributional bias when it comes to physical attractiveness. Dion, *et al.* (1972) have called this the 'what is beautiful is good' bias. A considerable literature has subsequently built up in relation to this bias. It seems to start in young children, as early as at nursery school (Dion and Berscheid 1974). The adult data point to a marked halo-effect, in which attractive people are seen to be: 'more successful, more intelligent, more poised, more exciting, more independent, and more sexual than their less attractive counterparts' (Aronson *et al.* 1994: 379).

Although it is remarkably consistent, the halo-effect can break down if attractiveness is seen to be misused. In a simulated sentencing study,

Sigall and Ostrove (1975) explored this for a female defendant on either an 'attractiveness unrelated offence' (burglary) or an 'attractiveness related offence' (a financial swindle on a middle-aged bachelor). For burglary, attractiveness brought recommendations for a more lenient sentence but for the financial swindle attractiveness brought harsher suggested penalties.

Bodyforming

As long as we accept that what is going on here is investigations into the conventions and folk-ways of US culture, and mainly white and middle-class culture at that, then it does seem to be the case that goodness is seen to be written on the body as attractiveness. In general people tend to assume that 'what is beautiful is good'. What, perhaps, is more of an issue is the impact that this can have when the pursuit of attractiveness becomes a powerful regulatory (and this includes self-regulatory) force. The marketplace has its influence here too. Crawford (1980) has argued that contemporary Western culture has become infiltrated by **healthism** – the pursuit of the optimally healthy and attractive body. What makes the situation concerning body ideals complex is that it has become interwoven with technological, medical and economic factors to a unique extent. The cocktail is highly irrational. For example, doctors promote weight loss because of data on the medical risks of obesity. Yet whereas it is men who tend to be most at risk, it is overwhelmingly women who diet. 'Fitness' is widely promoted and seems beneficial (particularly for the middle-aged). But is most often imposed on the young, for whom, particularly in sports such as rugby and gymnastics, serious injuries are far from rare. Sport itself is riddled with drugs scandals, but it is often in sport that role models are promoted (particularly to ethnic minorities). At the same time, anti-recreational-drug propaganda often stresses the health risks involved, even though some of these drugs (notably the amphetamine group) were originally prescribed by doctors as slimming aids. In all of this, there is a complex economic machine at work, operating, suggests Crawford (1984), on tensional cultural motifs of control and release (see Chapter 4) – 'the naughty but nice'. Psychologists are deeply involved in this economic complex in terms of sports, exercise and injury psychology (see Scully *et al.* 1998) and through their concerns in obesity, anorexia nervosa and bulimia.

Complex social factors are also strongly implicated in weight control and weight loss. Dieting can be regarded as a facet of a more general style known as 'restrained eating' which is contrasted with 'unrestrained eating'. 'Unrestrained eating' does not imply eating to excess but not consciously moderating food intake. Obese individuals tend to be 'restrained eaters' (Ruderman 1986). Dieting is not one of humankind's more successful exercises in self-control. Research and commonsense knowledge both suggest that women are, on the whole, less happy with their bodies than are men with theirs. Weight is central to this difference, and women are more likely to be judged by their size and how much they eat. Representations of thin women are judged as the most 'feminine', yet it is 'normal' men who are usually seen as the most 'masculine' (see reviews by Silverstein and Perdue 1988 and Leary *et al.* 1994). In other words, there is much more pressure on women to be slim than men. These differences may well be salient not only to normal weight regulation but also to eating disorders.

Eating disorders

Anorexia (loss of appetite) can be a temporary effect of many highly emotionalized experiences (notably, love and grief). It can also result from situations such as sea travel and chemotherapy. Hunger strikers and those on long-term religious fasts often report that hunger diminishes rather than increases as the fast prolongs. Finally, it is a common bodily response to seriously invasive cancer. For these reasons, we should, strictly, not use it as an abbreviation for anorexia nervosa.

Anorexia nervosa is defined as severe *self-induced* weight loss producing at least a 15 per cent drop below minimal normal weight. For women it is also usually associated with loss of menstruation. In post-industrial societies, about 1 per cent of the population may experience the disorder. However, that figure disguises a vastly greater frequency in women (by a factor of somewhere between 10 and 20:1), particularly young women. It is also more frequent in those from advantaged backgrounds (quite often described in such terms as 'talented' and 'sensitive'). We cannot be the first to point out that this constellation was also true of the early patients of psychoanalysis.

The relatively rapid build-up from the 1970s of reported cases of anorexia nervosa in the USA and Western Europe has led to it being regarded as a **culture-bound syndrome**. Anorexia nervosa is certainly enabled by food value labelling, the concept of dieting and the body politics of post-industrial societies. An example of a male culture-bound syndrome is *koro*, a syndrome found in South-East Asia, in which there is a morbid fear that the penis will withdraw into the abdomen with fatal consequences (Tseng *et al.* 1992).

Studies of body image show a marked gender difference. By and large young women tend to see themselves as somewhat fatter than the body shape they think men find attractive, and their ideal figure, they said, would be even thinner than that. Young men, by contrast, tend to see themselves as the size women find attractive, and close to their ideal weight (Fallon and Rozin 1985). Not surprisingly, this is manifested in a majority of young women becoming 'controlled eaters' – they are permanently on a diet. But with other forces at work, this tends to be regularly interspersed with forays into the sweet-shop and burger bars. This is a good example of Crawford's (1984) control/release concept (and precisely the kind of thing he was writing about). Perhaps most young women in mainstream US and UK culture constantly veer between control (carefully restricting their food intake) and release (indulging in chocolate, crisps and naughty-but-nice 'junk food' generally).

Never wanting to pass up a good market opportunity, the pathologizing-warrant machine was able to use this control/release to broaden its catchment, by arguing that more than half of US college women have some sort of eating problem (Betz and Fitzgerald 1993). This was achieved by drawing in another 'disorder': bulimia nervosa. Whereas anorexia nervosa sufferers often have a history of bulimia nervosa, the converse is not the case. Betz and Fitzgerald (1993) claim that between 2 per cent and 18 per cent of US college women met clinical criteria for a diagnosis of bulimia nervosa. Bulimia *per se* refers to insatiable hunger (for example, as the result of a brain lesion or tumour). **Bulimia nervosa** is defined as a condition (or constellation of behaviours) in which binge-eating is followed by purging through self-induced vomiting and/or the use of laxatives. This pattern was not unknown to the Romans who are said to have set aside space – a vomitarium – for such purposes.

Interestingly, in our own culture we tend *not* to apply the label of bulimia nervosa to the pattern of overeating combined with alcohol (the 10-pints-and-a-curry evening scenario) indulged in more by young men than by young women (although there are growing numbers of 'ladettes' taking part in this particular ritual). The label bulimia nervosa tends to be restricted to the control/release eating pattern that is more usual among young women, and therefore it is largely women (by a ratio of about 10:1) who are diagnosed as sufferers. About 4 per cent of the general female population is claimed to be bulimic (Hoek 1993), with younger women seen as particularly vulnerable. Unlike anorexia nervosa, the condition is fairly evenly spread across social class and ethnic divisions. Also unlike anorexia nervosa, bulimia nervosa is only rarely life-threatening, although it can lead to physical harm. The excessive use of laxatives may upset the body's potassium balance, leading to dehydration and a susceptibility to urinary infections. Teeth may also suffer from the ejected stomach acid. There is no shortage of analyses (feminist, psychodynamic and mainstream) of eating disorders. Lupton (1996), Malson (1997), Ussher (1997) and Grogan (1998) all offer up-to-date and sophisticated treatments from a climate of perturbation perspective.

Bodies that matter

Broader climate of perturbation approaches to the relationship between sex, gender and the body are also very topical at present. Possibly the best-known founding mother is Judith Butler. Indeed, her cult following has achieved the point where there is an academic fanzine called *Judy* devoted to her work, which is, mainly supported by those working in the women's studies field in the USA. Butler is notoriously difficult to understand (her work recently won a prize for the obscurity of its prose). New ideas are seldom easy, and a training in mainstream psychology may make the kinds of concepts being covered by Butler (1993) harder rather than easier to digest. Not the least of the problems is that the concepts throw up questions one may never have thought about before as a psychologist like: what shapes the discourse/language that shapes the subjects that make the world? Nevertheless, we will do our best to at least introduce some of her main ideas.

Butler views genderedness as always-ever present. She acknowledges that people may have some degree of agency over their gender, but is clear that they cannot choose it as they could, say, choose which clothes to wear. Vance (1992) offers a more accessible description of the argument being made here. She says that it is a misreading of social constructionism to 'suggest that individual sexual identity is easily changeable, much like a new outfit plucked from the closet at whim; that individuals have conscious control over sexual identity; that large-scale cultural formations regarding sexuality are easily changed' or that 'individuals have an open-ended ability to construct themselves, or to reconstruct themselves' (Vance 1992: 133).

In challenging the assumption that sexuality is determined by biology, social constructionism does not suggest that sexuality is not determined at all – that it is simply changeable at will. Rather, it draws attention to the impact of other kinds of determinants – to the tremendous influence of social, cultural and historical forces. However, even though their influence may be great, questions about biology and the material world (especially in terms of the material reality of the body) do not go away. We still need to account for their influence. Vance expresses it like this:

> Has social construction theory . . . made no room for the body, its functions and its physiology? . . . [H]ow do we reconcile constructionist theory with the body's visceral reality and our own experience of it? . . . And if we wish to incorporate the body within social construction theory, can we do so without returning to essentialism and biological determinism?
>
> (Vance 1992: 138)

Butler explores the relationship between two aspects of bodies: their materiality and their performativity. By **materiality** what Butler means is the physical presence and appearance of our bodies – their shape, size, colour and form; and their constituent parts of skin, hair, blood and organs. Many of these are 'givens' and relatively unchangeable. But other aspects (such as hair colour and shape and size) are (somewhat) changeable by what we do to them – such as cosmetic surgery, dieting and working out.

By **performativity** what she means is what we *do* with our bodies – how with them and through their actions we present ourselves. For Butler performativity is not simply a matter of adopting a social role (as in dramaturgical theories of human action, see Goffman 1959). She uses it much more in the way that speech act theory understands the term. Performativity, according to Butler, 'brings into being that which it proclaims' (as in 'I declare this game "null and void" '). Butler uses the distinction between materiality and performativity to point out that there is no simple one-to-one relationship between them. The materiality of our bodies affects who and what we are and what we can and cannot do. To be born with female genitalia, with blue eyes and blonde hair, and then to be badly injured in a car crash at the age of 17 – all of these could have profound consequences for the kind of person you would be, and the kind of life you would live. But these material features of a person's body would by no means be the sole – or even the most important – determinants of who they are. Who and what we strive to be and become, what we do and do not do with and to our bodies – these also determine our embodiment.

For Butler gender is *performative*. In this sense, genderness produces sex (and not, as is usually assumed, the other way around). Without gender, sex would not matter, and it is mattering that gives a construct meaning. It may be easier to understand this argument through applying it to race. It is not colour which produces racism, but racism that produces colour – in the sense of colour when it is used as a euphemism for 'racially different from white'. Without racism, the colour of a person's skin would not matter, and if it did not matter it would be no more meaningful than the absence or presence of earlobes (see Chapter 6).

The constructive activity through which constructs such as 'sex', 'sexuality' and 'race' are produced is a continuing process but never a 'perfect' one, resulting in 'gaps and fissures'. It is these gaps and fissures that leave space for human agency to operate. One (although Butler insists not *the*) site in which the potentially subversive character of performativity can be explored is in queer theory and practice (see Chapter 8). Hence, the appeal of the performance of 'gender as drag': 'drag . . . serves a subversive function to the extent that it reflects the mundane impersonations by which heterosexually ideal genders are performed and naturalized and undermines their power by virtue of effecting that exposure' (Butler 1993: 23).

In other words, what drag exposes is that heterosexuality is as much a performance as homosexuality. It is not some human quality lying immanent within the body (either in its biology or its psychodynamics), but gains its reality only through being acted out: 'the distinction between the "inside" truth of femininity, considered as psychic disposition or ego-core, and the "outside" truth, considered as appearance or presentation, produces a contradictory formation of gender in which no fixed "truth" can be established' (Butler 1993: 234).

Implications for psychology

- Although our bodies *have* a materiality (that is, they have existence in the material world) we cannot *know* it directly. Our meaning-making always gets in the way.
- Hence, although we may think we know about the materiality of our bodies, our biology and so on, we do not. All we can ever know about them are the products of human meaning-making.
- Most claim-making works through the use of warranting. Whenever somebody makes a claim, look to find the warrant. You will often learn something by exposing what it is.
- Psychology is good at using warranting to construct needs – for therapy, for intervention, for treatment. Always ask yourself who is gaining what out of such constructed needs.

Further reading

Books

Arthurs, J. and Grimshaw, J. (1998) *Women's Bodies: Identity, Discipline and Transgression*. Poole: Cassell.

Grogan, S. (1998) *Men, Women and Body Image*. London: Routledge.

Marsden, J. (1999) 'Cyberpsychosis: The feminization of the postbiological body', in A. Gordo-López and I. Parker (eds) *Cyberpsychology*. Basingstoke: Macmillan.

Martin, E. (1987) *The Woman in the Body*. Buckingham: Open University Press.

Price, J. and Shildrick, M. (eds) (1999) *Feminist Theory and the Body: A Reader*. Edinburgh: Edinburgh University Press.

Stam, H. (ed.) (1998) *The Body and Psychology*, especially Part Three: 'Sexed and Gendered Bodies'. London: Sage.

Ussher, J. (ed.) (1997) *Body Talk: The Material and Discursive Regulation of Sexuality, Madness and Reproduction*. London: Routledge.

Journals

Body & Society. London: Sage.

10 Sex crimes

My social life ended . . . my friends accepted his counterclaim that I had attempted to seduce him and made false accusations when rebuffed. They treated me as if I had contracted leprosy.

(Heterosexual man talking of the experience of being raped, cited by King 1992: 6)

Crime is one of those issues that is easy to see as both obvious and as obviously needing to be tackled. Murder, false-witness, theft and rape – all of these seem simple enough to define and to see as criminal. But by now you should be wary of anything that seems obvious, and recognize that crime is a socially constructed (and therefore socially contested) concept. There is one feature of crime, however, which sets it apart from many other contested notions. Crimes are codified by law. They are written down as relatively precise definitions of what constitute criminal acts. Law also codifies and regulates social policies that impinge on crime. This codification in law and the way in which the law is operated provide useful and informative social indicators of the way in which a particular society, at a particular time and in a particular location, thinks about and makes sense of human conduct. Lees (1996), writing from an explicitly feminist perspective, expresses this cogently in relation to rape: 'Rape trials can be seen as a barometer of ideologies of sexual difference, of male dominance and female inferiority. Rape can be seen as a metaphor for women's right to self-determination, their right to say "No", whether in regard to giving birth, having sex or making other choices' (Lees 1996: xxvi).

In this chapter we are going to use this barometer to explore recent British and US ideas about sexuality and gender, and how these are influenced by and influence psychology. We will concentrate on just one kind of sex crime: rape. We have had to be selective, and so, reluctantly, have left out other possibilities that are also instructive to the theme of gender and sexuality as they relate to social atmosphere: for example, what is defined in law as 'gross indecency' but basically means male homosexual sex acts that are carried out in 'public' places and/or between more than two men. Throughout the chapter, for simplicity, except where specifically mentioned, when we talk of 'the law' we will be referring to law in England and Wales, which is somewhat distinct from that of Northern Ireland, and can differ markedly from law in Scotland.

Rape

Legally the **rape** of a woman is defined according to the Sexual Offences Act (1956) as the penetration of the vagina by the penis without the woman's consent. Under the Criminal Justice and Public Order Act of 1994, this definition was expanded to include the penetration of a man's anus by another man's penis against his consent (penetration of a woman's anus by a man's penis without consent was already a criminal offence). Emission of semen is not required for a rape to have occurred. Where penetration has been attempted but has not succeeded, this is, legally, defined as 'attempted rape'. Under English law, for a man to be convicted of raping a woman, it must be proved, beyond reasonable doubt, that:

- sexual intercourse took place (that the woman's vagina was penetrated by the man's penis);
- the woman did not consent; and
- the man knew that she did not consent, or was reckless as to whether or not she consented.

Difficulties in defining rape

This strictly legal definition has been heavily criticized, especially by feminists (see, for example, Brownmiller 1978; Lees 1996). They argue that it diverts attention away from other acts which may be as devastating (or even more so) as rape, such as forced oral sex or the use of implements (some of which can cause horrific injuries). Many feminists also draw attention to the way that 'consent' is a highly problematic concept in a society that renders women powerless, dependent and open to manipulation. Some go so far as to argue that *all* heterosexual sex is, by its nature, 'compulsory' (Rich 1980; Wittig 1981; Epstein 1997), in the sense that there are powerful social and cultural forces which, in effect, make it extremely hard for women to resist men's sexual overtures. Butler calls this the **heterosexual matrix**, 'that grid of cultural intelligibility through which bodies, genders and desires are naturalised' (Butler 1990: 151). It includes the whole socio-cultural milieu in which heterosexuality is framed as what is 'normal' and 'natural' – sometimes called heteropatriarchy.

From this perspective, any act of heterosexual sex can be defined as rape, in that consent has already been undermined by generic cultural enculturation into gendered heterosexuality. This is one reading of the troubling slogan 'all men are rapists'. It does not need to imply that every man fantasizes about violently ravaging women, or that all men would rape if they thought they could get away with it. Rather, it is a deliberate attempt to shock; to draw attention to the way that men engage in sex with women in a patriarchal world (see Chapter 6). Heteropatriarchy is seen to facilitate men's sexual access to women, and makes available to them a range of strategies that they can (and often do) deploy to 'seduce' women. It positions women not only into accepting having sex with men, but also into thinking that they *want* to do so (because, for example, they are 'in love').

However, 'all men are rapists' also takes the meaning of a more obviously sinister reading of the politics of power. This is the view coming from feminists who take the slogan more literally, such as Brownmiller, who argues that 'rape . . . is nothing more than a conscious process of intimidation by which *all* men keep *all women* in a state of fear' (Brownmiller 1978: 5, our emphasis). The argument is that men *in general* benefit from women's fear of rape, even though only a minority of men commit legally defined rape. Walkerdine (1981) has pointed out that this power extends even to very small boys. She describes how two 3-year-old boys subjected their teacher to a barrage of sexual taunting about her 'bum' and her 'titties', to surprisingly intimidatory effect.

How prevalent is it?

Even with the strictly legal definition of rape, it is impossible to arrive at any objective estimate of how many rapes of women happen, how many women experience rape in their lives, or how many men commit rape. It is hardly surprising, then, that estimates vary widely. Hall (1985), who based her findings on a survey of 1236 completed questionnaires, arrived at the figure of one in five women having survived rape or attempted rape, at the time they completed the questionnaire. This figure is similar to the estimate arrived at by Koss *et al.* (1987) from a larger survey of more than 6000 US women college students, which concluded that one in four women had experienced rape or attempted rape. However, these estimates were criticized by Gilbert (1992). He pointed out that three-quarters of the women defined by Koss and her colleagues as raped did not, themselves, describe what had happened as rape; and that 42 per cent of the women defined as having been raped in the survey subsequently had consensual sex with the man concerned.

Hall's estimate is less vulnerable to this criticism, given that hers is based on reports of rape as defined by survey respondents. But her sample was likely to be over-inclusive, given that it was carried out by the campaigning group Women Against Rape, billed as a 'women's safety' survey, and based on 1236 returned questionnaires from a total of 2000. But even taking these caveats into consideration, what these studies do show is that rape (and even more so attempted rape) is more common than most people realize.

The experience of being raped

Acknowledging the methodological problems inherent in studying rape, it is still important to try to discover what goes on. Most people's understandings of rape are heavily influenced by reporting in newspapers and on television, which tends to give a distorted picture – it tends to highlight particular cases which are not necessarily typical. Some hit the headlines because famous people (such as Mike Tyson, the US boxing champion) are involved. Others because they 'touch a nerve', such as the case of Angus Diggle (one has to admit that his name must have played a part), who was convicted of attempting to rape a woman lawyer after he had taken her to a solicitors' ball. The press expressed interest in this case because it was about date rape – for some newspapermen a topic uncomfortably close to home. Even though Diggle was convicted, a headline in *The Times* (20 August 1993) described the case as 'Lawyer mistook "sex invitation" ', and the *Sunday Telegraph* (12 June 1994) devoted a one-page article to complaining about the 'miscarriage of justice' when the verdict was not reversed on appeal.

In an attempt to get beneath the 'media hype' about rape, and the myths that inform it, a number of researchers (see Kelly 1988 for a review) have tried to gather empirical evidence. Painter (1991) looked specifically at rape in marriage and cohabitation, and estimated that 14 per cent of the women surveyed reported being raped by their partner; 31 per cent reported being raped by another man.

A recent UK study carried out by Lees (1996) used a variety of methods to contact women who had been raped, and 116 of these women completed a lengthy questionnaire about their experiences. In this survey rape was defined as 'forced to have sex against your will' (note that this is not the legal definition). Of the total of 116 questionnaires returned, 100 conformed to the strictly legal definition of rape and were used as the basis for data analysis. There were a further 16 attempted rapes. As Lees acknowledges, it was a self-selected sample (for example, many of the women responded to advertisements or requests to take part from other participants in the study), and so it is difficult to generalize from the data obtained. But her data do suggest that the reality of rape is quite different from the impression given through press reporting.

Of the 100 women who reported on their experiences of being raped, almost half (44 per cent) were under 21 at the age of the assault. Eight per cent were single, 9 per cent cohabiting and 11 per cent were married. The relationships between the women and their assailants were:

complete stranger	14%
a man met within 24 hours of the assault	20%
general acquaintances	46%
person with whom they had had consensual sex previously	20%

Many people assume that a woman is most likely to be raped by a menacing stranger who attacks her when she is walking in a dark, isolated place, or who breaks into her home. But notice that three-quarters of the rapes reported were by men the women either knew socially, or had at least met and had some contact with before the assault. It is now much more commonly recognized, in part because of studies like this, that women are more at risk of rape from the men they know than from strangers.

Other data from Lees' study were less expected and more disconcerting. There was a lot of violence involved. More than 70 per cent of stranger and acquaintance rapes involved the man slapping or forcefully holding the woman down. More extreme violence was also used in most of the rapes by a stranger (69.6 per cent) or an acquaintance (63.9 per cent). Strangers were more likely to threaten to kill the woman than acquaintances (39 per cent compared with 14 per cent), and more likely to choke or attempt to strangle her (23 compared with 15 per cent). Twenty-four per cent of the women said they had been buggered as well as raped. Possibly the most disturbing statistic is that 14 of the 100 rapes described involved more than one assailant.

What are the effects of rape?

Of the 100 women in Lees' sample, all reported having been changed by the experience. Almost all became far more cautious, and said they felt less confident about going out on their own. Many of the women changed their lifestyles. Many moved home, took time off work or even gave up their jobs. Often their relationships with partners suffered, and many relationships did not withstand the impact of the rape and broke up. Twenty per cent of the women in the Lees study said they were virgins when raped, so it led to the loss of their virginity. Six became pregnant as a result of the rape (one woman with twins), 7 per cent contracted a sexually transmitted disease, and many were worried about HIV infection. Several of the women described feeling suicidal. One woman tried to kill herself, and several mutilated themselves. Other outcomes included depression; fear, anxiety and nightmares; and taking drugs and drinking excessively. Some respondents said the experience completely put them off having sex, others said they craved affection and became more promiscuous.

Holmstrom and Burgess (1978) have argued that there is a recognizable condition of 'rape trauma syndrome'. However, many women working in the field (for example, Foley 1994) reject this attempt to medicalize the impact of rape – to turn it into a pathology that requires medical treatment (see Chapter 6). Lees notes that her women respondents usually stressed that although the rape had affected them deeply, they were determined to rebuild their lives, and to try to avoid feeling humiliated or degraded. This finding may well reflect that many were contacted through self-help groups, which foster the identity of 'survivor' rather than 'victim'.

Rape as an instrument of war

The Latin word from which the term 'rape' (and rapacious) is derived means 'to seize and carry off'. It was used to describe how, in ancient times, bands of warring men would abduct women as part of warfare. This was a tradition in 35 per cent of the societies studied by Sanday (1981), and in 18 per cent of these rape was institutionalized or 'more than occasional'. These societies tended to show up other indicators of male aggression and lack of female power.

Recently, especially following the Bosnia-Hercegovina war in the former Yugoslavia, it has become clear that the practice of using rape as part of warfare continues today. Reliable reports claim that thousands of women, mostly Muslim women, were raped by Serbian soldiers during that war. A report by the European Community Commission investigating the Bosnia-Hercegovina war estimated that 20,000 women had been raped, and concluded that 'rape cannot be seen as incidental to the main purpose of the aggression but serving a strategic purpose in itself' (European Community Commission 1993: 5). The United Nations Commission, when it investigated the rapes, found in the larger clinics in Zagreb that there were 119 women pregnant as a result of rape, and concluded that rape was used as an instrument of **ethnic cleansing** (Amnesty International 1991).

Stiglmayer (1993) interviewed Muslim women from Bosnia-Hercegovina who had been forced at gunpoint into detention camps used as brothels, and concluded that men rape in war for a variety of reasons, each war providing its own specific motivations. She suggested that in the Bosnia-Hercegovina war, as well as rape used as ethnic cleansing, the women were raped for revenge and to celebrate male supremacy. But perhaps her most disturbing conclusion was about the men who perpetrated the rapes: 'Everyone [participated] in the rapes: regular soldiers as well as members of paramilitary groups, simple foot soldiers as well as high officers and commandants, policemen as well as friends, co-workers and acquaintances of the raped women – "ordinary Joes" ' (Stiglmayer 1993: 147).

Gang rape

Stiglmayer's assertion is supported by other work in connection with **gang rape** outside of the context of war. Lees cites a study by Amir (1971) conducted in the USA, who gathered data on 1292 men in Philadelphia who had been reported to the police for rape. Of these 43 per cent operated in pairs or gangs, and 71 per cent of the rapes were clearly planned. Lees comments on these data:

> Gang or pair rape, rather than being pathological, appears to be more about an extreme form of normative masculinity. It is in all-male communities such as the army, adolescent gangs, prison, college fraternities in America and competitive team sports that gang rape generally occurs.
>
> (Lees 1996: 38)

Rozee-Koker and Polk (1986) estimated that roughly one-third of rapes reported to the police in the USA were by gangs. Benedict (1985) suggested that it is particularly common among young men, as part of developing their masculine identity. Young men gang rape 'to prove themselves, to show off, to be part of the gang, or at best out of fear of being ostracised if they don't'. Warshaw (1988) has also stressed the 'social' elements:

> As they participate in gang rape, they experience a special bonding with each other, a unity of purpose that comes from the pride they feel in reducing the victim to nothing more than a collective vessel for their masculinity. Through the rape they prove their sexual ability to group members and underscore their status.
>
> (Warshaw 1988: 101)

Sanday (1990), in a study of gang rapes carried out on US university campuses by members of fraternities, suggested that what is going on in such rapes is that the college men were deploying the penis as a concrete symbol of masculine power and dominance. Also in the USA, Scully and Marolla interviewed gang rapists serving prison sentences, one of whom had this to say about the rape: 'We felt powerful, we were in control. I wanted sex and there was peer pressure. She wasn't like a person, no personality, just domination on my part. Just to show I do it – you know, macho' (quoted in Scully and Marolla 1985: 258).

Male rape

As was described at the beginning of the chapter, male rape became a specific criminal offence in England only in 1994. But sexual assaults on men by men have been long recognized as a problem in prisons (Sagarin 1976) and other male-dominated institutions (Goyer and Eddleman 1984). Gunby (1981) estimated that at least 9 per cent of men in US prisons are subjected to a sexual assault, many of them repeatedly over a number of years, and gang rape with extreme violence is common (Rideau and Sinclair 1982).

Reliable data are even harder to gather with respect to men who are raped than they are for women. For example, a study by Mezey and King (1989), despite strenuous efforts, was able to gather questionnaire data from only 22 respondents and, of these, only eight were eventually interviewed. Interestingly, though, the results show some similarities to those obtained by Lees in respect to women. For example, here too the assailants were by no means all strangers, although a larger proportion were people that the man had met only a matter of hours before, including some met explicitly for casual sex.

complete stranger	18%
a man met within 24 hours of the assault	22%
a men met explicitly for casual sex	14%
general acquaintances	27%
person with whom they had had consensual sex previously	14%
member of family	5%

As with rapes on women, stranger rapes were more likely to be violent, and the assailants were often angry, scornful and sadistic. Like women, men who are raped are usually strongly affected. All but two of the men in the Mezey and King study said they felt they suffered long-term psychological after-effects, including feelings of vulnerability, loss of self-respect, anxiety and social withdrawal. Several felt dirty and damaged, and two had attempted suicide and one had committed suicide, and eight of the men said they had begun to drink more. One man was subsequently given hospital treatment for drug addiction. Another man, when interviewed, said: 'The attack has made me feel really base – the lowest form of human life – it was the catalyst of my marriage break-up as heterosexual relations ceased and I became homosexually promiscuous' (cited in King 1992: 8).

There were differences, of course. Some of the heterosexual men faced confusions about their sexuality, especially the four for whom the rape had been their first sexual experience. Although most of the men were frightened of going to the police, the gay men were especially frightened. Some of the men said that they worried that the experience might predispose them to becoming sexually aggressive themselves. One commented: 'One fear was . . . that I might make someone do something against their will, that is become an unintentional rapist' (cited in King 1992: 7). In some ways, King suggests, there may be a more devastating impact of being made to feel vulnerable and weak, since many of the men were surprised by the attack, even though they had exposed themselves to a context (for example, by inviting a virtual stranger home) that most women would recognize as risky. King acknowledged a number of methodological shortcomings in the research, but none the less concluded: 'Despite these limitations, the results of this study demonstrate that male sexual assault is a frightening, dehumanising event, leaving men who have been assaulted feeling debased and contaminated, their sense of autonomy and personal invulnerability shattered. These effects were most devastating when the men were sexually inexperienced before the assault' (King 1992: 14).

Taking a critical stance

In this last section we will review three main ways that taking a critical stance to sex crimes can contribute to our understanding of sexuality and gender: the issue of consent; how biological and socio-cultural theories can be used and abused in relation to explaining sex crimes; and the need for a critical turn.

The issue of consent

As we saw at the beginning of the chapter, in law the issue of consent is crucial to defining rape. What turns having sex with somebody into rape is the lack of consent (either because it is not given, or because it cannot be given). Yet consent to sex does not operate in the same kind of a regulated domain as, say, consenting to medical treatment – which itself is a far from simple issue. Engaging in sex is seldom a matter of cool evaluation of the possible implications – a cerebral cost–benefit analysis of the options to give or withhold consent. It is, even where no overt coercion is involved, immanent with persuasion, enticement and 'leading on'. Indeed, sex that does not involve rituals of courtship and seduction is, for many people, sex that is cold, unfeeling and soulless.

What starts off as a simply biological definition (a matter, say, of penises penetrating vaginas or anuses) thus rapidly becomes a definition couched in terms of interpersonal negotiation, which is bound up with complex issues of power and freedom to act. As our exploration of the idea of compulsory heterosexuality has shown, radical and, especially, separatist feminists argue that women are enmeshed in a dominant order which renders them incapable of giving *informed* consent. Yet libertarian feminists, such as Roiphe (1993), reject this portrayal of women as 'victims':

> This is a portrait of the cowering woman, knocked on her back by the barest feather of peer pressure. Solidifying this image of women into policy implies an acceptance of the passive role. By protecting women against verbal coercion, these feminists are promoting the view of women as weak-willed, alabaster bodies, whose virtue must be protected against the cunning encroachments of the outside world. The idea that women can't withstand verbal or emotional pressure infantilizes them. The suggestion lurking beneath this definition of rape is that men are not just physically but intellectually and emotionally more powerful than women.
>
> (Roiphe 1993: 67–8)

In other words, to claim that women cannot consent to sex, or have an impaired capacity to negotiate consent to sex, is to collude with the very stereotype of feminine frailty and incompetence that feminism has fought so hard to challenge. At the same time, to deny that women are, in sexual matters as with many other aspects of their lives, often in positions of limited power is to collude with understandings of relationships between men and women which ignore issues of power.

As Bell (1993) has pointed out, therefore, the issue of consent is highly problematic for feminists: 'the notion of consent is in danger of disappearing from feminist work as women's own understanding of consent is elided' (Bell 1993: 156). The problem, Bell argues, is not that most feminists reject the possibility that women *can* consent to sex, but that they fear the consequences of such admissions. Bell writes of the need to recognize the 'forgotten whatness' of sexuality: the always problematic nature of *what* is going on? *what* is at stake? *what* are the implications and consequences? (There are strong parallels here to the kinds of questions asked in a postmodern approach to research, see Chapter 6.) At the very least a consideration of consent brings home to us that human sexuality is in no way simple, and that attempts to explain it away – whether through simplistic biological or through simplistic socio-cultural forces – is not just to miss that complexity but fails to recognize that explanations of these kinds are, in the very act of simplifying, potent tools that can be used to bring about particular consequences.

The use and abuse of biologically based theories

If we now turn to conventional understandings of why rape happens, we can see that embedded in these are many assumptions drawn from the biologically based theories of gender and sexuality that we examined in Chapter 1, especially those drawn from sociobiology and evolutionary psychology. It is one of the main reasons why such theorization is seen as 'dangerous' by feminists – because it can be used to provide a justification for rape. As an example, take this set of assertions made by Ann and Bill Moir in *Why Men Don't Iron*:

> Men, on average, have 400 per cent more erotic fantasies than women. Men dream of women, they daydream of women, they fantasize about women, and they do not fantasize about having cosy chats beside the fire. His fantasies are about sex. . . . He is sexually aroused far more easily than she is, and, as in the rest of his life, he craves novelty. He often finds that novelty in artificial stimuli, which is why he likes pin-ups, pornography and peepshows.
>
> (Moir and Moir 1998: 219)

The Moirs then go on to argue that

> The sexual drive in both women and men is fuelled by testosterone; and men have 1,000 per cent more. . . . Testosterone and sexual aggression are also linked. Sexual assaults by males peak at 17–25 years, but decline thereafter as the testosterone declines with age. There are more sexual assaults in the autumn when the male's testosterone peaks.

> Violent rape is associated with higher T levels, though the non-violent rapist generally has an average level. . . . While there is no proof at this time, it may be expected that a significant proportion of date rapes may be from steroid self-medication.
>
> (Moir and Moir 1998: 222–3)

It is easy to see where this argument is leading: when a man rapes a woman, he does so because he is suffering from a testosterone-fuelled, irresistible urge that he cannot control. His sexual desire, inflamed by a woman whose dress and behaviour send him 'misleading messages' (which, in any case, he cannot interpret because of his biologically determined inability to communicate with and understand women), becomes unstoppable. Aided by his testosterone-triggered aggression, he 'takes' her, by force if necessary.

Such an explanation comes dangerously close to suggesting that men who rape cannot help it. The propensity is just 'wired in' to some men, who, especially in their youth, or at certain times of the year, lurk around, souped-up on testosterone, waiting to pounce. This is hardly a flattering image of men, and also does not fit at all well with what we know about rape, especially rapes that are carried out by men in pairs or gangs.

The use and abuse of social theorization of masculine identity

When we considered gang rape and rape used in war, clearly there seemed to be much more going on than can be explained by levels of testosterone. Lees (1996) argues that these kinds of rape, in particular, are manifestations of the kind of masculine stereotype described in Chapter 2, but taken to horrifying limits. Think back to Robert Brannon's (1976) four main themes, from which he argues that stereotypical masculinity is woven:

No girlie stuff!	All feminine qualities are to be avoided.
Be a winner	Gain status, success and respect.
Be a tough guy	Be self-reliant, strong and confident.
Give 'em hell!	Never let anybody get the better of you, and use aggression or even violence if you need to.

It is obvious how each element can be seen to be reflected in what goes on in gang rape – it is a way to reject feminine qualities of intimacy and tenderness; to gain status; to prove strength; and to use aggression to get your own way.

The turn to critical theory

It is important to recognize what is being said here. It is no more helpful to argue that men are *inevitably* driven to rape by their masculine socialization than it is to argue that they are driven by their hormones. Rather, what is being argued by commentators such as Lees is that rape is made possible by the way that men are socialized into a form of 'macho' masculinity. It is a masculinity in which being 'a bit of a lad' is about being contemptuous of women, 'scoring' as often as possible and bragging about it, having no truck with 'soppy' feelings, taking risks and generally 'being a bad boy'. Within such an ethos, behaving in a sexually exploitative or coercive manner towards women, she argues, can be highly rewarding – a means of gaining status and respect as well as 'kicks'.

This, we believe, is why a turn to critical theorization and analysis is necessary. Mechanistic models, whether they are biological or socio-cultural, are insensitive to issues both of power and of human will. In relation to sex crimes, they portray men as victims either to their own base 'animal nature' or to their dysfunctional 'nurture', incapable of acting in anything but a sexually aggressive, exploitative macho manner. This can be quite explicit. Thornhill and Palmer have recently claimed:

> As bizarre as some of these facts may seem, they all make sense when rape is viewed as a natural, biological phenomenon that is the product of the human evolutionary heritage. . . . We fervently believe that, just as the leopard's spots and the giraffe's elongated neck are the result of aeons of past Darwinian selection, so is rape.
>
> (Thornhill and Palmer, cited in Ellison 2000: 4)

They portray women as victims of their own frailty and incompetence – either because of their biology or their socialization, unable to act assertively or to resist the attentions of men. Neither are very flattering images, nor do they offer a lot of optimism about the capacity for society to change.

Yet, at the risk of ire from some of our friends and colleagues, we will argue that not only is change possible, there is evidence that it is happening. In 1992 an episode of the BBC television series *Police* showing police officers' dreadful treatment of a raped woman shocked not only its general audience but many police officers themselves. It provided the impetus for far-reaching improvements in police procedures for dealing with rape. This changed climate has also led to training initiatives in the judiciary and for magistrates. The changes in the law making rape in marriage illegal have not been entirely successful, but are at least a move in the right direction.

Implications for psychology

- Psychological theories about gender and sexuality have the potential of being used to 'explain away' responsibility for sex crimes or to 'naturalize' them. We need to be critically aware of that potential.
- Viewing those who have been subjected to sex crime as doomed to experience a psycho-medical condition (such as rape trauma syndrome, or post-traumatic stress disorder) may serve the discipline but can pathologize and stigmatize (rather than help) the person concerned.

- Viewing sexual offenders as a type or profile and as 'suitable cases for treatment' may serve to perpetuate 'the problem' if it obscures the social and cultural resources (for example, in terms of the construction of masculinity) that enable sexual offending. Consent cannot simply be treated as a matter of individual or average cognitive competence or of rational decision-making, but must be considered in the context of power, and the constructed nature of age, gender and sexuality. This also goes for consent to research.
- Current sensibilities over sex and sexuality in childhood and adult responses to them should stimulate rather than inhibit informed research.

Further reading

King, M. (1992) Male sexual assult in the community, in G.C. Mezey and M.B. King (eds) *Male Victims of Sexual Assault*. Oxford: Oxford University Press.

Lees, S. (1996) *Carnal Knowledge: Rape on Trial*. Harmondsworth: Penguin.

Ward, C.A. (1995) *Attitudes Towards Rape*. London: Sage.

11 New men, new women, new relationships?

Traditional definitions of what it means to be a man or a woman are fading. . . . [W]e are in the middle of an historic change in the relations between men and women: a shift in power and values that is unravelling many of the assumptions not only of 200 years of industrial society, but also millennia of traditions and beliefs.

(Mulgan 1994: 1)

This assertion comes from the introduction to a report by the think-tank Demos, entitled *No Turning Back: Generations and the Genderquake* (Wilkinson 1995). Mulgan maintains that, in the Western world at least, women's emancipation and enfranchisement, both cultural and economic, have become deep-rooted and irreversible. In other words, the goals of first-wave feminism have been achieved, if not fully, then to a significant degree. He suggests that there have been two main drivers of this change: cultural shifts (especially shifts in values) affecting women's aspirations and vision of themselves; and economic forces, especially those affecting patterns of employment.

For all the benefits for women, however, Mulgan argues that these changes have had their downsides. They have aroused strong antagonism among some groups of men. And they have thrown up a number of problems, such as who will take on the traditional roles of looking after children and providing care for other dependent people, in a world where women no longer see these roles as their duty as wives, mothers, daughters and neighbours. Mulgan also notes that the debates and issues around these changes are becoming more complex. The emancipation and enfranchisement of women, together with changing values (especially against male misuse of power) and changing patterns of employment, have had a dramatic impact on the lives, life experiences and life opportunities of men. Consequently, the focus has shifted from a preoccupation with women's rights to a broader set of concerns which encompass, for example, the ways in which men may be disadvantaged, discriminated against and mistreated.

In this final chapter of the book we will look, in particular, at the impact of these changes and challenges on young men and young women – on who they are, how they see themselves, and what they want to do with their lives; and on their relationships with each other. To get into this examination we need, however, to look briefly at the more general ways in which the world has changed for today's generation of young people (roughly those in their teens and twenties).

Changes in values

Another Demos report, *Freedom's Children: Work, Relationships and Politics for 18–34 year olds in Britain Today* (Wilkinson and Mulgan 1995), describes a massive change in values among the 18–34-year-old UK generation. Overall, it seems that their values are changing in three main ways:

- Young people's values are undergoing an overall *generational shift*. Younger generations are expressing values that are *different from* those of older generations.
- Young people's values are *fragmenting*. We are seeing a shift from a situation where people living in the same community or social group (even the same country, to some extent) had a shared set of consensually held values, to a situation where this consensus is breaking down. One way in which this is manifested is a disengagement from party politics.
- Young people's values are undergoing *realignment*. New alliances are being formed, and new and different challenges are being made between different groups and world-views.

The generational shift in values

The US political scientist Ronald Inglehart (1990) suggests that we are seeing an intergenerational shift from what he calls materialist values (which stress security, material comfort and tradition) to non-materialist values (which are more concerned with personal freedom and quality of life). The survey conducted for Demos (Wilkinson and Mulgan 1995) showed that the picture is more complicated than this. It identified the following values as particularly salient to the young people who were aged 16–24 in 1995:

- a rejection of the authority of either the Church or State;
- a belief that people have a right 'to do their own thing', and not be 'told what to do' by parents or partners;

- an aspiration to 'authenticity' – a search for ways of being true to oneself and for relationships that are honest and open;
- a strong concern about the environment, combined with a belief that new technologies can help to resolve problems and will open up new opportunities; and
- an attachment to living life 'on the edge', to taking risks and to hedonism.

Some of these (such as risk-taking) may well be more to do with life stage than generation, but many do seem to represent a shift in values from those held by earlier generations. And it is not just happening with a privileged group, but happening across the board. Wilkinson and Mulgan stress that there is a 'remarkable degree of consistency across the class range. Although there are class differences . . . the rejection of tradition, more libertarian values and behaviours have spread to all classes' (1995: 47).

The fragmentation of values

At the same time they, and others who have researched young people's values (such as Furnham and Stacey 1991; Banks *et al.* 1992), have observed a fragmenting of values. Older generations tend to be committed to a common set of traditional values (such as respect for authority). Younger people, by contrast, tend to show much more diversity in the values they express. For example, the values espoused by 'young entrepreneurs' are very different from those who see themselves as 'eco-warriors'. And both are different from the values held by what Wilkinson and Mulgan have termed the **underwolves** – underdogs who are prepared to bite back. One manifestation of this fragmentation is that the ties that seem to bind most young people together into social groups are not old-style factors such as social class, ethnicity or even gender. It is not class or gender loyalty or a shared tradition that provides social cohesion, but rather a commitment to a particular ideology, religion or some other belief system, or concern about a particular set of issues.

Sometimes this is articulated around different patterns of consumption, such as of the music scene. Mitchell, for example, writes about the interplay between music and ethnic identities and communities, as Anglo-American rock 'split up into a series of fragmented, decentred musical forms which sometimes corresponded to or overlapped among particular youth subcultures' (Mitchell 1996: 12). Today (as we write, at least) these include house, hip-hop, techno, drum and bass, garage and jungle. The point here is not that different ethnic groups identify with different music genres (although there are some connections), but that there is a complex interplay between the consumption and production of different kinds of music and different alliances within and between ethnic identities (and, indeed, other identities, such as being gay) and communities. New spaces have thereby been created, whereby, for example, it is now not uncommon for young people to indulge in the **gender tourism** of 'visiting' gay culture. As noted in Chapter 8, cyberspace is another 'place' where this is possible.

Another manifestation of this is a shift from party politics to issue politics. Bhavnani (1991) interviewed young people about politics and found that almost without exception young people thought that party politics were boring, irrelevant and difficult to understand. Most of her interviewees also said that they would not bother to vote. This is borne out by voting statistics. In the UK four times fewer people under the age of 25 are registered to vote than in any other age group. The disengagement from party politics seems to be mostly to do with young people's disillusionment. They are becoming more:

- cynical and distrusting of the institutions which hold power – whether government, business, or indeed any other organisations that are seen as part of 'Them';
- discontented with the continued control over any 'real' power by the predominantly white, male, middle- and upper-class establishment; and
- frustrated in their aspirations – fed up with the growing gap between what they know is possible and available, and what they are likely to get.

The overall picture being painted is of a generation who are hostile towards 'the system', disenchanted with party politics, antagonistic to authority, stridently individualistic, and yet who are willing to take action (including breaking the law) about issues that matter to them and that they care about. Wilkinson and Mulgan speak of a 'politics of exclusion' which is not just driving growing numbers of young people out of the mainstream, but setting them up in conflict with it.

A realignment of values

The realignment of values is particularly noticeable in terms of gender. There seems to be a 'feminization' of young men's values and a 'masculinization' of young women's values. Young men, generally, are increasingly coming to reject machismo values and are becoming softer and more caring. Of course, there are exceptions. Indeed, Phillips *et al.* (1993) have argued that for some groups of young men the reverse is happening – especially those who feel that their identity is under threat, because, for example, their traditional roles as breadwinners and heads of the family are being challenged. Young women are not only becoming more likely to value success, their own enjoyment, and taking risks than did women in previous generations, they are also more 'into' these values than young men of the same age.

Changes in economics and employment

Work has become feminized. More women than men are now in paid work (Wilkinson 1995), although much of it is in poorly paid, part-time and insecure jobs. The male/female gap in earnings has narrowed, and among couples (married and living together) women's share in the household income has risen. It is now not at all unusual for the woman to have the higher salary. The sharpest rise in women's employment has been among women graduates. More women are entering professions previously seen as male, such as law, medicine and financial services. But it is not only women's increased participation in the workplace that has feminized it.

The nature of work has changed, from an emphasis on heavy manufacturing to a much greater proportion of the workforce employed in service industries and information technology. So too has the approach to work, which now involves more teamwork and often considerable 'emotional labour' (especially in the caring professions and service industries). The term emotional labour was devised originally to describe the work of flight attendants – the requirement to smile, and to be cheerful and calm, even in the face of customers behaving badly or making emotional demands. Consequently, men's traditional strengths – such as physical capacity and competitiveness – have become less valued; whereas women's traditional strengths – flexibility, adaptability, service and teamwork – have become more valued (Kanter 1993). This both makes women more employable, and puts pressure on male employees to become more feminine. The new conditions are also feminizing work organization, including delayering (that is, reducing the layers of management), greater openness, networking and a higher premium on interpersonal skills (Handy 1994). However, as Wilkinson (drawing on the work of Marlow 1996) has noted more recently, this feminization is limited, and large numbers of women who are fed up with the way they are treated by big business are turning to the option of setting up on their own:

> Female entrepreneurship has thrived partly because of the heady mix of female impatience and a corporate world which is considerably more reluctant to feminise its boardrooms than its service desks. . . . A younger more confident generation of women managers are voting with their feet and positively embracing a DIY culture of self-promotion. They are no longer content to be cast in the role of victims and for many the decision to leave is an assertion of power.
> (Wilkinson 1996: 14)

Alongside this feminization of work, a number of other economic forces have influenced gender relationships. Possibly the most important has been the combination of falling wages (in real and relative terms) among the lowest paid, together with a rise in expectations over living standards.

This has meant that for most families in the UK, it is no longer financially viable to rely solely or even mainly on the income of the male breadwinner if the family is to have the standard of living they would like. Many 'pin money' jobs taken by women to supplement the family income have come to be essential for the family budget. Increasingly, with rising levels of male unemployment, women have become the family's sole or main source of income. Many men have had to re-evaluate their job aspirations, and take on the kinds of part-time, insecure and poorly paid jobs that used to be thought of as 'women's work'. All of these factors together have influenced gender relations not only in the world of work, but in personal and family relationships too. In the view of many commentators, all this change has generated 'new men' and 'new women', who are quite different from the traditional stereotypes. We will move on now to look at these new species in some more detail.

New men

Moir and Moir (1998) are not too keen on the 'new man'. They describe him like this:

> He is more sensitive than the older model, more ready to help about the house or to spend time with his children. He is civilized, de-clawed and gentle. He can still be strong, of course, but his strength is manifested by patience and emotional warmth. This paragon sounds suspiciously like a female; indeed, it is often said that the new man is 'in touch with his feminine side'. The supposed compliment betrays a *fin de millnium* [*sic*] unisex ideal. It is RuPaul, supertransvestite, advertising M.A.C.'s Viva Glam lipstick (all profits to an AIDS charity). It is Generation X – with a splash of Calvin Klein's CKOne – cruising the line between sexual identities and possessing the best traits of both with none of the old male's inconvenient faults.
>
> (Moir and Moir 1998: 23)

(Mind you, this is nowhere near as scathing as their description of 'postmodern man', 'dressed to the hilt in academic theory . . . a boy-child of intellectuals who teach gender studies'.) But that aside, is the idea of new man nothing more than media hype and marketing strategy?

> Imagine yourself on Tottenham High Road on a winter Saturday afternoon. The pavements are blocked, but not with Christmas shoppers. A continuous stream of male youth are making for the Spurs ground. Look once and it might be the rituals of class played out unchanged since the 50s. Look again. It *is* 1987, not 1957. What has changed are the surfaces of the lads themselves, the way they carry their masculinity. Individuality is on offer, incited through the commodities and consumer display. From jeans: red tabs, designer labels, distressed

> denim. To hair: wedges, spiked with gel, or pretty hard boys who wear it long, set off with a large earring. And snatches of boy's talk I pick up are about 'looking wicked' as well as the game. Which is not to say violence is designer label! From Tottenham Court Road to *The Face*. Fashion spreads of Doc Martens and cycle shorts. Dole-style clothes for hanging around street corners. City wide boys and black rappers. Soul boys, wallies and razor partings dancing late at night. Soho clubs and metropolitan style. Something is happening to 'menswear'. Something is happening to young men.
>
> (Mort 1988: 193)

Mort argues that 'what is going on here is more subtle than advertising hype and profit motive. Young men are being sold images which rupture traditional icons of masculinity. . . . They are getting pleasures previously branded as taboo or feminine' (1988: 194). While accepting that the 'images put out by the advertising and marketing industries are important texts where today's youth – and now increasingly young men – learn about sex and gender' (1988: 213), he notes that this cannot happen in a vacuum. These images work only because they reflect young men's lived experience: at school and college, in the club and the pub, at the match and anywhere else young men congregate. Indeed, they only 'work' (that is, shift merchandise) because retailers do careful market research.

Traditionally men have been disembodied – their identities constructed around what they do and 'are', their rationality, intellect and power, rather than their physical attributes. Traditionally they have worn uniforms (either literally or figuratively), their clothes denoting status or occupation (pin-striped suit, white coat) rather than personal style. The aim was uniformity glossed with subtle signs of their position in the hierarchy. As their traditional roles and resources are diminishing, young men are becoming embodied. A number of commentators (see, for example, Pini 1997) have argued that this recent interest in 'dressing up' and other forms of bodily adornment (such as piercing) are examples of what Foucault called **technologies of the self**:

> Technologies of the self permit individuals to effect by their own means or with the help of others a number of operations on their bodies and souls, thought, conduct and way of being, so as to transform themselves in order to attain a certain state of happiness, purity, wisdom, perfection or immorality.
>
> (Foucault 1988: 88)

In other words, technologies of the self are means by which people construct their identities. McRobbie (1994) argues that young people today take on and play around with conventional images (such as conventional images of masculinity and femininity, being gay, being black and being white) to gain a sense of control over their lives in a world that offers them few other opportunities to do so. One of the most noticeable trends in young men's lives has been the loss of traditional job opportunities in manufacturing. Jobs in heavy industry have about halved over the past 50 or so years. Together with the rise in part-time and insecure work, and the rapid entry of women into what were, traditionally, 'men's jobs', young men – especially those without qualifications – are finding it harder and harder to get the kinds of jobs that would allow them to take on the traditional role of breadwinner (that is, to earn enough to support a wife/partner and a family).

Given that this life opportunity is simply not available to large numbers of young men, then where else are they to find any sense of identity? Pini suggests that they have turned to technologies of the self, that include managing both their bodies (for example, by working out) and their images (by the clothes they wear) and engaging in music and dance cultures: 'where job prospects and long-term planning become increasingly dismal, immediate bodily pleasure has arguably replaced far-sightedness' (Pini 1997: 163).

On the face of it, new men are having a hard time. Not all of them are, however, as the elite with the right backgrounds and a smallish number of entrepreneurs continue to thrive, and certain power-bases (such as the City) are still dominated not only by men but by male values and interests. Some men have gained considerably from opportunities to, for example, take periods out from paid work in ways their fathers could not have done. But for many the future looks quite bleak.

New women

Wilkinson (1995) describes the values to which young women today aspire as: androgyny, risk, excitement and hedonism. Together these have been encapsulated into the notion of the 'ladette', epitomized by media personalities such as Denise Van Outen.

> More than any previous generation they are rejecting the whole cluster of traditional values: authority, rigid moral codes of right and wrong, the emphasis on security (financial and otherwise), older parochial notions of community and the puritanism of the past. They are less attached to the family . . . and more likely to feel tied down by it.
>
> (Wilkinson 1995: 19–20)

She says these trends are strongest among 'career women', especially graduates. Young career women are now much less likely to feel the need for 'a man in their lives' than previous generations of women in similar situations, and much less likely to see having children as a life goal or a route to fulfilment. Work is important to these women, and they are planning their careers more, and delaying pregnancy to pursue them. This potential for success seems to be stimulating young women's performance in education. Wilkinson goes on:

> A sea-change is underway in younger girls' attitudes which is having a direct bearing on educational performance. School girls now have greater self-esteem, are happier than their male peers, are more ambitious, are more likely to want to continue in education and are less likely to want to have a family when they leave school than boys. Above all, perhaps, girls are much more positive about the future than boys. . . . Girls are now outperforming boys at GCSE level even in so-called 'male' subjects like science. They are outperforming boys at 'A' level, and now outnumber, and are outperforming, men at university.
>
> (Wilkinson 1995: 23)

These findings reported by Wilkinson are consistent with other research in this field (see, for example, Ferri 1993). Other features of the Demos research findings are more contentious. Wilkinson argues that young women today are showing what tend to be seen as male attributes. They are less emotional and more willing to take risks, and want excitement in their lives. They find this in activities such as parachuting, rock climbing and travelling to places that have previously been considered 'too risky' for women.

However, an aspect of Wilkinson's report which shocked a lot of people when it was first published were data from a market research survey (Wilkinson and Mulgan 1996) indicating that an increasing number of young women were seeing violence as legitimate, and suggesting that young women are becoming more tolerant of violence than young men. Responses to a questionnaire were used to derive a 'pleasure in violence' index, and the pattern observed over different age groups is instructive. It is shown in Table 11.1:

Table 11.1 'Pleasure in violence' index, by age and gender

Gender	*Age* 15–17	18–34	35–54
Female	3.35	1.36	0.55
Male	2.49	1.45	0.60

These data can be read as saying that whereas in older age groups women tend to show less pleasure in violence than men, among 15- to 17-year-olds, young women's pleasure in violence is higher than young men's. The first point to stress is that the index rather hides the fact that the proportions apparently valuing violence are still very small. The second point is that the terminology – *pleasure* in violence – seems almost to have been chosen to raise hackles. The index was crafted around responses to a number of statements, including 'it is acceptable to use physical violence to get something you want', but even this is not so much taking pleasure in violence as seeing it as sometimes pragmatically justified.

This aspect of Wilkinson and Mulgan's report does seem to be feeding into concern in the popular media about what is seen as an 'explosion' of crimes of violence perpetrated by young women, including traditionally 'male' crimes such as muggings of both old people and their peers. It is hardly surprising that the shift in young women's views on violence identified by Wilkinson and Mulgan therefore aroused considerable disquiet. Reid (1996), writing in the *Sunday Times* for example, called them 'chilling facts about the behaviour of modern women'. Note the words 'fact' and 'behaviour' there. Hopefully your reading of Chapter 7 will have alerted your suspicion about data being turned into 'facts'; and made you particularly suspicious about the turning of questionnaire responses *about* violence into 'the behaviour of modern women', implying that what had been found was evidence of violent behaviour itself. In the UK edition of *Cosmopolitan*, Lisa Brinkworth (1996) went even further, hyping the data into evidence that 'the new breed of violent female is threatening to unstitch the very fabric of society'.

It would seem that films such as *Thelma and Louise* and *Leon* have touched a nerve – it seems to be acceptable, even sexy, for young women to come across as ladettes, but not for them to actually adopt male attitudes to violence. However, young women themselves take a rather different view. Chappell (1997), in a Q methodological study of different understandings of young women and violence, found that only media images conform to the stereotype of the violent young woman as a 'bitter and twisted' psychopath (for example, the lead character in *The Hand that Rocks the Cradle*). When describing young women that they knew, the representations were much more mundane – the school bully, the attention-seeker, the girl who is 'stroppy' and the go-getter who loses her temper.

It is therefore important to distinguish between the evidence of changes in values and behaviour which does seem to be saying something meaningful (that young women are becoming more assertive and less prepared to accept traditional female passivity), and that which is being hyped up in an anti-feminist backlash campaign.

One way of looking at what is going on is to suggest that what we are seeing is a **third-wave feminism**. Think back to Chapter 5. Whereas first-wave feminism was mostly about taking action, second-wave feminism had much more to do with theorizing. Paglia has commented that it was 'text-driven. There were all kinds of theoretical polemicists people had to read and keep up on' (quoted in O'Brien 1998). Now a number of commentators are suggesting that feminism has entered a third wave which is being acted out not in academia but in the media, especially in music:

> In the US, they call it the Third Wave – a new feminism for a new generation. It is fuelled by popular culture in general and music in particular, and its icons are women with the right attitude, the right looks and a microphone.
>
> (O'Brien 1998: 8)

One of the major legacies of the permissive 1960s (see Chapter 4) has been a liberalization of performance, whether in the theatre or at a rock concert. At first this was used merely to present 'male gaze' spectacles, from the nude performers of shows like *Oh Calcutta!* to the excesses of guitars smashed up on stage. But more recently women have begun to use performance to open up 'the politics of the personal'. The kinds of 'in your face' young women that Wilkinson and Mulgan (1996) describe are epitomized by stand-up comics such as Jo Brand and singers like Tori Amos, Sinéad O'Connor and Ani DiFranco. All of these women have subjected to often fierce polemic topics ranging from contraception to abortion, child sexual abuse to rape, dieting to suntans, menstruation to menopause. And over time these performances have moved from the fringe to the mainstream:

> When I first started to get out there, some people thought: militant, angry, man-hating, puppy-eating feminist. Yikes! Now it's different. There's the industry hype of chick singers in rock, plus a lot of female-informed rock out there. People are getting more used to the idea of the girl with the big mouth.
>
> (Ani DiFranco, cited in O'Brien 1998: 8)

At the same time the distinction between performers and audience has become increasingly blurred – look on any dance floor and you will see some amazing performances. It is in spaces like this that 1980s and 1990s feminism has been acted out. Hebdige (1979) drew attention to the punk girl's laddered stockings and in-your-face hair and make-up, which offered a challenge to conventional femininity. McRobbie (1994) has pointed to the way that young women often dress up on the dance floor in a hyper-sexual, 'Barbie-doll' style which deliberately ironizes femininity. Icons such as Chrissie Hynde, Debbie Harry, Madonna and Skin of Skunk Anansie have provided potent role models for young women, showing them that women can be overtly (and even aggressively) sexual and outspoken while retaining their femininity. 'Girl power', for all its media hype and continued potential for exploitation both of its performers and consumers, effectively counters the stereotype of the 'sad, drab dyke' image of feminism.

We still need to be wary of the backlash argument (see Chapter 5) – that now the battle is won and girl power rules, there is nothing left for women to fight for. For all the successful career women breaking through the glass ceiling, for all the women entrepreneurs running their own businesses, many of the girls who dress up as babes on a Saturday night still return to a low-paid, no-future job on a Monday morning. And their well-paid sisters will find the going very tough indeed if and when they try to combine work with motherhood. They will still have problems getting doctors to take their 'women's problems' seriously, and may still be sexually harassed and subjected to violence in their relationships with men. Yet it can be argued that in its third wave, feminism has come of age. It is no longer restricted to a small elite of academics and political activists, but has passed into popular culture. Indeed, many aspects of feminism have become so familiar and taken for granted that new women do not see them as feminism at all – simply 'the way things are'.

New relationships

Turner (1954) argued that romantic love as a cultural form emerged (as far as Eurocentric history is concerned) in the complex social dynamics of the twelfth century. He claimed that it was a French invention with roots in Languedoc. 'Into this highly charged atmosphere rode the troubadours . . . singing of a new passion, of the ecstasies, and sorrows of unsatisfied desire' (Turner 1954: 24). There are, needless to say, other stories around, but the medieval romantic tale is the most common trail followed by historians of love. It has the additional advantage of being easily accessible through Eco's first novel (subsequently turned to film) *The Name of the Rose* (1984) in which Adso's 'love-sickness' is skilfully described.

Like gender and sexuality, love is culturally constituted – a want (a socially constructed desire) rather than a need (a biologically grounded drive, like hunger). One of the great true love stories of the medieval world is that between the scholar Abelard and his pupil Héloise. Her family were not amused and, even after the couple had regularized their affair by getting married, pursued them and castrated Abelard. Romeo and Juliet fared even worse. Indeed, what is surprising, given the notable lack of happy endings in romantic stories (Mills and Boon apart, of course), is that true love retains such popularity today. Even though our ideas of gender and sexuality have undergone such enormous change (as we have argued throughout this book) in the past 200 years since the birth of Modernism, true love seems to have stubbornly refused to give up and go away.

However, what have changed are the conventions and mores by which sexual encounters and relationships are acted out. To bring home the enormity of the change, consider Vera Brittain's (1933) description in her book *Testament of Youth* of the controls imposed on contact between men and women students at university. Writing of the time when she and her brother, Edward, first went to study at Oxford, she said:

> In the intervals between cocoa, Greek and religion, I saw something of Edward. On account of the strict chaperonage regulations of those days (always disrespectfully referred to as 'chap. rules') I was not allowed to go to his rooms in Oriel Street lest I should encounter the seductive gaze of some other undergraduate, but met him in cafés and at the practices of the Bach choir. . . . If ever he dropped

> in unexpectedly to tea with me at Somerville, I was obliged to hastily eject any friends who may be sitting in my room, for fear his tabood sex might contaminate their girlish integrity.
>
> (Brittain 1933/78: 111)

Within her social class and at that period in history, young men and women of twenty were recognized as sexually mature, in the sense that they were seen as capable of engaging in sex. Indeed, as Brittain wryly describes, the 'chap. rules' specifically drew attention to the 'dangers' that were feared to be lurking within young people's incipient sexuality. These rules were devised to keep what was seen as the danger of youthful sexuality under strict control. What was also different at that period in history compared with today – and profoundly different – was that sexuality was not only controlled by external regulation. Individuals exerted strong self-control too. A young woman of good character like Vera Brittain felt obliged to abstain from sex before marriage (although, as she goes on to describe later in the book, such attitudes were soon to change as a result of the First World War). Before her fiancé, Roland, was to be sent to fight (and ultimately to die) in France, he got leave so that they could spend some time together. She writes about how she considered the possibility of a speedy marriage before he left. But the idea of just meeting up and having sex with Roland outside of marriage simply did not arise. It was, quite literally, unthinkable.

Even in the 1950s two-parent families were the norm, and anything else tended to be seen by respectable people as distinctly undesirable. Getting a divorce or being an unwed mother were seen as shameful; cohabitation was viewed as living in sin; and women who became pregnant outside of marriage were made to feel that the best thing they could do for their babies was to have them adopted. Male homosexuality was illegal, and lesbianism was seen as sick and sinful when acknowledged at all – usually it was simply coyly ignored.

In Chapter 4 we saw how this kind of external and self-regulation over sexuality gradually and spasmodically gave way to sexual liberation (though conventional morality was never, of course, anything like universal). Divorce and single parenting have now become almost universally socially acceptable and common. Most heterosexual couples live together before marriage – and an increasing number of people have turned their back on marriage altogether. These days the traditional family of a heterosexual couple and their children represents only 23 per cent of households (Haskey 1994). And even in these traditional families, there have been considerable changes. People are, on average, marrying later. In about a third of families it will be a second marriage. The couple will, on average, have their children later, and, on average, fewer of them. The woman is much more likely to work more or less throughout the marriage, and her income is likely to make a crucial contribution to family finances – indeed, in a growing number of families it will be the major or only income. Housework and child care have become somewhat more shared, although the woman is still likely to do much more than the man. Alongside this there has been rapid growth in the number of one-parent families, and families composed of gay or lesbian couples. There are a number of factors that have brought about these changes, but possibly the most influential is a general liberalization of personal relationships which goes beyond sexual liberation.

In the 1990s first-time marriages were at their lowest level for more than a hundred years (Haskey 1994). Today, rather than being an automatic step for a (heterosexual) couple to take (as it was in the 1950s), marriage has now become, for most (in statistical terms) of today's generation of young people, a matter of personal choice, made (if at all) in the mid to late twenties or older, and generally following a period of cohabitation. There are exceptions, of course. In some communities and families early marriage is still the norm, and divorce rare. But the overall trend is very marked.

Alongside changed attitudes to marriage, expectations about the nature and purpose of couple relationships have undergone considerable shifts too (Lewis *et al.* 1992). In the marriage of the 1950s, the husband tended to be valued most for his breadwinning capacity and the wife for her home-making abilities. A good marriage was seen to be based on faithfulness, mutual respect, understanding and tolerance. But by the 1970s popular conceptions of couple relationships had undergone considerable change. Coupledom came to be seen as based on romantic love rather than pragmatics. Now what tends to be most valued in a good marriage or couple relationship is emotional intimacy, mutual affection and sexual fulfilment. Basically the shift has been from marriage-as-norm, seen as an institution, to coupledom, seen as a source of love, affection and personal satisfaction.

Remember, though, that one of the broader cultural shifts has been fragmentation. This also applies to relationships, as documented by Stenner and Watts (1997). In their study they identified a number of different understandings of what love is – an exchange, a cultural accommodation, a quest for fulfilment, a commitment, a partnership and a strategy for getting sex. These ways of telling love are part of our cultural stock of knowledge. Possibly more than any other understandings about human nature, they have been woven into the narratives which inform us about how to live our lives. We know them and need to know them, not only to be able to negotiate our relationships with others directly, but also to be able to make sense of soaps, pop songs, cinema and even opera. And perhaps it is there, as much as anywhere, we can begin to see how relationships are changing.

> If I was your girlfriend . . . [*sic*] so sings Prince on the hit single taken from his *Sign of the Times* LP. . . . Slithering between hetero and homosexuality, blackness and whiteness, masculinity and femininity. Simultaneously embodying a desire that in its urgency becomes disembodied, this song gives voice to an overwhelming want that pays no heed to sexual difference.
>
> (Moore 1988: 165–7)

As the old divisions, including distinctions of gender and sexuality, get perturbated (see Chapter 6) not just in academic theory but in popular culture, as old certainties about what love is dissolve, as gender and sexuality become not so much identities as performances, relationships become blurred. Is s/he my 'partner', my 'girlfriend', the 'love-of-my-life', my 'sexual friend', my 'lover' or my 'date'? Who knows?

Whatever next?

If everything is in flux – if we are now living in a world of new men, new women and new relationships – then is it possible to have any idea of where we are going, or (even trickier this one) where we *should* be going? It is all very well celebrating some sort of postmodern carnival, but, as they say, 'it doesn't pay the rent' (or for anything else).

Wilkinson and Mulgan (1995) offer at least one kind of practical response to the changes we are seeing. A new agenda is needed, he argues, to meet the needs, expectations and aspirations of the new generation of 18–34-year-olds. This new agenda must:

- redefine the balance between rights, freedoms and responsibilities of men and women;
- develop strategies which embrace and enable diversity as well as guaranteeing rights;
- rethink male and female roles in the context of the new economic climate and new patterns of employment and occupation;
- provide more supportive structures to help people to balance their wants, needs and responsibilities – to work, to care for others and to lead fulfilling lives.

That seems to us not a bad place to start.

Implications for psychology

- Traditional 'feminine' characteristics – such as submissiveness and interests in things like needlework – that were assumed by psychologists to be 'natural' aspects of femininity are clearly products of cultural and structural influences. For example, as the economics of the workplace change in ways that 'feminize' working practices, women's ways of working and thinking have become more valued. Hence, for example, the notion of 'submissiveness' (with its negative connotations) is being transformed into more positive qualities, such as 'cooperativeness'.

- Equally, traditional 'masculine' characteristics are coming to be viewed differently. But whereas what we understand by 'femininity' is changing – in the sense that women are redefining it – 'masculinity' appears to be more resistant to change. For some this heralds a 'crisis of masculinity', wherein men (especially young men) are facing an identity crisis and experiencing psychological problems in adjustment.
- Traditional psychological research into values is also being called into question. What were thought of as lawful connections (for example, that left-wing political values tend to emphasize equality, whereas right-wing values emphasize freedom) can now also be seen to be culturally mediated. As values fragment and realign, new connections are becoming apparent. Values must thus be seen as socially constructed.
- Theorization about interpersonal relationships is also in flux, as the nature of relationships between man and woman can be seen to be changing.
- Overall then, with both men and women redefining their gendered identities, and with values and interpersonal relationships in flux, psychologists are having to take a hard look at the assumptions that underpin their theorization and research in these fields.

Further reading

Epstein, D., Elwood, J., Hey, V. and Maw, J. (1998) *Failing Boys? Issues in Gender and Achievement*. Buckingham: Open University Press.

Petersen, A. (1998) *Unmasking the Masculine: 'Men' and 'Identity' in a Sceptical Age*. London: Sage.

Simon, W. (1996) *Postmodern Sexualities*. London: Routledge.

Staggenborg, S. (1997) *Gender, Family and Social Movements*. London: Sage.

Walby, S. (1997) *Gender Transformations*. London: Routledge.

Wilkinson, H. (1994) *No Turning Back: Generations and the Genderquake*. London: Demos.

Wilkinson, H. and Mulgan, G. (1995) *Freedom's Children: Work, Relationships and Politics for 18–34 year olds in Britain Today*. London: Demos.

Glossary

The **adolescent growth spurt** occurs during the transition from child to adult. It is when the child's bones (especially the long bones in legs and arms) and muscles suddenly grow a lot faster, so that the child relatively rapidly gains adult size and proportions.

Adrenogenital syndrome is a genetic disorder that can affect both XX and XY foetuses. It results from a reduction in adrenal cortisol (hydrocortisone), which in turn leads to an increase in adrenal androgens (male hormones). For boys the main impact is an accelerated onset of puberty. In girls, however, the excess of androgens leads to a masculinization of the body – an enlarged clitoris at birth (which may look like a penis) and the development of a sac resembling a scrotum. The internal sex organs are usually unaffected (see Box 1.4, page 20).

Ageing actress syndrome is a term devised by Wilson and Nias to describe the tendency for women who have been very attractive when young to become less happy than women of average attractiveness as they age.

Anal fisting (also simply called 'fisting') is a practice where sexual gratification is obtained by inserting the whole fist into another person's anus.

The **anal stage** is, according to Freud, the second stage of psychosexual development, where the anus is the primary site of sensuous pleasure. See Chapter 3 for more details.

Androcentrism means 'male centredness'. So, for example, an androcentric view of the world is one which is perceived from a male point of view.

Androgen insensitivity syndrome is a genetic disorder where, although the chromosomal structure shows the usual 46 chromosome, XY male pattern, the androgen (q.v.) receptors in the body do not 'recognize' the circulating androgens. The outcome is that at birth the individual looks female but there are actually no matching internal genitalia. The Müllerian system (q.v.)

does not develop. Individuals with this syndrome are infertile, and do not menstruate (see Box 1.4, page 20).

Androgens are male sex hormones (q.v.) – male in the sense that they are most active in men, although women also have them in smaller quantities.

Androgyny is usually defined as the state of having the most desirable qualities of both masculinity and femininity. In other words, a person who is androgynous is one who is neither strongly masculine nor strongly feminine, but has a balance of the best elements of both. See Chapter 4 for more details.

Anorexia means, literally, loss of appetite. However it is often used as a shortened form of anorexia nervosa (q.v.).

Anorexia nervosa is defined as severe *self-induced* weight loss producing at least a 15 per cent drop below minimal normal weight. See Chapter 9 for further details.

Anti-masturbatory devices were used in the nineteenth century to prevent children from masturbating. They were also devised for horses. They look like instruments of torture – one consisted of a leather ring to be tied around the penis, with sharp spikes pointing inwards.

Behaviourism is an approach to psychology which claims that all it can study is behaviour – since anything else (feelings, mental states and so on) is not accessible to objective study.

Biomode is a term devised by Colley to describe the degree of match between a person's gender and physique – for example, the way in which a powerful, muscular body typifies masculinity. See Chapter 2 for more details.

Biopsychology is an approach to psychology which emphasizes the biological determinants of human behaviour and experience.

B-love was Maslow's term for what he called 'being-love' – giving, unselfish, true love which is based on mutuality, respect and a genuinely caring attitude to the beloved.

Body dysmorphic disorder is a term devised by Phillips to describe a constellation of behaviours such as the overuse of or avoidance of mirrors, frequent and prolonged grooming, feeling bad because of how you look, and in more extreme cases, self-harm.

Bondage is any sexual practice which involves tying up, done to increase sexual arousal (either of the person doing the tying or the person being tied, or both) and/or to make the tied person unable to move – hence putting the other person in control. Bondage can also be used to affect sexual response (for example, tying up a woman's breasts to make them more sensitive) or sexual performance (for example, tying up a man's penis can help to retain his erection).

Boo-word is a term devised by Cranston to highlight the way that language can be used strategically, not just to describe but to deliberately indicate the required response from the reader or listener. A boo-word is one deliberately intended to evoke a negative reaction. Female genital mutilation is a good example.

Bowdlerize is a form of censorship. The term is derived from the way that Thomas Bowdler produced an expurgated edition of Shakespeare's works, in which all the references to sex and sexuality were discreetly removed to protect the sensibilities of, particularly, women and children.

Bulimia nervosa is defined as a condition (or constellation of behaviours) in which binge-eating is followed by purging through self-induced vomiting and/or the use of laxatives. See Chapter 9 for further details.

The **cerebral cortex** is the part of the brain that covers its top and looks a bit like a walnut kernel. It is divided into two halves – two hemispheres. It is the 'highest' part of the brain in its function – this is where all complex thinking occurs.

Chromosomal sex is the term given to an individual's sex – male or female – determined according to their chromosomes. Males have an XY pair of genes, females an XX pair, although other arrangements are possible which may lead to confusions over an individual's sex (see Box 1.4 for details, page 20).

Chromosomes are the structures in the nucleus of cells which contain genetic information. Humans have 46 chromosomes.

Circumcision means surgery on the genitals. Male circumcision involves the removal of the foreskin of the penis. Female circumcision varies in its form, but it usually involves the excision of the clitoris and may include the surgical closure (for example, with thorns) of the vagina in a way that leaves only a very small opening. See Chapter 9 for further details.

The **climate of perturbation** is a concept introduced by Stainton Rogers *et al.* (1995) to describe a growing fringe from mainstream thinking in the social sciences marked by its determination to stir up trouble and raise doubt about both their praxes and their epistemological, methodological and philosophical foundations. See the Introduction to Section 2 for more details.

Clitorectomy is the medical term for the surgical removal of the clitoris (q.v.). Its boo-word (q.v.) equivalent is 'female genital mutilation'. It was practised in England in the nineteenth century as a treatment for masturbation.

Clitoris is an organ sited at the top of the vaginal opening, between a woman's labia (q.v.), which is very sensitive to stimulation because it is richly supplied with nerves. It is for many women the site on their body most able to give them sexual pleasure. In a quiescent state it is covered by a hood of skin, which retracts when a woman becomes sexually excited.

Cognitive relates to thinking. In psychology the term cognitive implies higher-order thought which involves insight and reasoning.

Cognitive alien is a term adopted by Piaget's followers to stress the *qualitatively* different way that children think from adults.

The **cognitive revolution** in psychology was a theoretical shift from models of human thinking based on an analogy between the brain and a telephone exchange – the brain as an information processor – to models based on an analogy with a computer. These models view the brain as not only able to simply process information but also capable of applying knowledge stored in memory to inputs from the outside, thus perceiving the world in relation to pre-existing understanding.

Communes were popular in the 1960s. They consisted of households of a number of adults and often children living together, based on multilateral relationships (q.v.). They were intended as a direct challenge to conventional coupledom and families. They are rarer now, but still exist.

Conditioning is defined as the process through which organisms learn by associating a particular stimulus with a particular response. The classic example is from the work of Pavlov, who trained dogs to salivate when they heard a bell sounding. This he did by sounding a bell just before he fed them. Gradually the dogs developed a conditioned reflex – the sound of the bell became associated with the anticipation of food, and so they salivated whenever they heard it.

A **conflict view of gender** regards the different roles and positions of men and women as arising out of a conflict of interests. Feminism is the best-known theory which adopts this view.

A **consensus view of gender** sees the differences between men and women as manifestations of humankind's capacity to co-operate for the common good, and is based on structural functionalism (q.v.).

The **conventional level of moral development** is, according to Kohlberg, about achieving the middle ground of moral reasoning. At this level an individual views good and bad in terms of the conventions and rules of their culture and society.

The **corpus callosum** is a bundle of nerves that joins the two hemispheres of the cerebral cortex (q.v.).

Creata is a term devised by Andersen to ironize the word data, drawing attention to its constructed nature. See Chapter 7 for more details.

Critical psychology has emerged from the climate of perturbation (q.v.) to challenge mainstream psychology, both in terms of its politics and the inadequacy of its theorization.

A **culture-bound syndrome** is one which occurs only in a particular culture. An example is *koro*, a South-East Asian syndrome, in which men develop a morbid fear that the penis will withdraw into the abdomen with fatal consequences.

Cunnilingus is oral stimulation of a woman's genitals – for example by sucking and licking her clitoris (q.v.), vagina and her inner and outer labia (q.v.).

Différance is a term devised by Lacan to describe not simply a difference from a counterpart (for example, the difference between men and women) but the way in which the one is inherently opposed to its 'other'. See Chapter 5 for more details.

D-love was Maslow's term for what he called 'deficiency-love' – love that is based on a basic, selfish need to be loved rather than true love, which he called B-love (q.v.).

DNA (deoxyribonucleic acid) is the chemical name for genetic material. It has the shape of a twisted ladder, with the side-bars consisting of complex sugars and the cross-struts made up of interlocking nitrogenous bases: adenine, cytosine, thiamine and guanine.

The **Electra complex** is, in Freud's theory of psychosexual development, the girl's equivalent to a boy's Oedipus complex (q.v.). When a girl realizes that boys have a penis and she does not, she experiences penis envy (q.v.). She sees her vagina as the wound arising from the removal of the penis and this sense of 'having something missing' makes the girl feel inferior. She feels hostile to her mother because she blames her. So she transfers her affections to her father, but then surrenders her sexual desire for him and identifies with her mother. See Chapter 3 for more details.

Electrotherapy is therapy using electricity, popular in Freud's time.

Enculturation is the internalization (q.v.) of culture – the process by which individuals become members of their culture, familiar with its rules, conventions, customs and world-view.

Erotica is generally defined as explicitly sexual material (it can be images or text or, indeed, any other medium) designed to arouse sexuality and provide sensual pleasure, but which does not – unlike pornography (q.v.) – deprave or corrupt. It is also often called, these days, soft pornography – soft not in the sense of tumescence, but because it seems to show consensual sexual activity that does not involve violence.

Ethnic cleansing is an euphemistic term used in the Bosnia-Hercegovina war to describe the genocide, rape and forcible removal of Muslims by Serbs. See Chapter 10 for further details.

Evolution is defined as the process through which all the different species of living things (including humans) came to exist. Starting from very simple organisms, a combination of genetic mutation and natural selection (q.v.) brought new species into existence. Evolution is generally seen as progressive – that is, it has moved from simple organisms to more complex ones (see Box 1.1, page 12).

Excitement is the initial stage in human sexual response (see Box 1.6 for more details, page 29).

Existentialism is a philosophy which denies that there are any universal, objective values, and holds that individuals must construct values for themselves in the way that they act and live their lives.

Externalization is a term used by Berger and Luckmann to refer to the way in which cultures, societies and social groups of different kinds make sense of – and therefore 'make' – their social worlds, including a whole range of social institutions and constructs. See Chapter 6 for more details.

Extraverts According to Eysenck's theory of personality, **extraverts** are physiologically 'dampened' and so do not respond readily to external stimulation, and are not easily conditioned (q.v.). Hence they seek out stimulation – they tend to be sociable, talkative, lively and carefree when they are emotionally 'together'; but touchy, restless, aggressive, excitable and impulsive when they are not. See Chapter 3 for more details.

Family planning clinic – in the post-war period up until the 1970s contraception was not available from the UK National Health Service. At this time it was family planning clinics that provided access to contraceptive advice and services.

Fellatio is oral stimulation of a man's penis – for example, by sucking and licking.

Fin de siècle translated from the French means the period leading up to the end of a century.

First-wave feminism is primarily concerned with the material conditions of women's lives, a *civil political* crusade to gain equal treatment for women in terms of the law, in citizenship and welfare rights, and in the workplace. See Chapter 5 for more details.

Foetus is the term given to an immature mammal when it is developing in the uterus.

Follicle-stimulating hormone (FSH) at puberty stimulates the gonads to increase the production of oestrogens and androgens, which results in the maturation of the gonads. It is also active in the woman's cycle of fertility.

Follicular phase is the part of a woman's fertility cycle where the amount of follicle-stimulating hormone (q.v.) increases, stimulating ovarian follicles to grow around one or more ova. The follicles begin to release oestrogens, such as oestradiol. These oestrogens stimulate the hypothalamus to increase the production of luteinizing hormone and follicle stimulating hormone from the pituitary.

Free association was a technique used by Freud. It consists of giving the patient a word and asking them to respond with the first words that come to mind.

Gang rape is where a group of men act together to rape one or more women. See Chapter 10 for further details.

The **gay gene** is the term given to a speculative gene (q.v.) which is assumed to determine an individual's sexuality – hetero- or homosexuality. Its existence is contested and research evidence for it is weak (see Chapter 1 for more details).

Gender constancy is, according to Kohlberg, the stage of development at which a child recognizes that gender is unchanging.

Gender knowledge is, according to Kohlberg, the stage of development at which a child acquires accurate knowledge of the characteristics of female and male gender.

Gender labelling is, according to Kohlberg, the stage of development at which a child gains an understanding of the concept of gender sufficiently to be able to label people as male or female.

Gender role is the term given to the way in which people act out or perform their gender – if they have a male gender, for example, they act as a man is supposed to act, according to the customs and conventions of their culture and the society in which they live.

Gender schema theory is a development from Bartlett's theorizing about schema (q.v.). It was devised by Bem, and views children's acquisition of an understanding of gender as more complex than simple social learning.

Gender stereotyping – a gender stereotype is a schematized set of beliefs about the psychological traits and characteristics, as well as the behaviours expected of (and seen as appropriate for) men and women.

Gender tourism is a term used to describe a growing tendency for 'straights' to engage in gay culture – for example, by frequenting gay clubs, adopting gay forms of dress and, indeed, exploring their sexuality by having gay sex, without committing to 'being gay'. See Chapter 11 for more details.

Gendered identity is the term given to the way in which an individual's identity is gendered – the way 'being a woman', for example, is central to a particular woman's sense of her self as a person.

Gene is the term given to specific portions of genetic material which carry a particular segment of information.

Genetic inheritance is the process through which individuals are seen to acquire at conception and hence be born with particular qualities (such as their sex, pigmentation of skin, hair and eyes and susceptibility to certain diseases). These, being wired in to the genes, are seen as largely enduring and unchangeable (see Box 1.1, page 12).

The **genital stage** is, according to Freud, the fifth and final stage of psychosexual development, when sensuality becomes mature and is linked into adult sexuality – pleasure is gained through sexual intercourse. For a woman, in Freudian theory, this involves a transfer from clitoral to vaginal orgasm. See Chapter 3 for more details.

Gonads is the generic term for the reproductive organs – testes in the male and ovaries in the female.

Grundyism is the term used to describe a narrow-minded, busybody concern with the sexual morals of others. It derives from the play *Speed the Plough* by T. Morton.

Habituation is the simplest form of conditioning (q.v.). If a stimulus is repeated over and over again, the organism being stimulated tends to respond less and less. An example is putting on perfume. At first you will experience its smell quite powerfully, but after a while you will smell it less.

Harm warrants is a term devised by O'Dell to describe the way that psychological 'harm' is often used to warrant (q.v.) intervention. An example is the way that the harm attributed to child sexual abuse is used to warrant measures for child protection. See Chapter 9 for further details.

Healthism is a term devised by Crawford to describe the pursuit of the optimally healthy and attractive body. See Chapter 9 for further details.

The **heterosexual matrix** is a term devised by Butler to describe 'that grid of cultural intelligibility through which bodies, genders and desires are naturalised' (Butler 1990: 151). See Chapter 10 for further details.

Homoerotic describes sexual and/or sensual desire for members of the same gender.

Homophobia means, literally, fear of homosexuals, although it is usually taken to have a broader meaning which includes antagonism and prejudice towards homosexuals and homosexuality.

Hormones are chemicals that are produced by endocrine glands and travel around the body in the bloodstream. Particular organs in the body are receptive to particular hormones – they possess a biochemical receptor site which, when activated by a hormone, 'turns on' or 'turns off' a particular process (see Box 1.2 for more details, page 16).

Humaneering is a term devised by Tiffin *et al.* (1940) to convey the sense of modifying human society for the better – by analogy with the word 'engineering'.

The **humaneering mission** is a concept introduced by Stainton Rogers *et al.* (1995) to describe the way that psychology sees itself as a force for human betterment – its mission to go forth and discover new ills and heal them, new problems and solve them, new questions and answer them.

Humanistic psychology was devised in the 1960s to bring to psychology a more human 'third force' following disillusionment with its domination by behaviourism and psychoanalysis. It sought to find ways of exploring each individual's uniqueness rather than trying to formulate universal laws of human behaviour. It stressed the rights of individuals to make their own choices about the direction their lives will take. See Chapter 4 for more details.

Hurrah-word is a term devised by Cranston to highlight the way that language can be used strategically, not just to describe but to deliberately indicate the required response from the reader or listener. A hurrah-word is intended to evoke a positive reaction. The word 'natural' is often used as a hurrah-word – as in 'natural ingredients' or 'natural goodness'.

Hydrotherapy is therapy using water, popular in Freud's time.

The **hypothalamus** is a brain structure in the cerebral cortex which produces hormones that trigger the pituitary (q.v.) into action.

Hypothetico-deductive method is the basis of scientific research. It consists of devising a hypothesis – a speculation on what effect a particular variable will have – and then testing to discover whether or not it does have the hypothesized effect. Strictly, such a method cannot prove anything – all that it can do with certainty is disprove the hypothesis. In psychology, statistical techniques are used to judge the probability of an effect arising through chance.

Identification is a process described both in Freudian and social learning theory, by which children model themselves on another person, such as a parent.

The **imaginary order** is a term devised by Lacan to describe the system of unconscious desires, motivations and significances which contributes to our intersubjective world of meaning whereby our subjectivity is produced. See Chapter 5 for more details.

Instinct is behaviour which is genetically programmed and therefore automatic. An example is the 'dance' performed by bees to communicate the site of pollen to other bees. Human behaviour is seldom instinctual, but, for example, an infant's sucking response to being touched on the face by a nipple is instinctive.

Internalization – Berger and Luckmann define internalization as the process by which the objectified social world becomes known, understood and made familiar through processes of socialization and enculturation (see Chapter 6 for more details). An example is the way that children internalize the rules, conventions and customs of their culture, their community and their family. They not only learn to follow these, but they become 'part of them' – who and what they are as people.

Interpersonal politics are about what Foucault called the 'micro-politics of power' (q.v.). An example is the power differential between a woman patient and the doctors who have the power to agree (or not) to her having an abortion. Second-wave feminism seeks to open up these kinds of power differentials to scrutiny, contending that these forms of power can be as oppressive to women as their political and legal disenfranchisement.

Intersexuality (sometimes called hermaphroditism) is a rare genetic disorder, where a person is born with characteristics of both sexes. An individual may have, say, an ovary on one side of the body and a testicle on the other. Alternatively, both tissues may combine together to produce a structure called an ovotestis (see Box 1.4, page 19).

Introvert – according to Eysenck's theory of personality, introverts are physiologically sensitive to external stimulation, and so respond readily to input and are easily conditioned (q.v.). Hence they tend to avoid stimulation – they tend to be careful, thoughtful, peaceful, self-controlled, reliable, even-tempered and calm when they are emotionally 'together'; and moody, anxious, rigid, reserved when they are not. See Chapter 3 for more details.

The **Jonah complex** is a term devised by Maslow to denote the way that some people cannot achieve self-actualization (q.v.) because they fear the consequences of such self-knowledge.

Jouissance is a term devised by Cixous. It is a difficult word to translate, but contains elements of joyfulness and sensuous pleasure going beyond the purely erotic.

Klinefelter's syndrome is a genetic disorder that results from having one or more extra chromosomes – 47 or more instead of the usual 46. An XXY configuration disturbs male physiology. Males with this syndrome have male internal and external genitalia, but their testes are small and they are infertile, and have a lowered libido (see Box 1.4, page 18).

Kwolu-aatmwol is the New Guinea name given to a genetic disorder that is found there and in the Dominican Republic. It means 'male thing-transforming-into-female thing' and arises through a deficiency in the enzyme 5-alpha ructase, which prevents testosterone from producing the usual male genitalia at the foetal stage of development. Individuals born with this condition have genitals which are ambiguous – their penis looks more like a clitoris, and their scrotum is unfused and looks like labia. Often such individuals are raised as girls, although they are genetically XY. At puberty they produce testosterone, and become masculinized. Their penis grows, their testes descend, they grow facial hair and their musculature takes on a male shape. Such individuals seem to transform from girl children into men as they become adult (see Box 1.4, page 20).

Labia means literally 'lips', but in relation to sex usually means the inner and outer lips surrounding a woman's vaginal opening.

The **latency stage** is, according to Freud, the fourth stage of psychosexual development. It is a period when the child's sensuality is 'on hold'. See Chapter 3 for more details.

Lateralization is the process which occurs in childhood when the two hemispheres (halves) of the cortex of the brain become specialized in their function. Generally, the left hemisphere specializes in processing language, and the right hemisphere specializes in processing spatial information.

The **luteal phase** is the part of a woman's fertility cycle where, when the ovum is not fertilized, progesterone and oestradiol levels begin to fall.

Luteinizing hormone (LH) at puberty stimulates the gonads to increase the production of oestrogens and androgens, which results in the maturation of the gonads. It is also active in the woman's fertility cycle.

Materiality is a term devised by Butler to describe the physical presence and appearance of our bodies – their shape, size, colour and form, and their constituent parts of skin, hair, blood and organs. See Chapter 9 for further details.

Meiosis is a special kind of cell division that happens only in the gonads (q.v.). The usual number of chromosomes is reduced by half, passing into the sperm in males and the eggs in females. Thus when a sperm fertilizes an egg, the result is a full set of chromosomes.

Menopause is the term given to the stage in a woman's life when menstruation has ceased.

The **menstrual phase** is the part of a woman's fertility cycle which happens if the ovum has not been fertilized. The walls of the uterus are sloughed off as menstrual flow.

Methodolatry is a term devised by Curt to describe mainstream psychology's obsession with and worship of method, to the point that this comes to dominate research. Thus the questions being investigated may be trivial or unanswerable – but as long as the method is 'sound', the research is likely to get published.

The **micro-politics of power** is a term devised by Foucault to draw attention to the way in which power operates in interpersonal relations, both institutionally (for example, between a doctor and patient) and in personal relationships (for example, between a husband and wife).

Misogyny means, literally, women-hatred.

Mitosis is the process of ordinary cell division, by which cells replicate.

Modelling is a term used by Bandura to describe the process where children imitate the behaviour of the people around them.

Modernism, as we have used the term in this book, is the set of values and practices that emerged out of the eighteenth-century Enlightenment. It was motivated by the conviction that humankind can – and, crucially, *should* – create a better world through its *own* efforts (rather than, say, relying on the benevolence of God). Modernism, as an ideology, stresses reason and rationality. It contends that knowledge can be gained only by rational means, primarily through scientific methods of empirical inquiry. For more details, see the Introduction to Section 2.

Morphology is the process through which body form develops as a result of physiological influence (see Box 1.1, page 12).

The **Müllerian system** is a structure in an embryo that has the capacity to generate a female reproductive system – ovaries, a uterus and a vagina.

Multilateral relationships are sexual and/or romantic relationships that involve more than two people.

Natural selection is the evolutionary process by which the fittest survive long enough to produce offspring, thus passing on their genetic blueprint to the next generation. In this way new species are brought into existence.

Objectification is a term used by Berger and Luckmann to describe how our socially constructed realities are perceived as being 'out there', just as nature is out there. See Chapter 6 for more details.

Observational learning is a term used in social learning theory to describe the way that children learn how to behave by observing the actions of a role model. See Chapter 2 for further details.

The **Oedipus complex** is, according to Freudian theory, a crucial component of a boy's phallic stage of psychosexual development. Named after the Greek myth in which Oedipus ends up marrying his mother and killing his father, it arises from the boy's sexual feelings towards his mother, which he resolves by creating a powerful identification with his father. See Chapter 3 for more details.

Oestradiol is the most common oestrogen (q.v.).

Oestrogens are female sex hormones (q.v.) – female in the sense that they are most active in women, although men also have them in smaller quantities

Open marriage was a term much used in the 1960s (today we would tend to talk of an open relationship) to denote a marriage in which the couple agree to accept each other having sexual and/or romantic relationships with others.

The **oral stage** is, according to Freud, the first stage of psychosexual development, where the mouth is the primary site of sensuous pleasure. See Chapter 3 for more details.

Orgasm is the point in the human sexual response at which the climax happens (see Box 1.6 for more details, page 30).

Orientalism is a term devised by Said to draw attention to the way that the dominant culture of the West views its own knowledge as the norm and treats other forms of knowledge (such as that coming from the East – the Orient and the Arab world) as 'exotic' and other (q.v.).

Otherness is a term used to describe a process by which certain groups and individuals are treated as other – that is, 'not like us'. Haste, for example, describes it as the way that women are conceived within malestream knowledge as that by which men define themselves as not being. See Chapter 5 for more details.

Ovaries are the female reproductive organs, in which eggs are produced.

Ovulation is the part of a woman's fertility cycle when, in response to the surge of luteinizing (q.v.) and follicle stimulating (q.v.) hormones, one or more of the ovaries' follicles ruptures and releases the ovum. The ovum is then moved into the Fallopian tube and progesterone (q.v.) levels begin to increase.

Paedophile means, literally, one who loves children. However, it is generally used to describe an adult who has a sexual attraction to children.

Patriarchy is a social system that is dominated by men, where men's concerns and interests are met, men set the agenda and men wield most of the power.

Peak experience is a term devised by Maslow to describe the feeling of elation that can be achieved through self-actualization (q.v.). It is when a person is able fully to get in touch with themselves, in a spiritual sense, often triggered by a particular incident (for example, watching a beautiful sunset).

Penis envy is, in Freud's theory of psychosexual development, what happens when girls realize that boys have a penis and they do not. See Chapter 3 for more details.

Performativity is a term devised by Butler to describe what we *do* with our bodies – how with them and through their actions we present ourselves. See Chapter 9 for further details.

The **phallic stage** is, according to Freud, the third stage of psychosexual development, where, for a boy, his penis becomes primary site of sensuous pleasure – but also of anxiety. For a girl it is more complicated. She notices that she does not have a penis and experiences penis envy (q.v.). See Chapter 3 for more details.

Phallocentric means, literally, centred on the phallus, although it is usually taken to mean more generally male-centred.

Physics envy is an ironic term, playing on the concept of 'penis envy' (q.v.). It is what mainstream psychologists experience – realizing that they do not have the scientific credibility of a 'real science' like physics and therefore feeling incomplete and less potent.

Physiology is the body's chemical processes through which the genes (q.v.) are seen to exert their influence on human behaviour (see Box 1.1, page 12).

The **pituitary gland** is situated in the brain and produces a number of hormones, which, in turn, stimulate the release of other hormones. The action of the pituitary stimulates the gonads (q.v.).

The **plateau phase** is the stage in human sexual response that follows initial sexual excitement (q.v.) and precedes orgasm (see Box 1.6 for more details, page 29).

A **plesthysmograph** is a device for measuring a man's penile erection. It consists of a rubber sleeve that is fitted on to the penis and linked to a device to measure pressure. The larger and firmer the man's erection, the higher the measurement.

Pornography is defined, in law, as material (movies, images, shows and so on) in which the depiction of sex and sexuality is likely to 'deprave or corrupt'. The term is often used more loosely, however, to describe any material which portrays sex in an explicit manner.

Postmodernism differs from social constructionism through offering not only a challenge to the positivistic approach to knowledge, but an extensive and elaborate body of theorization about the processes involved in the making, maintenance and mongering of knowledge. It is also more ubiquitous than social constructionism. See Chapter 6 for more details.

The **preconventional level of moral development** is, according to Kohlberg, the crudest level of moral reasoning. It tends to be self-centred, starting with the simplistic idea that 'doing good' is about achieving good outcomes, and then moving on to seeing doing good as that which is good for oneself.

Premenstrual syndrome (PMS) is the term given to a collection of symptoms which may arise just before a woman menstruates. However, its existence is a hotly contested issue (see Chapter 1).

The **principled level of moral development** is, according to Kohlberg, the highest level of moral reasoning that an individual can achieve. Good and bad are judged by reference to the individual's own principles of right and wrong.

Progesterone is the most common progestin (q.v.). Its main function is to prepare a woman's body for pregnancy following fertilization, although men also secrete it in small quantities.

Progestins are sex hormones secreted by both males and females, although they are more active in females.

Pseudohermaphroditism is a genetic disorder that can arise from a variety of genetic 'bugs', the most common being androgen insensitivity syndrome (q.v.), adrenogenital syndrome (q.v.) and kwolu-aatmwol (q.v.) (see Box 1.4, page 20).

The **psy complex** is a term used by Rose to describe that set of institutions and professions (such as psychiatry, counselling and social work) which draw on psychological theory and methods to intervene in people's lives across a whole range of domains. See Chapter 6 for more details.

Psychometricians are involved in the study and measurement of individual differences, usually involving questionnaires or other scales (psychometrics).

Psychomode is a term devised by Colley to describe the extent to which attitudes are gender-appropriate – for example, the way that not liking people spitting typifies femininity. See Chapter 2 for more details.

A **psychotropic drug** is one which alters a person's psychological state. Examples include LSD, cannabis and Prozac.

Rape (of a woman) is defined, in a legal sense, according to the Sexual Offences Act (1956) as the penetration of the vagina by the penis without the woman's consent. However, other definitions are often used. One survey of rape, for example, defined it as being 'forced to have sex against your will'. See Chapter 10 for further details.

The **rape myth** is the assumption that women can enjoy being raped.

The **real order** is a term devised by Lacan for those aspects of our experience of the world that falls outside the domain of signification – where the psychic is felt rather than understood, for example, as a result of trauma. See Chapter 5 for more details.

Realpolitik means politics as they are practised, as opposed to what they are purported to be in rhetoric.

Resistance is a term coined by Foucault to describe the resisting of power by those in powerless positions.

The **resolution phase** is the stage in human sexual response following orgasm (see Box 1.6 for more details, page 30).

Riffraff theorizing is a term devised by Caplan to describe theorizing which seeks to make its case by discounting opponents as riffraff and their views as rubbish. See Chapter 4 for more details.

Role model is a term used in social learning theory to describe a person on whom a child models herself or himself.

Sadomasochism describes practices engaged in to obtain sexual pleasure through playing around with dominance and submission. Although the giving and receiving of pain is often involved, it is by no means always the case. Sadism – named after the Marquis de Sade – is the enactment of dominance; masochism is the enactment of submission. The variety of activities is enormous, varying from playful role play (for example, the 'sub' – submissive partner – acting as a 'pet' and being led around on a dog collar by the 'dom' – dominant partner) to practices which are clearly designed to give pain (for example, the use of clamps to hang a woman up by her nipples).

A **satellite relationship** is a term devised by Carl Rogers to describe extramarital love relationships, usually involving sex. Rogers believed that healthy marriages benefit from such relationships, and are secure enough for jealousy not to be a problem.

Schema is a term first developed by Bartlett to describe the conceptual frameworks through which people perceive and make sense of the world around them.

Scopophilia is the gaining of sexual pleasure through looking – for example, at erotica (q.v.) or in a mirror when having sex.

Second-wave feminism is primarily concerned with interpersonal politics (q.v.) – as in the slogan 'the personal is political' – what Foucault called the 'micropolitics of power' (q.v.). See Chapter 5 for more details.

Self-actualization is a term devised by Maslow to describe the capacity for satisfying one's innate curiosity about oneself and reaching one's unique potential. See Chapter 4 for more details.

The **semiotic order** is a term devised by Kristeva, drawing on the work of Lacan, to describe the pre-linguistic life stage when the child is trying to make sense of the inputs coming from the family and social structure. See Chapter 5 for more details.

Sex hormones (sometimes called gonadal hormones) are hormones that affect an individual's sexual development, sexual response and, in a woman, the fertility cycle.

Sex role is how early theorists (such as Talcott Parsons) referred to what we now call gender role (q.v.).

The **sexually dimorphic nucleus** is part of the cerebral cortex (q.v.). In rats it is much larger in males than females.

Slow masturbation is a sexual practice that involves tying up the recipient and then slowly teasing them to orgasm (see Comfort 1972 for more details).

Social constructionism involves taking a critical stance towards knowledge; seeing knowledge as history, culture and domain specific; viewing knowledge as created and sustained by social processes; and recognizing that knowledge implicates action. See Chapter 6 for more details.

Social exclusion is a term used to describe the process through which groups and individuals are excluded from the social benefits accorded to the majority – because of prejudice in different forms (such as racism, sexism or prejudice towards disablement) or, often, just a lack of thought or understanding.

Social learning theory is a development of more general learning theory, part of behaviourism (q.v.). In it the rewards and punishments that are seen to motivate people to learn are more complex than those that work for other animals – for example, a sense of achievement may act as a powerful reward, and a feeling of humiliation may act as a severe punishment. See Chapter 2 for more details.

Sociomode is a term devised by Colley to describe the extent to which people behave in gender-appropriate ways – for example, the way in which being 'warm and caring' typifies femininity. See Chapter 2 for more details.

Soixante-neuf is when two people mutually engage in oral sex, derived from the shape of the number 69.

Somatization is the term given in psychodynamic theory to a bodily manifestation of psychic distress. An example is coming out in a rash when anxious.

Standpoint describes the position being adopted in, say, the making of an argument or in theorizing. It is not just a matter of 'a point of view'. It has to do with the way that time and place, history and culture, social location and social status influence the position being taken. See Chapter 6 for more details.

Structural functionalism is a sociological theory which views social organization as coming about through a form of social evolution, in which particular social practices and customs evolve because they benefit the cohesion and smooth working of particular social groups and communities.

Super Femininity is a genetic disorder where females are born with one or more extra X chromosomes. They have a greater likelihood of learning disability, and some have menstrual irregularities and are sterile (see Box 1.4, page 19).

Super Masculinity is a genetic disorder that results from having one or more extra chromosomes – 47 or more instead of the usual 46, where there is an XYY pattern. It usually leads to making the male taller, and also raises the possibility of learning disability (see Box 1.4, page 19).

The **symbolic order** is a term devised by Lacan to describe the language-based social and intersubjective world of meaning we acquire through socialization and through which our subjectivity is produced. As used by Kristeva, it describes the stage at which the child severs dependence on the mother, becomes aware of the other and begins to construct their identity in relation to others. See Chapter 5 for more details.

Symptomologies is a term devised by O'Dell to describe how, in textbooks, authors provide lists of symptoms associated with a particular disorder or 'problem' (such as child sexual abuse) together with the scientific evidence cited to support each one. She argues that such symptomologies have the effect of making the disorder or problem seem more real. See Chapter 9 for further details.

Technologies of the self is a term devised by Foucault to describe strategies that people use to manage – or even to construct or reconstruct – their identities. It includes the way people manage their bodies (for example, by 'working out'), the images they create (by the clothes they wear) and, for example, their engagement in particular sports and pastimes (such as 'club culture'). See Chapter 11 for more details.

Techno-science is a term used to denote the complex of science and the technology it makes possible.

Testes (also known as testicles) are the male reproductive organs, in which sperm are produced.

Testosterone is the most common androgen (q.v.).

The **thalamus** is part of the cerebral cortex (q.v.).

The **thetic order** is a term devised by Kristeva, drawing on the work of Lacan, to describe the stage of development when the child starts to make sense of the world through meanings and when subjectivity and self-awareness begin to emerge. See Chapter 5 for more details.

Thingification describes the process whereby a set of coincidental events and occurrences get turned into a 'thing'. A good example is premenstrual syndrome.

Third-wave feminism is defined by O'Brien as 'a new feminism for a new generation. It is fuelled by popular culture in general and music in particular, and its icons are women with the right attitude, the right looks and a microphone' (O'Brien 1998: 8). See Chapter 11 for more details.

Transsexuals are people who see themselves as 'really being' the other gender – for instance, a man who feels that he is a woman locked in the body of a man. Such a man may seeks surgery to acquire the bodily characteristics of a woman. See Chapter 6 for more details.

Turner's syndrome is a genetic disorder where an X sex chromosome is missing from its couplet and this is usually denoted as XO (O = absence). Many embryos with this configuration are spontaneously aborted but where this does not happen the external genitalia are female in form although internally the ovaries fail to form. Ovulation is absent and there are no ovarian hormones to trigger puberty. Women with this syndrome are infertile (see Box 1.4, page 19).

Unconditional positive regard is a term devised by Carl Rogers to describe the giving of care, affection and affirmation to another, without requiring anything from them in return. Rogers believed that children who receive unconditional positive regard from their parents and caregivers grow up to be psychologically healthy.

Underwolves is a term coined by Wilkinson and Mulgan to describe underdogs who are prepared to bite back.

Urine play (also called water sports and golden rain) is a practice where sexual pleasure is gained by urinating/being urinated on.

Vaginismus is a conditioned response (see Chapter 3) in which a woman's vagina clenches up tightly when any attempt is tried to make her sexually aroused. It usually arises following painful or otherwise aversive sexual experiences, including sexual abuse in childhood. It makes penetration impossible.

Warrants are rhetorical devices which use language strategically to justify taking (or not taking) certain kinds of actions. See Chapter 9 for more details.

The **Wolffian system** is a structure in an embryo that has the capacity to generate a male reproductive system – a penis, testicles and so on.

Zeitgeist translates from the German as 'spirit of the age'. It is used to denote the dominant world-view of a particular time and place.

Bibliography

While every effort has been made to supply full and comprehensive references, this has not been possible in all cases.

ACSF Investigators (1992) AIDS and sexual behaviour in France, *Nature*, **360**: 407–9.

Adorno, T.W., Frenkel-Brunswick, E., Levinson, D. and Sandford, R.N. (1950) *The Authoritarian Personality*. New York: Harper Row.

Aldiss, B. (1971) *The Hand Reared Boy*. London: Corgi.

Alexander, R.D. (1974) The evolution of social behaviour, *Annual Review of Ecology and Systematics* **5**: 325–83.

Allen, V.L. (1965) Situational factors in conformity, in L. Berkowitz (ed.) *Advances in Experimental Social Psychology*, Volume 2. New York: Academic Press.

Allport, G.W. (1955) *Becoming*. New Haven, CT: Yale University Press.

Amir, M. (1971) *Patterns of Forcible Rape*. Chicago, IL: University of Chicago Press.

Amnesty International (1991) *Rape and Sexual Abuse: Torture and Ill-treatment of Women in Detention*. London: Amnesty International.

Andersen, M.L. (1994) The many and varied social constructions of intelligence, in T.R. Sarbin and J.I. Kituse (eds) *Constructing the Social*. London: Sage.

Arblaster, A. (1972) Liberal values and socialist values, *Socialist Register*, **9**: 83–104.

Archard, D. (1998) Can child abuse be defined?, in M. King (ed.) *Moral Agendas in Children's Welfare*. London: Routledge.

Archer, J. and Lloyd, B. (1982) *Sex and Gender*. Harmondsworth: Penguin.

Argyle, M. and Henderson, M. (1985) *The Anatomy of Relationships*. Harmondsworth: Penguin.

Aronson, E., Wilson, T.D. and Akert, R.M. (1994) *Social Psychology: The heart and the Mind*. New York: HarperCollins College Publishers.

Ashton, E. (1983) Measures of play behaviour; the influence of sex-role stereotyped children's books, *Sex Roles*, **9**: 43–7.
Asimov, I. (1964) *Second Foundation*. London: Panther, first published 1953.
Atwood, M. (1986) *The Handmaid's Tale*. London: Jonathan Cape.
Baker, R. (1996) *Sperm Wars: Infidelity, Sexual Conflict and Bedroom Battles*. London: Fourth Estate.
Bandura, A. (1986) *Social Foundations of Thought and Action: A Social Cognitive Theory*. Englewood Cliffs, NJ: Prentice-Hall.
Bandura, A. and Huston, A.C. (1961) Identification as a process of incidental learning, *Journal of Abnormal and Social Psychology*, **63**: 311–18.
Bandura, A. and Walters, R.H. (1963) *Social Learning and Personality Development*. New York: Holt, Rinehart & Winston.
Banks, M., Bates, I., Bracewell, G. *et al.* (1992) *Careers and Identities*. Buckingham: Open University Press.
Barbor, B.R. (1994) *An Aristocracy for Everyone: The Politics of Education and the Future of America*. Pakistan: Oxford University Press.
Bartlett, F.C. (1932) *Remembering*. Cambridge: Cambridge University Press.
Bass, E. and Davis, L. (1988) *The Courage to Heal: A Guide for Women Survivors of Child Sexual Abuse*. New York: Harper and Row.
Bayer, B.M. and Shotter, J. (eds) (1998) *Reconstructing the Psychological Subject: Bodies, Practices and Technologies*. London: Sage.
Beattie, J. (1966) *Other Cultures*. London: Routledge.
Bell, A.P., Weinberg, M.S. and Hammersmith, S.K. (1981) *Sexual Preference*. USA: Mitchell Beazley.
Bell, S. (1902) A preliminary study of the emotion of love between the sexes, *The American Journal of Psychology*, **13**: 325–54.
Bell, V. (1993) *Interrogating Incest: Feminism, Foucault and the Law*. London: Routledge.
Bem, S.L. (1974) The measurement of psychological androgyny, *Journal of Consulting and Clinical Psychology*, **42**: 155–62.
Bem, S.L. (1981) Gender schema theory: A cognitive account of sex typing, *Psychological Review*, **88**: 354–64.
Bem, S.L. (1985) Androgyny and gender schema theory: a conceptual and empirical integration, in T.B. Sonderegger (ed.) *Nebraska Symposium on Motivation, 1984: Psychology and Gender*. Lincoln, NE: University of Nebraska Press.
Bem, S.L. (1989) Genital knowledge and gender consistency in preschool children, *Child Development*, **60**: 649–62.
Benedict, H. (1985) *How to Survive a Sexual Assault for Women, Men, Teenagers, their Friends and Families*. New York: Doubleday.
Benedict, R. (1935) *Patterns of Culture*. London: Routledge.
Berger, P. and Luckmann, T. (1966) *The Social Construction of Reality*. London: Allan Lane.
Betz, N.E. and Fitzgerald, L.F. (1993) Individuality and diversity: theory and research in counseling psychology, *Annual Review of Psychology*, **44**: 343–81.
Bhavnani, K.-K. (1991) *Talking Politics: A Psychological Framing for Views from Youth in Britain*. Cambridge: Cambridge University Press.
Blackwell, E. (1885) *The Human Element in Sex*, 4th edn. London: J and A Churchill.

Blechman, E.A., Clay, C.J., Kipke, M.D. and Bickel, W.K. (1988) The premenstrual experience, in E.A. Blechman and K.D. Brownell (eds) *Handbook of Behavioral Medicine for Women*. New York: Pergamon, pp. 80–91.
Bowie, M. (1991) *Lacan*. Cambridge, MA: Harvard University Press.
Bowlby, J. (1951) *Maternal Care and Mental Health*. London: HMSO.
Boyle, M. (1997) *Re-thinking Abortion: Psychology, Gender Power and the Law*. London: Routledge.
Bradley Lane, M. (1880) *Mizora: A Prophesy*. Serialized in 8 instalments in the *Cincinatti Commercial* (1880–81).
Brannon, L. (1996) *Gender: Psychological Perspectives*. Boston, MA: Allyn and Bacon.
Brannon, R. (1976) The male sex role: our culture's blueprint for manhood and what it's done for us lately, in D.S. David and R. Brannon (eds) *The Forty-nine Percent Majority*. Reading, MA: Addison-Wesley, pp. 1–45.
Brehm, S.S. (1992) *Intimate Relationships*, 2nd edn. New York: McGraw-Hill.
Bremner, J. and Hillin, A. (1994) *Sexuality, Young People and Care*. Lyme Regis: Russell House.
Brinkworth, L. (1996) Angry young women: the rise of female violent crime, *Cosmopolitan*, February.
Bristow, J. (1997) *Sexuality*. London: Routledge.
Brittain, V. (1933) *Testament of Youth*. London: Victor Gollancz.
Broderick, C.B. (1966) Sexual behaviour among pre-adolescents, in A.M. Juhasz (1973) *Sexual Development and Behavior*. Homewood IL: Dorsey Press.
Brongersma, E. (1978) From the morality of oppression to creative freedom, *Civis Mindi*, **17**: 108–15.
Brooks, A. (1997) *Postfeminisms: Feminism, Cultural Theory and Cultural Forms*. London: Routledge.
Broverman, I.K., Vogal, S.R., Broverman, D.M., Clarkson, F.E. and Rosenkrantz, P.S. (1972) Sex-role stereotypes: a current appraisal, *Journal of Social Issues*, **28**(2): 59–78.
Broverman, J.K., Broverman, D.M., Clarkson, F.E., Rosenkrantz, P.S. and Vogel, S.R. (1970) Sex-role stereotypes and clinical judgements of mental health, *Journal of Consulting and Clinical Psychology*, 34: 1–7.
Brown, R. (1974) *Toward a Marxist Psychology*. London: Harper-Colophon.
Brown, R.C., Lang, W.C. and Wheeler, M.A. (1966) *The American Achievement*. Morristown, NJ: Silver Burdett.
Brown, S. (1980) *Political Subjectivity: Applications of Q Methodology in Political Science*. New Haven: Yale University Press.
Brown, S. (1997) The life of stress: seeing and saying Dysphoria. Unpublished doctoral dissertation, University of Reading.
Brownmiller, S. (1975) *Against Our Will: Men, Women and Rape*. London: Secker and Warburg.
Brownmiller, S. (1978) *Against Our Will*. Penguin: Harmondsworth.
Bryan, B., Dadzie, S. and Scafe, S. (1985) *The Heart of Race: Black Women's Lives in Britain*. London: Virago.
Bumiller, E. (1966) Elizabeth Dole is eager to keep strength subtle, *New York Times*, A1, A14.
Burgess, E.W. and Wallin, P. (1953) *Engagement and Marriage*. Philadelphia, PA: Lippincott.
Burman, E. (1994) *Deconstructing Developmental Psychology*. London: Routledge.

Burman, E. (1998) Deconstructing feminist psychology, in E. Burman (ed.) *Deconstructing Feminist Psychology*. London: Sage.

Burns, J. and Wilkinson, S. (1990) Women organising in psychology, in E. Burman (ed.) *Feminists and Psychological Practice*. London: Sage.

Burr, V. (1998) *Gender and Social Psychology*. London: Routledge.

Buss, D.M. (1990) Evolutionary social psychology: prospects and pitfalls, *Motivation and Emotion*, **14**: 265–86.

Buss, D.M. (1994) *The Evolution of Desire: Strategies in Human Mating*. New York: Basic Books.

Buss, D.M. (1996) Vital attraction, *Demos Quarterly*, **10**: 12–17.

Bussey, K. and Bandura, A. (1984) Influence of gender constancy and social power on sex-linked modelling, *Journal of Personality and Social Psychology*, **47**: 1292–1302.

Butler, J. (1990) *Gender Trouble: Feminism and the Subversion of Identity*. London: Routledge.

Butler, J. (1993) *Bodies that Matter: On the Discursive Limits of 'Sex'*. London: Routledge.

Butler, O. (1987) *Dawn*. London: Victor Gollancz.

Butler, S. (1872) *Erewhon*. London: Page.

Butler, S. (1901) *Erewhon Revisited*. London: Page.

Calderone, M.S. and Ramey, J.W. (1982) *Talking with your Child about Sex*. New York: Ballantine.

Cantril, H. (1940) *The Invasion from Mars*. Princeton, NJ: Princeton University Press.

Chapman, R. and Rutherford, J. (1988) *Male Order: Unwrapping Masculinities*. London: Lawrence and Wishart.

Chappell, S. (1997) Representations of violent young women, *Operant Subjectivity*, **20**(5): 62–72.

Charnas, S.M. (1980) *Motherlines*. London: Gollancz.

Cheater, A.P. (1969) *Social Anthropology: An Alternative Introduction*. London: Unwin Hyman.

Chesler, P. (1972) *Women and Madness*. New York: Avon.

Cixous, H. (1983) The laugh of the Medusa, in E. Abel and E.K. Abel (eds) *The Signs Reader: Women, Gender and Scholarship*. Chicago, IL: University of Chicago Press.

Clark, R.A. (1952) The projective measurment of experimentally induced levels of sexual motivation, *Journal of Experimental Psychology*, **44**: 391–9.

Cohen, S. (1972) *Folk Devils and Moral Panics: The Creation of the Mods and Rockers*. Oxford: Blackwell.

Cohn, C. (1987) Sex and death in the rational world of defence intellectuals, *Signs*, **12**(4): 687–718.

Colley, T. (1959) The nature and origins of psychological sexual identity, *Psychological Review*, **66**: 165–77.

Collins, P.H. (1990) *Black Feminist Thought: Knowledge, Consciousness, and the Politics of Empowerment*. London: Unwin Hyman.

Comfort, A. (1972) *The Joy of Sex*. New York: Crown.

Constantinople, A. (1973) Masculinity-femininity: an exception to the famous dictum?, *Psychological Bulletin*, **80**: 389–404.

Cranston, M. (1953) *Freedom: A New Analysis*. London: Longman.

Crawford, M. (1995) *Talking Difference: On Gender and Language*. London: Sage.

Crawford, M. (1998) 'Mars and Venus' gender representations and their subversion. Paper presented at the International Conference on Discourse and the Social Order, Aston University, Birmingham, July.

Crawford, M. and Maracek, J. (1989) Psychology reconstructs the female: 1968–1988, *Psychology of Women Quarterly*, **13**: 147–65.

Crawford, R. (1980) Healthism and the medicalization of everyday life, *International Journal of Health Services*, **10**: 365–88.

Crawford, R. (1984) A cultural account of 'health': control, released and the social body, in J.B. McKinley (ed.) *Issues in the Political Economy of Health Care*. London: Tavistock.

Cunningham, M.R. (1986) Measuring the physical in physical attractiveness: quasi-experiments on the sociobiology of female facial beauty, *Journal of Personality and Social Psychology*, **13**: 35–67.

Curt, B. (1994) *Textuality and Tectonics: Troubling Social and Psychological Science*. Buckingham: Open University Press.

Dabbs, J.M. Jr and Morris, R. (1990) Testosterone, social class and antisocial behaviour in a sample of 4,462 men, *Psychosocial Science*, **1**: 209–11.

Dabbs, J.M. Jr, Rubak, R.B., Frady, R.L., Hopper, C.H. and Sgoutas, D.S. (1988) Saliva testosterone and criminal violence among women, *Personality and Individual Differences*, **9**: 269–75.

Dabbs, J.M. Jr, de la Rue, D. and Williams, P.M. (1990) Testosterone and occupational choice: actors, ministers and other men, *Journal of Personality and Social Psychology*, **59**: 1261–5.

Dally, P. (1977) *The Fantasy Game*. London: Quartet.

Daly, M. (1978) *Gyn/Ecology: the metaethics of radical feminism*, in M. Daly (1979) *Gyn/Ecology: The Metaethics of Radical Feminism*. London: The Women's Press.

Daly, M. with Caputi, J. (1988) *Webster's First New Intergalactic Wickedary of the English Language*. London: The Women's Press.

Dan, A.J. and Beekman, S. (1972) Male versus female representation in psychological research, *American Psychologist*, **27**: 1078.

Darwin, C. (1859) *On the Origin of Species by Means of Natural Selection*. London: Murray.

Davies, C. (1975) *Permissive Britain*. London: Pitman.

Davis, S.N. and Gergen, M.M. (1997) Towards a new psychology of gender: opening conversations, in M.M. Gergen and S.M. Davis (eds) *Towards a New Psychology of Gender*. New York and London: Routledge.

Dawkins, R. (1976) *The Selfish Gene*. Oxford: Oxford University Press.

Dawkins, R. (1982) *The Extended Phenotype*. New York: Freeman.

Dawkins, R. (1988) *The Blind Watchmaker*. Harmondsworth: Penguin.

de Beauvoir, S. (1949) The second sex, in S. de Beauvoir (1972) *The Second Sex* (edited by H.M. Parshlay). Harmondsworth: Penguin.

Delany, S.R. (1977) *Triton*. London: Corgi.

DeLora, J.S. and DeLora, J.R. (eds) (1972) *Intimate Life Styles: Marriage and its Alternatives*. Pacific Palisades, CA: Goodyear.

De Lauretis, T., Huyssen, A. and Woodward, K. (eds) (1980) *The Technological Imagination: Theories and Fictions*. Madison: Coda Press.

Department of Health (1995) *Child Protection: Messages from Research*. London: HMSO.

Derrida, J. (1967) *'Speech and Phenomena' and Other Essays on Husserl's Theory of Signs* (translated by David B. Allison [1973]). Evanston, IL: Northwestern University Press.

Dewe Mathews, T. (1998) Sex: the final frontier, *The Guardian*, Friday Review Screen Section, 13 November, pp. 6–7.

Diamond, M. (1993) Homosexuality and bisexuality in different populations, *Archives of Sexual Behavior*, **22**(4): 291–310.

Dion, K. and Berscheid, E. (1974) Physical attractiveness and peer perception among children, *Sociometry*, **37**(1): 1–12.

Dion, K., Berscheid, E. and Walster, E. (1972) What is beautiful is good, *Journal of Personality and Social Psychology*, **24**(3): 285–90.

Dobash, R.E., Dobash, R.P. and Cavenagh, K. (1982) The contact between battered women and social and medical agencies, in J. Pahl (ed.) *Private Violence and Public Policy: The Needs of Battered Women and the Response of Public Services*. London: Routledge and Kegan Paul.

Dorkenoo, E. and Elworthy, S. (1992) *Female Genital Mutilation: Proposals for Change*. London: Minority Rights Group International.

Douglas, A. (1992) *The Beast Within*. London: Orion.

Duck, S. (1988) *Relating to Others*. Buckingham: Open University Press.

Dworkin, A. (1981) *Pornography: Men Possessing Women*. London: The Women's Press.

Eagly, A.H. (1996) Differences between women and men: their magnitude, practical importance and political meaning, *American Psychologist*, **51**(2): 158–9.

Eaves, L.J. and Eysenck, H.J. (1974) Genetics and the development of social attitudes, Nature, **249**: 288–9.

Eco, U. (1984) *The Name of the Rose*. London: Pan.

Eisenstein, H. (1984) *Contemporary Feminist Thought*. London: Unwin.

Elgin, S.H. (1985) *Native Tongue*. London: The Women's Press.

Ellenberger, H.F. (1970) *The Discovery of the Unconscious*. New York: Basic Books.

Ellis, A. (1949) A study of human love relationships, *The Journal of Genetic Psychology*, **75**: 61–71.

Ellison, M. (2000) The men can't help it, *The Guardian*, *G2*, 25 July, p. 4.

Engel, I.M. (1966) A factor-analytic study of items from five masculinity-femininity tests, *Journal of Consulting Psychology*, **30**: 565–78.

Epstein, D. (1997) Keeping them in their place: hetero/sexist harassment, gender and the enforcement of heterosexuality, in A.M. Thomas and C. Kitzinger (eds) *Sexual Harassment: Contemporary Feminist Perspectives*. Buckingham: Open University Press.

European Community Commission (1993) *Final Report of EC Investigative Mission into the Treatment of Muslim Women in the Former Yugoslavia*. Brussels: European Community Commission.

Evans, J. (1995) *Feminist Theory Today*. London: Sage.

Eysenck, H.J. (1967) *The Biological Basis of Personality*. Springfield, IL: Thomas Charles C Pub.

Eysenck, H.J. (1970) Personality and attitudes to sex: a factorial study, *Personality*, **1**: 355–76.

Eysenck, H.J. (1978) *Sex and Personality*. London: Abacus.

Eysenck, H.J. and Eysenck, S.B.G. (1964) *Manual for the Eysenck Personality Inventory*. London: University of London Press.

Eysenck, H. and Wilson, G. (1974) *The Experimental Study of Freudian Theories*. London: Methuen.
Eysenck, H.J. and Rachman, S. (1965) *The Causes and Cures of Neuroses*. London: Routledge.
Fagot, B.I., Leinbach, M.D. and O'Boyle, C. (1992) Gender labeling, gender stereotyping and parenting behaviours, *Developmental Psychology*, **28**: 225–30.
Fairburns, Z. (1979) *Benefits*. London: Virago.
Fallon, A.E. and Rozin, P. (1985) Sex differences in perceptions of desirable body shape, *Journal of Abnormal Psychology*, **94**(1): 102–5.
Faludi, S. (1992) *Backlash – The Undeclared War Against Feminism*. London: Chatto & Windus.
Farina, A., Fischer, E.H., Sherman, S. *et al.* (1977) Physical attractiveness and mental illness, *Journal of Abnormal Psychology*, **86**(5): 510–17.
Faust, B. (1981) *Women, Sex, and Pornography*. Harmondsworth: Penguin.
Feist, J. (1994) *Theories of Personality*. Fort Worth, TX: Harcourt Brace Jovanovich.
Feldman, R.S. (1998) *Social Psychology* (2nd edn) Upper Saddle River, NJ: Prentice Hall.
Ferri, E. (ed.) (1993) *Life at 33: The Fifth Follow-up of the National Child Development Study*. London: National Children's Bureau.
Fine, M. (1992) *Disruptive Voices: The Possibilities of Feminist Research*. Ann Arbor, MI: University of Michigan Press.
Firestone, S. (1979) *The Dialectic of Sex: The Case for Feminist Revolution*. London: The Women's Press.
Foley, M. (1994) Professionalizing the response to rape, in C. Lupton and T. Gillespie (eds) *Working with Violence*. London: Macmillan.
Foster, M.A. (1979a) *The Warriors of Dawn*. Middlesex: Hamlyn.
Foster, M.A. (1979b) *The Gameplayers of Zan*. Middlesex: Hamlyn.
Foucault, M. (1976/80) *History of Sexuality: Volume I*. Harmondsworth: Penguin.
Foucault, M. (1980) *The History of Sexuality Volume 1: An Introduction*. Harmondsworth: Penguin.
Foucault, M. (1988) Technologies of the self, in L.H. Martin and P.H. Gutman (eds) *Technologies of the Self*. London: Tavistock.
Fox, D. and Prilleltensky, I. (1997) *Critical Psychology*. London: Sage.
Frable, D.E.S. (1989) Sex typing and gender ideology: two facets of the individual's gender psychology that go together, *Journal of Personality and Social Psychology*, **56**: 95–108.
Franklin, M.B. (1997) Making sense: interviewing and narrative representation, in M.M. Gergen and S.N. Davis (eds) *Toward a New Psychology of Gender*. London: Routledge.
Freud, S. (1905/76) *Jokes and their Relationship to the Unconscious*. London: Pelican.
Freud, S. (1925/89) Some psychical consequences of the anatomical distinction between the sexes, in P. Gray (ed.) *The Freud Reader*. New York: Norton, pp. 670–8.
Freud, S. (1933/64) Femininity, in J. Strachet (ed. and trans.) *New Introductory Lectures on Psychoanalysis*. New York: Norton, pp. 112–35.
Friday, N. (1975) *My Secret Garden*. London: Quartet/Virago.
Fried Green Tomatoes at the Whistle Stop Cafe (directed by J. Avnet) (1991, Act III/Electric Shadow).

Friedman, R.C. *et al.* (1993) Neurobiology and sexual orientation: current relationships, *Journal of Neuropsychiatry and Clinical Neurosciences*, **5**: 1331–53.
Fromm, E. (1941) *Escape from Freedom*. New York: Rinehart.
Fromm, E. (1955) *The Sane Society*. New York: Holt, Rinehart & Winston.
Fromm, E. (1956) *The Art of Loving*. New York: Harper and Row.
Furnham, A. and Stacey, B. (1991) *Young People's Understanding of Society*. Routledge: London.
Garai, J.E. and Scheinfeld, A. (1966) Sex differences in mental and behavioural traits, *Genetic Psychology Monographs*, 77: 169–299.
Gavey, N. (1997) Feminist poststructuralism and discourse analysis, in M.M. Gergen and S.N. Davis (eds) *Toward a New Psychology of Gender: A Reader*. London: Routledge.
Gearheart, S.M. (1985) *The Wanderground*. London: The Women's Press.
Gentle, M. (1983) *Golden Witchbreed*. London: Arrow.
Gentle, M. (1987) *Ancient Light*. London: Arrow.
Gergen, M.M. and Davis, S.M. (eds) (1997) *Towards a New Psychology of Gender: A Reader*. London: Routledge.
Gerrard, N. (1997) Little Girls Lost, *Observer*, Review Section, 31 August.
Geschwind, N. and Galaburda, A.S. (1987) *Cerebral Lateralization*. Cambridge, MA: MIT Press.
Gibbons, A. (1991) The brain as 'sexual organ', *Science*, **253**: 957–9.
Giese, H. and Schmidt, A. (1968) *Studenten Sexualität*. Hamburg: Rowohlt.
Gilligan, C. (1982) *In a Different Voice: Psychological Theory and Women's Development*. Cambridge, MA: Harvard University Press.
Gilligan, C. and Attanucci, J. (1988) Two moral orientations, in C. Gilligan, J.V. Ward and J. McLean Taylor (eds) *Mapping the Moral Domain: A Contribution of Women's Thinking to Psychological Theory and Education*. Cambridge, MA: Harvard University Press.
Gilman, C.P. ([1915] 1979) *Herland*. London: The Women's Press.
Gleim, G.W. (1993) Exercise is not an effective weight loss modality in women, *Journal of the American College of Nutrition*, **12**: 363–7.
Goffman, E. (1959) *The Presentation of Self in Everyday Life*. Doubleday: New York.
Goleman, D. (1990) Aggression in men: hormone levels are the key, *New York Times*, section C, p. 1, 17 July.
Gorski, R.A. (1987) Sex differences in the rodent brain: their nature and origin, in L.A. Rosenblum and S.A. Sanders (eds) *Masculinity/Femininity: Basic Perspectives*. Oxford: Oxford University Press, pp. 37–67.
Goyer, P.F. and Eddleman, H.C. (1984) Same-sex rape in nonincarcerated men, *American Journal of Psychiatry*, **141**: 576–9.
Goodwin, J. and DiVasto, P. (1979) Mother-daughter incest, *Child Abuse and Neglect*, **3**: 953–7.
Gray, J. (1993) *Men are from Mars, Women are from Venus: A Practical Guide for Improving Communication and Getting What you Want in your Relationships*. London: Thorsons.
Gribbin, M. and Gribbin, J. (1998) *Being Human: Putting People in an Evolutionary Perspective* (2nd impression). London: Phoenix.
Griffin, S. (1981) *Pornography and Silence: Culture's Revenge Against Women*. London: The Women's Press.

Griffin, S. (1984) *The Roaring Inside Her*. London: The Women's Press.

Grogan, S. (1998) *Men, Women and Body Image*. London: Routledge.

Gross, E. (1992) What is feminist theory?, in H. Crowley and S. Himmelweit (eds) *Knowing Women: Feminism and Knowledge*. Cambridge: Polity.

Gunby, P. (1981) Sexual behaviour in an abnormal situation, *Medical News*, **245**: 215–20.

Haan, N., Smith, B. and Block, J. (1968) Moral reasoning of young adults, *Journal of Personality and Social Psychology*, **10**: 183–201.

Hadas, M. (1997) Faces of modernity. Men in films: a European versus an American model, *Replica: Hungarian Social Science Quarterly*, Special Issue: 171–84.

Hall, R. (1985) *Ask Any Woman*. London: Falling Well Press.

Hamer, D.H. (1993) A linkage between DNA markers on the X chromosome and male sexual orientation, *Science*, **261**: 321–7.

Handy, C. (1994) *The Empty Raincoat: Making Sense of the Future*. London: Hutchinson.

Haraway, D. (1984) Primatology is politics by other means, in R. Bleier (ed.) *Feminist Approaches to Science*. London: Pergamon.

Haraway, D.J. (1991) *Simians, Cyborgs, and Women*. London: Free Association Press.

Haraway, D.J. (1992) *Primate Visions*. London: Verso.

Harding, J. (1998) *Sex Acts: Practices of Femininity and Masculinity*. London: Sage.

Harding, S. (1986) *The Science Question in Feminism*. Ithaca, NY: Cornell University Press.

Harding, S. (ed.) (1987) *Feminism and Methodology*. Buckingham: Open University Press.

Hare-Mustin, R.T. and Maracek, J. (1990) On making a difference, in R.T. Hare-Mustin and J. Maracek (eds) *Making a Difference: Psychology and the Construction of Gender*. New Haven, CT: Yale University Press.

Harrington, D.M. and Anderson, S.M. (1981) Creativity, masculinity, femininity, and three models of psychological androgyny, *Journal of Personality and Social Psychology*, **41**: 744–57.

Hartley, R.E. (1959) Sex role pressures in the socialization of the male child, *Psychological Reports*, **5**: 456–62.

Hartsock, N.C.M. (1983) *Money, Sex and Power: Towards a Feminist Historical Materialism*. Boston, MA: Northeastern University Press.

Haskey, J. (1994) *Population Trends 78*, OPCS General Household Survey. London: OPCS.

Haste, H. (1993) *The Sexual Metaphor*. Hemel Hempstead: Harvester Wheatsheaf.

Hebdige, D. (1979) *Subculture: The Meaning of Style*. London: Routledge.

Hedgepeth, W. (1972) Maybe it'll be different here, in J.S. DeLora and J.R. DeLora (eds) *Intimate Life Styles: Marriage and its Alternatives*. Pacific Palisades, CA: Goodyear.

Heffner, R., Rebecca, M. and Oleshansky, B. (1975) Development of sex-role transcendence, *Human Development*, **18**: 143–58.

Heilbrun, A.B. (1978) An exploration of antecedents and attributes of androgenous and undifferentiated sex roles, *Journal of Genetic Psychology*, **132**: 97–107.

Helgeson, V.S. (1990) The role of masculinity in a prognostic predictor of heart attack severity, *Sex Roles*, **22**: 755–76.

Henslin, J. and Biggs, M. (1971) Dramaturgical desexualisation: the sociology of the vaginal examination, in J. Henshin (ed.) *Studies in the Sociology of Sex*. New York: Appleton-Century-Crofts.

Herdt, G. (1990) Mistaken gender: 5-alpha reductase hermaphroditism and biological reductionism in sexual identity reconsidered, *American Anthropologist*, **92**: 433–46.

Hergenhahn, B.R. (1988) *An Introduction to Theories of Learning*. Englewood Cliffs, NJ: Prentice-Hall.

Herrman, D.J., Crawford, M. and Holdsworth, M. (1992) Gender linked differences in everyday memory performance, *British Journal of Psychology*, **83**: 221–31.

Herzlich, C. and Pierret, J. (1984) *Malades d'hier, malades d'aujourd'hui: De la mort collective au devoir de guérison*. Paris: Payot. (Translation (1987) *Illness and Self in Society*.) Baltimore, MD: Johns Hopkins Press.

Hetherington, E.M. (1965) A developmental study of the effects of sex of the dominant parent on sex-role preference, identification and imitation in children, *Journal of Personality and Social Psychology*, **2**: 188–94.

Hetherington, E.M. and Frankie, G. (1967) Effects of parental dominance, warmth and conflict on imitation in children, *Journal of Personality and Social Psychology*, **6**: 119–25.

Hill, D. (1978) *The Shape of Sex to Come*. London: Pan.

Hirschfeld, M. (ed.) (1915) *Jahrbuch für sexuelle Zwischebstuffeb. Unter besonder Berücksichtigung der Homosexualität*. Leipzig: Max Spohr.

Hoek, H.W. (1993) Review of the epidemiological studies of eating disorders, *International Review of Psychiatry*, **5**(1): 61–74.

Hoffman, E. (1988) *The Right to be Human: A Biography af Abraham Maslow*. New York: St. Martin's Press.

Hollingshead, A.B. (1949) Cliques and dates, Chapter 9 in *Elmtown's Youth: The Impact of Social Classes on Adolescents*. New York: John Wiley & Sons.

Hollway, W. (1984) Gender difference and the production of subjectivity, in J. Henriques, W. Hollway, C. Urwin, C. Venn and V. Walkerdine (eds) *Changing the Subject: Psychology, Social Regulation and Subjectivity*. London: Methuen.

Hollway, W. (1989) *Subjectivity and Method in Psychology: Gender, Meaning and Science*. London: Sage.

Holmstrom, L. and Burgess, A. (1978) *The Victim of Rape: Institutional Reactions*. New York: John Wiley and Sons.

Home Office (1989) *Statistics on Offences of Rape 1977–87*, Home Office Bulletin. London: Home Office.

hooks, B. (1982) *Ain't I a Woman: Black Women and Feminism*. London: Pluto Press.

hooks, B. (1984) Reflections of a 'good' daughter: from black is a woman's colour, *A Scholarly Journal on Black Women*, **1**(2): 28–9.

Horner, M.S. (1969) Towards an understanding of achievement-related conflicts in women, *Journal of Social Issues*, **28**: 157–76.

Humm, M. (ed.) (1992) *Feminisms: A Reader*. Hemel Hempstead: Harvester Wheatsheaf.

Hunt, A.J., Davies, P.M., Weatherburn, P., Coxon, A.P. and McManus, T.J. (1991) Sexual partners, penetrative sexual partners and HIV risk, *AIDS*, **5**(6): 723–8.

Hyde, J.S. (1981) How large are cognitive gender differences: a meta-analysis using ω^2 and d, *American Psychologist*, **36**: 892–901.

Ibáñez, T. and Íñiguez, L. (1997) *Critical Social Psychology*. London: Sage.

Ingleby, D. (1985) Professionals as socialisers: the 'psy complex', in A. Scull and S. Spitzer (eds) *Research in Law, Deviance and Social Control*. New York: Jai Press, p. 7.

Inglehart, R. (1990) *Culture Shift in Advanced Industrial Society*. Princeton, NJ: Princeton University Press.

Irigaray, L. (1980) When our lips speak together, *Signs*, **6**(1).

Irigaray, L. (1985) *This Sex which is Not One*. Ithaca: Cornell University Press.

Jacklin, C.N. and Maccoby, E. (1978) Social behaviour at thirty-three months in same-sex and mixed-sex dyads, *Child Development*, **49**: 557–69.

Janoff-Bulman, R. and Frieze, I.H. (1987) The role of gender in reactions to gender victimization, in R.C. Barnett, L. Beiner and G.K. Baruch (eds) *Gender and Stress*. New York: Free Press.

Jolliffe, G. and Mayle, P. (1985) *Man's Best Friend*. London: Pan.

Juhasz, A.M. (1973) *Sexual Development and Behavior: Selected Readings*. Homewood, IL: Dorsey Press.

Jung, C. (1964) *Man and his Symbols*. London: Aldus.

Kalat, J.W. (1992) *Biological Psychology*. Belmont, CA: Wadsworth.

Kanter, R.M. (1993) *Men and Women of the Corporation*, 2nd edn. New York: Basic Books.

Kaplan, A.G. (1979) Clarifying the concept of androgyny: implications for therapy, *Psychology of Women Quarterly*, **3**: 223–30.

Kaplan, A.G. and Sedney, M.A. (1980) *Psychology and Sex Roles: An Androgynous Perspective*. Boston, MA: Little, Brown.

Katz, I. (1998) Is male circumcision morally defensible?, in M. King (ed.) *Moral Agendas in Children's Welfare*. London: Routledge.

Katz, P.A. and Ksansnak, K.R. (1994) Developmental aspects of gender role flexibility and traditionality in middle childhood and adolescence, *Developmental Psychology*, **30**: 272–82.

Kelly, J.A. and Worell, J. (1977) New formulations of sex roles and androgyny: a critical review, *Journal of Consulting and Clinical Psychology*, **45**: 1101–15.

Kelly, L. (1988) *Surviving Sexual Violence*. London: Polity.

Kiley, D. (1985) *The Wendy Dilemma: Do you Mother your Man?* London: Arrow.

Kimura, D. (1992) Sex differences in the brain, *Scientific American*, September: 119–25.

King, M. (1992) Male sexual assault in the community, in G.C. Mezey and M.B. King (eds) *Male Victims of Sexual Assault*. Oxford: Oxford University Press.

Kinsey, A.C., Pomeroy, W.B. and Martin, C.E. (1948) *The Sexual Behavior of the Human Male*. Philadelphia, PA: W.B. Saunders.

Kinsey, A.C., Pomeroy, W.B., Martin, C.E. and Gebhard, P.H. (1953) *The Sexual Behavior of the Human Female*. Philadelphia, PA: W.B. Saunders.

Kitzinger, C. (1987) *The Social Construction of Lesbianism*. London: Sage.

Kitzinger, C. and Perkins, R. (1993) *Changing Our Minds: Lesbian Feminism and Psychology*. London: Onlywomen.

Kohlberg, L. (1958) *The Development of Modes of Moral Thinking and Choice in the Years 10 to 16*. Chicago: University of Chicago.

Kohlberg, L. (1966) A cognitive-developmental analysis of children's sex-role concepts and attitudes, in E.E. Maccoby (ed.) *The Development of Sex Differences*. Stanford, CA: Stanford University Press, pp. 52–173.

Komarovsky, M. (1982) Female freshmen [*sic*] view their future: career salience and its correlates, *Sex Roles*, 8: 299–313.

Koss, M., Gidycz, A. and Wisniewski, N. (1987) The scope of rape: incidence and prevalence of sexual aggression and victimization in a national sample of higher education students, *Journal of Consulting and Clinical Psychology*, 55: 162–70.

Kristeva, J. (1984) *Revolution in Poetic Language* (trans. Margaret Waller). New York: Columbia University Press.

Kritzman, L.D. (1988) *Michel Foucault: Politics, Philosophy, Culture: Interviews and Other Writings 1977–84*. New York: Routledge.

Kuhn, D., Nash, S.C. and Brucken, L. (1978) Sex-role concepts of two- and three-year-olds, *Child Development*, **49**: 445–51.

Lacan, J. (1966) *Écrits*. Paris: Seuil.

Lacan, J. (1977) *Écrits: A Selection* (trans. Alan Sheridan). London: Tavistock.

Larousse Encyclopedia of Mythology (1960) London: Hamlyn.

Lane, M.E.B. ([1890] 2000) *Mizora: A Prophecy*. Syracuse, NY: Syracuse University Press.

Lavallee, M. and Pelletier, R. (1992) Ecological value of Bem's gender schema theory explored through females' traditional and nontraditional occupational contexts, *Psychologial Reports*, **70**: 78–82.

Lear, M.W. (1972) Save the spouses rather than the marriage, *The New York Times Magazine*, 13 August, p. 8.

Leary, M.R., Nezlek, J.B., Downs, D. and Radford-Davenport, J. (1994) Self-presentation in everyday interactions: effects of target familiarity and gender composition, *Journal of Personality and Social Psychology*, **67**(4): 664–73.

Le Guin, U. (1969) *The Left Hand of Darkness*. St Albans: Granada.

Le Guin, U. (1974) *The Dispossessed*. London: Gollancz.

Lees, S. (1996) *Carnal Knowledge: Rape on Trial*. Harmondsworth: Penguin.

Lefanu, S. (1988) *In the Chinks of the World Machine*. London: The Women's Press.

LeVay, S. (1991) A difference in hypothalamic structure between heterosexual and homosexual men, *Science*, **253**: 1034–45.

Levin, I. (1972) *The Stepford Wives*. London: Michael Joseph.

Levinson, D.J., Darrow, C.N., Klein, E.B., Levinson, M.H. and McKee, B. (1978) *The Seasons of Man's Life*. New York: Knopf.

Levy, D. (1989) Relations among aspects of children's social environments, gender schematization, gender role knowledge and flexibility, *Sex Roles*, **21**: 803–23.

Levy, G.D. and Fivush, R. (1993) Scripts and gender: a new approach to examining gender-role development, *Developmental Review*, **13**: 126–46.

Lewin, M. (1984a) 'Rather worse than folly?' Psychology measures femininity and masculinity: 1. From Terman and Miles to the Guilfords, in M. Lewin (ed.) *In the Shadow of the Past: Psychology Portrays the Sexes*. New York: Columbia University Press.

Lewin, M. (1984b) Psychology measures femininity and masculinity: 2. From '13 gay men' to the instrumental-expressive distinction, in M. Lewin (ed.) *In the Shadow of the Past: Psychology Portrays the Sexes*. New York: Columbia University Press.

Lewinsohn, R. (1958) *A History of Sexual Customs*. New York: Fawcett.

Lewis, J., Clark, D. and Morgan, D. (1992) *Whom God Has Joined Together*. Routledge: London.

Lightfoot-Klein, H. (1989) *Prisoners of Ritual: An Odyssey into Female Genital Circumcision in Africa*. Binghampton, NY: Harrington Park.

Lindenfield, G. (1992) *The Positive Woman*. London: Thorsons.

Lips, H.M. and Colwill, N. (1973) *The Psychology of Sex Differences*. Englewood Cliffs, NJ: Prentice-Hall.

Lipset, S.M. (1963) *Political Man*. London: Mercury.

Lord, C.G. (1997) *Social Psychology*. New York: Harcourt.

Lunneborg, P.W. (1972) Dimensionality of MF, *Journal of Clinical Psychology*, **328**: 313–17.

Lupton, D. (1996) *Food, the Body and the Self*. London: Sage.

Mac an Ghail, M. (1996) *Understanding Masculinities*. Buckingham: Open University Press.

Maccoby, E.E. and Jacklin, C.N. (1974) *The Psychology of Sex Differences*. Stanford, CA: Stanford University Press.

Maccoby, M. (1968) Polling emotional attitudes in relation to political choices. Unpublished paper.

MacDonald, G. (1981) Misrepresentation: liberalism and heterosexual bias in introductory psychology textbooks, *Journal of Homosexuality*, **6**: 45–60.

Macdonald, M. (1976) Homophobia: its roots and meanings, *Homosexual Counselling Journal*, **3**: 23–33.

Macey, D. (1993) *The Lives of Michel Foucault*. London: Vintage.

MacKinnon, C. (1983) Feminism, Marxism, method and the State: an agenda for theory, in E. Abel and E.K. Abel (eds) *The Signs Reader*. Chicago: Chicago University Press.

Malmquist, C.P., Kiresuk, K.J. and Spano, R.M. (1966) Personality characteristics of women with repeated illegitimacies: descriptive aspects, *American Journal of Orthopsychiatry*, **36**: 476–84.

Malson, H. (1997) *The Thin Woman: Feminism, Post-structuralism and the Social Psychology of Anorexia Nervosa*. London: Routledge.

Mandela, N. (1994) *Long Walk to Freedom: The Autobiography of Nelson Mandela*. Randburg, South Africa: Macdonald Purnell.

Marable, M. (1983) *How Capitalism Undeveloped Black America*. London: Pluto Press.

Marcuse, H. (1955) *Eros and Civilization*. New York: Vintage.

Martin, C.L. and Halverson, C.F. (1981) A schematic processing model of sex-stereotyping and stereotyping in children, *Child Development*, **52**: 1119–34.

Martin, C.L. and Little, J.K. (1990) The relation of gender understanding to children's sex-type preferences and gender stereotypes, *Child Development*, **61**: 1427–39.

Martin, C.L., Wood, C. and Little, J.K. (1990) The development of gender stereotype components, *Child Development*, **61**: 1891–1904.

Martin, E. (1987) *The Woman in the Body*. Milton Keynes: Open University Press.

Maslow, A.H. (1962) *Towards a Psychology of Being*. New York: Van Nostrand.

Masters, W.H. and Johnson, V.E. (1966) *Human Sexual Response*. Boston, MA: Little, Brown.

Masters, W.H., Johnson, V.E. and Kolodny, R.C. (1994) *Heterosexuality*. London: HarperCollins.

McCaffrey, A. (1972) *The Ship who Sang*. London: Corgi.

McCandless, B.R. (1970) *Adolescents: Behaviour and Development*. Hinsdale, IL.: Dryden Press.

McDougall, W. (1942) *An Introduction to Social Psychology*. London: Methuen.

McFarlane, J., Martin, C.L. and Williams, T. (1988) Mood fluctuations: women versus men and menstrual versus other cycles, *Psychology of Women Quarterly*, **12**: 201–23.

McGhee, P.E. and Frueh, T. (1980) Television viewing and the learning of sex role stereotypes, *Sex Roles*, **6**: 179–88.

McIntosh, M. (1968) The homosexual role, *Social Problems*, **16**(2): 182–92.

McRobbie, A. (1994) *Postmodernism and Popular Culture*. London: Routledge.

Mead, M. (1928) *Coming of Age in Samoa*. New York: Morrow.

Mead, M. (1930) *Growing up in New Guinea*. New York: Morrow.

Mead, M. (1935) *Sex and Temperament in Three Primitive Societies*. New York: Morrow.

Mead, M. (1949) *Male and Female*. New York: Morrow.

Medhurst, A. and Hunt, S. (eds) (1997) *Lesbian and Gay Studies: A Critical Introduction*. London: Cassell.

Meijer, G.A. *et al.* (1991) The effects of a 5 month endurance training programme on physical activity: evidence for a sex-difference in the metabolic response to exercise, *European Journal of Applied Physiology*, **62**: 11–17.

Meyer-Bahlburg, H.F.L. (1980) Sexuality in early adolescence, in B.B. Woolman and J. Money (eds) *Handbook of Human Sexuality*. Englewood Cliffs, NJ: Prentice-Hall.

Mezey, G.C. and King, M.B. (1989) The effects of sexual assault on men: a survey of 22 victims, *Psychological Medicine*, **19**: 205–9.

Mies, M. (1984) Towards a methodology for feminist research, in E. Altbacch, J. Clausen, D. Schultz and N. Stepphan (eds) *German Feminism: Readings in Politics and Literature*. Albany, NY: State University of New York Press.

Millar, S. (1998) Wonderland world on Internet porn, *The Guardian*, 13 September, p. 8.

Miller, A. (1986) *Thou Shalt Not be Aware*. London: Virago.

Miller, C. and Swift, K. (1976) *Words and Women: New Language in New Times*. Garden City, NY: Doubleday Anchor.

Miller, C. and Swift, K. (1981) *The Handbook of Non-Sexist Writing*. London: The Women's Press.

Miller, N.E. and Dollard, J. (1941) *Social Learning and Imitation*. New Haven, CO.: Yale University Press.

Millett, K. (1977) *Sexual Politics*. London: Virago.

Minogue, K. (1963) *The Liberal Mind*. London: Methuen.

Minsky, R. (ed.) (1995) *Psychoanalysis and Gender: An Introductory Reader*. London: Routledge.

Mirza, H.S. (1997) *Black British Feminism: A Reader*. London: Routledge.

Mischel, W. (1970) Sex-typing and socialization, in P.H. Mussen (ed.) *Carmichael's Manual of Child Psychology*. New York: Wiley.

Mitchell, T. (1996) *Popular Music and Local Identity: Rock, Pop and Rap in Europe and Oceana*. Leicester: Leicester University Press.

Mittwoch, U. (1973) *Genetics of Sex Differentiation*. New York: Academic Press.

Moir, A. and Moir, B. (1998) *Why Men Don't Iron: The Real Science of Gender Studies*. London: HarperCollins.

Money, J. (1986) *Venuses Penuses: Sexology, Sexosophy, and Exigency Theory*. Buffalo, NJ: Prothemus.

Moore, S. (1988) Boys' own, in R. Chapman and J. Rutherford (eds) *Male Order: Unwrapping Masculinities*. London: Lawrence & Wishart.

Morawski, J.G. (1990) Towards the unimagined: feminism and epistemology in psychology, in R.T. Hare-Mustin and J. Maracek (eds) *Making a Difference: Psychology and the Construction of Gender*. New Haven, CT: Yale University Press.

Morin, S.F. (1977) Heterosexual bias in psychological research on lesbianism and male homosexuality, *American Psychologist*, **19**: 629–37.

Morris, D. (1971) *The Human Zoo*. New York: Dell.

Mort, F. (1988) Boys' Own? Masculinity, style and popular culture, in R. Chapmen and J. Rutherford (eds) *Male Order: Unwrapping Masculinities*. London: Lawrence & Wishart.

Mrazek, P.B. and Mrazek, D.A. (1981) The effects of child sexual abuse: methodological considerations, in P.B. Mrazek and C.H. Kempe (eds) *Sexually Abused Children and their Families*. Oxford: Pergamon.

Mulgan, G.J. (1994) *Politics in an Antipolitical Age*. Cambridge, MA: Polity Press.

Mulkay, M. (1985) *The Word and the World: Explorations in the Form of Sociological Analysis*. London: George Allen and Unwin.

Mulvey, L. (1975) Visual pleasure and narrative cinema, *Screen*, **16**(3): 6–18.

Mulvey, L. (1992) Visual pleasure and narrative cinema, in *The Sexual Subject: A Screen Reader in Sexuality*. London: Routledge.

Nardi, P.M. and Schneider, B.E. (eds) (1998) *Social Perspectives in Lesbian and Gay Studies: A Reader*. London: Routledge.

Neisser, U. (1966) *Cognitive Psychology*. New York: Appleton-Century-Crofts.

Nelson, S. (1987) *Incest: Fact and Myth*, 2nd edn. Edinburgh: Stramullion.

Nettleton, S. and Watson, J. (1998) *The Body in Everyday Life*. London: Routledge.

Nicholas, K. and McGinley, H. (1986) Pre-school children's selective imitation of adults: implications for sex role development, *Journal of Genetic Psychology*, **146**: 143–4.

Nicholson, L. (ed.) (1997) *The Second Wave Feminism Reader: Feminist Theoretical Writings*. London: Routledge.

Nicholson, P. (1998) *Post-natal Depression: Psychology, Science and the Transition to Motherhood*. London: Routledge.

Norwood, R. (1986) *Women Who Love Too Much*. London: Arrow.

O'Brien, L. (1998) Rock'n'role, *The Guardian*, G2: 8–9.

Odeh, L.A. (1997) Post-colonial feminism and the veil: thinking the difference, in M.M. Gergen and S.N. Davis (eds) *Towards a New Psychology of Gender*. New York: Routledge.

O'Dell, L. (1997) Child sexual abuse and the academic construction of symptomologies, *Feminism & Psychology*, **7**(3): 334–9.

O'Dell, L. (1998) Damaged goods and victims? Challenging the assumptions within the academic research into the effects of child sexual abuse. Unpublished doctoral thesis, The Open University.

Olds, L. (1981) *Fully Human*. Englewood Cliffs, NJ: Prentice-Hall.

Orlofsky, J.L. (1977) Sex-role orientation, identity formation and self-esteem in college men and women, *Sex Roles*, **3**: 561–75.

Ortner, S.B. and Whitehead, H. (1981) *Sexual Meanings: The Cultural Construction of Gender and Sexuality*. Cambridge: Cambridge University Press.

Painter, K. (1991) *Wife Rape, Marriage and the Law*. Faculty of Economic and Social Studies, The University of Manchester.

Parlee, M.B. (1973) The premenstrual syndrome, *Psychological Bulletin*, **83**: 454–65.

Parsons, T. (1964) Age and sex in the social structure of the United States, in *Essays in Sociological Theory*. New York: The Free Press, pp. 89–103.

Parsons, T. and Bales, R.F. (1953) *Family, Socialization and Interaction Process*. London: Routledge and Kegan Paul.

Parton, N., Thorpe, D. and Wattam, C. (1997) *Child Protection: Risk and the Moral Order*. Basingstoke: Macmillan.

Pearson, J. (1990) Where no man has gone before: sexual politics and women's science fiction, Chapter 2 in P.J. Davies (ed.) *Science Fiction, Social Conflict and War*. Manchester: Manchester University Press.

Phillips, K.A. (1996) *The Broken Mirror: Understanding and Treating Body Dysmorphic Disorder*. New York: Oxford University Press.

Phillips, S.M. *et al.* (1993) Gender differences in leucine kinetics and nitrogen balance in endurance athletes, *Journal of Applied Physiology*, **75**(5): 2134–41.

Piedmont, R.K. (1988) An interaction model of achievement motivation and fear of success, *Sex Roles*, **19**: 467–90.

Piel Cook, E. (1985) *Psychological Androgyny*. New York: Pergamon.

Piercy, M. (1976) *Woman on the Edge of Time*. New York: Knopf.

Pinel, J.P.J. (1993) *Biopsychology*. Boston, MA: Allyn and Bacon.

Pini, M. (1997) Technologies of the Self, in J. Roche and S. Tucker (eds) *Youth in Society*. London: Sage.

Pizzey, E. and Shapiro, J. (1982) *Prone to Violence*. Feltham: Hamlyn.

Pleck, J.H. (1975) Masculinity-femininity: current and alternative paradigms, *Sex Roles*, **1**: 161–78.

Pleck, J.H. (1984) The theory of male sex role identity: its rise and fall, 1936 to the present, in M. Lewin (ed.) *In the Shadow of the Past: Psychology Portrays the Sexes*. New York: Columbia University Press.

Poppen, P.J. (1974) The development of sex differences in moral judgment for college males and females. Unpublished doctoral thesis, Cornell University.

Pringle, R. (1992) Absolute sex? Unpacking the sexuality/gender relationship, Chapter 4 in R.W. Connel and G.W. Dowsett (eds) *Rethinking Sex*. Melbourne: Melbourne University Press.

Probyn, E. (1997) Michel Foucault and the uses of sexuality, in A. Medhurst and S.R. Munt (eds) *Lesbian and Gay Studies: A Critical Introduction*. London: Cassell.

Raisman, G. and Field, P.M. (1971) Sexual dimorphism in the preoptic area of the rat, *Science*, **173**: 731–3.

Raskin, P. and Israel, A. (1981) Sex role imitation in children: effects of sex of child, sex of model, and sex-role appropriateness of modeled behaviour, *Sex Roles*, 7: 1067–77.

Raymond, J.C. (1980) *The Transsexual Empire*. London: The Women's Press.

Reich, W. (1983) *Children of the Future*. New York: Farrar, Strauss, Giroux.

Reid, S. (1996) Fair sex and foul play, *Sunday Times*, 5 May.

Reinharz, S. (1992) *Feminist Research Methods in Social Research*. Oxford: Oxford University Press.
Rich, A. (1980) Compulsory heterosexuality and lesbian existence, *Signs: Journal of Women in Culture and Society*, 5(41): 631–60.
Richards, M. (ed.) (1974) *The Integration of a Child into a Social World*. Cambridge: Cambridge University Press.
Richardson, D. (ed.) (1996) *Theorising Heterosexuality*. Buckingham: Open University Press.
Richardson, M. (ed.) (1987) *Maria W. Stewart, America's First Black Woman Political Writer*. Bloomington, IN: Indiana University Press.
Rideau, W. and Sinclair, B. (1982) Prison: the sexual jungle, in A.M. Scacco (ed.) *A Casebook of Sexual Aggression*. New York: AMS Press.
Roberts, H. (ed.) (1981) *Doing Feminist Research*. London: Routledge.
Rogers, C.R. (1972) *Becoming Partners: Marriage and its Alternatives*. New York: Delacorte Press.
Rogers, C.R. (1977) *Carl Rogers on Personal Power*. New York: Delacorte Press.
Roiphe, K. (1993) *The Morning After: Sex, Fear and Feminism*. London: Hamish Hamilton.
Rokeach, M. (1960) *The Open and Closed Mind*. New York: Basic Books.
Rorty, R. (1980) *Philosophy and the Mirror of Nature*. Oxford: Blackwell.
Rose, N. (1985) *The Psychological Complex*. London: Routledge.
Rose, N. (1990) *Governing the Soul: The Shaping of the Private Self*. London: Routledge.
Ross, L. (1991) The 'intuitive scientist' formulation and its developmental implications, in J.H. Havell and L. Ross (eds) *Social Cognitive Development: Frontiers and Possible Futures*. Cambridge: Cambridge University Press.
Rossi, A.S. (1988) *The Feminist Papers: From Adams to Beauvoir*. Boston, MA: Northeastern University Press.
Rozee-Koker, P. and Polk, C. (1986) The social psychology of group rape, *Sexual Coercion Assault*, **1**(2): 57–65.
Ruben, D. (1985) *Progress in Assertiveness, 1973–1983: An Analytical Bibliography*. Metuchen, NJ: Scarecrow.
Rubin, R.T., Reinisch, J.M. and Haskett, R.F. (1981) Postnatal gonadal steroid effects on human behaviour, *Science*, **211**: 1318–24.
Ruderman, A.J. (1986) Dietary restraint: a theoretical and empirical review, *Psychological Bulletin*, **99**(2): 247–62.
Rudin, J. (1969) *Fanaticism: A Psychological Analysis*. Notre Dame, IN: University of Notre Dame Press.
Rushton, J.P. (1989) Genetic similarity, human altruism, and group selection, *Behavioral and Brain Sciences*, **12**: 503–59.
Russell, D.E.H. (1989) *Lives of Courage: Women for a New South Africa*. New York: Basic Books.
Sagara, E. (ed.) (1998) *Embodying the Social*. London: Routledge.
Sagarin, E. (1976) Prison homosexuality and its effects on post-prison sexual behaviour, *Psychiatry*, **39**: 245–57.
Said, E. (1995) *Orientalism: Western Conceptions of the Orient*. Harmonsworth: Penguin.
Sanday, P.R. (1981) *Female Power and Male Domination*. New York: Cambridge University Press.

Sanday, P.R. (1990) *Fraternity Gang Rape: Sex, Brotherhood and Privilege on Campus*. New York: New York University Press.

Saussure, F. de (1916) *Course in General Linguistics* (Trans. Wade Baskin [1959]). London: Fontana.

Sawicki, J. (1991) *Disciplining Foucault: Feminism, Power and the Body*. London: Routledge.

Sayers, J. (1982) *Biological Politics: Feminist and Anti-feminist Perspectives*. London: Tavistock.

Schecter, M.D. and Roberge, L. (1976) Sexual exploitation, in R.E. Helfer and C.H. Kempe (eds) *Child Abuse and Neglect: The Family and the Community*. Cambridge, MA: Ballinger.

Schiavi, R.C. (1999) *Ageing and Male Sexuality*. Cambridge: Cambridge University Press.

Scully, D. and Bart, P. (1980) A funny thing happened on the way to the orifice: women in gynecology textbooks, in J. Ehrenreich (ed.) *The Cultural Crisis of Modern Medicine*. New York: Monthly Review Books.

Scully, D. and Marolla, J. (1985) Riding the bull at Gilley's: convicted rapists describe the rewards of rape, *Social Problems*, **32**(3): 251–63.

Scully, D., Kremer, J., Meade, M.M., Graham, R. and Dudgeon, K. (1998) Physical exercise and psychological well-being: A critical review, *British Journal of Sports Medicine*, **32**(2): 111.

Sears, R.R., Rau, L. and Alpert, R. (1965) *Identification and Child Rearing*. Stanford, CA: Stanford University Press.

Sedgewick, P. (1982) *Psychopolitics*. London: Pluto.

Segal, L. (1987) *Is the Future Female? Troubled Thoughts on Contemporary Feminism*. London: Virago.

Shaywitz, S.E., Shaywitz, B.A., Fletcher, J.M. and Escobar, M.D. (1990) Prevalence of reading disability in boys and girls. Results of the Connecticut Longtitudinal Study, *Journal of the American Medical Association*, **264**: 998–1002.

Shaywitz, B.A., Shaywitz, S.E. *et al.* (1995) Sex differences in the functional organization of the brain for language, *Nature*, 373: 67.

Sherif, C.W. (1987) Bias in psychology, in S. Harding (ed.) *Feminism and Methodology*. Milton Keynes: Open University Press.

Shields, S.A. (1975) Functionalism, Darwinism and the psychology of women: a study in social myth, *American Psychologist*, **30**: 739–54.

Showalter, E. (1992) *Sexual Anarchy*. London: Virago.

Sigall, H. and Ostrove, N. (1975) Beautiful but dangerous: effects of offender attractiveness and nature of the crime on juridic judgment, *Journal of Personality and Social Psychology*, **31**(3): 410–14.

Sigelman, C.K., Howell, J.L., Cornell, D.P. and Cutright, J.D. (1991) Courtesty stigma: the social implications of associating with a gay person, *Journal of Social Psychology*, **131**(1): 45–56.

Silverstein, B. and Perdue, L. (1988) The relationship between concerns, preferences for slimness and symptoms of eating problems among college women, *Sex Roles*, **18**(1–2): 101–6.

Simon, W., Kraft, D.M. and Kaplan, H.B. (1990) Oral sex: a critical overview, in B. Voeller, J.M. Reinisch and M. Gottlieb (eds) *AIDS and Sex: An Integrated Biomedical and BioBehavioural Approach*. Oxford: Oxford University Press, pp. 257–75.

Singh, D. (1993) Adaptive significance of female physical attractiveness: role of waist-to-hip ratio, *Journal of Personality and Social Psychology*, **65**(2): 293–307.

Sistrunk, F. and McDavid, J.W. (1971) Sex differences in conformity behaviour, *Journal of Personality and Social Psychology*, **17**: 200–7.

Slade, P. (1984) Premenstrual emotional changes in normal women: fact and fiction?, *Journal of Psychosomatic Research*, **28**: 1–7.

Smith, J.R. and Smith, L.G. (eds) (1974) *Beyond Monogamy*. Baltimore, MD: The Johns Hopkins Press.

Smith, V. (1998) *Not Just Race, Not Just Gender: Black Feminist Readings*. London: Routledge.

Spence, J.T. (1983) Comment on Lubinski, Tellegen and Butcher's 'Masculinity, Femininity and Androgyny Viewed and Assessed as Distinct Concepts', *Journal of Personality and Social Psychology*, **44**: 440–6.

Spence, J.T. and Helmreich, R.L. (1978) *Masculinity and Femininity: Their Psychological Dimensions, Correlates and Antecedents*. Austin, TX: University of Texas Press.

Spence, J.T. and Helmreich, R.L. (1979) The many faces of androgyny: a reply to Locksley and Colten, *Journal of Personality and Social Psychology*, **37**: 1032–46.

Spender, D. (1981) The gatekeepers: a feminist critique of academic publishing, in H. Roberts (ed.) *Doing Feminist Research*. London: Routledge.

Spock, B. (1963) *Baby and Child Care*. Montreal: Pocket Books.

Springer, S.P. and Deutsch, G. (1989) *Left Brain, Right Brain*, 3rd edn. New York: Freeman.

Stainton Rogers, R. (1997) The making and moulding of modern youth, in J. Roche and S. Tucker (eds) *Youth in Society*. London: Sage.

Stainton Rogers, R. and Stainton Rogers, W. (1992) *Stories of Childhood: Shifting Agendas of Child Concern*. Hemel Hempstead: Harvester Wheatsheaf.

Stainton Rogers, R. and Stainton Rogers, W. (1998) Word children, in K. Lesnik-Oberstein (ed.) *Children in Culture: Approaches to Childhood*. Basingstoke: Macmillan.

Stainton Rogers, R., Stenner, P., Gleeson, K. and Stainton Rogers, W. (1995) *Social Psychology: A Critical Agenda*. Cambridge: Polity.

Stainton Rogers, W. (1991) *Explaining Health and Illness: An Exploration of Diversity*. Hemel Hempstead: Harvester Wheatsheaf.

Stam, H. (ed.) (1998) *The Body and Psychology*. London: Sage.

Stangor, C. and Ruble, D.N. (1987) Development of gender role knowledge and gender constancy, in L.S. Liben and M.L. Signorella (eds) *Children's Gender Schemata*. San Francisco: Jossey-Bass.

Stephenson, W. (1967) *The Play Theory of Mass Communication*. Chicago: Chicago University Press.

Stiglmayer, A. (1993) *Mass Rape: The War against Women in Bosnia-Herzegovina*. Lincoln, NE: University of Nebraska Press.

Strickland, B.R. (1988) Sex-related differences in health and illness, *Psychology of Women Quarterly*, **12**: 381–99.

Sullivan, T. (1992) *Sexual Abuse and the Rights of Children: Reforming Canadian Law*. Toronto: University of Toronto Press.

Swaab, D.F. and Fliers, E. (1985) A sexually dimorphic nucleus in the human brain, *Science*, **228**: 1112–15.

Taussig, M. (1980) Reification and the consciousness of the patient, *Social Science and Medicine*, **14b**: 3–13.

Tavris, C. and Wade, C. (1984) *The Longest War: Sex Differences in Perspective*. New York: Harcourt Brace Jovanovich.

Taylor, J.M., Gilligan, C. and Sullivan, A.M. (1996) Missing voices, changing meanings: developing a voice-centred, relational method and creating an interpretive community, in S. Wilkinson (ed.) *Feminist Social Psychologies: International Perspectives*. Buckingham: Open University Press.

Thelma and Louise (directed by Ridley Scott) (1991, Pathé Entertainment).

Thornhill, R. and Palmer, C.T. (2000) *A Natural History of Rape: Biological Bases of Sexual Coercion*. Cambridge, MA: MIT Press Trade.

Tiffin, J., Knight, F.B. and Josey, C.C. (1940) *The Psychology of Normal People*. Boston: Heath.

Toulmin, S.E. (1958) *The Uses of Argument*. Cambridge: Cambridge University Press.

Townsend, C.W. (1896) Thigh friction in children under one year, quoted in H. Ellis (1910) *Studies in the Psychology of Sex*, Volume i (3rd Edn). Philadelphia, PA: Davis.

Tseng, W.S., Mo, K.M., Li, L.S. *et al.* (1992) Koro epidemic in Guangdong, China: a questionnaire survey, *Journal of Nervous and Mental Disease*, **180**(2): 117–23.

Turner, E.S. (1954) *A History of Courting*. London: Pan.

Turner, B. (1996) *The Body and Society*. London: Sage.

Unger, R.K. and Crawford, M. (1992) *Women and Gender: A Feminist Psychology*. New York: McGraw-Hill.

Urberg, K.A. (1979) Sex role conceptualization in adolescents and adults, *Developmental Psychology*, **15**: 90–2.

Ussher, J. (1989) *The Psychology of the Female Body*. London: Routledge.

Ussher, J.M. (1997) *Fantasies of Femininity: Reframing the Boundaries of Sex*. Harmondsworth: Penguin.

Vance, C. (1992) Social construction theory: problems with the history of sexuality, in H. Crowley and S. Himmelweit (eds) *Knowing Women*. Cambridge: Polity.

Veysey, L. (1974) Communal sex and communal survival, *Psychology Today*, **8**: 73–8.

Vickers, J. McCalla (1982) Memoirs of an ontological exile: the methodological rebellions of feminist research, in A. Miles and G. Finn (eds) *Feminism in Canada: From Pressure to Politics*. Montreal: Black Rose.

Voet, R. (1998) *Feminism and Citizenship*. London: Sage.

Waber, D. (1976) Sex differences in cognition: a function of maturation rate?, *Science*, **192**: 572–3.

Wachtel, A. and Scott, B. (1991) The impact of child sexual abuse in the developmental perspective, in C. Bagley and R.J. Thomlinson (eds) *Child Sexual Abuse: Critical Perspectives on Prevention, Intervention and Treatment*. Toronto: Wall and Emerson.

Wakeford, N. (1997) Cyberqueer, in A. Medhurst and S.R. Munt (eds) *Lesbian and Gay Studies*. London and New York: Cassell.

Walkerdine, V. (1997) *Working Class Women*. Basingstoke: Macmillan.

Walling, W.H. (1909) *Sexology*. Philadelphia, PA: Puritan.

Walster, E., Aronson, V., Abrahams, D. and Rottmann, L. (1966) Importance of physical attractiveness in dating behavior, *Journal of Personality and Social Psychology*, **4**(5): 508–16.

Warshaw, R. (1988) *I Never Called it Rape*. New York: Harper & Row.

Watkins, S.A., Rueda, M. and Rodriguez, M. (1992) *Feminism for Beginners*. Cambridge: Icon.

Watts, S. and Stenner, P. (1997) [Re]searching for love: subjectivity and the ontology of the Q factor, *Operant Subjectivity*, **20**(5): 22–9.

Weeks, J. (1981) *Sex, Politics and Society: The Regulation of Sexuality since 1800*. London: Longman.

Weeks, J. (1986) *Sexuality*. London: Routledge.

Weinberg, M.S., Williams, C.J. and Prior, D.W. (1994) *Dual Attraction: Understanding Bisexuality*. New York: Oxford University Press.

Weisner, T.S. and Wilson-Mitchell, J.E. (1990) Nonconventional family life-styles and sex typing in six-year-olds, *Child Development*, **61**: 1915–33.

Weissenstein, N. (1993) Power, resistance and science: a call for revitalized feminist psychology, *Feminism & Psychology*, **3**(2): 239–45.

Wellings, K., Field, J., Johnson, A.M. and Wadsworth, J. (1994) *Sexual Behaviour in England*. Harmondsworth: Penguin.

Wells, H.G. ([1898] 1968) *The War of the Worlds*. London: Heinemann.

Welter, B. (1978) The cult of true womanhood: 1820–1860, in M. Gordon (ed.) *The American Family in Socio-historical Perspective*, 2nd edn. New York: St. Martin's Press.

West, D.J. (1967) *The Young Offenders*. Harmondsworth: Penguin.

Wiggins, J.S., Wiggins, N. and Conger, J.C. (1968) Correlates of heterosexual somatic preference, *Journal of Personality and Social Psychology*, **10**(1): 82–90.

Wilkinson, H. (1995) *No Turning Back: Generations and the Genderquake*. London: Demos.

Wilkinson, H. (1996) *Parental Leave: The Price of Family Values*. London: Demos.

Wilkinson, H. and Mulgan, G. (1995) *Freedom's Children: Work, Relationships and Politics for 18–34 year olds in Britain Today*. London: Demos.

Wilkinson, S. (1997) Prioritizing the political: feminist psychology, in T. Ibáñez and L. Íñiguez (eds) *Critical Social Psychology*. London: Sage.

Wilkinson, S. and Kitzinger, C. (eds) (1993) *Heterosexuality: A Feminism & Psychology Reader*. London: Sage.

Williams, C.E. (1974) *Choice and Challenge: Contemporary Readings in Marriage*. Dubuque, IO: W.C. Brown Co.

Williams, F. (1989) *Social Policy: A Critical Introduction*. Cambridge: Polity.

Williams, J.E. and Best, D.L. (1990) *Measuring Sex Stereotypes: A Multination Study*. Newbury Park, CA: Sage.

Williams, J.H. (1977) *Psychology of Women: Behavior in a Biosocial Context*. New York: W.W. Norton.

Wilson, E.O. (1980) *Sociobiology*. Cambridge, MA: Harvard University Press.

Wilson, G.D. and Nias, D. (1976) *Love's Mysteries: The Psychology of Sexual Attraction*. London: Open Books.

Witkin, H.A., Mendrick, S.A., Schulsinger, F. *et al.* (1976) Criminality in XYY and XXY men, *Science*, **193**: 547–55.

Wittig, M. (1981) One is not born a woman, *Feminist Issues*, **1**(2): 46–54.

Woll, S. (1986) So many to choose from – decision strategies in videodating, *Journal of Social and Personal Relationships*, 3(1): 43–52.

Wright, R. (1996) The dissent of woman: what feminists can learn from Darwinism, *Demos Quarterly*, **20**: 12–17.

Yager, G.G. and Baker, S. (1979) Thoughts on androgyny for the counseling psychologist. Paper presented at the annual meeting of the American Psychological Association, New York, September.

Young, A. (1980) The discourse on stress and the reproduction of conventional knowledge, *Social Science and Medicine*, **14b**: 133–46.

Zimmerman, B. (1997) Feminism, in A. Medhurst and S. Munt (eds) *Lesbian and Gay Studies: A Critical Introduction*. London: Cassell.

Index

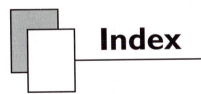

Page numbers in *italics* refer to boxes and tables, *g* denotes a glossary definition.

HEALTH PSYCHOLOGY
A TEXTBOOK: 2ND EDITION

Jane Ogden

> The additions and updates in this second edition will ensure that it maintains its well deserved position as a leading textbook . . . it provides a clear, comprehensive and up-to-date overview of a wide range of research and theory.
>
> John Weinman, King's College London

> . . . now that Jane Ogden's book has been published I feel that health psychology has finally come of age.
>
> Precilla Choi, *Psychology Teaching*

> . . . a great achievement . . . an excellent textbook.
>
> *Journal of Health Psychology*

Health Psychology: A Textbook will provide you with an accessible and comprehensive guide to all of the major topics in health psychology.

By reading this book, you will gain a historical and theoretical framework within which to study health psychology. The book focuses on how psychological theory has been applied in the area of health and explores how research can be used to influence and structure practice.

Health Psychology has already become established as a major textbook in the field, not least because it provides a strong coverage of European research as well as the US research which is the exclusive focus of many textbooks. The new edition includes a new chapter on the measurement of health status and new sections on professional issues, recant developments in social cognition models, body dissatisfaction and dieting, causes of obesity and the measurement of pain.

Health Psychology has been designed specifically with the needs of students and teachers in mind. It can form the basis for a complete health psychology course. Each chapter has been designed as the reading for a lecture, and the book contains many special features to aid learning:

- Focus on research sections describe specific studies which test theory
- Questions stimulate discussion and structure revision
- Assumptions in health psychology are highlighted
- Chapter overviews provide outlines of structure, aims and key points
- Figures and diagrams put essential information at your fingertips
- Further reading points to sources of further information and discussion
- Methodology glossary explains key methodological terms

If you are a student or researcher in health psychology, or if you are studying medicine, nursing or any other health-related course, *Health Psychology: A Textbook* is essential reading for you.

Contents

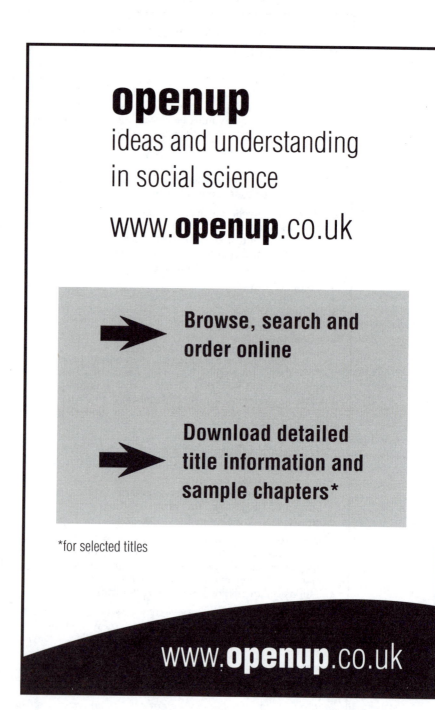